Young Children and the Environment

Early education
for sustainability

Second edition

Edited by Julie M. Davis

CAMBRIDGE
UNIVERSITY PRESS

CAMBRIDGE
UNIVERSITY PRESS

University Printing House, Cambridge CB2 8BS, United Kingdom

One Liberty Plaza, 20th Floor, New York, NY 10006, USA

477 Williamstown Road, Port Melbourne, VIC 3207, Australia

314–321, 3rd Floor, Plot 3, Splendor Forum, Jasola District Centre, New Delhi – 110025, India

79 Anson Road, #06–04/06, Singapore 079906

Cambridge University Press is part of the University of Cambridge.

It furthers the University's mission by disseminating knowledge in the pursuit of education, learning and research at the highest international levels of excellence.

www.cambridge.org
Information on this title: www.cambridge.org/9781107636347

First published 2010
Second edition 2015 (version 5, March 2018)

Cover designed by Anne-Marie Reeves
Typeset by Integra Software Services Pvt. Ltd.
Printed in Australia by Ligare Pty Ltd, March 2018

A catalogue record for this publication is available from the British Library

A Cataloguing-in-Publication entry is available from the catalogue of the National Library of Australia at www.nla.gov.au

ISBN 978-1-107-63634-7 Paperback

Young Children and the Environment

Early education for sustainability

Second edition

Young Children and the Environment is a practical resource that illustrates the difference that early childhood educators can make by working with children, their families and the wider community to tackle one of the most important contemporary issues facing the world today: sustainable living.

This second edition has been substantially revised and updated, with a new section exploring sustainability education in a variety of global contexts. Researched and written by authors recognised as leaders in their own countries, the chapters in this section provide readers with international resources and perspectives to further their teaching about early childhood education for sustainability.

The text engages with new curriculum initiatives that have placed greater emphasis on educating for sustainability, and endeavours to equip educators with the knowledge to teach this revised content. It remains accessibly written, with ample case studies, vignettes and 'provocations' to engage and enlighten readers, and to provide insights into how early childhood education for sustainability can be successfully implemented in practice.

This is an essential text for students at the beginning of their early childhood studies, as well as teachers and practitioners in a range of early childhood education and care settings.

Julie M. Davis is Associate Professor in the School of Early Childhood, Faculty of Education, at the Queensland University of Technology in Brisbane, Australia.

To all the world's children – today and tomorrow.

Contents

Contents

Contents

Contents

Foreword

It has been a pleasure to read the new edition of this book, the first edition published five years ago being a pioneer in an area that focuses on how early childhood education can contribute towards a more sustainable world. There are now seven new chapters and all the others have been updated. The chapters contain a balanced mix of facts, illustrative examples and provocative questions, with the authors aiming to actively engage the reader to become involved in changing him/herself as much as changing his/her ideas about teaching and learning. The different chapters focus on early childhood educational settings as places for children's actions related to the environment and sustainability and on related topics – such as health and wellbeing, embedding Indigenous perspectives, and community interactions – that are concerned with early childhood and children's lives in a wider sense.

Although the focus here remains on questions related to the natural environment, the text gives a much broader view of what education for sustainability can be like. The dimension of social sustainability is highlighted more in this edition, for example, although environmental sustainability remains central. Convincingly, the authors show how urgent it is to transform our education systems in order to be cross-disciplinary, authentic and closely related to children's everyday concerns and experiences. The reasons for this are global, in terms of justice, equality and equity, but also environmental, in terms of global climate change and issues such as food security.

While the book illustrates the need for global and community political commitments to sustainable living, it emphasises the importance of beginning with the youngest children. We know from years of research that the early years provide a window of opportunity to lay strong foundations for knowledge, skills and attitudes. We also know that there are international agreements and declarations that make commitments intended to guide policy, as well as everyday life for children, and those who work with children. One of these is the United Nations Convention on the Rights of the Child (1989). This Convention is the starting point for a theoretical framework of children's rights that is argued for in this book – a development of ideas presented in the first edition. This framework revises thinking about children's rights, proposing a multidimensional view that goes beyond the rights enshrined in the Convention, to consider more agentic and communal rights. This framework also proposes that rights belonging to beings other than humans is an idea that warrants consideration as an essential feature of early childhood education for sustainability.

Now, it looks like the United Nations has realised, in its work towards the post-2014 agenda following from the United Nations Decade of Education for Sustainable Development, that 'Children are the common basis for all dimensions of sustainable development. No advances in sustainable development will occur in the coming decades without multiple generations contributing to societal improvement' (Sustainable Development Solutions Network – A Global Initiative for the United Nations, 2014, *Young Children as a Basis for Sustainable Development*, http://unsdsn.org/wp-content/uploads/2014/02/ECD-Brief1.pdf, p. 1).

This book shows clearly that early childhood education of high quality is a good starting point for education for sustainable development, but that it is not enough in order to educate children for a more sustainable world and society. While the research field has expanded in recent years, and many more journals now include articles about early childhood education and sustainability, we still need to know much more, both through mainstream early childhood research, and through engagement in alternative cross-disciplinary research, methods and approaches, whereby the complexity of environmental and sustainability questions and issues can be explored.

This edition, like the first, will be of great value to pre-service teacher education all over the world, as well as to early childhood practitioners already in the field, to inspire them to change their practices. Researchers are another important target group, specifically those who want to approach this complex and challenging area of early childhood education and sustainable development. Last, but not least, this book will be of value to our politicians, who still need to become much more aware of how economy, social-cultural dimensions, and environment are intertwined and, in so doing, help create possibilities for working towards a sustainable world and society at all levels, beginning in the early years and proceeding throughout life.

Ingrid Pramling Samuelsson
UNESCO Chair of Early Childhood Education
and Sustainable Development
May 2014

Contributors

Eva Ärlemalm-Hagsér is Senior Lecturer in teacher education at Mälardalen University in Sweden. With a background as a preschool teacher, her main interests are early childhood education with a child-oriented approach, focusing on the lived curriculum. More recently, her research focus has been on outdoor play and learning, and education for sustainability (EfS). In 2013 Eva graduated from the University of Gothenburg with a doctoral thesis in EfS and young children. She has convened the Special Interest Group, Play and Learning, within the European Early Childhood Education Research Association (EECERA), since 2008. Eva is the Stockholm president of OMEP Sweden (Organisation Mondiale pour l'Éducation Préscolaire).

Sue Cooke (Susan M. Cooke) is a Brisbane-based educator, health promoter and climate activist, who has postgraduate qualifications in public health, education and environmental change. An advocate for 'green and healthy schools' (health-promoting and sustainable schools) over the 20 years since her children were little, she believes that early childhood and school settings can be powerful community generators for the transformational change needed to switch humanity's path towards healthy, just and sustainable futures.

Julie M. Davis is Associate Professor in the School of Early Childhood, Faculty of Education, at the Queensland University of Technology in Brisbane, Australia, where the focus of her work is integrating science, health, social and environment/sustainability education into early childhood education and teacher education. Julie has undergraduate qualifications in education and environmental studies, a master's degree in environmental education (focused on health-promoting schools) and a doctorate (focused on whole-school environmental education). Originally a local advocate for early childhood education for sustainability (ECEfS) for nearly 30 years, she now has extensive networks and research colleagues national and internationally.

Sue Elliott is Senior Lecturer in the School of Education at the University of New England in Armidale, Australia. She has been engaged in ECEfS advocacy and practice for more than two decades both nationally and internationally and is an acknowledged author in the early childhood field. Her publications include *The Outdoor Playspace: Naturally* (2008) and *Research in Early Childhood Education for Sustainability: International Perspectives and Provocations* (2014) and she is a consulting editor for the *International Journal of Early Childhood Environmental Education*. Sue has an ongoing involvement in research and consultancy in the areas of EfS and outdoor play in nature, including the development of forest preschool approaches in Australia.

Ingrid Engdahl is Deputy Head of the Department of Child and Youth Studies at Stockholm University in Sweden. Her academic interests are in EfS and early childhood education with a child-oriented approach, focusing on infants and toddlers. She lectures within teacher education programs and heads the International Program of Early Childhood Education at Stockholm Institute of Education. She serves as the national president of OMEP Sweden. Ingrid has a bachelor degree in psychology from Uppsala University, an early childhood education teachers' degree from Gothenburg Teacher College, and a doctorate in child and youth studies from Stockholm University.

Jo-Anne Ferreira teaches in the Master of Environment (Education for Sustainability) program at Griffith University in Brisbane. She was Editor of the *Australian Journal of Environmental Education* during 2002–09 and Co-Chair of the Sixth World Environmental Education Congress in 2011. She has worked in pre-service teacher education, and has developed and delivered professional development programs in Australia, South Africa and across the Asia-Pacific region. Jo has a number of doctoral students (researching school and community-based environmental/sustainability education) and is currently undertaking research on systemic approaches to change within pre-service teacher education and how environmental citizenship skills are taught and learnt through sustainability education.

Megan Gibson is a lecturer in the School of Early Childhood, Faculty of Education, at the Queensland University of Technology in Brisbane. Her key areas of research and teaching include teacher professionalism, leadership and management, policy, EfS, and health and wellbeing. An early childhood educator with nearly 20 years' teaching experience, Megan has worked across a diverse range of early childhood contexts. Her doctoral research focused on the production and maintenance of early childhood teachers' professional identities.

Louise Gilbert is a lead research associate on a project implementing a sustainable, community-wide, cross-disciplinary approach to promoting children's resilience and wellbeing through the use of Emotion Coaching at Bath Spa University in the United Kingdom. She is also involved in the development and delivery of the Attachment Aware Schools and Settings Project, which supports emotional wellbeing for vulnerable learners. Louise's working career is in health and education, having worked as a teacher, practised as a nurse, run a health promotion department and taught at the University of Gloucestershire in the position of Senior Lecturer in Early Years. She has co-written on early years education and training for sustainable futures and is currently writing a book with Dr Janet Rose on health and wellbeing in the early years. She is writing up her doctoral thesis on the transference of Emotion Coaching into community education practice.

Michiko Inoue is Professor in the School of Early Childhood, Faculty of Education at Osaka Ohtani University in Japan. She is a leader in environmental education and EfS at the early childhood level in Japan. More specifically, her interest is focused on conceptual understandings and the actual educational practices of educators in kindergartens and nursery centres to foster an ecological worldview. Currently, her research is concerned with comparing these aspects between Japan, Australia and Sweden.

Okjong Ji is Professor in Early Childhood Education at the Korea National University of Transportation in the Republic of Korea (South Korea, or 'Korea' for short). Her areas of interest are the Project Approach and nature-friendly education and, more recently, ECEfS. She is aiming to guide effective implementation of ECEfS in Korean kindergartens using the Project Approach. She is doing this as supervisor of the project learning community organised through the 'Chungbuk Early Childhood Educator's Community for Nature Appreciation', which consists of eight early learning institutions for young children. In 2012, the Maebong Park Project that was initiated by this group received certification from the Korean National Commission for UNESCO as an excellent case study of education for sustainable development.

Margaret Lloyd is Associate Professor in the Faculty of Education at the Queensland University of Technology in Brisbane. Her specialist area is information and communication technologies (ICT) in education. She has published widely and has recently been involved in the consultations around ICT in the Australian Curriculum, with a particular focus on making digital technologies both child- and teacher- friendly. She believes that technology has a critical role to play in sustainability and that it is time to embrace it as part of a creative solution rather than reject it as part of the problem.

Paulette Luff is Senior Lecturer in the Department of Education at Anglia Ruskin University (in Chelmsford and Cambridge) where she leads the MA in Early Childhood Professional Studies program and teaches in other undergraduate and postgraduate courses, particularly modules relating to curriculum and professional enquiry. For the past 10 years, her research has focused on child observation and its role in the planning, implementation and evaluation of early childhood curricula. She has spoken and written on this subject for various audiences, including co-authoring two books. She is now engaged in a new project examining understandings and uses of reclaimed resources in different types of early years settings. Paulette has worked in the field of early childhood as a teacher, foster carer, school–home liaison worker, nursery practitioner and adviser, and as a lecturer in further and higher education.

Nadine McCrea grew up in the Sierra Nevada foothills of California before arriving in Australia. She joined the University of New England in 1998 after lecturing at the Queensland University of Technology in Brisbane. Before that, Nadine worked in the early childhood education field in Victoria. Her focal interests include leadership approaches in children's services with an eco-angle; educative health promotion in early childhood settings; and early childhood eco-pedagogy focused on foodcycle learning. Nadine has a personal and professional commitment to sustainable awareness and eco-caring; she won a 2013 NSW Early Childhood Environmental Education Network (ECEEN) Sprouts Award for 'leadership in mentoring many'.

Melinda G. Miller is a lecturer in the School of Early Childhood, Faculty of Education, at the Queensland University of Technology in Brisbane. Her teaching and research interests include cultural studies, sustainability education, professional development and action research. Melinda's doctoral research focused on non-Indigenous educators' efforts to embed Indigenous perspectives in early childhood education curricula. The study highlighted how whiteness and racism continue to be mobilised in diversity work, even when educators' efforts are seen to be productive and inclusive, and despite the best of intentions. In recent years, Melinda has facilitated numerous year-long action research projects with educators in the before-school sector and formal years of school, around topics including culture and diversity, play and sustainability.

Lyndal O'Gorman is Senior Lecturer in the School of Early Childhood, Faculty of Education, at the Queensland University of Technology in Brisbane. Her university teaching focuses on arts and sustainability education in early childhood and primary school contexts and her research and writing also explores these areas. Lyndal taught as an early childhood teacher in urban and remote schools for 13 years prior to her academic career. She has undergraduate qualifications in early childhood education and a strong personal commitment to the arts, and environmental and social sustainability.

Robert Pratt has worked in education for more than 20 years, with his teaching career spent largely in the early years (kindergarten and preschool), both in Australia and overseas. For four years, from 2009 to 2012, he worked in a primary school setting. Although a valuable learning experience, it reassured him that his passion lies in early childhood education. Central to Robert's teaching approach is the concept of democracy. Robert's position is that all members of an education community should have opportunities to contribute to curriculum decision making. While he believes that curriculum should be child-orientated, he is of the view that curriculum content should emerge not only from the interests of children, but also from the contributions of teachers, parents and the broader community. Robert believes that participating actively in a democratic learning environment is integral to ECEfS.

Lesley Robinson is a senior lecturer for Te Tari Puna Ora O Aotearoa, the New Zealand Childcare Association. This organisation delivers initial teacher education for the childcare sector and advocates for quality early childhood education throughout New Zealand. Lesley has an interest in post-modern perspectives on EfS. As a teacher educator, she is interested in exploring transformative pedagogy and in bringing sustainability into the centre of curriculum in initial teacher education.

Janet Rose is Principal Lecturer and the Award Leader for the Early Childhood Education at Bath Spa University in the United Kingdom. She has more than 20 years' experience of working in the early years, both in England and internationally. In addition to her academic career, she has worked as a specialist early years teacher and for several local authorities developing training program for supporting young children. She has recently co-written a book on the role of the adult in early years settings and will soon publish a book on health and wellbeing in the early years. Janet is currently leading a research project that is implementing a sustainable, community-wide, cross-disciplinary approach to promoting children's resilience and wellbeing. She is also developing the Attachment Aware Schools and Settings Project, which is a comprehensive program of support for children affected by early attachment difficulties, trauma and neglect.

Sharon Stuhmcke is a Vocational Teacher in the School of Community Services at Southbank Institute of Technology in Brisbane. She is an experienced early childhood practitioner with more than 20 years' classroom experience, ranging from childcare and kindergarten to early primary teaching. Her key interest is EfS within early childhood contexts. Sharon has early childhood teaching qualifications and holds a master's degree in early childhood education. She recently graduated from the Queensland University of Technology with a doctoral degree in education focused on EfS, for which she received an Executive Dean's Commendation in 2013. Her chapter is derived from this doctoral research.

Sue Vaealiki is the Learning Programmes Director for Triplejump, a risk management advisory service company in Auckland, New Zealand, and is contracted to work with early childhood education services and tertiary organisations in a professional capacity as an adviser and monitor. For many years, Sue has been involved in developing initial teacher education programs that integrate EfS in holistic and thought-provoking ways based on the research she undertook when in the tertiary sector and through her involvement with early childhood centres in New Zealand.

Introduction

Introduction

As in the first edition, the following chapters provide a wealth of ideas, inspiration and provocations for those who have both the short-term and the long-term interests of young children at heart. This book covers a spread of birth to age 8 learning settings and highlights the potential for community learning arising from early childhood education for sustainability (ECEfS) initiatives that demonstrate that young children and their teachers and parents can be provocateurs for sustainability in their wider community.

While the main focus of the first edition was Australian and New Zealand experiences in ECEfS, in this edition authors come from further afield, with new chapters from Japan, Korea, Sweden and the United Kingdom. As the challenges of sustainability resonate globally, these wider perspectives make significant, additional contributions to ECEfS. As chapter authors were asked to include more examples of working within the domains of social and economic sustainability in this edition, I am hopeful that readers will appreciate that sustainability is more than a focus on the natural environment. Nevertheless, as we stated earlier, we make no apologies for treating nature with the respect it deserves.

In this edition, the book is divided into two parts. **Part 1** follows the basic structure of the first edition. It includes **Chapter 1** where I update concepts related to sustainability and education for sustainability (EfS) and discuss the recent expansion of ECEfS across the globe. I then develop ideas about sustainability challenges and how these relate to young children. The case is reiterated that early childhood education has a real contribution to make towards changing unsustainable patterns of living. **Sue Elliott** focuses **Chapter 2** on the underpinning relationship between children and their experiences in the natural world, and re-emphasises that children's experiences in nature are fundamental to their health, wellbeing, learning and development. Sue reiterates that early childhood educators have a key role in incorporating natural elements into children's play and learning environments and in sharing their enthusiasm and wonder about the natural world with children.

In **Chapter 3**, **Megan Gibson** updates her earlier chapter, examining transformational educational and organisational leadership as a key contributor to creating cultures of sustainability within early childhood education settings, re-emphasising 'whole settings' approaches, the creation of 'learning communities' for sustainable living, and recognition of young children as active and informed citizens and change agents. In **Chapter 4**, **Robert Pratt** again details his approach to implementing ECEfS, this time based on his current early childhood education context of Kenmore West Kindergarten. Robert weaves threads from his chapter in the first edition into this new chapter, as well as building in newer elements, such as connections to Aboriginal and Torres Strait Islander (that is, Indigenous) culture, and tackles the vexed issue of 'risk'. In **Chapter 5**, **Sue Vaealiki** and **Lesley Robinson**, from New Zealand, update their discussion of teaching and learning in ECEfS, linking these to ethics as a pedagogical principle that provides tools for learning to live with, and make decisions about, environmental, educational, social and cultural issues and topics. The revised chapter strengthens the view of children as rich and competent citizens of the present who already have capacities and capabilities to influence the future. **Chapter 6**, written by **Melinda G. Miller**, locates ECEfS initiatives within scholarship and practice that examines Indigenous perspectives and the aim of reconciliation between Indigenous and non-Indigenous Australians. She emphasises that examining EfS in this way helps to 'flip the lens' and garner fresh perspectives on our own lives and viewpoints.

Meanwhile, **Margaret Lloyd** in **Chapter 7** re-explores the 'virtual world', examining the potential of information and communication technologies (ICT) for EfS for young children. She comments that technology has a critical role to play in sustainability and that it is time to embrace ICT as part of creative solutions to sustainability rather than rejecting it as part of the problem. **Sue Cooke**, in **Chapter 8**, re-examines the synergies between ECEfS programs and projects, and international movements such as Health Promoting Schools, Child Friendly Cities and Transition Towns. The point is made that living sustainably is not only good for the planet but also for personal and community health and wellbeing.

Added to Part 1 are three new chapters. In **Chapter 9**, **Nadine McCrea** writes about food issues – a vital aspect of local, regional and global sustainability – using the concepts of young children's food learning and daily practices with food as springboards for discussion and practice. Nadine emphasises a clear distinction between nutrition and children learning holistically about food. The next new chapter, **Chapter 10**, is by **Lyndal O'Gorman**. Lyndal focuses on the arts and sustainability and discusses ways that these two areas can be successfully brought together in early education. She uses a 5-year-old's drawing project to exemplify her key points. The final chapter in **Part 1**, **Chapter 11**, is written by **Sharon Stuhmcke**. Sharon draws on her doctoral studies and illustrates effective use of the Project Approach to implement ECEfS. Sharon revises the concept, calling for a Transformative Project Approach that supports children as active agents of change for sustainability as a necessary step in addressing sustainability in early education.

Part 2 comprises a mix of new and updated chapters that provide an international perspective to ECEfS. **Chapter 12**, by **Eva Ärlemalm-Hagsér** and **Ingrid Engdahl**, examines ECEfS in Sweden. The authors provide an exemplar of ECEfS undertaken in a Swedish preschool focused on young children and their ideas and concerns about 'battery chicken' egg production. **Chapter 13**, by **Michiko Inoue**, discusses environmental education in Japan. She asks whether current conceptualisations, based in nature studies and resource conservation, are adequate for addressing the contemporary sustainability challenges in Japan. **Chapter 14** is by an author from South Korea, **Okjong Ji**, who outlines government and education initiatives in that country in relation to ECEfS. Okjong reports on an example where young children and their teachers use the Project Approach, in combination with new technologies, to learn about and engage the wider community in sustainability activism. **Chapter 15** is by three authors from the United Kingdom, **Louise Gilbert, Janet Rose** and **Paulette Luff**. These authors use the four strands of the Education for Sustainable Development initiative (2012) introduced by the United Nations Scientific and Cultural Organization (UNESCO) to shape their discussion about recent loss of momentum in the United Kingdom in the implementation of ECEfS initiatives. They comment that new opportunities, nevertheless, can emerge to keep EfS on the early childhood education reform agenda.

In the final chapter, **Chapter 16**, **Jo-Anne Ferreira** and **Julie M. Davis** update their ideas about systems approaches to creating educational change for sustainability. They re-emphasise the importance of research and whole-of-systems approaches in creating and strengthening the deep and wide cultural shifts necessary for EfS to become embedded in early childhood education.

Part 1

Chapter 1

What is early childhood education for sustainability and why does it matter?

Julie M. Davis

This book's purpose

As I wrote in the first edition of this text, this is not a book about the perils of global warming and its impact on children, although climate change provides an impetus for this text. Nor is it a response to issues that seeks to shift responsibilities from adults to children, asking next generations to fix what we leave behind. Instead, it is a book of positive ideas and actions that shows what early childhood education communities can do when children, teachers and parents work together to address perhaps the most serious issue of our times – how to live sustainably.

Since the first edition was published in 2010, scientific evidence of human causation of climate change has become virtually incontrovertible (Intergovernmental Panel on Climate Change [IPCC] 2013), despite the continuing 'unbelief' of a small number of vocal individuals, lobby groups and politicians. The authors of the *Summary for Policymakers* published in relation to the Fifth IPCC Assessment Report state: 'Warming of the climate system is unequivocal, and since the 1950s, many of the observed changes are unprecedented over decades to millennia. The atmosphere and ocean have warmed, the amounts of snow and ice have diminished, sea level has risen, and the concentrations of greenhouse gasses have increased' (IPCC 2013, p. 4). Nevertheless, and regardless of one's views about climate change, the matter of (un)sustainability has never really been in question – it is quite apparent that humans are living beyond the capacity of existing social, environmental and economic systems to function well or, clearly, equitably (United Nations 2013). The global financial crisis that took effect in 2008, for instance, exemplifies unsustainable economic systems that impact negatively upon societies, just as the 100 or so species of Australian flora and fauna that have become extinct since European settlement – with more than 1500 under threat – are evidence of unsustainable environmental systems. Increasing numbers of refugees leaving their homelands in leaky boats or risking travel across deserts and dangerous borders are evidence of unsustainable social/political/cultural systems.

Nevertheless, while many measures of global unsustainability paint a grim picture, it is gratifying to report that the early childhood field with regards to sustainability is in a significantly different place to where it was five years ago when the first edition of this text was published. Early childhood education for sustainability (ECEfS) has become an international movement, although it is fair to say that there are many parts of the world yet to engage and deep challenges remain. Perhaps the most significant challenge is the gross disparities in access to basic early childhood education that many young children and their families and communities experience. It is difficult to practise education for sustainability (EfS) if access to early education is missing in the first place, or you are an elementary teacher in charge of a class of 60 children, as I experienced recently in Papua New Guinea (PNG). In PNG, less than three hours by plane from wealthy Australia, the infant mortality rate is 40.84 deaths/1000 live births, 10 times that of Australia where the rate is 4.40 deaths/1000 live births (Index Mundi 2013). Not surviving to your first birthday constitutes the ultimate in unsustainability. But this text is not asking young children and early childhood educators to address such complex issues; that is primarily the role of nation states and the international community. However, it is about putting these issues in context and identifying the power of ECEfS as a catalyst for change, and the power of the very young as agents of change for sustainability. It is about learning, hope and taking action to 'make a difference' within the scope of children's own lives.

Why this book is important

Life on Earth is experiencing a critical period. While climate change has captured the headlines, the bigger issue is that humans are not living within the Earth's capacity to provide clean air, clean and adequate water supplies, fertile soils, productive oceans and ongoing resources for the world's human population, now more than 7 billion, and for the millions of non-human species. As the health of global ecosystems and the health of human populations are inextricably linked, the need for fundamental changes in how humans live is increasingly difficult to ignore. The crisis in the world's financial markets, first made evident in 2008, demonstrates what happens when we live on borrowed capital. 'The global financial crisis has drawn attention to the problem of borrowing from resources that do not exist' (University of Gothenburg & Chalmers University of Technology 2008). The impacts of this crisis were, and continue to be, worldwide; the most economically and socially vulnerable have become more vulnerable. Governments face new, deep and urgent challenges to maintaining economic stability and social cohesion. Coming on top of mounting ecological crises, deep cracks are showing in the way humans 'do business' on this planet.

The next generations – our children and grandchildren – are the recipients of the best and the worst that is passed on to them. There seem to be endless and exciting opportunities ahead for many children, particularly those born in the West. Nevertheless, even for rich nations (the over-developed world?), there is increasing concern about the state of the natural environment and the economic and social prospects for current and future generations if actions are not taken to reverse or, at least, ameliorate what is happening. As Lester Brown, formerly of the Worldwatch Institute, said, 'Nature has no reset button' (Brown 2000, para. 25).

What is sustainability and why does it matter?

Sustainability remains a confused and contentious topic with no universally accepted terminology or definition. A popularised description from the World Commission on Environment and Development's (1987) Brundtland Report – also known as *Our*

Common Future – describes sustainable development as that which 'meets the needs of the present generation without compromising the ability of future generations to meet their own needs' (p. 8). This is a definition that continues to resonate with me, and hence I continue to use it here. Perhaps, though, a more poetic way of capturing this complex concept is 'enough for all forever', a description used by a young person at an international conference in Australia that later shaped the *Statement on Sustainability for All Queensland Schools* (Education Queensland 2008).

In Australia and New Zealand, the term 'sustainable development' has largely been replaced by terms including 'sustainability' or 'sustainable living'. (In this text, I use 'sustainability' – and therefore 'education for sustainability' and 'early childhood education for sustainability' – as the descriptor to capture this concept.) This is preferred because of the implied assumption that development equates with economic growth, and that only after economic growth is achieved can environmental concerns be addressed. As many in the environment movement emphasise, supporting the growth and development of economies – especially through increasing mass consumption – in a world of finite resources and growing population is not a sustainable option.

As understood by all the chapter authors of this book, sustainability is a broad concept that is about so much more than addressing concerns related to the natural environment – important though these are. Therefore, in this second edition, authors were asked to highlight, more strongly, the dimension of social sustainability, although it is clear that environmental sustainability remains central to their thinking. We continue to hold to the idea that healthy people require a healthy planet, a concept recently advocated for in the 2014 statement 'From Public to Planetary Health: A Manifesto' published in *The Lancet*. Its authors call for the transformation of public health via 'a social movement to support collective public health action at all levels of society – personal, community, national, regional, global and planetary' (Horeton et al. 2014, p. 847). These are new and potentially powerful allies for efforts for which many of us have been agitating for decades.

Figure 1.1 illustrates this broad view.

In summary, sustainability emphasises the linkages and interdependencies of the social, political, environmental and economic dimensions of human capabilities. It is a view that acknowledges relationships between humans, and between humans and other species. It is also a view that is underpinned by critique of the ways humans use and share resources, and recognises intergenerational equity issues.

Sustainability is essentially an issue of social justice and fairness. The causes and effects of unsustainable living are disproportionate and unevenly distributed. Some humans enjoy the benefits of global economic development, industrialisation and new technologies; many people and many other species bear the risks and costs. Among human populations it is the poorest nations, and the poorest within nations, who are most at risk (Lowe 2006). As Nicholas Stern, author of the British government's report

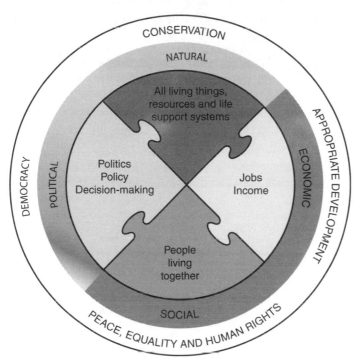

Figure 1.1 *The four dimensions of sustainable development*
Source: UNESCO (n.d.).

on the economics of climate change, commented, 'The poorest developing countries will be hit earliest and hardest by climate change, even though they have contributed little to causing the problem' (Stern 2006, p. xxvi). Furthermore, while efforts are (slowly) getting underway to reduce or reverse future climate change, the unequal distribution of benefit and risk is even greater for children who face the brunt of future consequences (a topic explored later in this chapter). Sustainability is concerned, therefore, not only with the state of the natural world but also with poverty, population, consumption, gender equity, indigenous issues, peace and reconciliation, community life and human health. It is about how we all live our lives now and into the future.

Provocation 1.1

Write or illustrate your own definition of sustainability. Consider personal, local and global dimensions as well as current and future perspectives.

Another way of capturing the ideas and ideals of sustainability has been realised through the Earth Charter (Earth Charter Initiative 2012). This document also integrates four dimensions, or pillars, of sustainability: social/cultural, economic, ecological and political. The development of the Charter was influenced by ways of thinking and knowing as diverse as science, indigenous peoples' knowledge, international law, religious and philosophical traditions, and United Nations' declarations and reports, and from examining good practices for building sustainable communities. In Chapter 4, Robert Pratt comments that the Earth Charter has had a strong and continuing influence in shaping his thinking and actions as an early childhood teacher for sustainability. There are even versions of the Earth Charter adapted for younger children, written in more accessible language.

Provocation 1.2

For an example of a Children's Earth Charter, go to www.littleearthcharter.org.

What does such an Earth Charter mean to you? Does it expand your thinking about how **you** live in the world? If so, how?

In what practical ways might you use a Children's Earth Charter in an early childhood education context?

Regardless of the still-evolving terminology for and definitions about sustainability, a clear underlying message is that the natural world's life-supporting capabilities must be sustained indefinitely, productively and equitably into the future. While the world has made some progress towards understanding what sustainability means, the overall situation has not improved; incremental progress in some areas is offset by worsening trends in others. For example, while the world's GDP is 10 times larger than in 1950 and average per capita GDP is four times larger, greater global wealth and technological capacity have not eliminated poverty and hunger nor prevented overall ecological decline. Many countries and peoples are trapped in persistent poverty, with 200 000 million more slum dwellers today than 20 years ago (United Nations 2013). Further trends described in the United Nations' *Global Sustainable Development Report* (2013) include the following:

- There are 740 million people who lack access to safe drinking water and 2.4 billion people who lack access to basic sanitation (650 million more than in 1990). Water pollution continues to claim the lives of millions, especially children.
- Biodiversity continues to decrease at rates 100 to 1000 times their pre-human level, with continuing losses to half of the world's forests, historically to domestication. Tropical forests declined at around 12–14 million hectares per year during both the 1990s and 2000s, and a similar amount was degraded.
- Local and regional freshwater shortages are common, with water stress occurring in one-third of the world.

- The proportion of overexploited fish stocks tripled from 10 per cent in 1970 to 30 per cent in 2012.

- Diversity of cultural heritage and traditions, traditional knowledge and 90 per cent of indigenous languages are threatened, although there are indications of some revivals.

- Affluence has increased amidst persistent poverty. While the world economy doubled from 1990 to 2012, consumption remains grossly inadequate for the poorest. There is growing income inequality in many parts of the world.

Additionally, world population reached 7.2 billion in mid-2013, with 80 million added each year, more than a threefold increase in just over 100 years. World population is projected to reach 8.1 billion in 2025, then to increase to 9.6 billion in 2050 and to 10.9 billion by 2100 (United Nations Population Fund 2013). High population growth rates prevail in many developing countries, most of which are on the United Nations' list of 49 least developed countries.

Put simply, the human species is living beyond its means. Profound shifts in thinking and acting are required to overcome current challenges and to prosper into the future. Governments must do more, and differently. New ways of building sustainable economies are essential – they need to stabilise the climate, protect habitats and environments, shift energy consumption to renewable forms, increase food production using less water and fewer chemicals, create jobs, build community cohesiveness and generate prosperity while achieving greater income equality. As Vanada Shiva, physicist, environmental activist and eco-feminist, remarked, 'sustainability demands that we move out of the economic trap that is leaving no space for other species and other people' (Shiva 2000).

How sustainable are you? Measure your ecological footprint

The term 'ecological footprint' has entered the lexicon in recent years as a way of measuring the impacts of human lifestyles on the planet and is measured by an ecological footprint calculator (Wackernagel & Yount 1998). A country's footprint is the sum of all the cropland, grazing land, forest and fishing grounds required to produce the food, fibre and timber it consumes, to absorb the wastes emitted when it uses energy and to provide space for its infrastructure.

Changes in the global footprint show a consistent trend. Overall, humanity's ecological footprint has doubled since 1966 (WWF Global 2010). In 2007, the most recent year for which data is available, the footprint exceeded the Earth's biocapacity, the area actually available to produce renewable resources and absorb CO_2, by 50 per cent. This is well beyond the level that the planet can regenerate on an annual basis. The impact is net environmental degradation. In other words, the total world population is engaged in unsustainable ecological overshoot.

Australia's ecological footprint has been calculated at 6.6 global hectares (gha) per person, which places Australia in the top 10 countries with the largest footprints and is three and a half times more than Australian environments have available. While such figures are useful, the important message related by ecological footprint measurements is that humanity's demand on the planet's living resources exceeds the Earth's regenerative capacity by about 30 per cent (WWF Global 2010). This is not sustainable and is a fundamental equity issue for our children and future generations.

Provocation 1.3

Calculate your own ecological footprint by going to www.footprintnetwork.org/en/index.php/GFN/page/calculators.

School children can calculate their footprint by going to www.kidsfootprint.org.

Young children and sustainability

As suggested earlier, exciting life opportunities lie ahead for many children, particularly those born in the wealthy West, even during turbulent economic times. The internet, for example, enables access to huge amounts of information, entertainment, commerce and communication possibilities across the globe, in rapid time. Children of developed nations have far more material possessions, and far more freedoms and rights in law, than at any time in the past. Individual options have been hugely expanded; choices seem endless. Nevertheless, even for 'well-off' children, there is increasing concern about the state of the world – in all its dimensions – if actions are not made, with some urgency, to reverse or ameliorate current trends.

A key driver impacting on children's future prospects is rapid urbanisation. According to a report by the United Nations Children's Fund (UNICEF), *Children in an Urban World* (2012), 'The day is coming when the majority of the world's children will grow up in cities and towns. Already, half of all people live in urban areas. By mid-century, over two thirds of the global population will call these places home' (p. 1). It is acknowledged that the more urban a country, the more likely it is to have higher incomes and stronger institutions. However, urban advances are uneven; millions of children live in marginalised urban settings that provide real challenges. A consequence of informal settlements and impoverished neighbourhoods is that children are excluded from essential services and social protection, and their survival rates, nutritional status and education access are severely compromised. Such environments are clearly unsustainable.

As McMichael (1993) has commented, 'Rapid urbanisation represents a profound transformation of human ecology – a transformation that is generally outstripping social and political responses' (p. 261), with the environmental by-products of large and concentrated urban populations posing direct threats to health and the quality of city life. In 2011, McMichael added to his remarks, stating that, in addition to the well-known health burdens that cities in the industrial era endure – toxic effluent chemicals in air, water and soil arising from huge increases in energy generation, industrial and agricultural chemicals, artificial food preservation and packaging and so on – new health threats are emerging. These are the ones arising from anthropogenic system–disrupting global environmental changes that include risks arising 'at the urban inter-faces with climate change, water shortage, rising seas and loss of community' (McMichael 2014, p. 52). Climate change, for example, brings heightened heat expo-sures amplified by the urban 'heat island effect' where huge, often treeless, agglomer-ations of masonry, steel and asphalt absorb much more heat than does the surrounding countryside, then traps it so that even night-time offers little relief.

For young children – and especially poor young children – these issues are com-pounded by their increased physical and social vulnerability, and the potentially limited provision of protective factors, such as meaningful relationships with adults, and positive cognitive and emotional stimulation. In addition, Tranter and Sharpe (2007) comment that, in relation to children and peak oil, 'It seems almost inevitable that one of the outcomes of peak oil [when cheap oil is no longer available] will be widespread poverty and an exacerbation of current inequalities' (p. 192) within urban areas, within nations and between nations. By many measures, our cities are not 'child-friendly' for rich or poor, a theme explored further in Sue Cooke's Chapter 8.

Provocation 1.4

If you were a city mayor or local area councillor, what would you do to make your city or neighbourhood more 'child-friendly'? What top five actions would you take?

Reporting specifically about climate change impacts on children, a growing list of authors and experts (for example, Farrant, Armstrong & Albrecht 2012) express mount-ing concern. Professor Fiona Stanley, an Australian epidemiologist noted for her work in public health and her research into child and maternal health, warned in April 2014 that climate change was expected to cause an increase in malnutrition among children as well as a rise in both old and new infectious diseases. Professor Stanley 'said the children and grandchildren of the next two generations would bear the brunt of climate change and expressed frustration that international and local efforts to mitigate global warming were not concentrating more on the public health effects' (Cox 2014).

Bartlett (2008) identifies a number of probable – and disproportionate – impacts of global warming on children, especially those living in cities. These are that:

- young children are at a stage of rapid growth and development and are less well equipped to deal with toxic levels of stress, deprivation and displacement

- their rapid metabolisms, immature organs and nervous systems, developing cognition, limited experience, and behavioural characteristics contribute to their vulnerability

- exposure to the various risks is likely to have long-term repercussions for children.

Such potential impacts are intensified by poverty. I argue that these impacts also apply to the broader range of environmental and sustainability issues that have been recognised for decades as injurious to human health and wellbeing (see, for example, Hicks 1996). Young children are already impacted by the physical and social effects of increased traffic, loss of green space, air and water pollution, and chemical exposures. The window of opportunity to act in time to avoid further dramatic impacts of unsustainable development is closing. The passage of time has not changed the underlying message of Timberlake and Thomas (1990), who wrote:

> We act as we do because we can get away with it: future generations do not vote; they have no political or financial power; they cannot challenge our decisions. But the results of the present profligacy are rapidly closing options for future generations. Most of today's decision-makers will be dead before the planet feels the heavier effects of acid precipitation, global warming, ozone depletion and species loss. Most of the young voters of today will still be alive (p. 11).

What is education for sustainability (EfS)?

It is a mistake, however, to think of children only as victims in the face of present and future sustainability challenges – and this is the key purpose of this book. With care, support and *education*, young children can be extraordinarily resilient and positive about the world and their place in shaping it. With growing international evidence of the benefits of children and young people being educated as active and informed participants who can respond to, and shape, the challenges in their lives (Berthelsen 2009; Penn 2009), I argue that even the very young can contribute ideas, energy and creativity to managing and solving local issues. This is where EfS and, particularly, ECEfS, plays its part.

While education has a key role in addressing sustainability concerns, it is important to emphasise that solving the world's problems cannot rest on the shoulders of educators alone, and certainly not on children's shoulders. Sustainability is everyone's business – politicians, civil servants, the media, doctors, plumbers, parents and grandparents. To change how we live though, first, we must change how we think. Bonnett (2002) calls for the exploration of sustainability as a 'frame of mind' (p. 9), a metaphysical transformation that qualitatively shifts outlook and relationships, where 'the attitude of sustainability is not a bolt on option but a necessity' (p. 19). Education and learning have clear roles in helping to create such shifts; 'across the globe there is a surge in interest in sustainability issues in governments, communities and organisations and in business and industry ... In response, new policies, legislation, forms of governance at the local, regional, national and international level and, indeed, new forms of education and learning are emerging that can help facilitate such changes' (Wals 2009, p. 7). However, while there have been such advances, it is apparent that many education policymakers remain unaware of the scale of the changes required if education is to play a significant and constructive role in achieving a more sustainable society (Sterling 2006). Indeed, in a number of countries, some politicians and policymakers are actively working to dismantle past advances.

Such fundamental reframing necessitates significant shifts in education – from fragmentary, short-term, 'here-and-now' thinking (Sterling calls this 'mechanistic') towards systemic, long-term, futures-oriented thinking ('ecological' thinking). An important element of the latter is the transcendence of discipline-bound knowledge. Living sustainably requires not just scientific and technological solutions but new social solutions and alternatives that blend science, sociology, psychology, health, economics, education, the arts and politics. Adopting interdisciplinary and, indeed, transdisciplinary ways of thinking and problem solving that are more than simply joining disciplines together is essential but a great challenge. Transdisciplinarity creates new knowledge, processes and perspectives that go 'beyond' the disciplines and offers new ways of looking at and responding to issues and problems.

A concept in evolution

Just as sustainability is a hard-to-define concept still being debated and clarified, so too is 'education for sustainability' a concept in transition. It is generally recognised that the first concerted effort to define environmental education and set out guiding principles and frameworks was at the Intergovernmental Conference on Environmental Education held in Tbilisi in 1977. The concepts and vision taken up at Tbilisi encompassed a broad spectrum of environmental, social, ethical, economic and cultural dimensions. The Tbilisi Declaration became the foundation for environmental education and has driven the call for environmentally educated teachers to be the 'priority of priorities'. The Brundtland Report, too, recognises that 'the world's teachers . . . have a crucial role to play in helping to bring about the extensive changes needed for sustainable development' (World Commission on Environment and Development 1987).

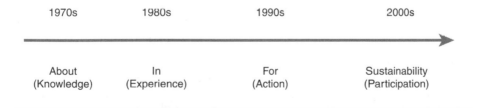

Figure 1.2 *Evolution of environmental education approaches*
Source: Tilbury, Coleman & Garlick (2005, p. 26)

Environmental education to EfS: A short history

EfS can be traced back to its basis in environmental education. Pivotal documents/initiatives that have contributed to environmental education/EfS include:

- Agenda 21 of the 1992 United Nations Conference on Environment and Development (Rio Earth Summit)
- the World Summit on Sustainable Development held in Johannesburg in 2002
- the United Nations Decade of Education for Sustainable Development (UNESCO 2005).

An early assumption of environmental education was that adequate knowledge and concern for the environment – generally derived through outdoor, science-based education – would create an appropriate environmental ethic leading to changes in behaviours that would be more 'environmentally friendly'. Research into links between environmental knowledge and values has indicated, however, little relationship between acquired knowledge and concern and values. Thus, in the 1990s, environmental educators began to refer to dimensions of environmental education that recognised these distinctions:

- education *about* the environment (understanding concepts and knowledge related to environmental processes and issues)
- education *in, through* or *from* the environment (direct experiences and field knowledge and skills)
- education *for* the environment (developing values and action skills, as well as knowledge and processes, aimed at learners making informed judgements, participating in decision making and taking action on environment-related issues).

The latter form of environmental education – education *for* the environment – subsumes education *in* and *about* the environment, but takes an overtly socio-political position. It is the form of environmental education that is closest to the more contemporary approach of 'education for sustainability'.

EfS – a socially transformative approach

EfS offers a vision of education that seeks to empower people to assume responsibility for creating a sustainable future. As Lang (2007) comments, EfS 'focuses on the interactions between people, and how these interrelationships affect the integrity of the environment and its functioning' (p. 6). This requires 'a deep understanding of ourselves, our neighbours, our societal and cultural processes, and how we are connected with the ecological systems for life'. EfS is founded on principles of critical inquiry, empowerment, participation, democratic decision making, action taking that supports sustainable living and aims for social change – it is transformative education. As such, there is recognition that education that delivers 'more of the same' is deeply inadequate in terms of contributing to the necessary social transformations required for sustainability. David Orr, a leading advocate of environmental education/EfS commented, and this still rings true, 'the crisis [of sustainability] cannot be solved by the same kind of education that has helped create the problems' (1994, p. 83).

This transformative orientation requires EfS to be implemented in such a way that it develops systemic curriculum, pedagogy and policy responses that go deep and wide (a topic returned to in Chapter 16), with the purpose of overcoming the fragmented, shallow and inconsistent approaches too often seen in educational settings. As growing international evidence indicates, an important element of a systemic approach is for EfS to be enacted through 'whole settings' approaches (Henderson & Tilbury 2004) aimed at transforming current [unsustainable] ways of thinking and acting with embedded 'cultures of sustainability' (see also Chapters 3 and 4 of this text).

Characteristics of EFS

Tilbury and Wortman (2004) identify the following skills as essential to EfS:

- *Envisioning* – being able to imagine a better future. The premise is that if we know where we want to go, we will be better able to work out how to get there.
- *Critical thinking and reflection* – learning to question current belief systems and recognise the assumptions underlying our knowledge, perspective and opinions. Critical thinking helps people learn to examine economic, environmental, social or cultural structures in the context of sustainability.
- *Systemic thinking* – acknowledging complexities and looking for links and synergies when trying to find solutions to problems.
- *Building partnerships* – promoting dialogue and negotiation and learning to work together.
- *Participation in decision making* – empowering people.

A further contribution to the discussion of what constitutes EfS for educators is offered by the United Nations Economic Commission for Europe Strategy for Education for Sustainable Development (2012). A number of key competencies for EfS, using three broad organisers, have been developed in the Strategy:

- *holistic approach*, which seeks integrative thinking and practice
- *envisioning change*, which explores alternative futures, learns from the past and inspires engagement in the present
- *achieving transformation*, which serves to change how people learn and the systems that support learning.

Beyond the United Nations Decade of Education for Sustainable Development (UNDESD) (2005–14)

A key driver of EfS worldwide has been the United Nations Decade of Education for Sustainable Development (UNDESD) (2005–14). This UNESCO-led initiative provided impetus for debates, discussions, agenda setting and concrete actions around sustainability and gave added strength to existing movements around the globe (see UNESCO

2002). In the schooling sector, a range of whole-school approaches to EfS got underway or were supported, variously called Sustainable Schools (Australia), Enviro-schools (New Zealand), Green Schools (USA), Green School Project (China), Green Flag (Sweden) and Eco-schools (Europe). Some of these – too few – welcomed the early childhood education sector into their programs.

Find out more about the achievements and challenges of the UNDESD

A range of UNESCO reports have been published over the past decade that examined the implementation and effectiveness of the UNDESD or contributed to greater discussion and awareness of EfS. Check out the following:

- *Good Practices in Education for Sustainable Development Using the Earth Charter* (2008)
- *Contribution of Early Childhood Education to a Sustainable Society* (2007)
- *Review of Contexts and Structures for Education for Sustainable Development* (2009)
- *Education for Sustainable Development: An Expert Review of Processes and Learning* (2011).

The end of the Decade, however, is not the end of global efforts to embed education for sustainable development/sustainability into international education systems. At the time of writing, a proposal for a Global Action Programme on ESD as a follow-up to the UNDESD has been developed 'to promote education for sustainable development and to integrate sustainable development more actively into education' (UNESCO General Conference 2013, p. 1). The overall goal of the draft Global Action Programme is 'to generate and scale-up action in all levels and areas of education and learning in order to accelerate progress towards sustainable development' (p. 1). Priority action areas are policy support, whole-institution approaches, educators, youth and local communities. These action areas offer affordances for early childhood education, especially as early childhood education has been identified in a number of reviews and reports (refer to the breakout box above) as requiring much greater efforts with regard to EfS. This is despite the fact there is increasing understanding of the importance of early childhood education to the realisation of sustainability.

A role for early childhood education for sustainability (ECEfS)

As discussed, there are still big gaps in the uptake of EfS principles and approaches within early childhood education. While still under-practised, under-resourced and under-researched, giant steps have been made in recent times.

Practitioners – the early drivers of this uptake – continue to engage with EfS, with increasing efforts being made to embed ECEfS into policy and research. Two reports that offer an international perspective of ECEfS efforts have been published: *The Contribution of Early Childhood Education to a Sustainable Society* (Pramling Samuelsson & Koga 2008) and *The Gothenburg Recommendations on Education for Sustainable Development* (University of Gothenburg & Chalmers University of Technology 2008). In some countries, such as Korea and Sweden, EfS is written into national early childhood education policy and curriculum frameworks. In other countries, there are pointers towards EfS in early childhood education, although these might not be as strong, yet, as one would hope.

Australian policy and EfS

Australia has two national policy documents that lend support to EfS in early childhood education:

1. *Belonging, Being and Becoming: The Early Years Learning Framework for Australia* (Australian Government, Department of Education, Employment and Workplace Relations 2009) sets the direction of early childhood education nationally. This document gives a slight nod to education for sustainability, but the conceptual understandings therein are rather vague and ambiguous. Children's agency is seen as connected to their own life, family and early childhood centre (that is, focused only on their social worlds), although the document does recognise that children should develop skills for active future citizenship in their early education.
2. The National Quality Standard (Australian Children's Education and Care Quality Authority n.d.) provides a legislative lever for the inclusion of EfS into early childhood education. Quality Area 3 (QA3) relates to a service's physical environment and makes direct reference to 'sustainable practices', stating that 'the service takes an active role in caring for its environment and contributes to a sustainable future'. Specifically, QA3 asks that:
   - 'Sustainable practices are embedded in service operations' (Element 3.3.1)
   - 'Children are supported to become environmentally responsible and show respect for the environment (Element 3.3.2).

In terms of ECEfS research, discussed in more detail in the final chapter, initiatives include the formation of an international network stemming from the two Transnational Dialogues in Research in ECEfS, and publication of the first international research text, *Research in Early Childhood Education for Sustainability: International Perspectives and Provocations* (Davis & Elliott 2014). Alongside steady growth in refereed journal articles, conference presentations, Masters and doctoral studies, a new international journal and various research projects in train, both practice and research in ECEfS is beginning to consolidate.

What is ECEfS?

ECEfS can be described as the enactment of transformative, empowering and participative education around sustainability issues, topics and experiences within early
education contexts. Such contexts take many forms – homes, childcare centres,
kindergartens, preschools, schools, environmental education centres, zoos, botanical
gardens, Indigenous heritage sites and a range of other community sites. Regardless
of the setting, what is advocated in this book is that ECEfS supports early learning
communities to create 'cultures of sustainability' that build or transform thinking,
practices and relationships around sustainability – an approach that occurs 'inside'
the setting, not imposed or mandated by external agents, and uses a whole-of-setting
approach. (Chapters 3 and 4 describe such an approach.)

It is important to emphasise that ECEfS is not about reducing or replacing
the more common play and learning events and experiences that characterise
early childhood education with learning and projects that are excessively focused
on environmental and sustainability issues. As is shown in Sharon Stuhmcke's
Chapter 11, the children in her kindergarten were engaged in typical learning
experiences while also having opportunities to learn through a sustainability-
oriented project. Traditional early childhood curriculum and pedagogical strategies –
dress-ups, puppetry, storytelling, singing, dancing, painting, digging, building with
blocks – remain 'the stuff' of early childhood education and will continue to provide
strong beginnings for young children in exploring, understanding and shaping their
worlds. What ECEfS is about, though, is enriching such experiences and overtly
building young children's knowledge, dispositions and skills to 'make a difference'
in their own lives on sustainability-related matters, now and into the future.

Why is ECEfS important?

Sometimes I am asked whether it is proper or appropriate to introduce young children
to sustainability concerns. Others ask, why put time, energy and resources into ECEfS?
Is it of value?

My response in 2014 is the same as it has been previously: sustainability issues and
topics are already part of children's lives. Many children have already seen graphic
images – perhaps they have experienced similar events firsthand – of dying birds,
drowning polar bears, choking smog, urban slums, war and civil upheaval, refugee
children and families aboard leaky boats, or the effects of droughts, floods and cyclones.
They already hear conversations and debates about these topics and events on the news
and within families. Who knows what ideas and impressions about such matters – and
about the future – young children are already formulating? Education is the *antidote* to
what is offered up. As a parent or educator, would you do nothing about classroom
bullying? Gender stereotyping? Playground racism? Would you ignore children's

questions about events such as a missing jet, gone for weeks or months, or the floods that devastated their town or city?

Provocation 1.5

What topical, perhaps uncomfortable, questions have you been asked by young children? How did you respond 'in the moment'? What teaching and learning strategies did you/could you use to provide a deeper, more enduring response to their queries?

What is the 'right' age to explore environmental and sustainability issues with young children? Is it 8, 10, perhaps 12 years? Delaying learning about such issues and topics reveals a 'blind spot' (Elliott & Davis 2009) about the realities of children's lives and the capabilities of young children to understand. This blind spot supports beliefs about young children that represent them as oblivious to – and quite separate from – the world in which they actually live; these beliefs imply that young children cannot understand complex ideas and are incapable of problem solving and acting within, and for, the environments in which they live. No matter how much we may wish it to be otherwise, children *are* exposed to, impacted upon and affected by real-world issues. Turning a 'blind eye' simply delays their ability to make sense of a world already known to them. Young children deserve early education that takes them and their capabilities seriously. ECEfS does this, and does it in positive, empowering ways.

ECEfS as transformative education

ECEfS is not 'doom and gloom' education. It is *transformative education* that values, encourages and supports children to be problem seekers, problem solvers and action takers in their own environments. It is explicitly about creating social change, and central to this change is the redistribution of power and authority. Empowerment can describe any transfer of power. As MacNaughton and Williams (2009) comment, 'it most often refers to the transfer of cultural, political, economic and social power between people' (p. 311), with the aim being 'to create greater social justice through participating in the transformation of their lives' (p. 312). In the context of early childhood education, empowerment provides greater opportunities for children to participate, make decisions and have choices; that is, it gives them the power (the ability) to do things (MacNaughton & Williams 2009).

When applied to ECEfS, empowerment and transformation mean creating changes in the ways children think, act and learn in relation to sustainability issues, topics and practices. Young children learn, for example, to be problem solvers and solution seekers around social and environmental issues and topics of meaning in their local context – they can plant and maintain gardens, care for local bushland, engage with indigenous elders to learn about local cultures and landscapes, or work with their council to enhance the local park for its citizens. As they engage in such thinking and actions, young children also learn the social and political skills of working together, resolving differences, making a case, quiet activism and the persistence required to harness the necessary resources to create changes and to implement their planned actions. At the same time, children learn to read and write for a purpose as they make signs and write stories, expand their vocabularies, learn to count, learn to 'do science', and learn to be physically active and comfortable outdoors. Many of their early thoughts and actions around sustainability topics and issues also have the potential to become habits that can be transferred into their lives outside of kindergarten or preschool, and that they take with them into the future as adults.

Linking early childhood education and EfS

In 1998, I wrote a paper (see Davis 1998) where I outlined the synergies between early childhood education and environmental education. Although discussions about environmental education and EfS have advanced considerably over the years, in many ways, this earlier discussion still provides a useful framework for thinking about contemporary ECEfS. At the time, I applied the '*in, about* and *for*' approaches of environmental education – described earlier – to early childhood educational practices. In summary, this discussion focused on:

- *Education* in *the environment* – a form of environmental education that employs the natural environment as a medium for learning, giving priority to the outdoors as a setting and learning resource. In early childhood settings, this often includes exploration of the outdoors, including nature studies, art play with natural materials, gardening, and playing with water, sand, mud, sticks and leaves. It seeks to provide foundational experiences that put children literally 'in touch' with nature to foster wonder, empathy and love for the natural environment.
- *Education* about *the environment* – a form of environmental education that encourages, for example, understanding the function of natural systems such as the water cycle (where rain comes from; why puddles dry up) or the carbon cycle (process of composting). It helps children appreciate and value the complexity of the natural world and interconnections between human and natural systems. Science learning including foundational scientific processes, such as observing and inferring, often underpins education *about* the environment.
- *Education* for *the environment* – environmental education with a socio-political dimension concerned with social action for change. Education *for* the environment involves, among other things, critical examination of social and environmental practices around, for example, the waste generated from lunch boxes, or children ostracising others who look or dress differently. Such critique is followed by collaborative problem solving and action taking to introduce more socially and environmentally sustainable strategies.

Generally speaking, early childhood services are quite good at offering opportunities for young children to play and learn *in* the environment. Learning *about* the environment is also engaged in reasonably well – young children generally have good groundings in the natural sciences through investigating plants, animals, soils, rocks, the water cycle, composting, gardening and the like.

I argue, though, that learning *in* and *about* the environment is not sufficient for laying the foundations for sustainability because they fail to explore human–environment interactions as causal in sustainability problems. They are also deficient, theoretically and practically, in helping to create current and future citizens who become agents of change for sustainability. It is hoped that the case studies provided throughout this text will give readers a stronger sense of what education *for* the environment and EfS within early childhood educational contexts might look like in practice.

Final thoughts: Children's rights in the age of (un)sustainability

In the first edition, I used this introductory chapter to explore and present ideas for a possible theoretical frame for ECEfS drawn from my teaching, research and scholarship in this field over many years. Since then, I have had the opportunity to think more about these ideas. As I stated earlier, ECEfS is essentially a matter of ethics and values, of teaching and learning framed by an understanding of, and commitment to, sustainability. As for early childhood education generally, children's rights are the foundation of ECEfS. However, prompted by the challenges of sustainability, I propose a revisioning of children's rights aimed at encouraging early education to better respond to these challenges. This revisioning offers a multidimensional approach to rights, illustrated in Figure 1.3. Further explanations of these dimensions can be found in Davis (2014). Here I provide a short overview for this text:

Dimension 1: This identifies children's *basic rights* to survival, protection and participation that are foundational rights as promulgated in the United Nations Convention on the Rights of the Child (UNICEF 1989).

Dimension 2: This highlights children's *agentic participation rights*, an expansion of participation rights beyond the right to express opinions, have a say and be heard. These rights promote children as active, capable participants in decision making and action taking.

Dimension 3: This dimension calls for greater recognition of *collective rights*, recognition that the complexities and scale of sustainability challenges demand social responses that serve collective interests, 'the greater good', if you will, rather than those that seek to maximise individual interests. Acknowledgement of collective rights means bringing people together – especially marginalised peoples and communities – for the common, shared purpose of healthy lives and long-term survival.

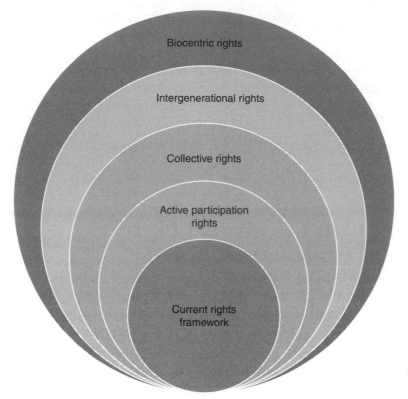

Figure 1.3 *Five dimensions of rights for early childhood education in light of the challenges of sustainability*
Source: Davis (2014, p. 23)

Dimension 4: This recognises *intergenerational rights*, an extension of collective rights that alerts us to the injustice of current generations taking and using the resources and capital of next generations, and leaving the planet less equipped to meet future generations' rights to strive for happy, healthy and secure lives.

Dimension 5: This dimension recognises *biocentric/ecocentric rights*. Biocentrism acknowledges that all biological species, not only human beings, have value and inherent rights to life. Ecocentrism extends these rights to the Earth's entire ecosystem conferring rights to elements such as air, soil and water, landscapes and ecosystems such as entire river catchments.

To summarise, in this proposal for revisioning children's rights, the United Nations Convention on the Rights of the Child remains the foundation for thinking about how children should be looked after and involved in society. However, I believe the Convention is no longer sufficient for thinking about children's rights given the necessity to live sustainably, now and into the future. Communal rights and the rights of all living things on the planet must also be taken into account if sustainability is ever to become a reality.

Conclusion

This chapter provides an overview of the role and potential of ECEfS, a synthesis of early childhood education and EfS. It highlights that ECEfS is rapidly gaining support and leverage, and that there is rapidly growing interest in the field across the globe. Now is the time for early childhood educators to fully engage with sustainability in its broadest sense – this is a moral and ethical imperative as well as an educational one. Professor Emeritus Peter Moss, a highly regarded researcher in early childhood education, commented in 2010: 'I want to argue that we, humankind, are in a period of crisis and peril … that we must review fundamentally the purposes of all education and, therefore, the values, qualities and practices needed of all educators, whether working with 15-month-olds or 15-year-olds (Moss 2010, p. 9). I couldn't agree more; early childhood education is beginning to 'make a difference', but has so much more to offer. It is now time for early childhood education to take bigger, bolder steps in creating healthy, just and sustainable futures for young children.

Review provocations

1. What ideas in this chapter have most impacted on you? Why?
2. Think about the world in 50 years' time. What do you think it will be like? How would you like it to be? What would you like your descendants to say about you and your contribution to the state of the world in 50 years?
3. Have you calculated your ecological footprint? What does this tell about your lifestyle? What aspects of your current way of living might you be able to change in order to reduce your ecological footprint? What practical steps can you take immediately to 'make a difference'?
4. Consider ways to address environmental topics and issues within your early childhood education context. Where might you start? Think about ways to engage the children in your centre or class. Who else can support you? What resources/information do you require? Start a curriculum plan.

References

Australian Children's Education and Care Quality Authority (n.d.). *National Quality Standard*. Sydney: ACECQA, www.acecqa.gov.au/national-quality-framework/the-national-quality-standard (accessed 1 May 2014).

Australian Government, Department of Education, Employment and Workplace Relations (2009). *Belonging, Being and Becoming: The Early Years Learning Framework for Australia*. Canberra: Department of Education, Employment and Workplace Relations for the Council of Australian Governments.

Bartlett, S. (2008). Factfile: Climate change and urban children. *Child Rights Information Network (CRIN)*, 22, p. 40.

Berthelsen, D. (2009). Participatory learning: Issues for research and practice. In D. Berthelsen, J. Brownlee & E. Johansson (eds), *Participatory Learning in the Early Years*. London & New York: Routledge.

Bonnett, M. (2002). Education for sustainability as a frame of mind. *Environmental Education Research*, 8(1), 9–20.

Brown, L. (2000). Information economy boom obscuring Earth's decline. *Worldwatch News Release*. Worldwatch Institute, www.worldwatch.org/news-releases?page=22 (accessed 16 February 2000).

Cox, L. (2014). Fiona Stanley attacks deniers and Tony Abbott, warns climate change is a serious health issue. *Sydney Morning Herald* (17 April), www.smh.com.au/federal-politics/political-news/fiona-stanley-attacks-deniers-and-tony-abbott-warns-climate-change-is-a-serious-health-issue-20140417-zqvvu.html (accessed 1 May 2014).

Davis, J. (1998). Young children, environmental education and the future. *Early Childhood Education Journal*, 26(6), 117–23.

Davis, J. (2014). Examining early childhood education through the lens of education for sustainability: Revisioning rights. In J. Davis & S. Elliott (eds), *Research in Early Childhood Education for Sustainability: International Perspectives and Provocations*. London & New York: Routledge.

Davis, J. & Elliott, S. (eds) (2014). *Research in Early Childhood Education for Sustainability: International Perspectives and Provocations*. London & New York: Routledge.

Earth Charter Initiative (2012). The Earth Charter, www.earthcharterinaction.org/content/pages/Read-the-Charter.html (accessed 1 May 2014).

Education Queensland (2008). *Statement on Sustainability for All Queensland Schools*, http://education.qld.gov.au/publication/production/reports/pdfs/statement-on-sustainability-all-qld-schools-enough-for-all-forever.pdf (accessed 14 May 2009).

Elliott, S. & Davis, J. (2009). Exploring the resistance: An Australian perspective on educating for sustainability in early childhood. *International Journal of Early Childhood*, 41(2), 65–77.

Farrant, B., Armstrong, F. & Albrecht, G. (2012). Future under threat: Climate change and children's health. *The Conversation* (9 October), http://theconversation.com/future-under-threat-climate-change-and-childrens-health-9750 (accessed 1 May 2014).

Henderson, K. & Tilbury, D. (2004). *Whole-School Approaches to Sustainability: An International Review of Sustainable School Program*. Report prepared by the Australian Research Institute in Education for Sustainability (ARIES) for the Department of the Environment and Heritage, Australian Government.

Hicks, D. (1996). A lesson for the future: Young people's hopes and fears for tomorrow. *Futures*, 28(1), 1–13.

Horeton, R., Beaglehole, R., Bonita, R., Raeburn, J., McKee, M. & Wall, S. (2014). From public to planetary health: A manifesto. *The Lancet*, 383, 847.

Index Mundi (2013). World population growth rate, www.indexmundi.com/world/population_ growth_rate.html (accessed 1 May 2014).

Intergovernmental Panel on Climate Change (IPCC) (2013). Summary for policymakers. In T. F. Stocker, D. Qin, G.-K. Plattner, M. Tignor, S. K. Allen, J. Boschung, A. Nauels, Y. Xia, V. Bex & P. M. Midgley (eds), *Climate Change 2013: The Physical Science Basis*. Contribution of Working Group I to the Fifth Assessment Report of the Intergovernmental Panel on Climate Change. Cambridge, UK & New York, NY, USA: Cambridge University Press.

Lang, J. (2007). *How to Succeed with Education for Sustainability*. Melbourne: Curriculum Corporation.

Lowe, I. (2006). Shaping a sustainable, healthy future. *VicHealth Letter: Healthy Planet, Healthy People*, Summer, 4–7.

McMichael, A. (1993). *Planetary Overload: Global Environmental Change and the Health of the Human Species*. Cambridge, UK: Cambridge University Press.

McMichael, A. (2014). Population health in the Anthropocene: Gains, losses and emerging trends. *The Anthropocene Review*, 1 (1), 44–56.

MacNaughton, G. & Williams, G. (2009). *Techniques for Teaching Young Children: Choices for Theory and Practice* (3rd edn). Frenchs Forest: Pearson Australia.

Moss, P. (2010). We cannot continue as we are: The educator in an education for survival. *Contemporary Issues in Early Childhood*, 11(1), 8–19.

Orr, D. W. (1994). *Earth in Mind: On Education, Environment, and the Human Prospect*. Washington, DC: Island Press.

Penn, H. (2009). International perspectives on participatory learning: Young children's perspectives across rich and poor countries. In D. Berthelsen, J. Brownlee & E. Johansson (eds), *Participatory Learning in the Early Years*. New York & London: Routledge.

Pramling Samuelsson, I. & Koga, Y. (2008). *The Contribution of Early Childhood to a Sustainable Society*. Paris: UNESCO.

Shiva, V. (2000). Poverty and globalisation. *Reith Lecture 2000*. British Broadcasting Corporation, http://news.bbc.co.uk/hi/english/static/events/reith_2000/lecture5.stm (accessed 22 January 2009).

Sterling, S. (2006). *Sustainable Education: Revisioning Learning and Change*. London: Green Books.

Stern, N. (2006). Executive Summary. In *The Economics of Climate Change* (pp. i–xxvii). London: British Government.

Tilbury, D. (2011) *Education for Sustainable Development: An Expert Review of Processes and Learning*. Paris: UNESCO.

Tilbury, D., Coleman, V. & Garlick, D. (2005). *A National Review of Environmental Education and its Contribution to Sustainability in Australia: School Education*. Canberra: Australian Government,

Department of the Environment and Heritage and Australian Research Institute in Education for Sustainability.

Tilbury, D. & Wortman, D. (2004). *Engaging People in Sustainability*. Gland, Switzerland: IUCN.

Timberlake, L. & Thomas, L. (1990). *When the Bough Breaks . . .Our Children, Our Environment*. London: Earthscan.

Tranter, P. & Sharpe, S. (2007). Children and peak oil: An opportunity in crisis. *International Journal of Children's Rights*. 15, 181–97.

UNESCO (n.d.). The four dimensions of sustainable development, www.unesco.org/education/ tlsf/mods/theme_a/popups/mod04t01s03.html (accessed 1 May 2014).

UNESCO (2002). *Education for Sustainability. From Rio to Johannesburg: Lessons Learnt from a Decade of Commitment*, http://unesdoc.unesco.org/images/0012/001271/127100e.pdf (accessed 1 May 2014).

UNESCO (2005). *United Nations Decade of Education for Sustainable Development*, Executive Board Report by the Director-General on the United Nations Decade of Education for Sustainable Development 172 EX/11. Paris: UNESCO.

UNESCO and Earth Charter International Secretariat (2007). *Good Practices in Education for Sustainable Development Using the Earth Charter*, www.earthcharterinaction.org/invent/ details.php?id=248 (accessed 22 January 2009).

UNESCO General Conference (2013). *Proposal for a Global Action Programme on Education for Sustainable Development as Follow-Up to the United Nations Decade of Education for Sustainable Development (DESD) after 2014*. 37th Session, Paris.

UNICEF (1989). *Convention on the Rights of the Child*, www.unicef.org/crc (accessed 1 May 2014).

UNICEF (2012). *The State of the World's Children 2012: Children in an Urban World*, www. unicef.org/publications/index_61789.html (accessed 1 May 2014).

United Nations (2013). *Global Sustainable Development Report. Executive Summary: Building the Common Future We Want*. New York: UN Department of Economic and Social Affairs, Division for Sustainable Development, http://sustainabledevelopment.un.org/globalsdreport (accessed 1 May 2014).

United Nations Economic Commission for Europe Strategy for Education for Sustainable Development (2012). *Learning for the Future: Competencies in Education for Sustainable Development*. Geneva: United Nations Economic Commission for Europe.

United Nations Population Fund (2013). Linking population, poverty and development, www. unfpa.org/pds/trends.htm (accessed 1 May 2014).

University of Gothenburg & Chalmers University of Technology (2008). *The Gothenburg Recommendations on Education for Sustainable Development*, www.esd-world-conference-2009.org/fileadmin/download/Gothenburg_RecommendationsAndBackground.pdf (accessed 5 February 2009).

Wackernagel, D. & Yount, J. (1998). The ecological footprint: An indicator of progress towards regional sustainability. *Environmental Monitoring and Assessment*, 51(1–2), 511–29.

Wals, A. (2009). *UNDESD: Review of Contexts and Structures for Education for Sustainable Development*. UNESCO. Paris, http://unesdoc.unesco.org/images/0018/001849/184944e.pdf (accessed 1 May 2014).

World Commission on Environment and Development (1987). *Our Common Future*. Oxford: Oxford University Press.

WWF Global (2010). *Living Planet Report*, http://wwf.panda.org/about_our_earth/all_publications/living_planet_report/living_planet_report_timeline/2010_lpr2 (accessed 1 May 2014).

Chapter 2

Children in the natural world

Sue Elliott

Editor's note

In this revised chapter, **Sue Elliott** reiterates the case for deep, authentic experiences in nature as foundational for young children's holistic and healthy growth and development. She emphasises that play in nature is fundamental to young children's learning. Sue argues that early childhood education has a long history that supports play in natural playspaces and that this must not be eroded. Indeed it must be strengthened.

Equally importantly, Sue argues that play in nature is not sufficient as early childhood education for sustainability (ECEfS) – it is just one aspect, though significant, of an holistic approach to relationships. Sue asks readers to contemplate their own relationships with nature and the outdoors while provoking them to deepen and widen their ideas and practices to take account of the challenges that living unsustainably on the planet confers. She argues that early childhood educators have a key role in embedding nature into children's play environments and sharing their own enthusiasm and wonder about the natural world with children. In so doing they lay a foundation for lifelong sustainable living.

Stories from the field

When visiting an early childhood centre during morning snack time, I asked the obvious question of a child munching on an apple: 'Where do you think apples come from?' The child replied promptly, 'The supermarket'. I then asked, 'Well, I wonder where the supermarket gets apples from?' She replied (demonstrating with her hands), 'Oh, they just get some yellow stuff and squash it all together, then they put more stuff on the outside'.

Early childhood educators are highly familiar with the somewhat amusing perspectives children express about how the world works. Should we, however, view this anecdote as a source of amusement or one of alarm? How disconnected from nature have children become when an everyday food item, such as an apple, is perceived as a manufactured product? *How would you promote understandings about human–plant–food relationships in an early childhood context?*

Introduction

This chapter builds on the ideas presented in the first edition of this text. It reinvestigates the literature that identifies nature as a human construct, and discusses the evolving relationships between humans and nature. It describes the erosion of children's connections with the natural environment and presents an argument for inclusion of nature in early childhood settings as a critical element contributing to children's health, wellbeing and development. A range of pedagogical strategies supports this argument. The chapter concludes by drawing links between children playing and learning in nature and the imperative of embedding education for sustainability (EfS) into early childhood settings.

Stories from the field

Some years ago I tried to create a sense of continuity for children by working with them to create a nature diary during a once-weekly, mobile early childhood program in a rural area. The focus of the nature diary was to document our experiences of nature in the open field that was our outdoor playspace. This field offered an indigenous acacia tree, oozing sap for hungry ants; a deciduous oak tree with collectable acorns; and some pine trees creating a blanket of pine needles for emerging mushrooms. There were also serendipitous natural events, such as flocks of cockatoos, fresh cow pats and the odd snake or lizard. To my dismay, the children often chose to record human-related experiences, such as aeroplanes flying overhead, or the passing of a truck or local school bus. Clearly, my understandings of nature were different from the children's; I felt challenged trying to define nature with these children. Since that time, I have often reflected on why our understandings differed. *Were the children so immersed in nature in their rural upbringing that nature was not seen as something separate within their daily lives that required a special label? Was it that the human-made elements created engaging novelty, or was it simply a reflection of other interests for that group at that time?* Perhaps it was my city upbringing that created the challenge, or my human (adult) need to categorise. I still reflect on how humans define nature and its importance in the lives of young children. This chapter, like that in the first edition, is an opportunity to refine these reflections and to inspire others to think seriously about the place of nature in early childhood education and, specifically, how it links to EfS.

Nature as a human construct and evolving human–nature relationships

In the past, humans and nature were so intertwined that notions of nature as separate or controllable by humans were irrelevant. Just as humans have evolved over time, their relationships with nature have also evolved. It is illuminating to reflect on where we have come from and recognise where we might be going, based on current anthropocentric constructs of nature. Successive reports on the state of the planet have highlighted our unique point in evolutionary history (Australian Government, Department of Climate Change and Energy Efficiency 2011). A critical factor at the crux of this discussion is our perceptions of the natural world.

What is nature?

I begin by asking the related questions: *What is nature?* and *What are common constructs of nature in human communities today?* Is nature:

- *wilderness – remote, untouched, uncontrolled?*
  This somewhat romanticised notion of nature is defined by people who venture off the beaten track, relishing the quietness and space away from human civilisation. Nature documentaries may lull us into complacency about wilderness, but as Kingsolver (2002) asserts, 'Wildness puts us in our place. It reminds us that our plans are small and somewhat absurd' (p. 40).

- *everything not made by humans?*
  This construct of nature, common since the Industrial Revolution, became necessary to distinguish between objects human-made and natural. Recently, the lines have become increasingly blurred as marketing campaigns convince us that we can buy 'natural' foods, cosmetics and fabrics. At the core of this misunderstanding is that, ultimately, everything comes from nature, even if highly processed.

- *the natural, physical world; for example, plants, animals, rocks and soil?*
  This construct arises from a scientific view of the world, whereby humans perceive they are in control of both the living and non-living elements of nature and employ

these for human benefit, such as mining or farming. Nature is distinguished from the built, physical world of cities where we create special nature spaces, such as gardens and parks.

- *planetary ecosystems that support all life?*
  This response acknowledges the critical role of nature in supporting life on the planet and the interdependent ecosystems that nurture all life, a view well supported by ecologists, biologists and systems theorists (Bateson 1979; Capra 1997). Nature is not about individual species (such as humans); rather, it is about the responsiveness, connectedness and intertwining that draws all species together. It is about perceiving humans as just one species – though an important and powerful one – among the multitude of interdependent species relationships. This perception sharply contrasts with the view of humans as disconnected, separate from and higher than other species, and above nature as a whole.

There is no single answer to the question *What is nature?* Answers may vary depending on past experiences and, in particular, childhood experiences. Kahn and Kellert (2002) coined the term 'generational amnesia' to describe how each generation of humans is becoming successively removed from nature and, in the process, redefining what nature is. Children who may have never experienced non-urban areas, whose understandings of nature might be limited to a local street tree or potted plant, demonstrate a potentially stark reality. As Beck (1994) states, 'the meanings of nature do not grow on trees, but must be constructed' (p. 39) and children actively construct their own nature understandings from their daily experiences. It is clear that a sustainable future lies in a deeper understanding of humans *in* nature, not *against* nature. This necessitates a revision of the pervasive human construct of nature as an exploitable resource that 'has rendered humans dysfunctional in so many ways' (Kellert 2012, p. 49). The power dichotomy and disconnectedness between humans and nature – generational amnesia – has no place in a sustainable future.

Provocation 2.1

How do you define nature?

What past experiences inform your definition of nature?

What signs of generational amnesia or disconnectedness from nature have you observed?

Relationships between humans and nature are evolving

From previous studies of geography, biology or history you may have an understanding of the evolutionary past of the Earth, and know that humans are a relatively recent species. In a novel approach to comprehending the scale of the Earth's history, Ornstein and Ehrlich (2001) tracked this history over just one calendar year, using each day to represent 12 million years. Their condensed time scale shows:

1 January   – origin of the Earth
mid-February – first simple bacterial life forms
20 November – first complex life forms, fish
10 December – dinosaurs arrive
25 December – dinosaurs disappear

Then, lastly:

31 December   – first human ancestors
31 December 11.45 pm – Homo sapiens/humans emerge
31 December 11.59 pm – all recorded history, as we know it, occurs only in the last minute!

The last minute is where it all happens for humans, and only in the last half-second or less (about 50 years in real time) has awareness of human impacts on the environment, and the need to demonstrate responsibility for the planet, been realised. McKibben (Thoreaux with McKibben 1997) states: 'What nature provides is scale and context, ways to figure out who and how big we are and what we want' (p. xix). This is what this condensed time scale does; it demands that we ask questions about scale and context, including: *How have we caused so much damage to this planet in such a brief time?* and *What can we do to address the situation?*

Coulter (2008) describes the last second in this time scale as an unprecedented period of exponential human population growth. He argues that population growth is the key determinant of the global environmental crisis and, when compounded by the inequitable overuse of resources, our human footprint is beyond the Earth's biocapacity (Flannery 2008). A sustainable future is dependent on slower population growth, reduced resource demands and finding solutions to distribution inequities. Sustainability is more than fixing our relationships with nature; it is a complex social, cultural, political and economic concern on a global scale.

Further compounding these concerns is the concept of 'old mind' described by Ornstein and Ehrlich (2001), who highlight that humans evolved in very different environments to those of today. For most of human evolution, the key to survival was quick responses to imminent dangers and needs, such as thirst, rather than addressing longer-term threats. Williams and Nesse (1991, p. 1) affirm that 'human biology is designed for Stone Age conditions'. Consequently, comprehending our longer-term impacts on the Earth and the actions required for sustainability are a significant challenge (Ornstein & Ehrlich 2001; Ehrlich 2000). Such is the influence of human 'old mind' habits on the Earth that a new geological epoch, 'Anthropocene', has been proposed (Crutzen &

Stoermer 2000). This epoch aptly describes the multiple impacts of humans on the Earth's natural systems. When considered from the perspective of a global evolutionary time scale, the critical need for change at many levels is apparent – not just in how we live on Earth, but how we think about our place in evolution.

Differing interpretations of evolution

The global evolutionary time scales described above are only one interpretation of the past. People of different cultures and religions have alternative interpretations from which all civilisations may learn. *What alternative interpretations of the Earth's time frame are shared by you or by your peers?*

Morgan, Mia and Kwaymullina (2008), for example, in their collection of Australian Aboriginal stories, *Heartsick for Country*, about connections with the land, provide this salient advice:

> If we are to solve the multitude of environmental problems that we face, then we must begin with our connection to country. We must repair and regrow relationships between peoples and peoples, and people and country that have been damaged by dispossession. Despite the environmental devastation that has been wreaked on Australia, this ancient continent continues to nourish and sustain all who live here. It gives us our water and food and it protects us in ways we do not often imagine. We cannot survive here without a loving land that cares for us, and all Australians, Aboriginal and non-Aboriginal alike are bound to its rise and fall (p. 19).

Extending the evolutionary perspective, E. O. Wilson's biophilia theory (Kellert & Wilson 1993) states that our innate relationship with nature is primal to our being, and to ignore this ancient biological relationship jeopardises human survival. Drawing on this theory, Rivkin (1995) suggests that 'children reared apart from nature are necessarily limited' (p. 6). Innate relationships with nature are strongly evident in early childhood; water, rocks, plants and animals are the raw palette from which children construct their meanings of, and relationships with, nature. Chawla and Derr (2012) and Munoz (2009) align children's innate connectedness with nature with desires to play in nature. Play in and with nature just seems 'absurdly logical' (Lester & Maudsley 2006).

At some point in time, worldviews as described above became marginal to human existence, and the current Western anthropocentric views emerged. Fell and Russell (1994), inspired by Maturana (Maturana & Varela 1987), suggest that at about 4500 BC a 'nature-trusting, peaceful and sharing culture' was destroyed by an 'appropriative, patriarchal, warlike culture' (para. 62). Further, they speculate that 'the existence within us of vestiges of that nature-trusting emotional base appears to have come into conflict with our appropriative culture of today – this contradiction could be what generates so much of our human suffering' (para. 62). For example, would the clear felling of native forests for timber, or whaling for meat, be issues if there were not some people willing to actively demonstrate their vestiges of nature trusting? To reinvigorate these emotional vestiges, children must experience acquaintanceship with nature, 'a direct, intimate and tacit knowledge that affects us' (Bonnett 2004, p. 93). Such acquaintanceship occurs through play in nature, exploring the senses, discovering play affordances, and experiencing a sense of wonder in and of the natural world.

A gift of whales

In some families, values about nature and relationships with nature are actively explored as illustrated by this parent responding to an interview question about how she sought to foster her child's awareness of nature.

We were in New Zealand the Christmas before last and my son and I went whale watching. And to hear him talk about the experience of seeing killer whales and dolphins out on this boat was just so special. Like I only saw my first killer whale when I was in my 20s, and for my son to get that connection when he was only five, is one of the best gifts I could give him (Elliott 2012, p. 84).

Currently, there are increasing calls for a biocentric or ecocentric, rather than an anthropocentric, worldview. A biocentric worldview can be described as a view where all life is equally valuable and the human species, while unique, is not the central focus. An ecocentric worldview is broader, encompassing all living and non-living elements of the Earth. Kellert (2012) states: 'Until we achieve a fuller understanding of where we fit into the world that embraces a new consciousness and ethic toward nature, we will continue to generate environmental and social problems that no technology or government policy can ever resolve' (p. xiv). As early childhood educators, we are uniquely placed to ensure children play out their primal drives for connections with nature, create nature-trusting relationships, and are supported to construct new worldviews aligned with sustainable futures.

Children's connections with nature are eroding

Louv (2005) first coined the provocative phrase 'nature deficit disorder' (p. 34) to describe a generation of children so disconnected from the natural world that they experience symptoms such as diminished sensory engagement, attention difficulties, and physical and emotional illnesses. Louv's concerns are increasingly supported (Chawla & Derr 2012; Kellert 2012; Planet Ark 2011) and a popular groundswell has led to establishment of the international Children and Nature Network. Often adults fondly recall their own childhood opportunities for playing outdoors in nature. However, there are now a multitude of factors contributing to the erosion of childhood opportunities for outdoor play and contact with nature. Key factors are outlined below.

Time to play is being eroded

According to Hofferth and Sandberg (2001), children's free playtime dropped by an estimated 25 per cent between 1981 and 1997; the rise of more structured playtime and adult-directed activities are causally linked. Skar and Krogh (2009) reinforce these concerns, noting that in an increasingly competitive and materialistic world, play is commonly regarded as frivolous and a waste of time.

More importantly, reduced time for free play correlates with reduced time playing outdoors; for example, Clements' (2004) research indicated a 39 per cent drop in the frequency of daily outdoor play between generations. Perhaps more concerning is that this downward trend is also evident in educational contexts for children aged 2–11 years in the United Kingdom (Waite 2010). One may well ask the question: *When do children freely engage in outdoor play if not at home or in their educational setting?* Early childhood educators understand the significance of play in children's lives and have a critical role in advocating for outdoor play, given the increasingly hurried lives of children.

Access is evaporating

Even if children do have time to play outdoors, the accessibility of places to play is a growing concern. As Rivkin (1995) stated almost two decades ago, 'children's access to outdoor play has evaporated like water in sunshine' (p. 2). A multiplicity of factors has contributed to this diminished access. These include car-friendly, as opposed to child-friendly, streets; urban development that prioritises buildings over outdoor playspaces; negative attitudes towards inclement weather and getting dirty; and parents' perceived safety concerns. Also, as children are increasingly transported in cars and engaging less in independent active walking, the serendipitous opportunities for play are being lost (Malone 2007). In light of reduced access, early childhood educators have a responsibility to ensure outdoor play opportunities are provided every day. *Where else can children build bush cubby houses and make mud pies?*

Provocation 2.2

As an early childhood educator, how do you/will you promote access to outdoor play?

Are indoor and outdoor learning environments equally valued? Is this demonstrated through planning and opportunities for children to choose their preferred play setting?

Are children playing outdoors when parents deliver or collect their child? How might this be used as an opportunity to convey to parents the value of outdoor play?

Is the value of both indoor and outdoor environments demonstrated by similar amounts of funding and time devoted to ongoing maintenance, for example, cleaning and gardening?

Technology is taking over

Children are exposed to an ever-increasing array of screen-based technologies, at younger and younger ages. Questions are now being asked about the impacts of such media saturation. Impacts on children's behaviour, emotional wellbeing, social skills, eyesight, consumer orientation, cognitive development and body weight are cited as potential risks from overuse of technologies (French et al. 2013; Kimbro, Brooks-Gunn & McLanahan 2011; Moore & Marcus 2008).

For example, in the United States, one in five children aged birth to 2 years and one in three children aged 3–6 years have a television in their bedrooms (Vandewater et al. 2007). In a United States' study of fifth-grade students' perceptions of nature, when asked 'Do you ever see nature yourself when it's not on TV?' one student unsurprisingly replied, 'Not really. Umm, not really' (Aaron & Witt 2011). We are reminded by McKibben that nature 'provides reality, in place of the endless electronic mirages and illusions that we consider the miracle of our moment' (Thoreaux with McKibben 1997, p. xix). In progressing from an 'either nature or ICT' position, Kahn (2011) proposes a middle ground where direct experience and ICT combined may facilitate nature connections. The issue is to ensure that children do have opportunities to experience the richness of outdoor play and learning in nature; a balanced, somewhat precautionary, approach is required. In Australia, such an approach is promoted by government guidelines (Australian Government, Department of Health 2014) that stipulate no screen-based activity for children under 2 years of age and a maximum of one hour per day for 2- to 5-year-olds.

Stories from the field

An educator shared her experience of a parent questioning the content of the 3-year-olds' program at the kindergarten. In effect, the parent was asking when the 'real' learning would begin. As the educator began to explain the opportunities for learning through play, the parent revealed that she was teaching her child mathematics by sitting her in front of a computer for three hours every day, using a mathematics software program.

What is this story communicating about family beliefs concerning young children and their learning? How would you respond as an early childhood educator?

Safety concerns outweigh the need for risk and challenge in play

Gill (2007) has stimulated ongoing international discussion about how children are missing out on opportunities to manage risk because they are 'bubble-wrapped' and surrounded by 'helicopter parents' (those who hover around their children to ensure they never experience any physical or emotional risks). While parents do need to promote children's safety, it is argued that popular media has fostered disproportionate perceptions about dangers (Furedi 2001). Both parents and educators in many societies seem to have become intolerant of 'normal' play risks, failing to recognise that some risk – whether physical, cognitive, social or emotional – is inherent, if not essential, in play and life. Many researchers and commentators suggest that children's health and development is being compromised by *not* positively engaging children in risk taking (Brussoni et al. 2012; Eager & Little 2011). A revised approach, based on risk–benefit analysis (Ball, Gill & Spiegal 2008) and making playspaces 'as safe as necessary, not as safe as possible' (Guldberg 2009), is gaining support. Robert Pratt's Chapter 4 provides a practical example of risk–benefit analysis in action.

Provocation 2.3

What were your risky childhood play experiences?

Were your parents from the 'helicopter' or 'benign neglect' school of thought?

If risk is inherent in play, how do you manage risk in an early childhood setting in which play is an omnipresent activity?

How can you promote risk–benefit analysis in an early childhood context?

How do you convey the benefits of risk to parents who may be denying their children fundamentally important learning experiences?

Misperceptions about places for play

Not so long ago, a diverse range of places for play were readily defined by children in their local area: the inviting pile of builder's sand, the refuge of an old hollow tree or the challenges of a disused quarry. Such places directly communicated play affordances to children that frequently adults could not see. The notion of a playspace as synonymous with fixed, manufactured equipment evolved only in the mid 20th century, with the advent of purpose-designed playspace equipment, improved engineering and technology, and efforts to get children off busy streets (Frost 2007). Consequently, many adult perceptions of appropriate outdoor playspaces have become focused on fixed equipment from a manufacturer's catalogue. It is not surprising that children often describe these spaces as boring (Veitch et al. 2005). Concerns are also evident regarding unsustained play episodes (Luchs & Fikus 2013), social exclusion and less creative play (Dyment & O'Connell 2013). In early childhood education settings, there are significant opportunities to break with these precedents and create landscape-based or natural playspaces in which children can safely engage in diverse play opportunities. Many services in Australia, well supported by the Early Years Learning Framework (Australian Government, Department of Education, Employment and Workplace Relations 2009), are (re)creating natural playspaces. These are '*landscapes for children to embroider with the loose threads of nature*. In such landscapes children can create meaning, develop a sense of place, connect with the natural world and feel empowered to live healthy, sustainable lives' (Elliott 2008, p. 12; emphasis in the original).

Provocation 2.4

How do you define a playspace for young children?

What was your favourite playspace as a child and why?

How could you promote alternative perceptions of playspaces to parents, management committees and the wider community?

In summary, a range of factors are eroding children's connections with nature outdoors; only some are highlighted here. Early childhood educators must be advocates for children's play outdoors in nature, before another generation succumbs to nature-deficit disorder and generational amnesia.

Nature: A critical element in children's health, wellbeing and development

Research that directly supports nature as a vital element contributing to children's health, wellbeing and development is now increasingly evident. There is no single literature base to draw on here; psychologists, evolutionary biologists, developmental theorists and educationalists all provide some support, either theoretically or directly from research. The following paragraphs offer an overview (see Sue Cooke's Chapter 8 for more on this topic).

Links to mental health and wellbeing

The impacts of nature on adult mental health and wellbeing are well documented (Townsend & Weerasuriya 2010). In particular, Kaplan and Kaplan's (1989) Attention Restoration Theory suggests that green, leafy spaces have a restorative function for the human brain. This theory defines restorative places by the following criteria: they are places where one has a sense of fascination and curiosity; a sense of being away from usual settings; a sense of being part of a larger whole; and where there is compatibility with an individual's needs. These criteria appear highly applicable to natural playspaces in early childhood settings, which might well have a restorative function for all who play in them. Also, several studies have revealed positive health and wellbeing impacts on children from direct exposure to green, leafy spaces (Faber Taylor & Kuo 2011; Wells 2000). Further research is needed, but the initial signs indicate that natural spaces do have positive impacts on children's mental health and wellbeing.

Links to physical and sensory play opportunities

Play opportunities are more diverse and numerous in natural playspaces, when compared with built playspaces (Bagot 2005; Fjørtoft, Kristoffersen & Sageie 2009). In turn, more play implies greater physical activity, a critical point when reduced activity is often cited as a major causal factor in childhood obesity (Kimbro, Brooks-Gunn & McLanahan 2011). Furthermore, forest-based programs promote improved physical health and skills according to Borradaile (2006) and Fjørtoft (2001). Physically active play promoted by natural playspaces may well be part of the obesity solution. Moreover, nature is not intended to be an element for young children to explore vicariously through electronic media. From birth, direct, intimate sensory experiences with nature – such as feeling grass underfoot or smelling a scrunched leaf – are essential. Children require immersion in 'a sea of natural sensory stimuli' (Elliott & Davis 2004, p. 5) to build a broad sensory repertoire in nature, thus promoting the nature-trusting relationships described earlier. The potential benefits of play in nature also include the promotion of sensory integration processes (Sebba 1991). We might speculate that contact with nature outdoors is as important for health and wellbeing as are daily food and sleep for children. Daily access to nature outdoors in early childhood settings is an imperative; 'the cure for the lifestyle maladies of contemporary childhood seems glaringly obvious and simple: outdoor play in nature' (Moore & Marcus 2008, p. 160).

Links to a sense of agency and place

The sense of agency and place promoted by the manipulability of natural materials creates a deep sense of connectedness. Having a place in the world and a belief in one's abilities to alter or manipulate immediate surroundings is linked to wellbeing. As Sobel (1990) states: 'If we allow people to shape their own small worlds during childhood, then they will grow up knowing and feeling they can participate in shaping the big world tomorrow' (p. 12). In a similar vein, evolutionary biologists Heerwagen and Orians (2002) predict that young children – just beginning to venture into the world – will actively seek places of refuge. They propose that this is the basis of cubby building: a primal drive for children to create hiding spaces or places – a vestigial survival strategy. Kirkby (1989) states that refuges fulfil children's 'need to see without being seen' (p. 7). Recently, Moore (2010) has substantiated secret refuges as an ongoing requirement in children's playspaces.

In summary, a natural playspace can fulfil primal drives, promote feelings of agency or empowerment, and support a child's sense of place in the world.

Provocation 2.5

What contributions do experiences with nature make to children's learning and development?

What might be the long-term impacts of childhood connections with nature?

How can the benefits of outdoor play in nature be conveyed to parents who express concerns about dirty clothes and safety?

The argument supported by pedagogy

The previous sections may have convinced you of the fundamental importance of contact with nature outdoors in childhood. Further support can be gained by considering the alignment between early childhood pedagogy and the opportunities offered by play in nature.

Precedents for nature in early childhood education

The notion of children playing in nature is not new, and can be traced to Froebel's original conception of the kindergarten as a 'garden for children', where educators were seen as gardeners. 'He envisioned children being educated in close harmony with nature and the nature of the universe' (Morrison 1995, p. 54). Similarly, Montessori noted that 'to place humans in contact with nature can never be a useless act, for in order to live well humans must get in touch with nature' (Feez 2013, p. 177). Early childhood practitioners have inherited traditions such as nature tables, keeping pet animals and growing plants. Nevertheless, it is no longer enough to keep a pet mouse or grow vegetables in isolation from broader understandings of nature and the relationships between humans and nature. The challenge today is to expand on these precedents in meaningful and authentic ways relevant to sustainability imperatives.

Play affordances with/in nature

Play is fundamental in early childhood education, and play in or with nature enhances the potential for learning through play. The alignment between children's innate drive to play and their desire to connect with nature is evident. The following points highlight these pedagogical links from an early childhood practitioner's perspective:

- Nature provides the loose parts (Nicholson 1971) for play that can be investigated, manipulated and symbolically used in imaginative scenarios. Natural materials are open-ended; there is no single right way to use a natural material, but many possibilities limited only by the imagination of the player. For example, a leaf might become a fairy's seat and a pebble may be used as a sandcastle decoration. Play with natural materials also supports cultural inclusion – the symbolic play value of items such as leaves and twigs is created by the player through their own socio-cultural lens.

- Natural elements, more so than ergonomically designed structures, suggest play challenges that engage children's risk appetites. Natural shapes, textures and scales are not so predictable, require concentration, and challenge both the senses and physical skills, as in, for example, jumping over a dry creek bed or climbing a tree. 'Cognitive climbing' emphasises the potential for cognitive as well as physical skill development when climbing in nature.

- Real work is part of play for children, an opportunity to suspend childhood and take on the important roles of farmer, builder or civic participant. There are many potential real-work projects for children, such as creating vegetable gardens, building bird boxes, constructing a frog pond or participating in local environmental causes – see Robert Pratt's Chapter 4 and Sharon Stuhmcke's Chapter 11 for further examples. A bonus of real-work projects is the potential to engage interested and/or skilled parents in a shared learning journey and for children to be visibly present and authentically engaged in real life (Nimmo 2008).

- Nature is ever-changing and unpredictable. In natural playspaces, there is always something new for children to discover and respond to. Daily discoveries may stimulate new interests and program directions or create learning challenges; educators need to be responsive to the possibilities. For example, a rain puddle or the first summer tomato could be a unique and fulfilling discovery for a child.

  Play experiences in nature provide the opportunity for diverse activities that challenge, engage, inspire and provoke. In a natural setting, there is space for each individual child to experience a sense of agency and resilience and to explore their particular interests and abilities.

Special places for nature connections in early childhood

Natural outdoor playspaces are the most obvious context for connecting with nature, and many publications support the design and development of natural playspaces in early childhood centres (Elliott 2008; Gamson Danks 2010). Features such as significant plantings, creek beds (dry or wet), trees for climbing, bush cubbies and manipulable rocks and logs are typical of natural playspaces. Here, some special places that offer opportunities for connecting with nature, both within an early childhood centre and in the wider community, are identified:

- Natural play materials can extend beyond the outdoors to indoors; for example, gravel or water trays, baskets of seed pods or shells, and potted indoor plants that improve air quality and create a green backdrop. Careful and creative use of such materials as part of imaginative play, construction or sorting experiences can inspire nature connections. For further inspiration consult Aitken et al. (2013) and Kolbe (2007).

- Productive gardens created by children, parents and educators present a unique opportunity to explore human relationships with nature. Children can sow seeds, nurture plants, observe growth, harvest and prepare garden produce to eat, and then return any waste to a compost or worm farm for recycling. (See Nadine McCrea's Chapter 11 for more on this topic.) While space in some early childhood settings can be limiting, even a few pots or garden boxes of potatoes or lettuces hold promise. Perhaps an ongoing partnership with a local community garden or farm can provide gardening opportunities for children. References to support gardening projects include Alexander (2012) and Nuttall and Millington (2008). Often, useful guides are local 'green thumbs' experts, such as plant nursery workers, permaculture gardeners and community gardeners.

- Excursions into the wider community can offer different kinds of connections with nature. Excursions might be to major venues, such as botanic gardens or farms, but could equally be a local walk to explore community gardens or parks. In some services, a regular bush excursion might reflect the Scandinavian forest preschool approach that is now a worldwide trend (Elliott & Chancellor, in press; Knight 2013; Williams-Siegfredsen 2012). Such excursions may also be part of an investigation into a local environmental issue or provide the impetus for advocacy and action. Sharon Stukmcke's Chapter 11, Michiko Inoue's Chapter 13 and Okjong Ji's Chapter 14 describe how excursions and incursions were integral to projects about local environmental/sustainability issues enabling children to become empowered and visible advocates in their communities.

The role of adults

Relationships with adults are a cornerstone of early childhood pedagogy, where adults are variously described as co-learners, interpreters and role models. With respect to nature, this relationship requires responsiveness, wonder, curiosity and authentic caring for nature. Research by Chawla (2006) and Wells and Lekies (2006) confirms that, beyond direct experiences with nature, significant adults who share nature experiences with children have the greatest impact on lifelong nature dispositions. Significant adults are those who model, mentor, share and interpret positive connections with nature, not those who only teach the facts of nature. Chapters 4 and 13 provide excellent examples of adults whose roles support children learning in nature.

Rachel Carson summarised the role of the significant adult in stating: 'If a child is to keep alive his inborn sense of wonder . . . he needs the companionship of at least one adult who can share it, rediscovering with him the joy, excitement and mystery of the world we live in' (Carson 1956, 1998, p. 55). Her essay was written at a time when children were generally free to roam in nature and her sentiments are still critically relevant. I urge you to be the significant adult in promoting children's connections with nature. In the longer term, we must remember that 'creating conditions for children to learn to care for the environment has the potential to benefit not only children but all ages and all other living things as well' (Chawla & Derr 2012, p. 551).

Drawing links between children in nature and EfS

Intuitively, it seems clear that children's experiences in nature are linked to EfS. One cannot imagine being divorced from nature yet impassioned about advocating for and implementing sustainable practices. As Dighe (1993) states, 'one can hardly imagine a generation of persons with neither interest nor knowledge of the outdoors making responsible decisions about the environment' (p. 62). Further, Chawla and Derr (2012) comprehensively link direct childhood experiences and active participation in nature, with environmentally active adults. Bonnett (2002) suggests, however, that we need to view sustainability not as isolated practices, policy or curricula, but as a 'frame of mind' that underpins all decision making about the way we live. One can speculate that a sustainability frame of mind informed by childhood nature experiences has particular advantages. Thus, in reflecting more broadly on this chapter, specific links between children in nature and EfS emerge:

1. Children's experiences in nature inspire an affective knowing of the natural world or an acquaintanceship with nature (Bonnett 2004). Affective knowing can be a key motivating force when making decisions about sustainability that may have far-reaching impacts. Direct experiences in nature during childhood can personalise the possibility of living sustainably and add a deeper layer of meaning to the bigger picture.

2. In early childhood, *affective knowing* is obvious in the curiosity and enthusiasm children demonstrate when investigating the natural world. However, *cognitive knowing* of facts and information is important too. With a revised contemporary image of children as capable and competent, and pedagogies based on children's emerging interests, there are many possibilities for cognitive knowing. Educators, as significant mentors, can scaffold cognitive knowing about the natural world in positive and meaningful ways. Such understandings provide a sound basis for decision making from a sustainability frame of mind.

3. Play in nature offers the potential for developing many cognitive, social and physical skills relevant to creating sustainable futures for all. Skills including collaboration, problem solving, investigation and risk management are honed in diverse, unpredictable and dynamic natural outdoor play contexts. Practising these skills in a supportive early childhood setting with peers and adults provides a strong skills base for ongoing engagement with sustainability.

4. A sustainability frame of mind requires not only an ability to make decisions about best possible living, but also a willingness to question, enact, engage with challenges and demonstrate resilience. The sense of place and agency afforded by play in nature provides real-life experiences as well as a training ground for the bigger questions and decisions of adulthood. In small ways, children can be supported to believe in their own agency and in their abilities to participate in society and change the ways in which humans live in nature for a sustainable future.

In summary, some specific links between children's experiences in nature and sustainable living have been outlined here, but perhaps there are other links yet to be revealed. Ärlemalm-Hagsér (2013) argues there is a disjuncture in early childhood practice between promoting children's stewardship of the environment and the need for critical discussion about human relationships with nature and for children to be vocal participants in this discussion. There is a window in early childhood to set the scene for more than simply stewardship; lifelong advocacy and action with a sustainability frame of mind is the goal. Chawla (1998) summarises that 'there is no single all potent experience that produces environmentally informed and active citizens, but many together' (p. 381). Restating this in terms of young children and nature, I suggest that *there is no single experience in nature that creates a sustainability frame of mind, but many experiences over time, crucially beginning in early childhood.*

Conclusion

This chapter was introduced by reflecting on my own early teaching experiences. After reviewing the literature again for this second edition, I feel even more committed to the place of nature in children's lives and, specifically, in early childhood education settings. Connections with nature are foundational to embracing EfS and, in early childhood, there is a unique opportunity to create nature foundations. These foundations will contribute significantly to the wellbeing of current and future human generations and the health of the planet as a whole. I invite you to be goaded by the provocations presented here, to engage further with the literature cited and, most importantly, to become a vocal advocate for young children in nature.

Review provocations

Reflect on your lifetime of experiences in nature.

1. How have your experiences informed your relationship with nature?
2. What relationships with nature will you foster in the children you work with?
3. Is there just one right relationship with nature that will promote a sustainable future?
4. Envision children's future relationships with nature. What do you imagine for the future?

References

Aaron, R. F. & Witt, P. A. (2011). Urban students' definitions and perceptions of nature. *Children, Youth and Environments*. 21(2), 145–67.

Aitken, J., Hunt, J., Roy, E. & Sajfar, B. (2013). *A Sense of Wonder*. Melbourne: Teaching Solutions.

Alexander, S. (2012). *Kitchen Garden Cooking with Kids*. Melbourne: Lantern, Penguin.

Ärlemalm-Hagsér, E. (2013). Respect for nature: A prescription for developing environmental awareness in preschool. *Center for Educational Policy Studies Journal*, 3 (1), 25–44.

Australian Government, Department of Climate Change and Energy Efficiency (2011). *Australian Climate Commission Report: The Critical Decade*, Canberra. Department of Climate Change and Energy Efficiency.

Australian Government, Department of Education, Employment and Workplace Relations (2009). *Belonging, Being and Becoming: The Early Years Learning Framework for Australia*. Canberra: Department of Education, Employment and Workplace Relations for the Council of Australian Governments.

Australian Government, Department of Health (2014). Australia's Physical Activity and Sedentary Behaviour Guidelines, www.health.gov.au/internet/main/publishing.nsf/content/health-pubhlth-strateg-phys-act-guidelines (accessed 1 May 2014).

Bagot, K. (2005). The importance of green play spaces for children – aesthetic, athletic and academic. *Eingana*, 28(3), 12–16.

Ball, D., Gill, T. & Spiegal, B. (2008). *Managing Risk in Play Provision: Implementation Guide*. London: Crown/Play England/Big Lottery Fund.

Bateson, G. (1979). *Mind and Nature: A Necessary Unity*. Ballantine Books: New York.

Beck, U. (1994). *Ecological Politics in an Age of Risk*. Cambridge, UK: Polity Press.

Bonnett, M. (2002). Education for sustainability as a frame of mind. *Environmental Education Research*, 8 (1), 9–20.

Bonnett, M. (2004). *Retrieving Nature: Education for a Post-Humanist Age.* Oxford: Blackwell Publishing.

Borradaile, L. (2006). *Forest School Scotland: An Evaluation.* Edinburgh: Forestry Commission Scotland.

Brussoni, M., Olsen, L. L., Pike, I. & Sleet, D. A. (2012). Risky play and children's safety: Balancing priorities for optimal child development. *Environmental Research and Public Health*, 9, 3134–48.

Capra, F. (1997). *The Web of Life: A New Synthesis of Mind and Matter.* London: Harper Collins.

Carson, R. (1956, republished 1998). *The Sense of Wonder.* New York: Harper and Row.

Chawla, L. (1998). Significant life experiences revisited: A review of research on sources of environmental sensitivity. *Environmental Education Research*, 4(4), 369–83.

Chawla, L. (2006). Learning to love the natural world enough to protect it. *Barn* 2, 57–78.

Chawla, L. & Derr, V. (2012). The development of conservation behaviours in childhood and youth. In S. D. Clayton (ed.), *The Oxford Handbook of Environmental and Conservation Psychology.* New York: Oxford University Press.

Clements, R. (2004). An investigation of the status of outdoor play. *Contemporary Issues in Early Childhood*, 5(1), 68–80.

Coulter, J. (2008). *Population and Sustainability: A Global Role for Australia. Australian Options*, 52, Autumn Edition.

Crutzen, P. J. & Stoermer, E. F. (2000). The 'Anthropocene'. *Global Change Newsletter*, 41, 17–18.

Dighe, J. (1993). Children and the Earth. *Young Children*, 48(3), 58–63.

Dyment, J. & O'Connell, T. S. (2013). The impact of playground design on play choices and behaviours of preschool children. *Children's Geographies*, 11(3), 263–80.

Eager, D. & Little, H. (2011). Risk deficit disorder. Presentation at the International Public Works Conference (IPWEA) Canberra, Australia, 21–25 August.

Ehrlich, P. (2000). *Human Natures: Genes, Cultures and the Human Prospect.* New York: Penguin.

Elliott, S. (2012). Sustainable outdoor playspaces in early childhood centres: Investigating perceptions, facilitating change and generating theory. PhD thesis, University of New England, Armidale, NSW.

Elliott, S. (ed.) (2008). *The Outdoor Playspace: Naturally.* Sydney: Pademelon Press.

Elliott, S. & Chancellor, B. (in press). From Forest Preschool to Bush Kinder: An inspirational approach to preschool provision in Australia. *Australasian Journal of Early Childhood*.

Elliott, S. & Davis, J. (2004). Mud pies and daisy chains: Connecting young children and nature. *Everychild*, 10(4), 4–5.

Faber Taylor, A. & Kuo, F. (2011). Could exposure to everyday green spaces help treat ADHD? Evidence from children's play settings. *Applied Psychology: Health and Well-Being*, 3(3), 281–303.

Feez, S. (2013). *The 1913 Rome Lectures: First International Training Course. The Montessori Series: Volume 18*. The Netherlands: Montessori-Pierson Publishing.

Fell, L. & Russell, D. (1994). An introduction to 'Maturana's' biology. In L. Fell, D. Russell & A. Stewart (eds), *Seized by Agreement, Swamped by Understanding*. www.pnc.com.au/~lfell/book.html (accessed 1 May 2014).

Fjørtoft, I. (2001). The natural environment as a playground for children: The impact of outdoor play activities in pre-primary school children. *Early Childhood Education Journal*, 29(2), 111–17.

Fjørtoft, I., Kristoffersen, B. & Sageie, J. (2009). Children in schoolyards: Tracking movement patterns and physical activity in schoolyards using global positioning system and heart rate monitoring. *Landscape and Urban Planning*, 93(3) 210–7.

Flannery, T. (2008). *Now or Never: A Sustainable Future for Australia*. Melbourne: Black Inc.

French, A. N., Ashby, R. S., Morgan, I. G. & Rose, K. A. (2013). Time outdoors and the prevention of myopia. *Experimental Eye Research*, 114, 58–68.

Frost, J. (2007). A brief history of American playgrounds. *IPA Playrights Magazine*, 2, 10–13.

Furedi, F. (2001). Making sense of parental paranoia, www.frankfuredi.com/site/article/112 (accessed 1 May 2014).

Gamson Danks, S. (2010). *Asphalt to Ecosystems: Design Ideas for Schoolyard Transformation*. Oakland, CA: New Village Press.

Gill, T. (2007). *No Fear: Growing up in a Risk Averse Society*. London: Calouste Gulbenkian Foundation.

Guldberg, H. (2009). *Reclaiming Childhood: Freedom and Play in an Age of Fear*. Abingdon, UK: Routledge.

Heerwagen, J. H. & Orians, G. H. (2002). The ecological world of children. In P. H. J. Kahn & S. R. Kellert (eds), *Children and Nature*. Cambridge, MA: The MIT Press.

Hofferth, S. L. & Sandberg, J. F. (2001). Changes in American children's time, 1981–1997. In S. L. Hofferth & T. Owens (eds), *Children at the Millennium*. Amsterdam: Elsevier.

Kahn, P. H. J. (2011). *Technological Nature: Adaptation and the Future of Human Life*. Cambridge, MA: MIT Press.

Kahn, P. H. J. & Kellert, S. R. (2002). *Children and Nature*. Cambridge, MA: The MIT Press.

Kaplan, R. & Kaplan, S. (1989). *The Experience of Nature: A Psychological Perspective*. New York: Cambridge University Press.

Kellert, S. R. (2012). *Birthright: People and Nature in the Modern World*. New Haven: Yale University Press.

Kellert, S. R. & Wilson E. O. (eds) (1993). *The Biophilia Hypothesis*. Washington, DC: Island Press.

Kimbro, R. T., Brooks-Gunn, J. & McLanahan, S. (2011). Young children in urban areas: Links among neighborhood characteristics, weight status, outdoor play and television watching. *Social Science and Medicine* 72(5), 668–76.

Kingsolver, B. (2002). *Small Wonder*. New York: HarperCollins.

Kirkby, M. (1989). Nature as refuge in children's environments. *Children's Environments Quarterly*, 6(1), 7–12.

Knight, S. (2013). *International Perspectives on Forest School: Natural Places to Play and Learn*. London: Sage Publications.

Kolbe, U. (2007). *Rapunzel's Supermarket: All about Young Children and their Art* (2nd edn). Paddington, NSW: Peppinot Press.

Lester, S. & Maudsley, M. (2006). *Play, Naturally: A Review of Children's Natural Play*. London: Children's Play Council.

Louv, R. (2005). *The Last Child in the Woods: Saving our Children from Nature Deficit Disorder*. New York: Algonquin Books.

Luchs, A. & Fikus, M. (2013). A comparative study of active play on differently designed playgrounds. *Journal of Adventure Education and Outdoor Learning*. 13 (3), 206–22.

Malone, K. (2007). The bubble-wrap generation: Children growing up in walled gardens. *Environmental Education Research*, 13(4), 513–27.

Maturana, H. & Varela, F. (1987). *The Tree of Knowledge: The Biological Roots of Human Understanding*. Boston: New Science Library/Shambhala Publications.

Moore, D. (2010). 'Only children can make secret places': Children's secret business of place. Master's thesis, Monash University, Melbourne.

Moore, R. C. & Marcus, C. (2008). Healthy planet, healthy children: Designing nature into the daily spaces of childhood. In S. R. Kellert, J. Heerwagen & M. Mador (eds), *Biophilic Design: The Theory, Science and Practice of Bringing Buildings to Life*. Hoboken, New Jersey: Wiley.

Morgan, S., Mia, T. & Kwaymullina, B. (2008). *Heartsick for Country*. Fremantle, WA: Fremantle Press.

Morrison, G. (1995). *Early Childhood Education Today* (6th edn). New Jersey: Merrill.

Munoz, S. (2009). *Children in the Outdoors: A Literature Review*, www.educationscotland.gov.uk/images/Children%20in%20the%20outdoors%20literature%20review_tcm4-597028.pdf (accessed 1 May 2014).

Nicholson, S. (1971). How not to cheat children: The theory of loose parts. *Landscape Architecture*, 62, 30–4.

Nimmo, J. (2008). Young children's access to real life: An examination of the growing boundaries between children in child care and adults in the community. *Contemporary Issues in Early Childhood*, 9 (1), 3–13.

Nuttall, C. & Millington, J. (2008). *Outdoor Classrooms: A Handbook for School Gardens*. Eurnundi, Qld: Nuttall and Millington.

Ornstein, R. & Ehrlich, P. (2001). *New World New Mind: Moving Towards Conscious Evolution* (2nd edn). Boston: Malor Books.

Owens, T. & Hofferth, S. L. (eds) (2001). *Children at the Millenium*. Amsterdam: Elsevier.

Planet Ark (2011). *Climbing Trees: Getting Aussie Kids Back Outdoors*. Sydney: Planet Ark.

Rivkin, M. (1995). *The Great Outdoors: Restoring Children's Rights to Play Outside*. Washington, DC: NAEYC.

Sebba, R. (1991). The landscapes of childhood. *Environment and Behaviour*, 23(1), 395–422.

Skar, M. & Krogh, E. (2009). Changes in children's nature based experiences near home: From spontaneous play to adult controlled, planned and organised activities. *Children's Geographies*, 7 (3), 339–54.

Sobel, D. (1990). A place in the world: Adult memories of childhood's special places. *Children's Environments Quarterly*, 7(4), 5–13.

Thoreaux, H. D. with McKibben, B. (1997). *Walden*. Boston: Beacon Press.

Townsend, M. & Weerasuriya, R. (2010). *Beyond Blue to Green: The Benefits of Contact with Nature for Mental Health and Well-being*. Melbourne: Beyond Blue Limited.

Vandewater, E. A., Rideout, V. J., Wartella, E. A., Huand, X., Lee, J. H. & Shim, M. (2007). Digital childhood: Electronic media and technology use among infants, toddlers and preschoolers. *American Academy of Pediatrics Journal*, 119(5), 1006–15.

Veitch, J., Bagley, S., Ball, K. & Salmon, J. (2005). Where do children play? A qualitative study of parents' perceptions of influences on children's active free-play. *Health and Place*, 12(4), 383–93.

Waite, S. (2010). Losing our way? The downward path for outdoor learning for children aged 2–11 years. *Journal of Adventure Education and Outdoor Learning*, (10)2, 111–26.

Wells, N. (2000). At home with nature: Effects of 'Greenness' on children's cognitive functioning. *Environment and Behaviour*, 32, 775–9.

Wells, N. M. & Lekies, K. S. (2006). Nature and the life course: Pathways from nature experience to adult environmentalism. *Children, Youth and Environments*. 16(1), 1–24.

Williams, G. C. & Nesse, R. M. (1991). The dawn of Darwinian medicine. *Quarterly Review of Biology*, 66 (1), 1.

Williams-Siegfredsen, J. (2012). *Understanding the Danish forest school approach*. Oxon, UK: Routledge.

Chapter 3

Leadership for creating cultures of sustainability

Megan Gibson

Editor's note

In this revised chapter, **Megan Gibson** again discusses the vital role of leadership in creating change for sustainability in an early childhood education and care (ECEC) setting. Megan was the Director of Campus Kindergarten, a long day care centre in Brisbane, in the Australian state of Queensland, when it initiated its Sustainable Planet Project (SPP) in the late 1990s, a time when ECEfS was in its infancy. Megan reflects on her personal experiences at the centre and outlines the theoretical underpinnings that helped to shape her work as an innovative leader and a leader of innovation in ECEfS.

Megan also updates her discussion of the four frames of leadership, organisational culture, professional development and organisational change and how they can contribute to creating and shaping whole-centre approaches to ECEfS. She re-emphasises that educational and organisational leadership *style* plays an essential role in creating cultures of sustainability within a centre and community, and that teacher professional development within a collaborative learning community is a vital aspect for creating change.

To our children's children
The glad tomorrow
by Oodgeroo Noonuccal   (formerly Kath Walker, 1970, p. 40)

An opportunity to lead for EfS

For close to a decade I had the privilege to work within the Campus Kindergarten community[1] – a unique place for children, families and teachers. This community's interest in environmental issues led to the development of the SPP. From its inception at a staff professional development retreat, this project permeated the everyday 'lifeworld' (Sergiovanni 2003, p. 16) at the centre.

The SPP was actively embraced by staff, children and families at Campus Kindergarten, and slowly evolved over time. My role as Director provided an opportunity and a responsibility, as I saw it, to set the conditions that would value and empower people in this learning community. These would in turn support the growth of the SPP, and at the same time engender a stronger sense of collegiality. These conditions created the space in which to bring about a revolution in thinking and actions in regard to EfS. So deep were the changes that they provided a platform for a shift in the centre's culture. Some years on from the inception of the SPP, I now lecture in early childhood teacher education, mainly in the area of leadership. What I initially practised and wrote about in the earlier version of this chapter in the first edition of this text remains ingrained in my work, and worthy of restating. It is important to note, too, that the early childhood policy landscape in Australia has shifted considerably since I was Campus Kindergarten's Director. The national Early Years Learning Framework (Australian Government, Department of Education Employment and Workplace Relations 2009) and the National Quality Framework (ACECQA n.d.) include requirements that early childhood centres afford attention to EfS. This was not previously the case and when the SPP was conceived there were no legislative requirements for centres to work with principles of EfS.

Introduction

This chapter focuses on the role of leadership in creating a culture of sustainability. It is based on my former position as Director at Campus Kindergarten and the leadership that was brought to the centre's SPP. In this discussion, the significant leadership roles of staff, parents and children are explored and interfaced with the literature. The first part of this chapter sets the scene by providing the contextual background of the early childhood centre and the origins of the SPP. In the second part of the chapter, Campus Kindergarten's SPP is further explored through the four frames of *leadership, organisational culture, professional development* and *organisational change*. Rather than being distinct frames, each works as an organiser and builds upon the others, creating deep and connected ways of understanding the SPP. Throughout these four frames, vignettes of the project from my time as Director highlight examples of practice that created a culture of sustainability.

---

[1] I am appreciative of the Campus Kindergarten Board of Management, the team of staff, parents and children who afforded me the opportunity to work with an extraordinary community of people (1996–2005).

As the reader, you are encouraged to engage with the 'provocations' interspersed throughout the chapter, to support your thinking and meaning making around leadership for creating cultures of sustainability. Through updating and retelling this story, I hope to provide a window into the structures and systems that supported the project and to share insights into how to bring about collective change so that a community of people feel empowered and have ownership. Therefore, this chapter explores some of the conditions, systems and structures that enable EfS to grow in an early childhood setting.

Part one: The context

Campus Kindergarten is an ECEC centre situated on the St Lucia campus of the University of Queensland in Brisbane, Australia. It is located in a 'green corridor' on the university's site map, and has expansive outdoor playspaces, dominated by gum trees and open spaces. The kindergarten building was the original university caretaker's cottage, and has been extended and renovated since the centre's opening in 1971. The building houses three main kindergarten rooms, bathrooms, kitchen and storerooms. Verandas wrap around the building and, due to the warm climate in Brisbane, there is a strong focus on the outdoors, with links between the indoor and outdoor environments.

During my time as Director, the centre operated dually as a long day care centre and a kindergarten/preschool and opened from 8.00 am to 5.30 pm, Monday to Friday during school terms. Children were enrolled from 2.5 years of age to approximately 5 years of age, or school-entry age. Approximately 70 per cent of families who accessed the centre were engaged in work or study at the university, with families coming from a

Figure 3.1 *Campus Kindergarten, University of Queensland (2002)*

wide range of language and cultural backgrounds. Approximately 80 children across three age groups attended weekly. At the time of my directorship, the teaching team comprised 19 full-time and part-time staff, including teachers, group leaders, assistants and those working in administrative roles.

Integral to Campus Kindergarten's operation was families' involvement and contributions, which enabled a strong sense of community. There were varied ways through which families were able to be formally involved, including sitting on the Board of Management. This group of both past and present parents, together with people outside the Campus Kindergarten community who offered particular skills to the centre's operation (for example, an early childhood professional and an accountant), met approximately five times during the year. A systematic and strategic system for policy development and review supported a strong organisational structure. Another formal way for parents to participate was through the 'class reps' system. Each of the three classrooms had two parent representatives who met together regularly to coordinate centre-based social and fundraising events. Parents were also encouraged to contribute informally by spending time in the centre, sharing interests, skills and hobbies. Both formal and informal levels of families' involvement were important aspects of the centre's approach to EfS.

During my directorship, there was strong philosophical debate and program critique at Campus Kindergarten, which contributed towards program evolution and renewed approaches to pedagogy. The centre's educational philosophy drew upon a number of theorists, including Malaguzzi (1998), Rinaldi (2006), Gardner (2006), Dahlberg, Moss and Pence (2007) and Vygotsky (1993). Key elements that were embedded into the centre's philosophy at the time I was Director were that educational and management practices be child-centred, holistic and futures-oriented. Key organisational values of rights, respect and trust were articulated through centre policy and curriculum documents and staff enactment of the culture and program (Campus Kindergarten 2004). Children's rights and *their* say in what happens in the centre were integral in these values. In a practical sense, this meant that the teachers made connections between their care and concern for children's wellbeing, with concern and respect for the centre's natural *and* built environments, and that these were embedded into everyday practices. A strong sense of democracy, shared decision making and consultation were key features in the centre – within classrooms and within centre management. These qualities underpinned all facets of Campus Kindergarten's organisation and culture, including the SPP.

Origins and first steps of the SPP

When I first commenced as Director of Campus Kindergarten in 1996, I joined a team of long-serving staff who had experienced five changes of Director over a five-year period. I was mindful of the impact of these changes upon staff collegiality and cohesiveness.

Further, I found myself working with a highly dedicated team of people who brought rich qualities to their respective roles; however, my observation was that people were pulling in different directions. With such a skilled team of staff, there was potential to harness people's interests and motivation, so that the team was pulling in the *same* direction.

Setting the conditions for change

I sensed that there needed to be time and space for people to discuss, connect with each other and create ideas. Therefore, one of the first goals that I made in my early months as the new Director was to bring staff together for a retreat where there would be opportunities, together, to reflect, review and develop shared visions for the centre's future. At the time, I was working towards my Master of Education with a double major in leadership and management and ECEC. It was fortuitous that my thesis supervisor was enthusiastic about working with me to plan the staff retreat. The centre's Board of Management was very supportive of this initiative and provided a small, though significant, amount of funding. This support became a valuable platform for what was to be, I believe, a turning point for Campus Kindergarten's evolution as an organisation, and our journey into EfS.

The staff retreat

The staff retreat, or 'team-building weekend', was carefully structured to support centre growth and staff development. A professional development opportunity that aims to bring staff together, where there is dedicated time to explore ideas and concepts, provides a valuable context to create 'radically transforming professional learning spaces' (Bredeson 2003, p. 5) at both an individual staff and an organisational level.

A great deal of planning went into the program, which included opportunities for staff to spend time together, with music, food and wine providing great opportunities to build connections. The location was approximately one hour outside of Brisbane – at a mountain resort with beautiful views from our conference room. The purposeful arrangement of room furniture to *face* the floor-to-ceiling windows that framed a view of mountains and rainforest provided staff with scope for connecting with nature, and not feeling 'cooped up' as one might at a two-day intensive conference.

A key focus was on team building. As mentioned earlier, the team-building exercises revealed that the teachers were seeking a project through which to build team work and create a shared purpose. They also showed that many staff wished for greater complementarity between their personal and working lives. The significance of creating a co-owned vision in cultural change is identified by Fullan (2010), who explored this idea through the importance of collaboration – where staff have the opportunity to have a say and have 'buy-in' into what happens in their everyday classroom practices.

As a past staff member commented, 'I felt that I wasn't putting enough of my own personality into the room. It was great to give towards the children but there was none of me in there'.

A facilitator was engaged for the weekend retreat, with acknowledgement that this person should have an understanding of ECEC and leadership/team building, as well as a strong sense of how early childhood centres work. For these reasons, my then-thesis supervisor was considered a 'good fit'. Through the strategies she used, important recurring themes were drawn upon throughout the weekend. A real turning point for staff team development – and for Campus Kindergarten's future directions – came about when a number of staff identified 'the environment' as a topic that they were passionate about. By tapping into a collective interest, a shared vision for the centre (Fullan 2010), and its future growth and operation, began to emerge. This shared interest became a catalyst for further discussions about people's experiences in life, and in ECEC in relation to the environment. Sparks were ignited as people contributed ideas and brainstormed about how we, as an ECEC centre, might embrace principles and practices of EfS. This discussion continued well into the course of the retreat, and so it was that the Campus Kindergarten SPP was born.

Provocation 3.1

What might be your first steps to motivate people within an ECEC centre to develop a project about EfS?

Following up

Upon our return from the retreat, staff were noticeably more communicative, cohesive as a group, and inspired to enact the plans for the SPP. Follow-up staff meetings provided further opportunity to discuss ideas and implement plans to start the project. Bredeson's (2003) conception that professional development is a 'journey not a credential' (p. 8) offers scope to reposition professional growth and learning as part of an ongoing continuum. Likewise, the team-building weekend that was designed for the Campus Kindergarten staff was considered a core component of an ongoing program of professional development.

The vision and goals of the SPP were shared through the centre newsletter, and generated interest and enthusiasm from children and families. There were overwhelming offers of support, and people were ready to commence hands-on projects. Within a month of returning from the retreat, a whole-centre 'working bee' was planned for a Saturday. The largest number of centre families ever attending a working bee was present, with children, parents and staff working side by side, planning a permaculture garden, building a chicken coop (known as the 'Chook Hilton') and creating a worm farm. These small steps provided the building blocks for the project.

Under the banner of the SPP, individual staff members were able to 'add value' to their work as early childhood educators by including their personal interests, such as gardening, wildlife conservation and recycling, into their day-to-day work at the centre. The project had an action-oriented focus, encapsulated in the project's subtitle, 'Saving our planet: Become a conscious part of the solution'. This collective advocacy and activism provided a strong framework for staff and the centre's community to work together.

The practical projects

Once the concept was formulated and the initial working bee held, staff continued to work with the centre's children and families on a number of small-scale, mini-projects that were allied with their own particular environmental interests. These included:

Swings and roundabouts

There was considerable success with the project in those early days, but there were also several operational challenges. A significant barrier was the variable levels of knowledge, experience and commitment among the staff with regard to environmental matters. This led to periods of great activity and times when interest and energy waned as other topics, issues and priorities took precedence. There were also frustrations with the level of parental commitment to some initiatives.

Figure 3.2 *Initial mini-projects in the Sustainable Planet Project*
Source: Campus Kindergarten teachers (1997)

For example, the centre's 'litterless lunch' program was met with varying levels of support from families. This initiative encouraged parents to pack lunches for the children – brought daily from home – in ways that minimised food packaging. Some parents resisted the concept, seeking to explain why changing their lunch-making habits was an unreasonable demand applicable to others but not to themselves. As a result of such reactions in these early days, the teachers became more prepared for some resistance and, hence, sought to work more collaboratively with families to assist them to understand the issues, rather than adopting a strict policy position.

One tangible and positive outcome of the litterless lunch program, together with the related composting project, was the considerable reduction in the amount of refuse produced by the centre. Being part of the university community meant that garbage bins (referred to locally as 'wheelie bins') were emptied daily. Wheelie bins have a capacity of 240 litres each, so a reduction in refuse from three wheelie bins per day to half a wheelie bin per day was a significant achievement. This outcome was acknowledged and celebrated with the children and highlighted in the centre's newsletter to families. Such success provided the centre community with the motivation to maintain and further develop the SPP.

As time progressed and the project evolved, all the mini-projects encompassed in the overarching SPP became inculcated into everyday routines at the centre, with new projects continually being added. In effect, the centre worked with an environmental or sustainability ethic that became part of its organisational and social culture.

Provocation 3.2

What potential obstacles might hinder the development of EfS in early childhood educational settings?

How might these pitfalls be overcome?

Key points from part one

- ECEC centres provide immense opportunities for developing EfS projects.
- Campus Kindergarten developed the SPP following a staff professional development retreat.
- The SPP grew and evolved for over a decade, with leadership being integral to its evolution.
- The project was multifaceted, with shared responsibilities taken on by staff, parents and children, and inputs made by the wider community.
- Momentum in the project varied, resulting in intense periods of growth and development, and times when energy waned.

Part two: Leadership matters

In this section, the four frames of *leadership, organisational culture, professional development* and *organisational change* are used to consider how an ECEC centre might support EfS.

Frame one: Leadership for sustainability

Leadership in ECEC is distinctive, to a large extent because of the unique workplace contexts in which leaders operate (Rodd 2013; Waniganayake et al. 2012). The different funding structures, policies and professional roles and the very nature of work with families contribute towards leadership in ECEC being qualitatively different from that experienced in broader public and private arenas, where much of the literature and most research about leadership is focused (Hard, Press & Gibson 2013; Rodd 2013). As the Director of Campus Kindergarten, I was aware of my role and my responsibility to support the SPP in practical as well as more visionary ways. Opportunities were provided for staff members to create goals and dreams for what could be, or was, possible, rather than limiting their aspirations. Notably, time was formally allocated so that visionary thinking could occur during staff meetings and centre professional development days/retreats. Thus, where and how professional development occurred was not constrained by traditional notions of 'seminars' and 'conferences' (Bredeson 2003). Professional learning for staff and the centre also occurred in different ways in different places and times. Additionally, opportunities were created for people to share ideas informally; for example, during meal breaks staff were provided with comfortable communal spaces, and they were encouraged to collaborate during weekly whole-room-team 'planning-time' discussions.

Staff at Campus Kindergarten were listened to, their ideas valued and their thinking genuinely respected. The rights of people, including those of staff, parents and children, were paramount in this process. This attention to rights enabled debate, dialogue and exploration of key philosophical ideas (Rinaldi 2006). Thus, possibilities were created for individual and centre growth, with the SPP serving as a sturdy vehicle through which we, as a staff, engaged in rich growth and learning. My role as leader was central to this, though equally important were the leadership roles that other staff, parents and, indeed, children actively took on and were supported to enact. For example, a pre-schooler, Greta, became a leader in the centre's water conservation project. A teacher, Robert (author of Chapter 4), became the leader of the overall SPP. He worked on a number of mini-projects with groups of children while also taking on the pivotal coordination role of managing and leading across the whole project. At a broader level as Director, I also provided leadership, supporting and developing the project.

Leadership provides opportunities that can either constrain or support an organisation's operations and evolution. The process of leadership is essentially about vision and influence, and can occur within an organisation in a number of ways (Rodd 2013; Waniganayake et al. 2012). An overview of approaches to leadership (see breakout box 'Types of leadership') provides a viewpoint from which to further consider what happens in an organisation, and specifically in a long day care centre.

Types of leadership

Transactional leadership relies on influencing people through rewards and sanctions (Oldroyd 2005; Sinclair 2007). A transactional leader creates a clear, formalised structure whereby expectations are made transparent and compliance is rewarded. Disciplinary procedures, or punishment, are clearly outlined and understood.

Transformational leadership (Waniganayake at al. 2012) brings about change and organisational growth through leadership that inspires and motivates. This approach to leadership empowers staff and sees an aligning of the values within the organisational culture with that of the leader (Schein 2010; Sergiovanni 2000).

Shared or distributive leadership (Rodd 2013) is conceptualised as a relational process, dependent on social interaction and networks of influence, with a focus on all staff being equal. Under such a model, power is shared and leadership becomes a participative process.

Provocation 3.3

What styles of leadership have you experienced (in ECEC contexts or other workplaces)?

How did/do you feel about operating within this style?

What style(s) of leadership sit(s) comfortably with you?

Rather than looking to select one type of leadership over another, thereby making distinctions between these leadership approaches, the concept of fostering leadership at many levels should be seen as one of an educational leader's main roles (Fullan 2010). A skilled transformational leader, for example, can implement elements of distributive leadership as a means of empowering staff, while also reaping immense benefits for organisational culture. This more fluid type of leadership is encapsulated in Senge's (2006) concept of a 'learning organisation'.

Leading a learning organisation

In a learning organisation, people continually develop their own and the group's capacity to work together and create what has the potential to be deeply influential (Senge 2006). Senge (2006) describes that in a learning organisation, people at all levels, individually and collectively, are continually increasing their capabilities to produce results around matters they really care about. This approach has synergy with Campus Kindergarten's SPP, as it was indeed a project and organisational focus about which staff were passionate.

Within a learning organisation framework, a central role of all people is to work together, inspire one another and enhance the growth of the organisation; taking risks is integral to this. Leadership is fundamental in this framework. Fullan (2010) comments that effective leaders are energy creators who create harmony, forge consensus, set high standards and develop a 'try this' futures orientation. In reflecting on my role as leader within the centre, in an interview conducted some years into the SPP, I commented: 'I've been mindful of giving staff support and encouraging understanding ... I've tried to motivate them so that they have felt they've got time to participate and coordinate projects and that they have understood what the project is about.' This 'learning' approach was corroborated by one of the teachers, who said of me: 'She really encourages us to think ... and you actually work through a lot of issues' (Davis et al. 2005).

Leadership and staff relationships

One way of understanding leadership is to pay attention to relationships between people as central to strong, effective and responsive communities (Rinaldi 2006; Rodd 2013; Waniganayake et al. 2012). Too little emphasis is placed on the 'human factor' in many ECEC centres. The nature of these relationships can be explored and critiqued by considering the paradigm of organisational culture (Sergiovanni 2003; Limerick, Cunnington & Crowther 2002). Loris Malaguzzi, founder of municipal preschools in Reggio Emilia, Italy, asserted the significance of relationships when he stated: 'I believe there is no possibility of existing without relationship. Relationship is the necessity of life' (Malaguzzi 1998, p. 287). The relationships that exist within an ECEC organisation, particularly those 'relations' (Rinaldi 2006) between staff, provide a strong platform for considering EfS initiatives.

The link between leadership and organisational culture

Leadership is inherent in an organisation's evolution and trajectory. The role that leaders take, the approach they have to leading, managing people, creating relationships and developing a sense of team collegiality is paramount to the culture of an organisation. The connection between organisational culture and leadership is considered to be so close that Schein (2010) purports they are 'two sides of the same coin' (p. 7). When a leader enters an organisation, that person constructs a culture through the creation of groups and sub-organisations. It follows that when a culture already exists, the criteria for leadership and, therefore, who will be a leader in that context, is predetermined. In other words, the existing culture supports a particular type of leader in order to continue the evolution of that culture. The relationship, therefore, between organisational culture and leadership is of great relevance in understanding organisations, mapping what happens and developing a shared understanding of its inner workings. Campus Kindergarten had a long history of program critique and evolution and, together with a strong base for community involvement, provided a foundation for building the SPP.

By establishing a deeper understanding of cultural issues within groups and organisations, it is possible to identify priorities for leaders and for leadership (Schein 2010). Indeed, one of the key roles of leaders that Schein (2010) highlights is the role played in creating and managing culture. This involves the ability to not only understand, but also to work within a culture. In making a distinction between leaders and managers, Schein emphasises that leaders create and change cultures, while managers live by the culture. Therefore, a leader needs to bring a dynamic and open approach to cultivating the organisational culture.

Key points on frame one

- Leadership in ECEC is unique and requires particular consideration.
- Leadership can enable visions to be articulated and ideas to grow. Different types of leadership can work to enable or constrain these. In a 'learning organisation', leadership is shared and projects have a strong sense of shared ownership.
- Fostering and supporting relationships is pivotal to strong and effective leadership.
- Leadership and organisational culture are closely related.

The conditions that foster inclusive, democratic leadership can be explored through understandings of organisational culture. Therefore, the second frame to be considered in this chapter in support of embedding EfS in organisational culture.

Frame two: Organisational culture as a basis for sustainability

The culture of an organisation is unique, diverse and complex. To try to understand what happens in an organisation is not a simple process. However, insight into an organisation's culture provides a valuable window into 'what makes that place tick', what inspires people, what motivates people and, in essence, what makes that place unique. Sergiovanni (2003) offers that 'with shared visions, values, and beliefs at heart, culture serves as a compass setting, steering people in a common direction' (p. 14).

Unravelling the complexities of an organisation's culture reveals a number of aspects that Schein (2010) refers to as artefacts, espoused values and basic underlying assumptions. How these are understood and enacted is critical in exploring and mapping organisational culture. In the case of Campus Kindergarten, the culture was imbued with the values of trust and respect. Early on in my role as Director, I articulated to staff that it was the people in the community who were valued above all else. As such, the relationships between people in the centre's community were what gave the place 'heart and soul'.

Further exploration and understanding of organisational culture help explain some of the less tangible aspects of staff teams and relationships within organisations.

Understanding organisational culture

Ongoing discussion over the definition of culture has resulted in a number of approaches to studying and defining it. Understanding the levels or layers of artefacts, espoused values and basic underlying assumptions (Schein 2010) provides insight into these core concepts and complexities in exploring organisational culture.

Artefacts: These are the visible organisational structures and processes in an organisation. They are products of the group and include, for example, the layout of the physical environment, group language, and its style as seen in clothing, manners of address, myths and stories, and published values (Schein 2010). Because of the nature of these artefacts, they are actually readily observed, though difficult to interpret. The suggested research strategy for understanding and making meaning of an organisation's artefacts is to spend prolonged periods of time within the group and to engage in an anthropological study (Schein 2010). In the case of Campus Kindergarten, I was well positioned as the Director to identify, along *with* the staff, what it was that made the centre unique.

Values: The values that a group espouses become shared when there is ownership and people feel that they have had the opportunity to have some level of input (Schein 2010). It is how these values are transformed into *shared* values that become the values that are promoted as those of the whole organisation, or reflective of the culture, that is important. In the case of the SPP, all staff contributed to the centre's values. However, it was in my role of Director that I provided the impetus, foundations and 'glue' to bind people together.

Basic assumptions: These are often so much a part of the fabric of a workplace that they are not questioned or challenged; people accept and enact them in their daily relationships and interactions. Basic assumptions provide another viewing platform into the core of an organisation's culture. It is these underlying basic assumptions that are considered to be the essence of the culture – those taken-for-granted, invisible and 'outside of consciousness' aspects (Schein 2010; Owens 2004).

In summary, the elements of organisational culture – its artefacts, values and assumptions – are developed over time by staff. They are informed, even inspired, by the leader, or leaders, within that organisation. It is these shared elements that amalgamate and eventually become a culture.

While mapping an organisation's culture is valuable for providing an insight into that organisation, it needs to be remembered that each organisation or community is unique. This uniqueness suggests that trying to find sameness, or even commonalities, in cultures is complex, and needs to be sensitive to diversity. In considering organisational culture, therefore, there is a risk in seeking one truth, formula or recipe of how organisations should be. Rather than looking for superficial constructs of culture, it is important to build on a deeper, more complex model. Moving beyond superficial constructs enables a clearer understanding of the hidden and complex aspects of organisational life.

As already noted, at a deeper level the culture of the organisation is about people – what they bring to the culture and how they enact that culture. A central element of culture, therefore, is the accumulated shared learning of a given group or team that encompasses behavioural, emotional and cognitive elements of the group's 'total psychological functioning' (Schein 2010). A shared sense of history, underpinned by shared learning, supports and sustains organisational culture (Owens 2004). These attributes are further supported by relatively low staff turnover, which enables a culture to be developed, enacted and passed on. Staff stability is also an important factor in supporting shared learning, which, in turn, supports the growth of an organisation. The implication is that an organisation with high staff turnover impacts directly on the culture (or lack thereof) of an organisation. The staff at Campus Kindergarten embraced the SPP as a vehicle through which a stronger team and staff collegiality could be built. This, in turn, positively affected the evolution of a richer and more complex organisational culture. In time, the project enhanced the centre's culture and, reciprocally, the culture strengthened the project. In other words, the relationship between the SPP and the organisational culture of the centre contributed to a stronger sense of staff cohesion, ownership of the project and, more broadly, people's work within a diverse team.

Provocation 3.4

From reading the above section, what is important to consider in building an organisational culture for EfS?

Organisational culture and staff motivation

A key component of organisational culture is staff motivation. The culture of an organisation plays a significant role in how people feel about their work, their level of motivation, commitment and, in turn, job satisfaction. A strong organisational culture brings to the surface people's energy to perform, their loyalty and, at a deeper level, emotional bonds of attachment to the organisation (Owens 2004). The ways in which a centre inculcates its philosophy and practices, in and with staff, suggests a highly developed and refined culture that is enacted both consciously and subconsciously.

To 'drill down' further into how a deep culture may be embedded in an organisation, attention to people, relationships and leadership is required. The ways in which the Campus Kindergarten staff developed, collaborated and shared the experiences in the SPP provided a sense of empowerment and collective belief in this project, and in themselves as individuals and as members of a team.

Organisational culture and 'lifeworld'

The concept of 'lifeworld' (Sergiovanni 2003, p. 16) provides another insight into organisational culture by considering meaning and significance. Sergiovanni (2003) offered that 'the lifeworld provides the foundation for the development of social, intellectual, and other forms of human capital which then enriches the lifeworld itself' (p. 17). For Campus Kindergarten, the lifeworld was the everyday ways in which the centre was experienced by the people within it. The interrelationship between what is the lifeworld and what contributes to that lifeworld was an important part of EfS at the centre. This did not happen by chance: it involved careful planning and ongoing reflection. These planning and review processes are considered through the third overarching frame: professional development.

Key points on frame two

- Organisational cultures are unique and complex.
- An exploration of organisational culture includes looking at artefacts, values and assumptions.
- Mapping an organisation's culture provides a valuable insight into that context as a unique workplace. The mapping is done from inferences and direct observations.
- A strong organisational culture (that is, one that is clearly defined and supportive of both staff and organisational growth) sets the tone for higher levels of staff motivation.

Frame three: Professional development

Professional development provides opportunities for an organisation to reflect, grow and change. This cyclic process can be eclectic, with little focus or planned intention or, at the other end of the continuum, can involve systematic, sustained planning. In this latter approach, ideally professional development is planned so that there is synergy between the organisation's and individual staff members' directions and needs. This third frame considers professional development and, in doing so, explores aspects of policies to support professional development, namely centre-based professional development, succession planning and career planning.

Opportunities to take risks and to venture into unknown terrain provide for immense growth for both the organisation and individual staff. When the traditional design of professional development is challenged, it opens up possibilities to create new ways of thinking about learning occurring as part of an ongoing journey (Bredeson 2003), where participants are beckoned 'to travel in directions untrodden and [this] promises new realms of being and experiencing' (Ehrich 1997, p. 287). In this sense, professional development becomes a basis for individual and organisational growth and provides scope for creating synergy for these two sets of goals.

Campus Kindergarten developed policies to support professional development over a period of many years, with a clear and strategic focus on centre-based professional development programs. These policies provided motivation for staff and empowered people to take risks, embrace challenges and enact projects. The SPP was a core project that benefited from these policies.

Centre-based professional development

Centre-based professional development programs provide opportunities for staff to connect, share experiences and engage in visionary thinking. At Campus Kindergarten, a carefully planned, annual, centre-based professional development program included these three components:

- *Staff retreats* – these were either whole-day or weekend residential in format, with a clear focus and purpose, and developed in consultation with staff and the Board of Management.

- *Staff meetings* – at these meetings 'administration' was left to a whiteboard or staff memo. Instead, this precious time focused on professional growth. At staff meetings and team planning sessions, issues of curriculum and pedagogy were regularly discussed and debated.

- *Weekly room 'planning sessions'* – during these times people had numerous opportunities to learn about and critically reflect upon their teaching and learning. Teachers also commented that they learnt a great deal from each other in lunchroom conversations and other informal exchanges.

In addition, external professional development was encouraged that aligned with career-planning pathways (see below). This included, for example, support to attend conferences and workshops, undertake courses to upgrade qualifications, and networking through professional associations. The SPP was often the beneficiary and the impetus for both centre-based and external professional development activities.

Together, both formal and informal approaches to professional development generated a 'grassroots' collaborative learning culture, which supports learning for everyone – children, teachers, families and the community at large.

Provocation 3.5

In what ways can professional development support EfS projects? Consider both centre-based professional development and external professional development.

Succession planning

Succession planning is another aspect of professional development that is often given little consideration. Understandably, organisations are often so busy keeping up with the daily work life that limited attention is given to planning for the future, particularly in regard to staffing. Considered investments to support the emergence of new leaders, both from within and external to an organisation, go some way to supporting this process (Fullan 2010). At Campus Kindergarten, the centre-based professional development program provided opportunities for individual staff to take on leadership roles. In the case of the SPP, specifically, many staff embraced the opportunities to take responsibility for one or more project components, while others took on leadership or coordination roles. The centre-based, staff career-planning sessions provided occasions to identify and refine these roles and responsibilities.

Career planning

Career planning provides opportunities for staff to consider future career directions, goals and needs. Ideally, there is alignment between career planning, professional development and the organisation's directions. Career planning is considered to be an integral part of professional development, as staff seek to engage in professional growth that enriches career trajectories.

Career-planning sessions at Campus Kindergarten were offered in a relaxed, outdoor café environment, where staff members were supported in self-reflection and centre reflection. The process was facilitated by me as Director, and the Chair of the Board of Management (who brought extensive understandings of staff support processes). These one-hour sessions were instrumental in opening up opportunities for personal development and centre development, including policy development. One important area of development was the ongoing evolution of the SPP and the elaboration of the centre's environmental education policy.

Key points on frame three

- Well-managed and carefully planned professional development can provide opportunities for both organisational and staff growth.
- Policies for professional development are integral in supporting the strategic growth and evolution of both the organisation and individual staff.
- Centre-based professional development is instrumental in fostering organisational and staff growth.
- Succession planning provides for future-oriented planning in which systems and frameworks are put into place to support the ongoing growth of an organisation.
- Career planning is able to provide opportunities for valuable reflection, and for centre and staff development.

Frame four: Organisational change for sustainability

This section considers ideas concerned with the process of organisational change. It explores the notion of 'evolution rather than revolution' as a viable change strategy for embedding EfS into a centre's culture.

Creating a learning culture for change

Creating change at Campus Kindergarten was a slow, evolutionary process, advancing incrementally in small steps over more than a decade. Explanations for how and why organisational change is more likely to happen in this manner, rather than as a rapid revolutionary process, are provided by educational change theorists – for example, Fullan (2010) – who have applied complexity theory to social systems such as schooling. A key idea is that change *emerges* from within the organisation and the people in it (Fullan 2010), rather than being imposed. Through emergent change, the people in the organisation have a strong capacity to support and bring about collective change; however, this calls for the visionary leadership that was explored earlier in this chapter. A characteristic of emergent change is that the pace of collective change is likely to vacillate between stability and disorder as people grapple with competing demands. Thus, organisational change is more likely to be slowly emerging, but deeper-rooted, rather than fast-paced and revolutionary.

Further, the introduction of an innovation such as EfS into an already established organisational culture is more likely to result in numerous 'small wins' that build over time, rather than the creation of momentous change that sweeps away old patterns and ushers in new ones (Fullan 2010). These small-scale successes reflect the complex, dynamic nature of the setting and need to be interpreted as important accomplishments, not reform failures. Ultimately, small wins have the potential to set in motion further processes for continued small wins – a strategy that strengthens organisational capacity and the ability to solve larger-scale problems.

As the story of change at Campus Kindergarten has shown, the SPP had a slow, somewhat erratic evolution, characteristic of organisational change underpinned by complexity. Along the way, these slow changes led to creativity, engagement, critique and ongoing change within this learning organisation. A strong, shared vision of what a sustainable ECEC centre might look like was translated into small but realistic goals and achievements where, ultimately, a culture of sustainability permeated the program, operation and lifeworld of the centre.

The slow pace of the change initiated through the SPP, coupled with the shared sense of ownership, also provided a platform for change at the deepest level of the centre's practices and philosophy. It is this deep change, identified by Sergiovanni (2003), that led to a fundamental realignment of relationships and that changed understandings of curriculum, pedagogy, how children learn, and teachers' skills and behaviours. Inherent in the changes was a strong grounding in, and emphasis on, the centre's cultural values, particularly its focus on rights and respect. These cultural values not only informed the project but provided reciprocal inspiration for the broader, ongoing evolutionary changes within the organisation. It was through such devolved, dynamic and inclusive processes that a 'professional learning community' (Senge 2006; Fullan 2010) was created and sustained. This was not a top-down change process but a uniquely situated process where the participants had ownership, individually and collectively, for what happened.

Provocation 3.6

How can early childhood centres bring about deep and systemic change that is embedded in their culture?

Key points on frame four

- Incremental organisational change can reap significant, long-term rewards with deep and long-lasting impacts.
- Change is complex, with developments occurring in dynamic and, at times, unpredictable ways.
- Staff and centre-based ownership of change is important.
- Evolutionary change is a key to organisational growth. Small steps can equal significant gains in the long term.

Conclusion

This chapter has explored the SPP at Campus Kindergarten through four frames: leadership, organisational culture, professional development and organisational change. Insights into each of these frames provides ways of understanding the complexities of organisations such as ECEC centres, and how EfS can be developed and embedded in the everyday lifeworld of a centre.

With people as the most valuable part of an organisation, relationships are considered central to the growth and evolution of individuals and the organisation. A culture that supports rights and respect underpinned and enabled the SPP's evolution so that sustainability was lived and breathed within the centre's everyday life. Effective leadership was central to the changes. While my role as Director at Campus Kindergarten has been profiled in this chapter, the varying and diverse leadership roles that many people embraced were also instrumental in the project's evolution. The SPP simply would not have emerged without the tenacity of an extraordinary team of staff, who worked in a unique early childhood centre.

Rather than ignoring the critical issue of sustainability, the teachers at Campus Kindergarten engaged the support of children, families and the broader community in making changes – 'small wins' – to their day-to-day practices. These changes came about because a culture of sustainability was created. This culture was built on an educational philosophy that deeply valued young children as active participants in a learning community, and where open and trusting relationships permeated the teachers' work. Engaging in a broad range of professional and community education activities enabled staff to encourage others to think about sustainability – thus further supporting *their* learning and actions. In summary, this chapter has illuminated the work at Campus Kindergarten as a learning community where an organisational culture was created that deliberately engaged in pro-people, pro-environment and pro-futures EfS.

Review provocations

1. How do you see leadership as contributing to EfS?
2. What 'type' of leader do you think you are or will become?
3. How will your leadership style support and develop EfS with early childhood education?

References

Australian Children's Education and Care Quality Authority (n.d.). National Quality Standard, http://acecqa.gov.au/national-quality-framework (accessed 1 May 2014).

Australian Government, Department of Education, Employment and Workplace Relations (2009). *Belonging, Being and Becoming: The Early Years Learning Framework for Australia*. Canberra: Department of Education, Employment and Workplace Relations for the Council of Australian Governments.

Bredeson, P. V. (2003). *Designs for Learning: A New Architecture for Professional Development in Schools*. Thousand Oaks, CA: Corwin Press.

Campus Kindergarten (2004). *Prospectus*. Brisbane: Campus Kindergarten.

Dahlberg, G., Moss, P. & Pence, A. (2007). *Beyond Quality in Early Childhood Education and Care: Languages of Evaluation* (2nd edn). London: Taylor & Francis.

Davis, J., Rowntree, N., Gibson, M., Pratt, R. & Eglington, A. (2005). Creating a culture of sustainability: From project to integrated education for sustainability at Campus Kindergarten. In W. L. Filho (ed.), *Handbook of Sustainability Research*. Germany: Peter Lang Publishing.

Ehrich, L. (1997). Principals' experience of professional development and their response to teachers' professional development: A phenomonological study. PhD thesis, Queensland University of Technology.

Fullan, M. (2010). *Motion Leadership: The Skinny on Becoming Change Savvy*. Thousand Oaks, CA: Corwin Press/School Improvement Network/Ontario Principals' Council/American Association of School Administrators/National Staff Development Council.

Gardner, H. (2006). *Multiple Intelligences: New Horizons*. New York: Basic Books.

Hard, L., Press. F. & Gibson, M. (2013). 'Doing' social justice in early childhood: The potential of leadership. *Contemporary Issues in Early Childhood*, 14(4), 324–33.

Limerick, D., Cunnington, B. & Crowther, F. (2002). *Managing the New Organisation: Collaboration and Sustainability in the Post-Corporate World* (2nd edn). Crows Nest, NSW: Allen & Unwin.

Malaguzzi, L. (1998). History, ideas and basic philosophy: An interview with Lella Gandini. In C. Edwards, L. Gandini & G. Forman (eds), *The Hundred Languages of Children: The Reggio Emilia Approach – Advanced Reflections*. Greenwich: Ablex Publishing Corporation.

Oldroyd, D. (2005). Human resources for learning. In M. Coleman & P. Earley (eds), *Leadership and Management in Education: Cultures, Change and Context*. Oxford: Oxford University Press.

Owens, R. G. (2004). *Organisational Behavior in Education: Adaptive Leadership and School Reform*. Boston: Pearson Education Inc.

Rinaldi, C. (2006). *In Dialogue with Reggio Emilia: Listening, Researching and Learning*. Oxfordshire, UK: RoutledgeFalmer.

Rodd, J. (2013). *Leadership in Early Childhood: Pathways to Professionalism* (4th edn). Crows Nest, NSW: Allen & Unwin.

Schein, E. (2010). *Organizational Culture and Leadership* (3rd edn). San Francisco: John Wiley and Sons.

Senge, P. M. (2006). *The Fifth Discipline: The Art and Practice of the Learning Organisation* (rev. edn). Milsons Point, NSW: Random House.

Sergiovanni, T. J. (2003). The lifeworld at the center: Values and action in educational leadership. In N. Bennett, M. Crawford & M. Cartwright (eds), *Effective Educational Leadership*. London: Open University Press in association with Paul Chapman Publishing.

Sinclair, A. (2007). *Leadership for the Disillusioned*. Crows Nest, NSW: Allen & Unwin.

Vygotsky, L. (1993). *The Collected Works of L. S. Vygotsky. Volume 2: The Fundamentals of Defectology* (Abnormal Psychology and Learning Disabilities) (R. W. Rieber & A. S. Carton, eds of English translation). New York: Plenum Press.

Walker, K. (1970). *My People*. Brisbane: Jacaranda Press.

Waniganayake, M., Cheeseman, S., Fenech, M., Hadley, F. & Shepherd, W. (2012). *Leadership: Contexts and Complexities in Early Childhood Education*. South Melbourne: Oxford University Press.

Practical possibilities and pedagogical approaches for early childhood education for sustainability: The Kenmore West story

Robert Pratt

Editor's note

Here, **Robert Pratt** presents a new chapter based on his work in ECEfS at Kenmore West Kindergarten, Brisbane, Australia. Building on the philosophy, ideas and practices that underpinned his work at Campus Kindergarten (see Chapter 4 of the first edition) Rob translates and extends these into another early childhood setting. He shares just a small part of the extensive repertoire of day-to-day teaching ideas and strategies that make the work at Kenmore West Kindergarten successful. As outlined in this chapter, the foci of the teaching and learning are management, eco-friendly resource choices, and community and nature connections, including embedding Indigenous perspectives into the learning environment. It is important to note that Rob and his colleagues were working with EfS concepts and practices long before the current Australian Curriculum and quality initiatives were introduced. Their work was exemplary then, and today continues to set a benchmark for high-quality ECEfS in Australia and internationally.

At the heart of Rob's approach is a commitment to the health and integrity of natural environments and to children's right to a sustainable future. Hence, engaging children in learning about complex sustainability issues and topics is central to this work, where children are seen as competent and capable learners well able to solve problems and take actions to deal with environmental and sustainability issues of relevance to their lives.

Introduction

... early childhood education for sustainability is a transformative and empowering process actively engaged in by children, families and educators who share an ecocentric worldview (Elliott 2014, p. 15).

In this chapter I focus largely on the practical possibilities and pedagogical approaches that support ECEfS, drawing on my experiences at Brisbane's Campus Kindergarten (see Chapter 4 of the first edition of this text for more details), where I worked as a teacher for 11 years and, more recently, at Kenmore West Kindergarten (KWK) (also in Brisbane), where I have been working since January 2013.[1] At Campus Kindergarten, in addition to my responsibilities as a classroom teacher in charge of the development and implementation of an early childhood education program, I held a significant leadership role in supporting the centre's ever-evolving Sustainable Planet Project – the title given to all initiatives and practices that support ECEfS at Campus Kindergarten. At KWK I have played a similar leadership role. However, in this latter case, many of the initiatives that support EfS had already been introduced by the pre-existing teaching team. This chapter is a reflection of our combined strategies.

Campus Kindergarten and KWK are both community-based, not-for-profit early childhood education services managed by a volunteer parent committee or board of management. During my employment at Campus Kindergarten, it operated jointly as a community kindergarten affiliated with the Creche and Kindergarten Association of Queensland and as a long day care centre. KWK is also a community kindergarten affiliated with the Creche and Kindergarten Association of Queensland; however, it does not offer long day care. KWK has just one classroom and two groups of 22 children aged 3–4 years. One group attends on Monday and Tuesday and alternate Wednesdays while the other group attends on alternate Wednesdays and each Thursday and Friday. KWK is situated in a quiet suburban street in western Brisbane. Like the families at Campus Kindergarten, those at KWK are generally well educated and reasonably affluent.

In the first part of this chapter I re-articulate the philosophical beliefs that underpin my work as an early childhood teacher who is committed to EfS. In the second part, I present a range of practical strategies that support the development of a culture of sustainability, predominantly focusing on KWK. As noted above, these strategies are a reflection of the work of everyone in the teaching team.

My philosophy

My teaching approach and educational philosophy have evolved through the course of my teaching career, now stretching over 22 years. I have been influenced by my

---

[1] I acknowledge the staff, children and families at both Campus Kindergarten and Kenmore West Kindergarten for allowing me to share the experiences and knowledge I gained during my employment at these centres.

teaching colleagues, the children with whom I have interacted over the years, the communities in which I have worked, and various educational advocates and researchers in education, early childhood education, EfS and ECEfS. Those in the latter category include the following: in education, Gardner (1993, 2006) and Vygotsky (1993); in early childhood education, Malaguzzi (1998) and Rinaldi (2006); in EfS, Fien (2005); in ECEfS, Davis and Elliott (2003). A new influence is the work of Tim Gill, who argues that contemporary childhood is being undermined by the growth of risk aversion that is intruding into every aspect of children's lives (Gill 2007). His work helps educators navigate their way through and around the complexities of risk management and its apparent limitations on children's play and learning.

In the first edition, I illustrated my teaching approach through a model called 'Campus Kindergarten's teachers' model of curriculum and culture'. This has not fundamentally changed. For details of the original model, please refer to the first edition of this text.

I continue to be strongly influenced by the Earth Charter (Corcoran 2005) and its four guiding principles:

1. Be kind to each other, to the animals and the plants.

2. Take good care of the environment.

3. We are all equal.

4. Say yes to peace and no to violence.

These principles continue to resonate closely with my personal values, key ideas about sustainability, and my early childhood teaching practice. In summary, I believe in an holistic approach to teaching young children. This is an approach that fosters a healthy self-image, respectful relationships and respect for the world in which we live. In my new teaching context, the centre encapsulates this by seeking to create a culture that will 'support and nurture a community of reflective learners who are passionate, respectful, responsible and active citizens' (Kenmore West Kindergarden Handbook 2014, p. 12). We articulate our own context-specific principles as follows:

- *Democracy* – inputs and participation are valued from all members of the community (children, staff, families and local and global communities).

- *Active citizenship* – all community members feel empowered and have the capacity to act upon their beliefs and values.

- *Critical reflection and creative thinking* – these are important aspects of problem solving, applying as much to the children as to the adults in the KWK community.

- *A negotiated and emergent curriculum* – curriculum content emerges from the interests and events having an impact on the members of the KWK community.

- *A fully integrated curriculum for EfS* – learning about the environment is not an add-on, but is embedded into all curriculum areas.

- *Sustainability* – this is embedded in all aspects of centre practice, as well as into the daily lives of members of the KWK community.
- *Indigenous connections* – we actively seek to strengthen relationships with our local Indigenous communities, to learn about their values and beliefs, and to contribute to reconciliation.

Provocation 4.1

List the key influences on your teaching philosophy.

What are your core values? How do they influence your teaching practice?

How strongly do you believe in the capabilities of young children in making decisions and participating in actions that contribute towards a sustainable future?

In the context of the curriculum at KWK, the teaching team utilises the organiser developed in the first edition. ECEfS encompasses three broad elements; they are interconnected and of equal importance (see Figure 4.1).

This model illustrates three central elements of ECEfS as we aim to enact them in our work with young children at KWK. These are the centre's physical environment, its curriculum/program and its culture/philosophy.

1. *Physical environment*: This refers to both built and natural elements. To support sustainable operations and to promote the modelling of sustainable practice, buildings should incorporate elements of sustainable design, including water tanks, solar energy, insulation and greywater treatment. Outdoor playspaces should aim

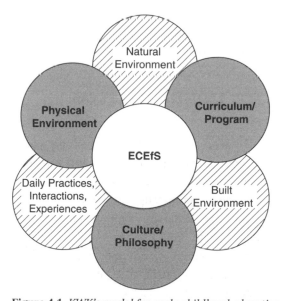

Figure 4.1 *KWK's model for early childhood education for sustainability*

to be as natural as possible, providing opportunities for children to immerse themselves in the richness of nature.

2. *Curriculum/program*: The aim is for EfS content and processes to be fully integrated into the education program. Practices promoting sustainable living need to become an everyday part of our lives. Children should have extended opportunities to connect with nature, learn about the environment and human impacts upon it, deepen understandings through recognition of Indigenous peoples and perspectives, and develop skills and action capacity to care for others and the environment. Daily practices could include appreciating each other and our community's diverse histories and cultures, protecting the local natural environment, maintaining an organic fruit and vegetable garden, and investigating water and energy conservation strategies within the service.

3. *Culture/philosophy*: A key aim of ECEfS is to promote a culture of sustainability whereby all members of the community (children, teachers and families) become more ecologically, socially, economically and politically aware (Fein 2005). As Julie Davis discusses in the Introduction to this second edition, sustainability is largely an issue related to relationships and equity. Therefore, it is critical that a philosophy or culture develops that embraces active citizenship and recognises and values the inputs of all community members, especially children. Core values should promote equity in all respects: between generations, between humans as individuals or communities, and between the human and non-human species that inhabit this planet.

Provocation 4.2

Does the model above resonate with your teaching approach? Explain.

List the attributes that **you** view as integral to ECEfS.

Teaching and learning possibilities and practices

Life in the 21st century is presenting humanity with many challenges, including economic recession, food shortages, poverty, global warming and ethnic and religious conflict. As this chapter demonstrates, I believe that children as young as 3 or 4 years (possibly even younger) already possess significant knowledge and understanding about such issues. Equipped with further knowledge, skills and support, children are able to develop resilience and the capacity to deal with these challenges. I believe that educators are doing children (and nature and humanity) an injustice if they seek to shelter young children, or 'bubble wrap' them, in order to protect them from knowing about and engaging with such challenges in positive ways.

This chapter explores the multitude of teaching possibilities that early childhood educators can implement to ensure that young children *are* equipped – now and into the future – to deal with environmental and sustainability challenges. In the first edition of this text, there were five main headings that I used to encapsulate these teaching and learning possibilities. These were:

- waste and resource management
- connecting with nature
- efficient use of natural resources
- wise chemical use and green cleaning
- sustaining sustainability.

In this chapter there is a streamlined focus with just two key topics:

- resource management and promoting eco-friendly resource choices
- community/nature connections.

The following sections provide teaching and learning examples involving young children at KWK as they explored and took actions connected with these topics. Each section is then followed by more general examples and suggestions that strengthen a 'whole-centre' approach. Much of the recent information and ideas in this chapter come from the learning documentation that teachers and children at KWK constructed together about a topic or project. Using images, dialogue and explanations of the projects, supported by relevant research and connections to current curriculum documents including the national Early Years Learning Framework, the National Quality Standard and C & K's *Building Waterfalls* (2011), the teachers and children 'tell the story' of a particular topic, project, experience or event. The documentation is presented in various forms, including PowerPoint presentations, posters and folios. By making learning and thinking visible for children, teachers and families, documentation is also an effective tool for curriculum/program evaluation and reflection.

Provocation 4.3

What additional strategies, methods or techniques could you use as an early childhood educator to document children's learning and thinking? How would you evaluate their effectiveness?

Teaching and learning for resource management and promoting eco-friendly resource choices

The resources we use and how they are disposed of have a significant impact upon people and the environment. Carefully considered waste and resource management practices will save money and help reduce an early childhood service's carbon emissions and environmental footprint, while also providing valuable opportunities for children to learn about ways to be more sustainable. Through active engagement in decision-making processes and practices in waste and resource management, children can be encouraged to develop foundational values, skills and strategies for lifelong, environmentally responsible living. It is essential to include children, staff and families in discussions, investigations and actions regarding waste and resource management, in order to deepen and widen community understandings of these issues. The following two projects undertaken at KWK illustrate how this can happen:

1. Where Does All the Garbage Go? The Kenmore West Kindy Story
2. Beyond the Kindy Gates – the Creek Excursions.

Project 1: Where Does All the Garbage Go? The Kenmore West Kindy Story

In the first edition of this text, I told the story of how I introduced the concept of sustainable waste management to a group of children at the beginning of the year. On that occasion, I initiated the conversation by asking, *Where does all our rubbish go?* This led to a discussion and the reading of the story *Where Does All the Garbage Go?* by Melvin Berger (1992). At KWK, we follow a similar process, but expanded on it based on prior experiences.

Since the first edition, the inclusion of recycling bins, compost bins and other sustainable waste management initiatives have become much more commonplace in people's homes and in early childhood services. Consequently, many of the children at KWK are already familiar with such practices when they commence enrolment at the beginning of the year. In considering this change, the teaching team has approached the topic with additional goals in mind. As well as introducing the concept of sustainable waste management to the children and familiarising them with the equipment and practices we have at kindy, we also have the goal of fostering a sense of stewardship for the Earth as a whole. Our aim is for the children to take the knowledge and skills they are developing at kindy and apply them outside the kindy gates.

Therefore, when introducing the topic in early 2013 at our morning meeting, I simply presented to the children the various waste bins we currently use (recycling, rubbish and compost), along with a poster made with the children that demonstrated how to use the bins appropriately. I then let the conversation flow. Thus, in this informal way, the children started to share their knowledge, such as:

Nic: That's a recycling bin. It's for paper.
Blake: That one's for the chooks and worms.

A number of children were quite knowledgeable while others had obviously had less experience. I asked questions to provoke further conversation:

Robert: What other rubbish do we have at kindy? What can we do to help make less rubbish?

The conversation continued for a short while before evolving into an imaginary role-play game where each child 'imagined' a piece of rubbish they might produce at kindy then imagined themselves placing it in the appropriate bin. When a child was uncertain about which bin to use, a group discussion/debate would begin, with each child sharing their opinion before a shared decision was reached.

On finshing the session, I read the children's book *Michael Recycle* (Bethal 2008), which tells the story of a superhero who travels the world educating and empowering people to clean up their towns. The following day we revisited the discussion and reflected on what we had spoken about the day before, recalling what we had learnt, specifically which bin to use with particular types of rubbish. We then went on to read *Where Does All the Garbage Go?* again, which led to further discussions about what we could do at kindy and at home to 'make less rubbish in the world'. Suggestions from the children included picking up rubbish in the street, buying less plastic 'stuff' and making our own food.

Through this learning experience, the group achieved a range of positive outcomes. Not only did the children develop a deeper understanding of sustainable waste management practices, but also a sense of agency. They felt like they could take action. Consequently, we saw the amount of recyclables, reuseables and compostables that had previously ended up in the kindy rubbish bin (but later removed by teachers) reduce by approximately half. The amount of food materials placed in the worm/chook scrap and recycling bins correspondingly increased. As noted earlier, though, our goal was not only for the children to learn more about sustainable waste management at kindy, but to take this knowledge beyond the kindy gates. Parents reported increased awareness and participation in sustainable waste management practices at home by both children and adults. The story told in Project 2 describes how the children were further developing their sense of stewardship for the Earth and how they applied their emerging values, knowledge and skills while on a kindy excursion.

Provocation 4.4

Do you view the above example as an effective way to introduce sustainable waste management practices to a group of young children? What else could you do? List some possibilities.

Project 2: Beyond the Kindy Gates – the Creek Excursions

Several weeks after the initial discussions about sustainable waste management and our practices at kindy, the teaching team began to consider taking the children on an excursion to a nearby creek and bushland. In doing so, we had regard to the following questions:

- What are the overall benefits of this experience?
- How are we going to navigate the complexities of 'risk management' and the rules and regulations that can make conducting such an excursion a challenge?

In answer to the first question, we decided that the benefits were:

1. connecting with our local community
2. connecting with nature

3. exploring our local environment
4. developing a greater understanding of natural environments and Earth stewardship
5. learning to manage risk
6. physical exercise
7. lots of fun.

I also considered that it would be a valuable opportunity for accompanying parents to see the richness of learning that can occur in the outdoors, and how capable their children are at negotiating challenging physical or potentially 'risky' activities, such as climbing across fallen logs and tree climbing.

In considering the second question, we decided to turn to the work of Tim Gill and his strategies to help us manage potential risks. Gill advocates for a balanced approach to risk management in which the potential hazards of an activity are weighed up against the benefits (Gill 2010). We developed our own risk–benefit assessment (Appendix 1) that helped us ensure that we had taken a 'balanced approach' to managing risk on our excursion. With the risk–benefit assessment complete, safety guidelines developed with the children, parent permission forms signed, parent helpers briefed (Appendix 2) and first aid kits packed, we embarked on our excursion. Immediately after leaving, and while still in the kindy carpark, one of the children noticed plastic rubbish in among the bushes.

Luci: We have to pick it up.
Noah: Yeah, we have to look after the Earth.

Figure 4.2 *Children picking up rubbish in the carpark*

Figure 4.3 *Children crossing creek*

Luci and Noah, as well as several other children, went on to pick up all the rubbish they could find in and around the kindy carpark. We then continued on our walk to the creek, collecting several items of rubbish along the way.

Over the course of the next few hours, the children spent their time exploring the bush, climbing trees, throwing rocks in the creek, investigating wildlife, navigating fallen logs across the creek (and falling in!) and picking up numerous items of rubbish, including car tyres, broken pipes, building materials, broken glass, plastic bottles and lots of plastic bags.

Participating in experiences that engage children within the local community further expands learning possibilities and takes opportunities for environmental protection beyond the kindergarten's gates. In so doing, such opportunities also support wider recognition of children as active, engaged citizens capable of creating positive change in their environment.

Provocation 4.5

How do you feel about children climbing trees? Do you perceive this as an unsafe activity?

What strategies, procedures and guidelines could you put in place to minimise risk to children when climbing trees?

How would such guidelines be developed? Who would be involved in the decision-making process? Children, teachers and/or parents? How might you specifically engage the children in developing risk-minimising strategies?

Whole-centre practices for resource management and promoting eco-friendly resource choices

If early childhood educators wish to encourage others to take up sustainable waste and resource management practices, they must model appropriate practices. This means including children and families in discussions, investigations, decision making and actions regarding waste and resource management. The list of possibilities included in the first edition of this text remains relevant. They include the following:

With regard to resource management:

- Adopting the philosophy *Respect, Rethink, Reduce, Reuse, Recycle*. Encourage all members of the community to *rethink* their purchasing and waste management practices in order to *reduce* the use of non-renewable resources (for example, energy and water), *reduce* the use of materials that harm the environment (for example, plastics and cleaning products) and *reduce* the amount of waste in landfill.

- Buying locally made products that support the local community and reduce fuel use and carbon emissions produced in the transportation of products over long distances.

- Introducing a low-waste lunch program.

- Encouraging sustainable transport initiatives, such as walking to kindy, carpooling or cycling.

With regard to heating/cooling:

- Opening windows and doors to maximise ventilation during hot weather.

- Installing insulation.

- Using fans to increase air circulation. Fans are much more economical than air-conditioning.

- Using air-conditioning only if absolutely necessary.

With regard to water conservation:

- Installing a water tank and connecting it to toilets, the washing machine and irrigation. Ensure the tank has a gauge that children can access.

- Installing a greywater treatment system.

- Installing water-saving fittings on taps and dual-flush toilets.

- Ensuring the dishwasher and washing machine are not turned on until full. Use the 'eco' cycle for greater water efficiency.

- Buying water-efficient products (for information on the the Water Efficiency Labelling and Standards [WELS] scheme, go to www.waterrating.gov.au).

- Encouraging children and staff to pour any contaminant-free waste water, including excess drinking water, used waterplay water, and washing-up water, into the garden (but first check restrictions with your local council).

- Planting native plant species and ensuring they are adequately mulched for water retention.

- Installing drip irrigation to reduce evaporation.

- Considering what goes down the drain – chemicals, paints, bleached toilet paper and so on.

- Conducting scientific investigations, including understanding the water cycle and properties of water, as well as exploring the question 'where does water come from?'

- Educating families about water conservation through newsletters, displays, and through the children's communication with their families.

- Providing a wide range of resources to support investigations, such as storybooks, reference books, games, role-play props, and digital and web-based resources.

- Modelling water-conservation strategies by adults.

With regard to wise chemical use and green cleaning:
Here, I re-articulate and summarise my first edition chapter. Recognising that barriers continue to exist in many early childhood settings around 'safe' cleaning, and drawing on the works of Gardner (2008), Kinsella (2007) and the Kindergarten Union's Environment Policy (2004), as well as my own experiences, I make the following suggestions:

- Research green cleaning practices and gather evidence to support such practices.

- Find out from other services in your area what products and practices they are using.

- Ensure practices meet licensing and accreditation requirements.

- Make changes in small, incremental steps. Phase in green-cleaning products one at a time. Get rid of the worst first. Discuss green-cleaning practices with children. Share what they do at home.

- Share your ideas with families – through newsletters, through the children, and so on.

- If your service uses a contract cleaner, ensure they use appropriate products. Adopt the philosophy of 'removing' rather than 'killing' germs.

- For surface cleaning, use 1 part soap to 10 parts warm water in a squeeze bottle.

- For tougher stains, try equal parts of plant-based, petrochemical-free laundry detergent and bicarbonate of soda (bicarb). Rub with a scourer (onion bags make great scourers). Try health food stores for good quality, plant-based, petrochemical-free cleaning products. Some supermarkets also sell such products.

- Consider using microfibre cleaning products. These do not use water or chemicals.

- Avoid using aerosols. Buy products in bulk and use refillable spray and squeeze bottles.

- Investigate other environmentally friendly cleaning products. There are countless websites and publications that address this topic. Many traditional products and practices that 'grandma used to use' can be effective and appropriate in early childhood services.

- Use a chemical analysis guide, such as Bill Statham's (2006) *The Chemical Maze: Shopping Companion*, to ascertain whether products contain potentially harmful chemicals. Other essential reading includes Dr Sarah Lantz's (2009) *Chemical Free Kids*.

- Consult the useful Fresh Green Clean website (www.freshgreenclean.com.au).

- Avoid the use of antibacterial handwashes and gels.

- Conduct a chemical audit of all the chemicals in use in your centre – both indoor and outdoor. Check warning labels on products.

- Consider the products you are using in your washing machine or dishwasher. Are they high in phosphates, sodium or other harmful chemicals? Investigate alternatives.

- Consider the presence of potentially toxic chemicals in products such as paints (both children's paints and building/furniture paints), pens and whiteboard markers, pest-control products, furniture and building materials, and plastics. Investigate alternatives, such as non-toxic paints, furniture and buildings constructed with non-treated timber (or less heavily treated processed timber, such as medium-density fibreboard, or MDF), and insect repellents made with natural ingredients, such as essential oils.

- In the garden, consider using natural pest-control methods, such as companion planting and other permaculture strategies. Use natural plant fertilisers, such as worm castings and compost.

- Consider the quality of drinking water. Should it be filtered?

- Does the service provide food? Has it been sourced locally? Local food uses fewer transport miles. Has it been grown organically? Fewer or no artificial chemicals are used in organic food production.

Teaching and learning to connect with nature/community

As this topic has been explored in depth in Chapter 2, further explanatory detail is not required here. Suffice to say, I fully recognise the importance of creating natural playspaces and providing many opportunities for young children to connect with nature in early childhood services. It is my belief that humans are deeply connected with nature and the earth, and that our futures depend upon recognising, understanding and valuing that connection (Gill 2007; Louv 2005; Suzuki 2007). Hands-on contact with nature is vital if children's attitudes, values and full appreciation of the importance of such connections are to be fostered. The following project illustrates the way that nature connections have been integrated into the curriculum at KWK.

The 'Discovering Wildlife at Kenmore West Kindy' book

> Teaching a child not to step on a caterpillar is as important for the child as it is for the caterpillar (Bradley Miller, cited in Wilson 2008, p. 14).

The KWK outdoor playspace is fortunate in that it has many native trees and shrubs that support a rich habitat of native animals. Notable inhabitants include blue-tongue lizards, water dragons, bush stone curlews, scrub turkeys and native bees. The natural playspace, and the wildlife within it, have long provided a wealth of learning opportunities for the teachers and children. The *Discovering Wildlife at Kenmore West Kindy* book documents some of the interactions with nature experienced by the children at KWK since 2012. It has become an important resource book for the KWK community.

The inception of this book occurred at a morning planning meeting in February 2012, when many of the children stated that they would like to explore the bamboo forest. Thomas said he would like to find spiders. Tash (teacher) suggested the children use magnifying glasses to help look for such creatures. The children's explorations continued throughout the morning. Along the way, some of the children recorded their findings through drawings (for example, Asha's lizard footprints).

Later, at the second planning meeting, Tash asked the children to share what they had found with the rest of the class. Many children drew the creatures they had found on the whiteboard: lizards, spiders, ants, toads, snakes, butterflies, turkeys, beetles ... and monsters! At this point, Tash made the suggestion of recording all their discoveries in a book. The children were all familiar with a local publication, *Wildlife of Greater Brisbane* (Queensland Museum 2007), and therefore decided to call their book *Discovering Wildlife at Kenmore West Kindy*. Digital cameras were made available for the children to photograph their discoveries and, over the following days, the first entries were made in the book. Children continued to contribute to the book in the later years and it has now become a valuable resource for all members of the KWK community wanting to learn more about the creatures that may be found in the kindy playground.

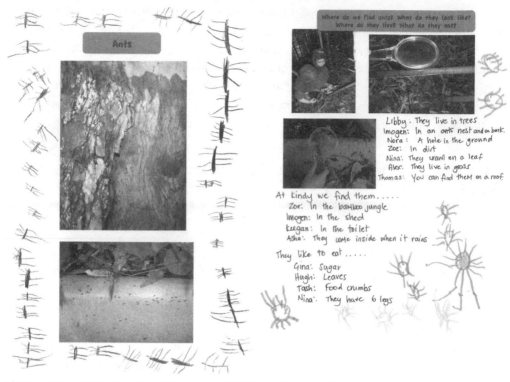

Figures 4.4 and 4.5 *Pages from* Discovering Wildlife at Kenmore West Kindy

Adding depth to human/nature connections – embedding Indigenous perspectives

Recognising and valuing the strong connection to nature experienced by Indigenous Australians has become an integral component of teaching and learning at KWK. In its first few years, KWK was attended by a group of Aboriginal children who were bused to the kindy from outlying suburbs (Pascoe 2012). In 2012, in commemoration of the 40 years of KWK, we embarked on an Indigenous art project, in recognition of the kindergarten's beginnings. We wanted this project to reflect our kindergarten's wildlife, environment and community, an investigation reflective of the social pillar of sustainability as much as its environmental aspects. With the help of Aboriginal artist Peter Mulcahy, we created a visual feature in the central area of our carpark, a notable meeting point for the kindergarten community. Peter created designs that represented animals connected to the stories of the Dreaming, interwoven with children's handprints. The children also placed river rock artworks of their own designs in a concrete central

Figure 4.6 *Image of the Indigenous art feature*

circle that was part of the feature. Two native trees, a lillypilly (Syzygium sp.) and a wattle (Acacia sp.), were also planted.

Below is Peter's story, which describes this feature and its significance.

Maran Gaarrimay

At the centre of this work we have our Gaarrimay (the nest). As the children are central to our existence, we hold them closest, to provide and protect. These little ones, these little eggs are the culmination of every ancestor that has ever come before them. They are and will be the storytellers of all that you do. They are the link between you and the generations you will never come to see.

The Sandstone boulders represent you, the parents and the teachers, ever guiding and providing. You too, like the sandstone are the layered culmination of thousands of generations and now stand as protectors of the nest. Remember they can only be what your gentle guidance allows them to be.

Next are the Australian Cypress timbers, they stand as sentinels, as totemic teachers.

These four figures start with Gugurrgaagaa (the Kookaburra). He is the Awakener, the one who calls the sun to rise each day. He does this with joy in his heart, in the hope that this joy is spread with one another every day of our lives. Gugurrgaagaa faces the east so the sun will rise each day for these little ones.

Opposite him we have the figure of Yabba (the carpet snake). He faces the west in recognition of my Jut Ju Uncle Paddy Djeripi Gerome and my kin connection to the Waka Waka peoples of the North West. Yabba stands for spiritual power and strength. He teaches us that the shedding of things does not diminish us, but it is exactly that which allows us to become something greater. Yabba teaches us of growth, strength and fluidity.

The third sentinel is that of the blue-tongue lizard. He is a local to the Kindy and his dreaming stories will reveal his teachings as an aspect of the creator father and the Dreaming itself.

The last Watcher, representing the totemic teachers and our ancestors who watch over this most ancient of lands and all its people, is Bala Balaa (the Butterfly). This image faces your little ones' Kindy as a reflection of all that lies ahead of them. Bala Balaa was the first creature to prove life after death. This little caterpillar passed through a cocoon of darkness to re-enter the world as a Butterfly.

May all our children grow strong and beautiful, and in opening their wings to eventual adulthood, never forget the child within. Like Bula Bulaa, who will forever remain the little caterpillar with her beautiful adult wings.

(Source: Peter Muraay Djeripi Mulcahy)

Maran Gaarrimay has become a special part of the physical and social environment for the KWK community. Teachers often visit the site with small groups of children to simply sit and reflect. We tell new groups of children the story of KWK's Indigenous history, Peter's artwork, and the significance of the animals depicted within it. Since the creation of Maran Gaarrimay and the celebrations for KWK's 40th anniversary, the teaching team has continued to foster an ongoing relationship with Peter and other members of our local Indigenous communities. For example, Sharron 'Mirii' Lindh of 'Indigenous Insights' has become a regular visitor to KWK, with Sharron conducting Indigenous culture awareness workshops for children and adults.

Through these connections the children and teachers have developed much deeper understandings, not only of Indigenous Australian culture, but also of human–nature connections, and the importance of our role as Earth's custodians.

Provocation 4.6

Early childhood educators often find it difficult to include Indigenous perspectives in their programs in meaningful and non-tokenistc ways.

What are your feelings? Can you think of other authentic strategies or techniques for embedding Indigenous perspectives into an early childhood education program?

Figure 4.7 *Image of Sharron 'Mirii' Lindh conducting a workshop at KWK*

Whole-centre practices for connecting community and nature

Some other projects related to community–nature connections that can be embedded in the everyday life, teaching and learning of an early childhood service include:

- coordinating a native plant regeneration project, both within a service's grounds and in the local community
- supporting neighbourhood clean-up days, such as 'Clean-up Australia Day'
- organising community bushwalks or camping trips
- maintaining an organic vegetable garden
- keeping chickens
- building worm farms and compost bins
- opening a 'Worm Wee Shop' with the children; that is, selling worm castings (a worm farm by-product) as fertiliser
- building and installing possum, bird and bee boxes, with children and families
- establishing a frog pond
- using natural materials (inside and outside), thereby reducing use of plastic toys/products.

Provocation 4.7

It is a common adult misconception that 'real learning' occurs indoors while outdoor play is 'just for fun', with little or no real value. **What do you believe?**

I often hear parents make comments about the 'dangers' of outdoor play, with concerns expressed about, for example, insects, sticks and dirt (germs). Others worry about their children getting dirty or sandy. **How would you respond to these kinds of parental concerns?**

Sustaining sustainability: Whole-centre organisation and management possibilities

Throughout this chapter, a range of possibilities to support sustainability has been discussed, derived from my experiences at both Campus Kindergarten and, more recently, at Kenmore West Kindergarten. With so many ideas available, the moral pressure to 'do something' for the environment and sustainability, statutory demands through the National Quality Standard to embed sustainable practices into early childhood centre practices, and the countless other responsibilities of early childhood educators, it can feel overwhelming to begin the process of addressing sustainability in *your* early childhood setting. Therefore, based on my own background and experiences as an early childhood educator for sustainability, I have developed the following suggestions to guide you through this process. These ideas provide a set of change strategies to make 'sustaining sustainability' more achievable and to 'spread the load'. (Refer, also, to Megan Gibson's chapter on leadership for further ideas about creating sustainable change for sustainability.)

- Establish a Sustainability Committee in your centre to coordinate all EfS initiatives and strategic planning. The committee should include parents, children and staff.

- Develop a Sustainability Action Plan based on your centre's collaboratively derived priorities.

- Compile and use sustainability checklists to guide your actions (see first edition).

- Conduct a comprehensive audit of energy, water, chemical use, cleaning practices, and waste and resource management.

- Calculate the centre's ecological or carbon footprint – see McNichol, Davis and O'Brien's study (2011) for ideas. Their project was based on research undertaken at Campus Kindergarten.

- Review your service's policies related to sustainability; for example, play and the natural environment, cleaning policies, waste management policies, and health and wellbeing policies. Update these to take account of sustainability issues.

- Think about how you might authentically embed Indigenous perspectives into your centre's plans and actions (read Melinda Miller's Chapter 6 for more on this important aspect).

- Take small steps initially – one goal at a time! Celebrate every success.

- See challenges as opportunities for learning and for strengthening and sustaining community participation.

- Access funding to support your EfS program. Local, state and federal levels of government offer varying types of support, as do a range of non-government organisations.

- Maximise opportunities to engage in EfS research with educational institutions and other relevant bodies. These people and organisations can help stimulate thinking and promote your good work to a wider audience.

- Establish and maintain networks with like-minded organisations, services and professional associations (see Appendix 3).

- Provide continuing professional development and information sessions for all staff members and families. These sessions should explore the service's culture/philosophy in terms of sustainability, help build EfS concepts and practices, and offer practical strategies (see Megan Gibson's Chapter 3 for motivating ways to think about professional development and learning).

- Review your available resources and teaching materials. Prioritise the use of those that support sustainability concepts and practices. Obtain additional materials to fill the gaps.

- Visit useful websites for further education and information (see Appendix 4).

- Visit early childhood services already implementing sustainable practices and EfS in order to learn and share. Joining or starting a local ECEfS network is a great way to do this.

- For the longer term, advocate and lobby government and non-government organisations at all levels to support ECEfS with research, resources and pre-service and in-service education. Again, this is more easily done through the collective activities of network participation.

Conclusion

Taking action on just some of the educational and practical possibilities that early childhood educators might consider as relevant to EfS will help to make small steps towards creating more sustainable futures for us all. Such actions also provide opportunities for children to develop greater understandings of their roles and capabilities in helping to achieve this goal. For an EfS program to reach its full potential, however, a shift in the way children are perceived and taught is required. It is no longer acceptable for children to be thought of as unknowing or uninformed about sustainability matters or as passive recipients of knowledge and for adults to make all the decisions about their learning. Children must be actively engaged in the learning process, and safe in a democratic environment in which they can share ideas and contribute towards decision making and action taking. In such a learning environment, children have the potential to develop a sense of agency and to 'make a difference'. These are important first steps in being knowledgeable, active and empowered citizens, now and into the future.

Review provocation

Now it's your turn! Whether you are a practising teacher or in pre-service education, develop a Sustainability Action Plan for an early childhood workplace and/or your home. Involve others in your plan. Start with a few small steps, a few actions you can take towards creating sustainable futures.

References

Australian Children's Education and Care Quality Authority (n.d.). National Quality Standard, www.acecqa.gov.au/national-quality-framework/the-national-quality-standard (accessed 1 May 2014).

Australian Government, Department of Education, Employment and Workplace Relations (2009). *Belong, Being, Becoming – The Early Years Learning Framework for Australia.* Canberra: Department of Education, Employment and Workplace Relations for the Council of Australian Governments.

Berger, M. (1992). *Where Does All The Garbage Go?* London: Macmillan.

Bethal, E. (2008). *Michael Recycle.* California: Worthwhile Books.

Corcoran, P. B. (ed.) (2005). *The Earth Charter in Action: Toward a Sustainable Development.* Amsterdam: KIT Publishers.

C&K (2011). *Building Waterfalls* (2nd edn). Brisbane: C&K.

Davis, J. & Elliott, S. (2003). *Early Childhood Environmental Education: Making it Mainstream.* Canberra: Early Childhood Australia.

Elliott, S. (2014). *Sustainability and the Early Years Learning Framework.* Mt Victoria, NSW: Pademelon.

Fien, J. (2005). *Teaching and Learning for a Sustainable Future.* CD-ROM, Version 4.0. Paris: UNESCO.

Gardner, B. (2008). *SASIclean: The Safe and Sustainable Indoor Cleaning Report,* http://zetec.co.nz.pdfs/SASI_Clean Project Results report.pdf (accessed 1 May 2014).

Gardner, H. (1993). *Multiple Intelligences: The Theory in Practice.* New York: Basic Books.

Gardner, H. (2006). *Multiple Intelligences: New Horizons.* New York: Basic Books.

Gill, T. (2007). *No Fear: Growing up in a Risk Averse Society.* London: Calouste Gulbenkian Foundation.

Gill, T. (2010). *Nothing Ventured: Balancing Risks and Benefits in the Outdoors*. United Kingdom: English Outdoor Council.

Kenmore West Kindergarten Handbook (2014). Brisbane: Kenmore West Kindergarten.

Kindergarten Union (2004). *Kindergarten Union's Environment Policy*. Sydney: Kindergarten Union.

Kinsella, R. (2007). *Greening Services: Practical Sustainability*. Watson, ACT: Early Childhood Australia.

Lantz, S. (2009). *Chemical Free Kids*. Buddina, Qld: Joshua Books.

Louv, R. (2005). *Last Child in the Woods: Saving our Children from Nature-Deficit Disorder*. Chapel Hill, NC: Algonquin Books of Chapel Hill.

McNichol, H., Davis, J. M. & O'Brien, K. R. (2011). An ecological footprint for an early learning centre: Identifying opportunities for early childhood sustainability education through inter-disciplinary research. *Environmental Education Research*, 17(5), pp. 689–704.

Malaguzzi, L. (1998). History, ideas and basic philosophy: An interview with Lella Gandini. In C. Edwards, L. Gandini & G. Forman (eds), *The Hundred Languages of Children: The Reggio Emilia Approach – Advanced Reflections*. Greenwich: Ablex Publishing Corporation.

Pascoe, B. (2012). *The Little Red Yellow Black Book: An Introduction to Indigenous Australia* (3rd edn). Canberra: Australian Institute of Aboriginal, Torres Strait Islander Studies (AIATSIS).

Queensland Museum (2007). *Wildlife of Greater Brisbane*. Brisbane: Queensland Museum.

Rinaldi, C. (2006). *In Dialogue with Reggio Emilia: Listening, Researching and Learning*. Oxfordshire, UK: Routedge Falmer.

Statham, B. (2006). *The Chemical Maze Shopping Companion*, West Sussex, UK: Summersdale Publishers.

Suzuki, D. (2007). *The Sacred Balance: Rediscovering Our Place in Nature*. Crows Nest, NSW: Allen & Unwin.

Vygotsky, L. (1993). *The Collected Works of L. S. Vygotsky. Volume 2: The Fundamentals of Defectology* (Abnormal Psychology and Learning Disabilities) (R. W. Rieber & A. S. Carton, eds of English translation). New York: Plenum Press.

Wilson, R. (2008). *Nature and Young Children*. London: Routledge.

Appendix 1: Risk–benefit assessment for creek excursion

A risk assessment matrix with Likelihood on the vertical axis and Impact on the horizontal axis:

	Minor	Moderate	Major
Very likely	Medium 2	High 3	Extreme 5
Likely	Low 1	Medium 2	High 3
Unlikely	Low 1	Low 1	Medium 2

What is the chance it will happen?

Local Bushland Excursion

Date activity planned to start:	August 2013	**Frequency of activity**:	Occasionally
Today's date:	July 2013	**Certified Supervisor**:	Robert Pratt
Brief description of the experience/ event/equipment:	Excursion to a small bush and parkland consisting of a shallow flowing creek, open grassed area, small children's playground and a small treed area centred around a magnificent old fig tree. Facilities include: two drinking water fountains, rubbish bin, lots of natural shade and picnic tables. There are toilet facilities at the nearby Kenmore High School if required. The bushland is accessed by a gentle 10-minute walk (pedestrian footpaths all the way) crossing five quiet suburban streets and one busy Moggill Rd (with pedestrian crossing).		
Costs:	No cost		
Benefits of the activity:	1. Connecting with local community 2. Connecting with nature 3. Exploring our environment 4. Developing greater understanding of natural environments and earth stewardship 5. Learning to manage risk 6. Physical exercise 7. Lots of fun!		

Risks associated with the activity:	Risks	Hazard rating	Action
	1. Road crossings	2	Maintain direct supervision by Certified Supervisor and 1:4 ratio. Discussions with children about road safety
	2. Trips/falls	1	Ongoing safety discussions with the children – develop rules prior to excursion
	3. Cuts from broken glass, sharps	1	Ongoing safety discussions with the children – develop rules prior to excursion
	4. Drowning	2	Maintain direct supervision by an adult and ensure 1:4 ratio at all times. Discussions with children about water safety
	5. Child separated from group	1	Maintain direct supervision by an adult and ensure 1:4 ratio at all times

What is already in place?	1. Road crossings will only take place at designated areas or as instructed by the teacher 2. An adult–child ratio of at least 1:4 will be maintained 3. All staff are trained in first aid 4. First aid equipment will be carried 5. Ongoing safety discussions with the children – develop rules prior to excursion 6. Attending parents and staff will be given comprehesive safety instructions, including which children they will be supervising 7. Mobile phone with all children's parent contact details will be taken on excursion
Consultation with children:	Safety issues regarding the excursion will be discussed with the children prior to and during the excursion. Together we will develop safety rules. These may include: • Stay immediately with a teacher/adult • Use walking feet when crossing roads and along footpaths • Listen to all adult instructions • Wear shoes and other appropriate clothing, e.g. hat, long-sleeved shirt, long pants • Ask adults before picking up any unknown objects or rubbish (staff will take gloves, bags etc.) • (Attach rules when complete)

Action plan:	What?	Whom?	By when:
	1. Conduct site analysis	Rob Pratt	Completed 31 July
	2. Develop rules with children	Teachers/ Children	Prior to excursion
	3. Complete Parent Permission Form	Teachers/ Parents	Prior to excursion

4. Set up excursion backpack (suncream, spare clothes, water, plastic bags, gloves, first aid, epipens, Zyrtec, drawing stuff, mobile phone)		Teachers	Prior to excursion
5. Complete Excursion Log		Teachers	Following excursion

Final decision: Have risks been reduced as far as reasonably practicable?	Yes
Stakeholders:	Teachers/Parents/Children

Final approval by: President's name:		Sign:	Date:
Final approval by: Director's name:		Sign:	Date:

Evaluate: (after activity) Was activity successful or not and why. Do changes need to be made?	

Appendix 2: Parent guidelines for creek excursion

Excursion Parent Helper Guidelines

Dear

Thank you for volunteering to help on our excursion. You can help ensure our excursion is as safe and enjoyable as possible by:

- being aware of the whereabouts of the children you are responsible for

- letting a staff member know if you become aware of any danger or hazard

- letting a staff member know if any sort of incident occurs – injury, altercation and so on

- letting a staff member know if you need to leave the group for any reason

- giving the children space to explore and investigate whilst still being present to extend their thinking with questions and provocations.

The children you are responsible for are:

Appendix 3: Professional organisations that support ECEfS

- Australian Association for Environmental Education (AAEE) – www.aaee.org.au
- Australian Science Teachers Association – http://asta.edu.au
- Early Childhood Australia – www.earlychildhoodaustralia.org.au
- Environmental Education in Early Childhood (Victoria) – www.eeec.org.au
- Little Green Steps – www.gosford.nsw.gov.au
- Nature Action Collaborative for Children – www.worldforumfoundation.org/working-groups/nature
- NSW Early Childhood Environmental Education Network – www.eceen.org.au
- Queensland Early Childhood Sustainability Network – www.qecsn.org.au
- UNESCO, 'Teaching and Learning for a Sustainable Future' – www.unesco.org/education/tlsf
- World Organization for Early Childhood Education – www.omep.org.gu.se/English

Appendix 4: Useful websites

Organisations

- Australian Government, Department of the Environment – www.environment.gov.au
- Children and Nature Network – www.childrenandnature.org
- Earth Charter Initiative – www.earthcharterinaction.org/content
- Planet Ark – www.planetark.com

Specific topics

Green cleaning

- Fresh Green Clean – www.freshgreenclean.com.au

Energy conservation

- Aurora Energy, 'Energy saving hints and tips' – www.auroraenergy.com.au/Your-Home/Help-and-advice/Energy-saving-hints-and-tips
- EnergyAustralia, 'Energy saving tools' – www.energyaustralia.com.au/residential/energy-efficiency-safety/energy-saving-tools
- Equipment Energy Efficiency Program – www.energyrating.gov.au
- GreenPower – www.greenpower.com.au

Recycling

- Clean Up Australia – www.cleanup.org.au
- RecyclingNearYou – www.recyclingnearyou.com.au

Water conservation

- Queensland Government, 'Water: Learn it for life!' – www.nrm.qld.gov.au/waterwise/education

Ethics and pedagogy at the heart of early childhood education for sustainability

Lesley Robinson and Sue Vaealiki

Editor's note

In this updated chapter our two New Zealand authors, **Lesley Robinson** and **Sue Vaealiki**, again highlight *ethics* as an essential guide that provides tools for teaching and learning about environmental, educational, social and cultural issues and topics. They identify the ethics of *care, listening, participation* and *hope* as central to ECEfS and justify why this is so. They propose a set of early childhood pedagogies that have resonance with ECEfS. These are *interdisciplinary learning, co-constructing 'working theories' for living sustainably, building respectful relationships* and *participating in communities of action*. It is the authors' belief that (re)consideration of the ethical and pedagogical foundations of early childhood education to ensure that sustainability issues and topics are addressed requires new professional journeys for early childhood educators and their communities. These journeys offer challenges and great rewards for those who believe that children – in collaboration with their families and communities – can be rich and competent citizens of the present who already have capacities and capabilities to influence the future.

Introduction

While setting off on a journey is often exciting, it may also be full of challenges. The journey of implementing an ECEfS curriculum is often more challenging and complex than one ever imagines. We hope that this revised chapter will assist you to reflect on some of the underpinning ethical principles that not only will act to anchor your journey but will also provide direction and inspiration. These principles are *care, listening, participation* and *hope*. We also discuss four transformative pedagogical approaches: *interdisciplinary learning, co-constructing 'working theories' for living sustainably, building respectful relationships* and *participating in communities of action*. These four approaches align with the ethics discussed in this chapter, the sustainability goals of ECEfS, and our belief that transformative pedagogical approaches hold the most promise for confronting the intertwined social, economic, cultural and environmental issues facing our world. For further reading on ways to enact ECEfS pedagogies, also refer to Chapter 2, where Sue Elliott discusses the necessity of learning and teaching in and with nature; Chapter 7, where Margaret Lloyd discusses ICT to encourage learning and teaching related to sustainability; and Chapter 11, in which Sharon Stuhmcke outlines a project approach to ECEfS.

Ethical principles for ECEfS

First, let's consider the general notion of ethics in teaching and learning, and why ethical principles are relevant to ECEfS.

Thinking about the ethics of teaching

Teaching ethics are principles that form the basis of teaching and learning practices and decisions. They speak of deeply held core values and teaching beliefs. Ethical principles include personal codes – as revealed by Robert Pratt in Chapter 4 – and professional codes (established by governments and/or the teaching profession; see provocation 5.1) that guide an educator's work.

We like the description of using ethical principles to inform teaching and learning as 'a way of travelling' (Hydon 2007, p. 7). When travelling, we use a compass to guide the path we take. While a journey is a uniquely personal experience, it is often shared with others. Therefore, ethical teaching decisions are often collective understandings and/or cultural wisdoms that provide direction for the pedagogical practices of an individual or a group. Sometimes these collective understandings are expressed formally in a Code of Ethics framework that provides a set of governing principles for the teaching profession. A limitation of generic principles, however, is that they

Figure 5.1 *Exploring composting to learn about the natural world*

frequently have less relevance within a particular community context, may privilege one culture over another, and may constrain the ethical choices that educators may wish to make.

One possible way to avoid such limitations is for educators to take a personal and active approach to evaluating issues and making decisions with the local context in mind. Dahlberg and Moss (2004), in their discussion of postmodern ethics, state that 'rather than seeking the truth, these new approaches to ethics foreground wisdom, which involves an active practice to decide what is best in a concrete situation' (p. 69). For instance, if educators choose to purchase locally produced food for the children in their early childhood centre, they would make these decisions by involving their broader community and taking account of cultural perspectives and aspirations. While the decision-making process becomes more complex, it is likely to lead to sustained and responsive actions that have influence beyond the early childhood setting (Vaealiki & Mackey 2008).

Provocation 5.1

Review a Code of Ethics developed in your state/country. Discuss its relevance to your local early childhood context. In what ways does the Code of Ethics inform decisions regarding ECEfS?

Here are two links:

For New Zealand, go to www.teacherscouncil.co.nz/content/code-ethics-registered-teachers-0.

For Australia, go to www.earlychildhoodaustralia.org.au/code_of_ethics/early_childhood_australias_code_of_ethics.html.

At the United Nations Earth Summit held in 1992, Agenda 21 – a comprehensive blueprint for environmental action – challenged governments around the world to reorient their education systems to promote ethical ways to sustain life on the planet (Fien & Tilbury 2002). An important question for educators to ask is: *What are the ethical ways to sustain life on Earth?* Each person's answer to this question is filtered through their own attitudes, experiences, histories and culture, leading each of us to value different solutions and choose different pathways for responding to the challenges. One of the ways that early childhood educators can promote sustainable practices is to make ethical choices about resources and curricula. Such choices are not without tensions and dilemmas. There is complexity in every choice as we weigh up the benefits and disadvantages to people and to the environment. A deeper understanding of the ethics inherent in our choices can help to simplify, to some extent, the decisions that we make.

Provocation 5.2

Debate the following:

- use of cloth nappies versus disposable nappies
- provision of vegetarian menus versus non-vegetarian menus
- use of plastic toys versus wooden toys.

Consider the social, cultural, economic and environmental dimensions of each of these choices.

Provocation 5.3

Sustainable decisions are never easy, but can be empowering. Reflect on the notion of power in this quotation from Barbara Kingsolver (2002) as she explores her personal choice to purchase ethically grown food.

I understand the power implicit in these choices. That I have such choices at all is a phenomenal privilege in a world where so many go hungry, even as our nation uses food as a political weapon, embargoing grain shipments to places such as Nicaragua and Iraq. I find both security and humility in feeding myself as best I can and learning to live within the constraints of my climate and seasons. I like the challenge of organizing our meals as my grandmother did, starting with the question of season and which cup is at the moment running over (p. 117).

Unpacking the four ethical principles

As an early childhood educator implementing ECEfS, you will find that there are tensions and competing aspirations related to environmental and sustainability issues that require negotiation with other educators, families and children. Anchoring your practice with ethical principles will assist you to take this journey with more assurance.

Ethic of care

'Care' is a well-used term in early childhood education that requires deeper reflection than is current practice. Caring is an essential part of being human, and how we care for each other is an ethical action that carries obligations and responsibilities. Within societies, obligations and responsibilities are carried out in diverse ways shaped by cultural understandings and practices.

In advocating for ECEfS, Simonstein Fuentes (2008) suggests two core ethical aspects – equity and human rights – that need to be given greater prominence in early childhood education. He suggests that by caring for others *and* the natural world, each of us has the potential to create an identity of peace. In early childhood education educators, children and families should experience what it means to care and to receive care, thereby strengthening dispositions such as empathy, harmony, mutual respect and responsibility towards people and the earth.

One of the weaknesses of the more traditional, developmentalist view of children that has been strongly critiqued over the past two decades is that it positions educators and children in a relationship that is problematic and unequal (Brennan 2007; Cannella 2002; Fleer 2003; Jordan 2009). Educators are seen as the 'carers' who are responsible for doing the caring, while children are seen as the 'cared for', less able to provide care (Moss & Brannen 2003). This deeply ingrained view of the child as 'needing care' and not yet able to care may constrain many educators' beliefs about the environmental and social responsibilities that can and should be shared with young children.

While it is challenging to let go of deeply held ideas about what children can and cannot do, cultural research demonstrates that young children are, indeed, able to care in significant ways. Woodhead (2000) explains that in some nomadic communities, young children take responsibility for the care of their family and animals in ways that would not be thought possible in some other communities. Many indigenous cultures around the world view care as a shared responsibility, placing strong emphasis on relationships with family, and interdependence with the natural world (see also Chapters 2 and 6). Children are taught from an early age about care through the practices, stories and songs of their communities. The Maori, the indigenous people of New Zealand, have many words to express the notion of care, such as *manaakitanga*, *whakawhanaungatanga* and *kaitiakitanga*. The following quotation explores the concept of *kaitiakitanga*.

Provocation 5.4

Kaitiakitanga is the Maori view of sustainable living in the whole sense of the word. In the traditional sense, Maori see the world as being interrelated: the trees, the birds and plants, the fish, the mountains, the rivers, the seas, the lakes, the stones, the rocks, all things living and inanimate, the divine and the human. Hence, people's relationship to their mountain, their river or lake is deep and very real. These values are carried onto their children and in turn grandchildren. **Whanau, hapu** and **iwi** endeavour to pass on the similar threads and values of deep respect for the land and knowledge of how to care for it to their **uri whakatipu** (Ruka Te Korako 2005).

How do your cultural beliefs inform your view of children as carers? What words do you have to describe care, and what different meanings do you ascribe to these words?

Research in New Zealand demonstrates that teachers find their teaching of sustainability deepened by the inclusion of indigenous world views. Examples of teaching practices are the celebration of traditional times for planting and the telling of myths and legends about the earth. Such practices not only enrich practice but importantly strengthen social sustainability as they show respect for indigenous values and beliefs and in doing so support healthy indigenous communities (Rau & Ritchie 2011).

An ethic of care that emphasises interdependence is highly relevant to ECEfS as interdependence informs the concept of guardianship (particularly our responsibility to care for the earth). This interconnected approach to caring defines caring as 'a species activity that includes everything that we do to maintain, continue and "repair" our world so that we can live in it as well as possible' (Tronto 1993, cited in Dahlberg & Moss 2004, p. 74). We would add that an ethic of care in early childhood educational settings must also reflect the cultural values of families, including those of indigenous communities, so that 'home' cultures are sustained, enriched and strengthened; that is, are 'cared for' (Ritchie et al. 2010).

Ethic of listening

As identified by Julie Davis in her Introduction, the core of ECEfS is democratic decision making; the ethic of listening strengthens educators' resolve to make space for children and their families to contribute ideas and to have a say in making decisions. It is important for educators to reconsider the notion of listening and to reinvest in deeper and richer meanings that inform and strengthen their practice.

The term 'to listen' most often emphasises the importance of children *listening to the teacher*. There is high value placed on educators transmitting knowledge to young children; this is underpinned by a view of children as 'empty vessels' who need to be 'filled up' with knowledge (Dahlberg, Moss & Pence 2007). Listening to the views and ideas of young children is seen as less significant if this view of listening has primacy. Even with recent shifts to a child-centred curriculum, many educators are still positioned as experts whose job it is to make important decisions on behalf of children (Cannella 2002). For example, while children are often involved in making simple decisions, such as which vegetables they might grow in the garden, it is less common for educators to intensely listen to their ideas and involve them in making decisions about more complex issues, such as over-consumption of resources or ways to reach out to the wider community (see Chapters 4 and 11 for ways to listen to and engage young children in such decision making).

A postmodern view of listening, as espoused by Rinaldi (2005), creates an 'open space' within which children and families have a voice in decision making. In such a space, educators see listening as a form of 'welcoming' – that is, an openness to dialogue. This presents a challenge to let go of fixed ideas and assumptions about others. Rinaldi (2005) reminds educators that it can be confronting to remove our 'blinkers' and to be non-judgemental:

> Listening is not easy. It requires a deep awareness and at the same time a suspension of our judgments; it requires openness to change. It demands that we have clearly in mind the value of the unknown and that we are able to overcome the sense of emptiness and precariousness that we experience when our certainties are questioned (p. 20).

Warming (2005) explains that not all current practices in early childhood education settings acknowledge children's voices, despite the belief that this is, indeed, the case. Observation, for example, is commonly thought of in relation to listening to children Teachers listen to what children say and do, then interpret this data according to their theories of learning and development. Warming (2005) makes a clear distinction between observational listening, evaluation and assessment, and a way of listening whereby children's contributions are truly heard and valued. ECEfS promotes the view

Figure 5.2 *Active listening between generations*

that children must have an authentic voice that allows opportunities for children to influence their world. ECEfS, therefore, requires educators to listen and really hear what children and families have to say about sustainability issues, and for this listening to lead to action. Accordingly, children's competencies are enhanced as educators notice and respond to their ideas and creativity and encourage children's participation in decision making and action taking.

Ethic of participation

The concept of participation is firmly established in the United Nations Convention on the Rights of the Child, and strengthens the right of children to participate in the sustainability issues that affect them and the world (Pramling Samuelsson & Kaga 2008; Vaealiki & Mackey 2008). ECEfS embraces the concept of early education as a democratic, participatory process. Therefore, an ethic of participation in ECEfS considers the quality of the relationships educators have with young children and their families. Such relationships should be based on a willingness to share knowledge, respect difference, and hear and act upon children's and families' ideas and solutions.

Implementing democratic participation in an early childhood community is often a difficult and complex process, particularly given the dominance of developmental views that restrict adult thinking about young children's competency. Yet, research undertaken in early childhood centres suggests that young children's competence to advocate for, and take a position on, sustainability issues expands as children participate with their families and educators in addressing real-life issues in their own communities (Davis 2005; Vaealiki & Mackey 2008).

It is important to think more deeply about children's participation, however. Hart's (1997) view of children's participation clearly distinguishes between participation that is genuine and that which is tokenistic. Tokenistic participation occurs when adults make all the decisions and use children to promote their (adult) concerns. For instance, a teacher might decide that the local council should provide more recycling options, so she instructs the children at her kindergarten to draw paintings of rubbish that she then includes with her letter in support of her cause. In this example, the children's drawings are merely used to evoke an emotional response. The power dynamic is heavily weighted in favour of the teacher. Genuine participation supports children's choices and shares power (Driskell 2002; Hart 1997). This means that, where possible, children are invited to share in curriculum decisions and are involved in exploring appropriate solutions and actions. For instance, when children express a concern about an issue, educators could invite them to brainstorm ideas about how to deal with the situation and then help them find some collective ways to respond (Davis 2005).

Finally, we consider the importance of the educator's own participation in sustainable practices in educational settings. Ethically, it would be hard to justify promoting sustainable practices to children without the educators and their early childhood centre 'walking the talk'. Siraj-Blatchford (2008) wisely reminds us:

> Young children have always learnt the most from our actions; they have learned from what we do, more than from what we say. It will therefore always be through the sustainability of our own day to day practices that we are the most influential to them (p. 68).

This is a challenge if educators and their early childhood centre or service are only at the beginning of their own journeys towards sustainability with few sustainable practices or systems in place. Initially, small, but visible, collaborative steps that support sustainable practices will indicate this ethic in action.

Ethic of hope

Hope is a vitally important ethic to hold on to, especially as climate change and environmental and sustainability threats can adversely impact on children. There are growing concerns about the impact of despair, worry and helplessness on the emotional and psychological wellbeing of children (Ojala 2012). One study carried out with Australian children, for example, found that a quarter of children questioned believed that the end of the world would take place in their lifetime (Tucci, Mitchell & Goddard 2007). It follows that an ethic of hope is vital in ECEfS, and that hopefulness is nurtured and strengthened from an early age. Hope is essential as it enables individuals to look towards the future with confidence, even though the future is uncertain. If developed from an early age, a sense of hope helps provide impetus for becoming more knowledgeable and competent in dealing with sustainability issues. Having hope is not about denying difficulties, but about facing challenges. Importantly, hope also supports children to withstand and endure, and to be resilient. The disposition of resilience is crucial as it is 'the tendency to engage with challenges, to persist with activities despite adversity or difficulties, and to be willing to make mistakes and recover from them'

Figure 5.3 *Balinese spiritual flags: hope for the future*

(Smith 2013, p. 232). It is in facing adversities that resilience is fostered. Mental toughness and the ability to 'bounce back' are important qualities for forging the paths to sustainability because there will undoubtedly be setbacks and unexpected obstacles.

When discussing environmental and sustainability concerns, there is often a tendency to focus on negative impacts, such as global warming, biodiversity losses or growing gaps between rich and poor. Such foci may lead some educators to refrain from addressing sustainability with young children, believing that sustainability issues are just too depressing and 'too big and too awesome to be "dumped" on young children' (Pramling Samuelsson & Kaga 2008, p. 11). Such resistance to teaching sustainability is understandable given that, generally speaking, educators wish to protect children and provide them with a safe haven as they begin to grow and learn.

Hope, though, is a key ethic to utilise when sharing issues of sustainability with children, as it empowers children, educators and families to action. Hope leads to the belief that there are solutions to problems, and builds capacity and confidence to act. Walker (2006) describes hope 'as a way of feeling that propels you and your learning community forward' (p. 6). When we take a postmodern view of children and childhood, we see children as strong and competent and able to engage with sustainability issues. We see children as already living in the real world, and thereby avoid overprotecting them. Fritze et al. (2008) explain that 'when people have something to do to solve a problem, they are better able to move from despair and hopelessness to a sense of empowerment' (p. 7). In sum, it is critical that educators nurture a sense of hope in children, as hope motivates action to 'make a difference'.

Importance of ethical principles

Ethical principles provide guidance for early childhood educators journeying on the pathway of ECEfS. Each principle assists educators to reframe their philosophical approaches, core values and assumptions about working with children and families.

ECEfS pedagogies

In this section, we first discuss the concept of pedagogy, and then consider four early childhood pedagogical approaches that align with ECEfS.

Thinking about pedagogy

Pedagogy is often described as the 'art' or 'science' of teaching and refers to the way that an educator enacts the theories that guide their practice. The term 'pedagogy' has its origins in ancient Greece, describing the care and education by slaves of their master's children; the literal meaning of the term is 'to lead the child'. Throughout history, pedagogy has been constantly reinterpreted and theorised, influenced by the philosophical views about the purpose and value of education that are current at the time. As Moss and Petrie (2002) discuss, pedagogy can never be regarded as neutral; rather, it is 'a political and ethical minefield in which choices are to be made' (p. 136).

In more recent times, 'pedagogy' has expanded in meaning to include 'the learner', thus recognising that teaching has a powerful effect on the learning trajectories of children and their families (Watkins & Mortimore 1999). For those teachers choosing to reorient their teaching within the framework of education for sustainability, it is essential to consider a shift towards more critical and transformative pedagogies that not only lift consciousness of sustainability issues but also involve children and their families in advocacy and action.

Pedagogies for ECEfS

Key aims of ECEfS are to build social justice values and attitudes; strengthen a sense of curiosity and inquiry about the environment; seek creative solutions; develop social and ecological literacy; and create skills for advocacy and action (Elliott 2010). With these in mind, we have chosen to discuss four pedagogical approaches that have resonance with contemporary early childhood education. These are *interdisciplinary learning, co-constructing 'working theories' for living sustainably, building respectful relationships* and *participating in communities of action.*

Interdisciplinary learning

The value of this approach:

- invites creative, holistic thinking
- capitalises upon children's learning strengths and interests
- encourages shared learning experiences and peer scaffolding
- provides opportunities to solve issues, using a range of perspectives and knowledge
- creates opportunities for families and community members to share their expertise
- values indigenous practices and understandings.

Early childhood education has a long history of incorporating holistic and integrated curriculum approaches. Such approaches can cross traditional subject boundaries – for example, maths and literacy – and draw on different domains, such as the spiritual and emotional. This idea resonates with a core principle of ECEfS that learning is connected and transcends bodies of knowledge in order to generate creative and innovative solutions (Parliamentary Commission for the Environment 2004). Taking an interdisciplinary approach to heart, early childhood teachers can maximise their learning environments by exploring sustainability issues with young children that concern both people and the environment. Such experiences are enriched when families' cultural and local subject knowledge is utilised to deepen exploration of these issues. See Chapters 11 and 14 for examples of ways that local sustainability issues can be addressed in interdisciplinary ways.

Making it possible: Teaching roles and strategies

- Broaden children's knowledge with literature and resources that expand their social, cultural and environmental ideas.

- Discuss with children a range of local issues that may spark their interest; for example, water conservation, concern for a local animal species, and playspaces in the neighbourhood.

- Infuse indoor and outdoor learning spaces with diverse environmental resources that invite children's participation, creativity and resourcefulness and make them aware of indigenous perspectives – for example, native plants for weaving, indigenous artefacts and designs and natural cloths for decoration.

- Organise and encourage regular visits from family and community members so that children can discuss their ideas with a wide range of people and learn from the expertise and experiences of those people.

Stories from the field

I bought some prayer flags for our kindergarten. This morning I hung them in the trees before children arrived. Outside, the children noticed them straight away, flapping brightly in the windy weather. Brigette was one of a small group who were very interested and asked what they were. I explained they were prayer flags, and that you could say a prayer for people you wanted to send thoughts of love and care to, maybe someone who was unwell or unhappy. Brigette told me about her grandmothers: one had a broken arm and was wearing a sling that was ok to get wet; her other grandmother had a sore leg. The children and I stayed looking at the prayer flags for a while and then we all went off on our separate ways. An hour or so later Brigette came outside to show me what she had been making. I was deeply moved by what she had to share with me. She had made two prayer flags: one for each grandmother, each different, beautiful and strung up on a piece of wool. After talking about how beautiful her flags and thoughts were, we discussed what Brigette would like to do with her flags. Brigette decided she would like to hang them outside with the other prayer flags. We did this together and talked more about her grandmothers, and how proud they would be of her.

Since writing this story I have been thinking more of making the area where the prayer flags are a beautiful, peaceful space where we can be, contemplate and connect with nature.

Spirituality is important to us at our kindergarten, where we all have our own beliefs and values that are diverse and varied. Therefore, it is an important part of our community's wellbeing and learning that we acknowledge and treasure the diversity of these beliefs and values.

Co-constructing working theories[1] for living sustainably

The value of this approach:

- Children increase their ability to theorise about sustainability issues from an early age.

- Children and adults work collaboratively towards testing possible solutions.

- Children and adults construct knowledge and understandings that increase eco-literacy.

- Children's different perspectives assist teachers to consider alternative solutions.

As the world changes and sustainability issues come increasingly to the fore, it is clear that humans will need to be creative in developing new ways of living that sustain both human communities and the natural environment. We now recognise that very young children are able to consciously articulate a desire to care for their world, and that this is increased when we adults show willingness to engage with their interests and take their ideas seriously. As educators, we are in a unique position to provide children with opportunities to imagine and construct new approaches and/or solutions as children express their own working theories. Earlier, we talked about an ethic of listening; here, we re-emphasise the importance of this principle when responding to the emergent speculations and hypotheses of children. As Rinaldi (2005) highlights, 'any theorisation, from the simplest to the most refined, needs to be expressed, to be communicated, and thus to be listened to, in order to exist' (p. 19).

Making it possible: Teaching roles and strategies

- Take children's ideas seriously, understand their perspectives and validate their contributions.

- Engage in joint projects with children focusing on relevant real-life sustainability issues.

- Create more sustainable early childhood settings so that children's learning occurs within a relevant context.

- Seek resources and information for sharing from the local community and especially from its indigenous people.

- Restore children's access to an authentic range of indoor and outdoor experiences, thus increasing opportunities for them to play with natural materials and access cultural tools.

---

[1] Contemporary early childhood education places a strong emphasis on children constructing their ideas about the world and learning how it works, which has led to the concept of 'working theories'. The New Zealand early childhood education curriculum document *Te Whāriki* (Ministry of Education 1996) states that early childhood settings should provide an environment in which children 'develop working theories for making sense of the natural, social, physical, and material worlds' (p. 82).

Stories from the field

There have been many conversations initiated by the children after their imaginations were sparked by a movie about penguins shown in the local cinema. In response their teacher located some calendars with photos of the Antarctic, and laid these out on the floor in the book corner. This led to lots of interesting questions and conversations concerning penguins, particularly about how the penguins might survive in the future and what would happen when the ice caps melt. The teacher listened and encouraged the children to express their ideas.

Sitting in the background was a child who often remained at the periphery of group interactions. This child was playing with a construction set and building what appeared to be a complicated machine. After about 30 minutes, the child went to stand by the teacher and quietly explained that he had an idea to help the penguins. The teacher listened carefully and, aware of his shyness, shared his ideas with the other children. The boy's idea was a machine that was a penguin-saving device with long ladders that could reach across the icebergs. The teacher decided to document the child's ideas and took a photo of his machine to go on the wall with the penguin display. Over the following week, with this encouragement, the child completed several drawings related to his ideas and upgraded the machine with more complex additions.

Building respectful relationships

The value of this approach:

- Encourages respectful, reciprocal and responsive dialogue and action.
- Provides opportunities to consider inequity and fair resolution.
- Opens up dialogue about fair ways to act in the early childhood centre and in the local community.
- Identifies shared ways to make a difference.

The emphasis that ECEfS places on relationships is in keeping with a socio-cultural approach that views interactions as the basis for children's learning and development (Rogoff 2003). All learning is seen as taking place within relationships, with the nature of these relationships being critical to how and what children learn. *Te Whāriki* goes as far as to state that 'children learn through responsive and reciprocal relationships with people, places, and things' (Ministry of Education 1996, p. 43).

We cannot emphasise enough that educators in early childhood settings have a pivotal role in promoting social sustainability by building relationships with and between children, families and communities. This extends to helping children shape their identities as active carers of both people and the environment. As teachers, it is critical to communicate with children about how to live in peaceful, just and sustainable ways, raising awareness of their interactions with each other and ways to resolve differences peacefully (Simonstein Fuentes 2008).

Frequently, educators experience resistance when introducing a sustainability focus into the curriculum. Barrera and Corso (2002) suggest an approach called 'skilled dialogue', which is based on three elements. First, it is suggested that teachers acknowledge the different views and beliefs held by others, and resist trying to immediately change viewpoints to reflect their own perspectives, as differences are experienced as boundaries or markers between ourselves and others. Disregard for boundaries and differences may lead to mistrust. Paradoxically, relationships strengthen when we acknowledge our differing perspectives, as acknowledgement builds confidence and trust. Second, Barrera and Corso (2002) identified reciprocity as an essential quality in relationship building. A balance of power is achieved more easily when each individual's contribution is seen to be equally valuable and worthy. Therefore, it is important when working on sustainability issues that we welcome all contributions, and avoid positioning ourselves as experts and gatekeepers of curriculum, thereby limiting others' involvement and contributions. 'In reciprocal relationships everyone has something to offer that enriches not only the persons involved but also the outcome of their interactions. Every interaction is both giving and receiving' (Barrera & Corso 2002, p. 6). Responsiveness, the third element, is about being open to uncertainty and recognising that one does not have all the answers. As educators, we can sometimes become uncomfortable with not knowing and being unsure. Having all the answers does not leave space for others' contributions, so it is important we invite others to participate in seeking new or alternative solutions.

Making it possible: Teaching roles and strategies

- Provide forums whereby children come together as a community to discuss issues that are important to them, their families and communities.

- See children as active agents capable of providing care and support. Support them to act in ways that 'make a difference' for others.

- Nurture positive dispositions towards diverse cultures so that cultural diversity is not seen as problematic, but as richness.

- Share issues that arise out of everyday living with children in ways that help to:
  - reflect on the fairness or unfairness of a situation

  - problem solve how situations can be made fairer

  - consider equity related to topics such as consumerism, water availability and poverty

  - make reasonable and responsible decisions.

Stories from the field

In recent years, an early childhood centre has been forging close relationships with its immediate neighbours. The children and staff have built a special relationship with one elderly woman who lives alone. This neighbour keeps an eye on the centre in the evenings and at weekends, and rings the manager at home if anything seems amiss. The neighbour also spends time in the centre, bringing her little dog along with her. In return, the staff and children keep an eye on her house and property when she is away. At Christmas time the children give her a present of edible treats, such as chocolate balls, made by the children and teachers. When this neighbour recently returned from a stay in hospital, the children and staff made a special visit, taking a gift of chutney made with produce from the centre's garden.

Participating in communities of action

The value of this approach:

- Recognises the right of young children to be involved in democratic decision making.
- Builds community capacity and action competency.
- Solutions and actions are futures-focused and relate specifically to the community.
- Children, families and educators engage in collaborative learning.
- A sustainable community is imagined and implemented.

  Fien and Tilbury (2002) described education for sustainability as:

  a process of local empowerment that enhances the ability of people to control their own lives and the conditions under which they live. This involves learning and action to ensure that as many people as possible participate in making decisions about the issues and problems that need addressing and work collaboratively to implement them (p. 6).

The notion 'think globally, act locally' brings attention to the idea that the best starting point for sustainability for local communities is in addressing concerns in their 'own backyard'. In this way, the skills of advocacy and decision making, and the knowledge needed to understand complex environmental and social issues, are learnt at a grassroots level and help build the community's capacity (Maser 1996, cited in Fien & Tilbury 2002).

A community approach that favours inclusive and collaborative relationships by involving children and families is much more likely to achieve relevant local solutions to environmental and social concerns. 'Going it alone' to achieve such change would be impossible, anyway. ECEfS supports the position that the – often-intertwined – social, environmental and economic concerns of children and families should be the starting point for community action. Whatever the concern, this 'needs to be rooted in the local, concrete reality of young children if it is to have real meaning and impact' (Pramling Samuelsson & Kaga 2008, p. 12). The investigation of a local concern, and the planning, advocacy for and implementation of possible solutions become the foci of the curriculum. When an early childhood centre undertakes to address a sustainability concern that arises within an early childhood centre – for example, water or energy conservation, or fair play – the involvement of parents and children leads to broader community development of action competencies and dispositions. Vaealiki and Mackey (2008) have identified that 'openness to consider alternative practices, the confidence to advocate for and express a desired outcome' (p. 10) are just some of the competencies that children, families and educators can demonstrate when they all work collaboratively on local issues. Perhaps one of the most challenging aspects of young children's participation is finding ways for children to have an authentic voice as it is often difficult for them to communicate complex ideas.

Making it possible: Teacher roles and strategies

- Use mapping techniques whereby children draw a preferred environment or solution to a concern (Hart 1997).

- Invite children to express their ideas/solutions through 3D construction – for example, carpentry, collage, blocks, ICT.

- Pay attention to children's actions as they often implement solutions without verbalising them.

- Make provision for dramatic play using environmental props to facilitate reenactment of sustainable activities – for example, shells, driftwood, mini-compost bins, ranger/hiking, dress-up clothes.

- Encourage discussion of sustainability issues during 'circle times' or meetings. Include adults from the broader centre community.

- Document the learning journey and sustainable achievements of your early childhood setting so that success can be celebrated, contributions acknowledged and actions reflected upon.

Stories from the field

Given the drought conditions in the local area, there is a need to conserve water in the sandpit at the early childhood centre. One day, a conversation arose from the children's wishes to use water in the sandpit. The teacher responded by providing a limited amount of water and reminding the children that 'once this is all gone, there won't be any more'. Sensing the children's disappointment, it was decided that collecting and reusing water could be an alternative solution. The children were asked to think about what might be possible.

One child responded: 'Why don't we get it from the sky?'

In the following weeks, there was ongoing discussion about the issue. By chance, one of the teachers found an article about rain harvesting in India. She brought the article to the centre and discussed the idea with the children, encouraging them to think about how they might harvest the water from the sky. The article inspired many suggestions. One of the most practical ideas seemed to be to collect water from the roof of the outdoor shed. The teachers shared this idea with the parent committee. There was much enthusiasm for this idea and, once an agreement was reached on how to progress the project, a local contractor visited the centre while the children were present. This provided an opportunity for the children to see and contribute to the plan for guttering and a storage system. Parents were invited to contribute recyclable materials, in order to keep the costs as low as possible.

Conclusion

Aligning ethical principles and teaching and learning approaches within a critical and transformative framework will enable you to stay true to the key tenets of ECEfS. We hope that your early childhood educational setting becomes a place where educators, young children and families learn and work together to build a more sustainable future.

Finally, some educators share their thoughts about ECEfS:

Yes! I believe we have a responsibility to teach about sustainability – to guide our *tamariki* [children] into the future. We should want them to live in a world that is 'green'. *Ko te whenua te wai u mo nga uri whakatipu* – the land provides the sustenance for the coming generation.

Children need to understand that you don't take more than what you replace – because it is going to be their world.

In 50–100 years this generation of educators won't be living in the world – but if we have inspired children to care, nurture and protect, hopefully the world will be a better place.

Teaching is about change – a constant journey. Sustainability is part of this journey. You can't teach and ignore the fact that the world is changing and we have a responsibility to introduce our *tamariki* [children] to these changes.

By teaching children now when they are very young it becomes part of their everyday culture.

Review provocations

1. What does the concept of 'listening' mean to you, and what does this look like when you are teaching?
2. What opportunities can early childhood educators and communities provide for children so that they take an active part in caring for others and the environment?

3. Are there additional ethical positions that you believe could / should underpin ECEfS? If so, describe how these could be implemented in practice.
4. Reflect on one of the four pedagogical approaches discussed above. Using this approach, how would you embed additional sustainable practices in your centre? What would need to change?

References

Barrera, I. & Corso, R. (2002). Cultural competence as skilled dialogue. *Topics in Early Childhood Special Education*, 22(2), 103–13.

Brennan, M. (2007). Beyond child care – how else could we do this? Sociocultural reflections on the structural and cultural arrangements of contemporary Western childcare. *Australian Journal of Early Childhood*, 32(1), 1–9.

Cannella, G. (2002). *Deconstructing Early Childhood Education: Social Justice and Revolution*. New York: Peter Lang Publishing.

Dahlberg, G. & Moss, P. (2004). *Ethics and Politics in Early Childhood Education*. Oxfordshire, UK: RoutledgeFalmer.

Dahlberg, G., Moss, P. & Pence, A. (2007). *Beyond Quality in Early Childhood Education and Care: Languages of Evaluation* (2nd edn), London: Routledge.

Davis, J. (2005). Educating for sustainability in the early years: Creating cultural change in a child care setting. *Australian Journal of Environmental Education*, 21, 47–55.

Driskell, D. (2002). *Creating Better Cities with Children and Youth: A Manual for Participation*. London: UNESCO.

Elliott, S. (2010). Essential not optional: Education for sustainability in early childhood centres. *Childcare Information Exchange*, 32(2), 34–3.

Fien, J. & Tilbury, D. (2002). The global challenge of sustainability. In D. Tilbury, R. B. Stevenson, J. Fien & D. Schreuder (eds), *Education and Sustainability: Responding to the Global Challenge*. Gland, Switzerland: IUCN.

Fleer M. (2003). Early childhood education as an evolving 'community of practice' or as lived 'social reproduction': Researching the taken for granted. *Contemporary Issues in Early Childhood*, 4(1), 64–79.

Fritze, J., Blashki, G., Burke, S. & Wiseman, J. (2008). Hope, despair and transformation: Climate change and the promotion of mental health and well-being. *International Journal of Mental Health Systems*, 2(13), 1–10.

Hart, R. (1997). *Children's Participation: The Theory and Practice of Involving Young Citizens in Community Development and Environmental Care*. London: Earthscan and UNICEF.

Hydon, C. (2007). A way of travelling: the environment and our code of ethics. *Every Child*, 13(1), 7.

Jordan. B. (2009). Scaffolding learning and co-constructing understandings. In A. Anning, J. Cullen & M. Fleer (eds), *Early Childhood Education; Society and Culture* (2nd edn). London: Sage.

Kingsolver, B. (2002). *Small Wonder*. New York: HarperCollins Publishers.

Ministry of Education (1996). *Te Whāriki: He Whāriki Mātauranga mō ngā Mokopuna o Aotearoa: Early Childhood Curriculum*. Wellington: Learning Media.

Moss, P. & Brannen, J. (eds) (2003). *Rethinking Children's Care*. Buckingham, UK & Philadelphia, USA: Open University Press.

Moss, P. & Petrie, P. (2002). *From Children's Services to Children's Spaces: Public Policy, Children and Childhood*. London: RoutledgeFalmer.

Ojala, M. (2012). Regulating worry, promoting hope: How do children, adolescents and young adults cope with climate change? *International Journal of Environment & Science Education*, 7(4) 537–61.

Parliamentary Commission for the Environment (2004). *See Change: Learning and Education for Sustainability*, www.pce.parliament.nz/assets/Uploads/Reports/pdf/See_change_report.pdf (accessed 1 May 2014).

Pramling Samuelsson, I. & Kaga, Y. (eds) (2008). *The Contribution of Early Childhood Education to a Sustainable Society* (pp. 9–17). Paris: UNESCO.

Rau, C. & Ritchie, J. (2011). Ahakoa he iti: Early childhood pedagogies affirming Māori children's rights to their culture. *Early Education and Development*, 22(5), 795–817.

Rinaldi, C. (2005). Documentation and assessment: What is the relationship? In A. Clark, P. Moss & A. T. Kjřrholt (eds), *Beyond Listening: Children's Perspectives on Early Childhood Services*. Bristol: Policy.

Ritchie, J. Duhn, I., Rau, C. & Craw, J. (2010). *Titiro Whakamuri, Hoki Whakamua. We Are the Future, the Present and the Past: Caring for Self, Others and the Environment in Early Years' Teaching and Learning*. Wellington: NZCER, Teaching and Learning Research Initiative, www.tlri.org.nz/sites/default/files/projects/TLRI-Ritchie-et-al-summary_1.pdf (accessed 1 May 2014).

Rogoff, B. (2003). *The Cultural Nature of Human Development*. New York: Oxford University Press.

Ruka Te Korako, M. (2005). *Whiri i te tai: AO – making connections with the natural world*, unpublished manuscript.

Simonstein Fuentes, S. (2008). Education for peace in a sustainable society. In I. Pramling Samuelsson & Y. Kaga (eds), *The Contribution of Early Childhood Education to a Sustainable Society*. Paris: UNESCO.

Siraj-Blatchford, J. (2008). The implications of early understandings of inequality, science and technology for the development of sustainable societies. In I. Pramling Samuelsson & Y. Kaga (eds.), *The Contribution of Early Childhood Education to a Sustainable Society*. Paris: UNESCO.

Smith, A. B. (2013). *Understanding Children and Childhood: A New Zealand Perspective* (5th edn). Wellington: Bridget Williams Books Ltd.

Tucci, J., Mitchell, J. & Goddard, C. (2007). *Children's Fears, Hopes and Heroes: Modern Childhood in Australia*. Melbourne: Australian Childhood Foundation.

Vaealiki, S. & Mackey, G. (2008). Ripples of action: Strengthening environmental competency in an early childhood centre. *Early Childhood Folio*, 12, 7–11.

Walker, K. (2006). Fostering hope: A leader's first and last task. *Journal of Educational Administration*, 44(6), 540–69.

Warming, H. (2005). Participant observation: A way to learn about children's perspectives. In A. Clark, P. Moss & A. T. Kjȓrholt (eds), *Beyond Listening: Children's Perspectives on Early Childhood Services*. Bristol: Policy.

Watkins, C. & Mortimore, P. (1999). Pedagogy: What do we know? In P. Mortimore (ed.), *Understanding Pedagogy and its Impact on Learning*. London: Paul Chapman.

Woodhead, M. (2000). Towards a global paradigm for research into early childhood. In H. Penn (ed.), *Early Childhood Services: Theory, Policy and Practice*. Buckingham: Open University Press.

Chapter 6

Reconciliation and early childhood education for sustainability: Broadening the environmental paradigm

Melinda G. Miller

Editor's note

This revised chapter, like the earlier version it updates, is provocative and challenging. The links between Australia's sustainability and Aboriginal and Torres Islander (that is, Indigenous) perspectives on country – both past and present – are clear but complex. **Melinda G. Miller**, a non-Indigenous author with a background in early childhood education and whiteness studies, challenges those of us working in ECEfS to resist privileging the environmental dimension of sustainability over social, economic and political dimensions. Particularly for Australian early childhood educators working in EfS, she challenges us to make reconciliation (bringing together Indigenous and non-Indigenous Australians) a central tenet of our thinking and pedagogies. Melinda asserts that, as interest in this field heightens, ECEfS offers a unique opportunity for early childhood educators to put reconciliation front and centre and, in so doing, contribute to repairing the Earth, healing the shared but fractured histories of Indigenous and non-Indigenous Australians, and creating new and sustainable futures for all Australians.

Introduction

The uptake of sustainability initiatives in early childhood education curricula continues to gain momentum in Australia and internationally. Growing awareness about the fragility of natural environments in local and global contexts, along with the prioritising of sustainability in educational policy, has resulted in more broad-scale responses to sustainability in early years settings. To address issues of sustainability, many childcare centres and schools focus on environmental initiatives, such as garden projects, recycling and water conservation. While important, such initiatives respond to just one dimension of sustainability. Taking a broad definition of sustainability into account, the environmental dimension of sustainability sits alongside social, political and economic areas of concern. Collectively, these four dimensions generate an holistic understanding about sustainability, described by UNESCO (n.d.) as four interdependent dimensions that require simultaneous and balanced progress (see Figure 1.1 in Chapter 1). With expanding focus on sustainability initiatives in early childhood education, it is timely to consider why the environmental dimension receives the most attention and what this means for the social, political and economic areas of concern.

In this chapter, I raise questions about the scope and purpose of ECEfS and the ways in which its main tenets are enacted in practice. This is to highlight why social, political and economic dimensions should be central in ECEfS, alongside an environmental focus. Specifically, this chapter establishes the place of reconciliation within ECEfS since this remains one of the most pressing ethical, social, political and economic issues for Australia. The chapter begins with commentary on the current scope and direction of ECEfS in Australia, focusing on the dominance of an environmental paradigm. Following this, I establish a link between reconciliation and sustainability and outline some of the complexities inherent in the application of reconciliatory acts within an environmental framework only. These complexities include essentialist and 'practical reconciliation' approaches that can produce tokenistic and inequitable responses in practice. Examples of how early childhood educators might work to bring environmental initiatives and reconciliation together in practice to move beyond a tokenistic approach are outlined. The chapter concludes with discussion about the positioning of sustainability in early years policy in Australia for both the before-school sector and the formal years of school.

It is important to note that this chapter is conceptually different from others in this text. In a collective sense, this second edition, like the first, is both a testament to the growing momentum around sustainability in early years policy and curricula, and a response to the history of marginalisation of both environmental education and EfS in early childhood education. This history of marginalisation was documented in *Patches of Green* (Elliot 2003), the first national review of the scope, status and direction of early childhood environmental education in Australia. While this publication demonstrates the continuing growth and expansion of thinking and practices in ECEfS in Australia and beyond, I continue to be concerned about what is marginalised or left out of mainstream conceptions of sustainability and sustainability education. In response, I present a critical review of current approaches, and discussion about ways to redefine the scope and direction of ECEfS. This draws attention to ideologies and practices around sustainability that, in my view, continue to be too narrow and that have potential to replace 'patches of green' with patches of reconciliation.

ECEfS: Broadening scope and potential

In Australia, social, political and economic issues such as reconciliation with Indigenous Australians, place-based pedagogy, fairness and inclusion have been discussed as part of a broad sustainability agenda for some time (see Baker, Davies & Young 2001; Newman 2001; Sisely 2003; Somerville 2010; Somerville & Green 2011; Zink 2007). In their commentaries, these authors acknowledge reconciliation as one of the most pressing issues on the Australian socio-political landscape. Collectively, they call for responses to reconciliation at both an individual and institutional level, in order to further long-term social sustainability and partnerships for sustainable development. As an holistic view of sustainability is concerned as much with the social, political and economic as it is with the environmental, reconciliation should be part of any conversation about sustainability and sustainability education in Australia.

In Australian early childhood education literature and practice, some consideration has been given to links between sustainability and social, political and economic themes of social justice, equity, and cultural practices (for examples see Nucifora 2007; Magiropoulos & Giugni 2007; Miller 2013a). However, discussion has focused mainly on environmental conditions and greening initiatives that are, primarily, responses to environmental concerns. As Davis (2008) has highlighted, there is also a political element to environmental education initiatives because adults and children are encouraged to become involved as activists and advocates for environmental/sustainability change. ECEfS is promoted as 'a time for providing [children with] significant groundings for adult activism around environmental issues' (Davis 2008, p. 20). Elements of social and political areas of concern are connected with ideals of activism and building foundations for later social action, but in the current scope of ECEfS in Australia, this potential remains somewhat restricted. Consequently, the emerging ECEfS literature and practice continue with too few explicit links between sustainability and broader social, political and economic issues, including reconciliation.

In early childhood education contexts, the enactment of ECEfS has translated predominantly as greening practices that include gardening projects, landscaping, the use of environmentally friendly products, rubbish reduction, recycling, and water and energy conservation practices (such as the installation of water tanks and solar panels), although this second edition has attempted to redress this. It is evident that the field at large is committed to sustainability principles and initiatives, although these can be somewhat one-dimensional. It is apparent that, while many children are being supported to be 'change agents' who contribute to positive change through environmental initiatives, and who influence others in their social circles to generate changes in behaviours and attitudes (Davis 2008), many are still not having opportunities to explore broader social, political and economic issues that always form part of environmental concerns (Hickling-Hudson & Ferreira 2004).

In recent years, intersections between environmental issues and social and political elements, including culture, race and ethnicity, have received some attention in environmental education literature internationally. This body of work, framed typically as intercultural dialogues, has called for a focus on the co-existence of different groups in societies beyond a celebration of difference (Gundara & Portera 2011; Nordström 2008). This occurs both in terms of an inward look at one's own ethnicity (including whiteness) and related cultural positioning, and an outward look at the standpoints and perspectives of individuals and various cultural groups. The key premise is to engage people in challenging stereotypes and ongoing effects of racism and discrimination in order to develop more inclusive attitudes and behaviours in their personal and professional lives (Gorski 2008). Intercultural dialogues promote strategies for thinking critically about relations between different groups. This includes how power and the distribution of resources between groups are bound by historical circumstances that influence the present. Conley and Bryan (2009) frame this as embracing 'different paradigms and often uncomfortable truths' (p. 22). For people in mainstream cultures, it is particularly vital to actively question what informs one's worldview and what is silenced in the stories and histories one attends to in the present.

Broadening the scope and potential of ECEfS in Australia relies, in part, on educators understanding how Western orientations of sustainability link historically with notions of development that focus on economic, social and political gain. In Chapter 1 of this volume, Davis outlined how 'development' in a Western paradigm is often toxic in form, having adverse impacts on social, political, environmental and economic systems on a global scale. In Australia, a Western (or industrial) paradigm of development is founded on acts of dispossession of Indigenous peoples from their lands, premised on hostile occupation and subsequent development and gain for the invading European population (Behrendt 2003; Broome 2010). The land now known as Australia was viewed by European 'settlers' as a material asset to be possessed and sold for economic, social and political gain.

A Western standpoint on development is widely divergent from an Aboriginal worldview of the land as 'a sacred entity' that is 'not property or real estate' (Graham 2008, p. 181). As Graham (2008) explains, 'the relation between people and land become[s] the template for society and social relations' (p. 181). Tracing inequities in social, political, economic and environmental systems in contemporary Australia to historical events supports educators to deepen their understandings about issues of sustainability relevant to their own local and national context. Through this process, explicit links between sustainability and reconciliation can be made. Early childhood educators can then locate the relevance of reconciliation in ECEfS initiatives, and consider ways to enact reconciliation on a personal and institutional level.

Reconciliation and sustainability

Reconciliation and sustainability are both concerned with relationships between groups of people and relationships between people and place. In the Australian context, reconciliation holds different, and often contested, meanings within and across groups of people, but is concerned primarily with the relationship between non-Indigenous and Indigenous Australians, and reparation for the relationship between Indigenous peoples and place. Reparation relates to the dispossession of Indigenous peoples from place or country since colonisation – dispossession being an act of institutional decision making founded on Western notions of occupation, ownership and (ab)use of land for economic, social and political gain (Behrendt 2003). The dispossession of Indigenous peoples from their lands following colonisation began a history of social and political fragility in Australia that continues to the present day. This history rivals the urgency attached to current concerns with environmental fragility, yet receives different forms of public and personal attention and response in non-Indigenous and Indigenous circles.

Reconciliation processes

In a broad sense, reconciliation processes have translated as various government strategies linked with Indigenous rights to sovereignty rights. Many have argued that few Indigenous peoples have benefited from reconciliation processes because of imposed European systems of law that do not legitimise existing models of Indigenous governance (Baker, Davies & Young 2001; Behrendt 2003; Birch 2007; Broome 2010; Moreton-Robinson 2007). Lawful recognition of the cultural and political sustainability of Indigenous sovereignty is central to effective reconciliation processes – a fact unacknowledged or left undisclosed by successive Australian governments (Birch 2007).

Reconciliation processes are complex because they are about knowledge and the disclosure of facts related to political atrocities, as well as appropriate forms of reply (Short 2008). The Rudd Government's Apology to Australia's Indigenous Peoples in 2008 is an example of reconciliation in the form of public acknowledgement. Short (2008) describes such a process as an extension of 'truth as acknowledgement' (pp. 13–14), meaning facts about political atrocities and rights violations are already known, but have been previously denied in political and public discourse. Public acknowledgement moves an act of denial to an act of disclosure, sometimes in fragmented or misrepresented form, although more at a political and public level than at a personal level.

Translating the Apology to acts of reconciliation, at least in local contexts, requires educators to think critically about what a public acknowledgement means for them at a personal and professional level. To think critically is to use sources and theories that enable thinking about scenarios and situations from different viewpoints – or, as Schön (1983) labels it, making the familiar strange. As an example, I have found it useful to draw from the work of Sara Ahmed (2004, 2012) to consider how I, as a non-Indigenous person, can (ab)use a public apology to lessen personal responsibility for acts of reconciliation. This is because the nation has admitted wrongdoing on my behalf and 'individual guilt' can be replaced with 'national shame', thus detaching recognition of wrongdoing from individuals who can claim they had no part in historical events (Ahmed 2004, para. 22). This implies that history is not personal. Ahmed (2004) makes a critical point that personal attachment to an act of wrongdoing is optional for some, but not for those directly affected by the act. For Indigenous peoples, stories of political atrocities are personal and relate directly to their histories. For non-Indigenous people, there is no formal requirement to understand and personalise the burden of past events, particularly when individuals can make use of a national apology in place of a personal and professional response.

Provocation 6.1

Locate a copy of the Apology to Australia's Indigenous Peoples, presented to the House of Representatives in 2008 by then Prime Minister Kevin Rudd. Reflect critically on your personal response to the Apology. How is your response connected with your personal history as an Australian? What informs your response and what other sources and theories could be used to deepen your response in your personal life and professional practice? As an educator, consider how acts of reconciliation feature in your thinking about the role of education in combating racism in Australia and how EfS can provide multiple entry points for reconciliatory work.

In early childhood education, sustainability education and related initiatives provide scope, space and possibilities for educators to acknowledge and enact the Apology at a personal and professional level. This becomes possible because of the focus on relationships and responsibilities between groups of people and environments that is core to both EfS and reconciliation processes for non-Indigenous and Indigenous people (Reconciliation Australia 2009). I suggest, however, that social and political action goals can only be achieved in ECEfS when possibilities are created for centralising reconciliation alongside environmental concerns. Reconciliation is a crucial element of ECEfS because it is a primary ethical responsibility for non-Indigenous people to seek and enact reconciliatory practices with Indigenous populations, particularly in the local context. In post-Apology Australia, this responsibility is gaining recognition as non-Indigenous people achieve greater comprehension about the ramifications of acts of dispossession and denials from successive governments. Nevertheless, reconciliation, to date, has not featured strongly in ECEfS. As previously stated, when this does occur, it is understood primarily from within an environmental framework.

Reconciliation in an environmental framework

In many respects, environmental reconciliation is framed in global terms, connecting individuals with their responsibilities as global or 'planetist citizens' (Ellyard 1999). Acts of environmental reconciliation occur most often in local sites, but a broader focus on a 'global picture' can enable non-Indigenous people to conceptualise and explain their actions as being for the good of the planet – of *all* people. This broad, planetary focus may serve to diminish making connections with social, political and economic concerns about rights, ownership and the past and present treatment of Indigenous peoples in the local and national context.

To date, the notion of reconciliation in ECEfS has encouraged individuals to reconcile their lifestyles with natural environments or ecosystems, somewhat in isolation from broader understandings about the political, social and economic factors that impact local contexts. When an environmental focus is isolated from other sustainability dimensions, inequities will occur. This is because any environmental issue will have 'important political, cultural and social concerns that need to be considered as well' (Hickling-Hudson & Ferreira 2004). Nordström (2008) supports this idea in questioning whether environmental education and multicultural education are too close to be separate, further stating that 'strategies of environmental education need to be tailored to the cultural context' (p. 134). In defining similarities in objectives, values and content, Nordström (2008) outlines shared characteristics of environmental education and multicultural education, including respect, belonging, and goals for individual, institutional and social reform. Similarly, Burnett and McArdle (2011) view EfS as offering 'new discursive nodes around which educators can regain pedagogical traction for many of the original tenets of multiculturalism' (p. 51). This statement is drawn from recognition that educators' understanding about sustainability often marginalises goals of multicultural education and broader sustainability themes, including cultural diversity, peace, human security and gender equity. The prevailing focus on ecological or greening initiatives can limit broader potential around educators' conceptualisations of EfS and its uptake in educational contexts (Burnett & McArdle 2011). A more holistic response to sustainability supports reconciliatory processes that are broader in scope and purpose and that can become a filter for sustainability initiatives (see Figure 6.1).

Political
Social
Environmental
Economic

Reconciliation

Australian
ECEfS

Sustainability

Figure 6.1 *Reconciliation as a 'filter' for early childhood education for sustainability in Australia*

Reconciliation in ECEfS: Complexities and cautions

Both theoretical and practical complexities underlie reconciliation in ECEfS; for example, essentialism and 'practical reconciliation' are two approaches to reconciliatory acts that undermine social and political action goals. Complexities with reconciliation often stem from a lack of deep knowledge about the relationship between one's personal history and the histories of Indigenous peoples in Australia. Phillips (2012) explains that non-Indigenous and Indigenous Australians have a shared history from the point of colonisation, although social and political atrocities endured by Indigenous peoples have largely been silenced 'through other stories: the arrival of the First Fleet, Federation in 1901, the "heroic" deeds of Ned Kelly and settler perspectives of the pioneering of Indigenous land' (pp. 12–13). These stories continue to shape notions of Australian identity and are reproduced in mainstream realms, including education, the media and popular culture. As a result, colonial stories are mobilised by non-Indigenous people in the present in different ways, but usually with the result that Indigenous peoples and cultures remain largely unknown in non-Indigenous domains (Phillips 2012). However, repeated exposure to misrepresentations of Indigenous peoples and cultures does not excuse inaction in terms of developing knowledge and understanding, and acting in ethical and genuine ways in shared interactions.

Essentialism

Essentialist notions about a group of people focus on supposed 'fixed' traits or characteristics belonging to the group. Essentialism denies diversity *within* particular groups and fails to recognise how group cultures and identities are complex and dynamic constructs that are continually changing. Within cultural groups, individual experience will also be dynamic, multiple and fluid, with a wide range of practices, identities and politics employed by group members (Diller 2011).

For many non-Indigenous people, essentialist forms of thinking extend from repeated exposure to mainstream projections that Indigenous peoples have a 'fixed' or collective identity. There is concern in reconciliation processes that non-Indigenous people may attempt to fill in 'gaps' created by misrepresentations of Indigenous identities and knowledges in place of Indigenous voices and local perspectives. In enacting reconciliation, educators and institutions should work from the understanding that 'Indigenous communities are diverse in culture and circumstance' (Behrendt 2003, p. 87). Reconciliation processes at the local level will look different in diverse communities, serve different purposes, and invite different forms of participation from non-Indigenous and Indigenous groups.

At a curriculum level, essentialist approaches to Indigenous perspectives position difference as being 'exotic'. This tokenistic form of curriculum only affords children what Derman-Sparks (1989) refers to as a tourist curriculum, in which 'children visit non-white cultures and then "go home" to the daily classroom, which reflects only the dominant culture' (p. 7). Aspects of Indigenous cultures constructed as 'exotic' often include art, music, food and dance. In isolation, a focus on these aspects of culture is tokenistic, resulting in educators including them in curricula for a one-off activity or Indigenous 'focus week'. Within this approach, Indigenous peoples and cultures remain largely unknown because of the emphasis on 'acceptable' or 'safe' explorations of culture (for example, corroborees, dot paintings and bush tucker) that do not disrupt the reproduction or status quo of mainstream stories and structures (Phillips 2012). Tokenistic curricula approaches are limited in charter to cultural affirmation and only serve to reinforce underlying racism in education because of their failure to genuinely address it (Kalantzis 2005). In ECEfS, this often translates as the essentialising of Indigenous knowledges separate from broader understanding of Indigenous spirituality and worldviews about relationships and responsibilities between people, land and related elements (see Martin 2005).

While Indigenous perspectives are starting to appear in environmental practices in ECEfS, these are sometimes in misrepresented or tokenistic forms, and often in isolation from related cultural, social, political and economic issues. Here, I present a transcript from a conversation between a non-Indigenous educator (Miriam) and a 5-year-old child (Albert) that shows how educators and children *can* engage in deep and broad thinking about issues of occupation and ownership at a local level, with a commitment to further research that takes in national circumstances. In this excerpt, both individuals are dedicated to critical thinking about reconciliation.

Albert:	(Touching the ground.) This is Aboriginal land of the Gadigal people and their bones and souls are here.
Miriam:	Yes, but Council owns the land that our centre is built on, as well as our playground and the park next door.
Albert:	Even the road and the train tracks?
Miriam:	Yes, they are owned by government departments.
Albert:	(Albert picked up a blade of grass and held it in his hand. He cupped it gently and took it to Miriam.) This is Aboriginal grass, but this is Council grass. We have a problem.
Miriam:	Yes. That is why we need to think about reconciliation all the time. That's why we need to think about this as Gadigal land, to think carefully about this issue of ownership.
Albert:	Me and Bob can draw a sign to show Gadigal land.

(Mundine & Giugni 2006, p. 17)

Here, an educator and a young child make explicit the relationship between local environments and issues of ownership connected with historical, social and political acts of dispossession. This conversation led to a study of cartography in which children explored land and place from both an Aboriginal and a colonial perspective using maps of Australia in a comparative fashion (Mundine & Giugni 2006). In this work, social, political and environmental dimensions of sustainability were central, simultaneously. It would also be possible to introduce discussion about economic issues in terms of the imbalance between non-Indigenous and Indigenous land ownership (seen through the mapping exercise) that has resulted in the most economically productive lands and resources being 'owned' and used by non-Indigenous people (Baker, Davies & Young 2001). Conversations such as this provide a reminder about the rights of children to engage with broader sustainability themes that introduce them to concepts of culture, diversity and equity between groups of people in the places in which they live.

In Australia, this includes a right for *all* children to engage with the histories and cultures of Indigenous peoples and to be supported by educators and others to think critically about the shared history of Indigenous and non-Indigenous groups (Craven 1999; Dodson 2010; Skerman 2013). Collectively, the explorations outlined in the above example allow for deep and broad thinking on a local and national scale – thinking that counters essentialist viewpoints and encompasses and makes explicit each of the four interrelated dimensions of sustainability.

Practical reconciliation

Another complexity of reconciliation in ECEfS relates to the notion of practical reconciliation. Practical reconciliation was originally installed by the Howard Government (1996–2007) as an alternate (or deviant) agenda to suggestions put forward in the Final Report by the Council for Aboriginal Reconciliation in 2000 (Borrows 2004). Suggestions included in the report called for distinct rights for Indigenous peoples via legislation to recognise a right to self-governance and customary law, and compensation and reparation for acts of dispossession following European colonisation (Borrows 2004). These issues continue to dominate Australia's political landscape, regardless of which political party holds the balance of power.

Practical reconciliation is underpinned by two strategies: the injection of funds into recognised areas of need (for example, education, employment, housing and health) and a human rights framework (Behrendt 2003). Opinions on practical reconciliation generally point to grave concern about the denial of human rights through reconciliation processes that are concerned more with the management of existing issues rather than symbolic or systemic change (Behrendt 2003; Huggins 2003; Human Rights and Equal Opportunity Commission 2003). In this sense, practical reconciliation is non-performative (Ahmed 2004) because there is little opportunity to disrupt existing structures of governance, despite this approach being constructed as a moral and ethical response to issues faced by various Indigenous groups. By default, practical reconciliation is seen to respond to human rights, but does so through government channels that do not invite genuine forms of participation or empowerment for Indigenous peoples (Huggins 2003).

ECEfS brings into play parts of the educational component of practical reconciliation, as well as a rights-based agenda to early education. ECEfS is premised on human rights, but, as pointed out earlier, the framing of human rights in ECEfS is generally on a global scale – for the good of *all* people sharing life on Earth. The enactment of ECEfS that currently privileges the environmental dimension of sustainability also maintains a focus on practical measures for managing existing and foreseen environmental concerns. Within an environmental framework, practical measures are often promoted systemically, although this typically relates to whole-centre or whole-school responses to environmental issues, such as the installation of water tanks or a commitment to reduce energy consumption. As explained by Huggins (2003), practical measures for reconciliation (as seen in environmental reconciliation) shift the focus away from systemic rights-based issues of reconciliation. I argue that social, political and economic themes of reconciliation should become core to a rights-based agenda in ECEfS to shift from the practical to the systemic, and to encompass all dimensions of sustainability. For example, environmental reconciliation that centralises Indigenous perspectives and knowledges (including local knowledge and elder knowledge) attends more to issues of social justice, including marginalisation and power relations between different groups, at least in local contexts. Bowers (2001) frames such an approach as eco-justice. In explaining differences between eco-justice and the mainstream environmental paradigm, Bowers (2001) states:

> The crux of the problem is that the mainstream environmental movement has not sufficiently addressed the fact that social inequality and imbalances of power are at the heart of environmental degradation, resource depletion, pollution and even overpopulation. The environmental crisis can simply not be solved effectively without social justice (p. 23).

Within an eco-justice framework, there are four key principles: greater attention to relationships between ecological and cultural systems; attention to environmental racism, including geographical dimensions of social injustice (for example, dispossession); recognising traditions of different groups in non-commodified ways; and adapting lifestyles in ways that will not further jeopardise the environment for future generations (Bowers 2001). In the next section I draw on examples of practice in ECEfS to show ways of broadening an environmental paradigm to include elements of an eco-justice framework and intercultural dialogues in sustainability initiatives.

ECEfS in practice

Figures 6.2 and 6.3 show efforts by non-Indigenous educators in an urban childcare centre to make connections between environmental issues, embedding Indigenous perspectives and forming relationships with Indigenous persons (see Miller 2013b). Figure 6.3 also shows differences between practical and systemic forms of reconciliation, with a shift from curricula experiences in the short term, to the long-term involvement of Indigenous persons in decision making, including as members of staff.

To enrich such practices further, educators could explore historical circumstances and connect Indigenous and non-Indigenous relations to the specific geographical location of the early education centre. In relation to the particular centre where these examples of practice were enacted, the building is located in close proximity to Boundary Street, Brisbane, which has historical and ideological significance in terms of colonial forms of urban development. In some Australian cities, 'Boundary Streets' were used as a colonising place value that demarcated 'civilised' areas from which

Sunday 12th Oct

I went to GREENFEST to take a look at Solar Panels + Solar Hot Water. There is good rebates 4 solar hot water. I collected heaps of information plus I got some awesome posters to help teach the children about Green Power. They need to be laminated first. I also got a book called "Nyingari and Energy". It is a book about an Aboriginal Girl learning about energy so it crosses over in both the sustainability and the Indigenous section of the cultural project.

Figure 6.2 *Making links between sustainability and Indigenous knowledges and perspectives (handwritten note)*

Short term
- Small excursion to [Indigenous artist's] workshop
- Visiting [a local Indigenous childcare centre]
- Visiting Ngutana-Lui Indigenous Education Centre
- Resources (books, music, posters)
- Aboriginal [and] Torres Strait Islander flags

Long term

Find out about Elders [in the local community]

↓

[Elders] involved in decision making

↓

Indigenous staff employed at centre

Figure 6.3 *Making plans – educators' efforts to shift from practical to more systemic forms of reconciliation in local sites*

Aboriginal peoples could be excluded (Greenop & Memmott 2007). The street name itself represents a lived experience for Indigenous peoples. For the educators who now occupy the building, there is no formal requirement to recognise Indigenous and non-Indigenous relations as they relate to the geography of the local area. However, a commitment to do so enriches understanding about the significance of reconciliatory acts to sustainability initiatives enacted in this particular location. This provides a starting point for thinking about the significance of the local area for Indigenous groups and how past experiences influence the present.

Skerman (2013) discusses a similar scenario in reference to her participation in a yarning circle (Yarn Up: Tok Blo Yuni) built around six reflective practice sessions aimed at exploring ways to work effectively with Indigenous Australians. In speaking about how the sessions supported educators to know, understand and learn, Skerman (2013) describes how the group explored the local history of the Mackay region (located in tropical North Queensland, Australia) and came to understand how Aboriginal groups have been treated in the region over time. In researching the history of the local area, the educators learned of shooting parties organised by local pastoralists, issues of starvation and introduced diseases, and how a place called the City Gates (the gates are no longer standing) was locked at night to exclude Aboriginal people from inner-city boundaries. Learning about local history and the impact of this history on Aboriginal groups enabled the educators to build greater understanding and empathy and to consider how historical circumstances impact different cultural groups in the present (Skerman 2013). While ECEfS is often oriented around a futures perspective, it is valuable – also – to look to the past to understand how environment/sustainability issues manifest in the present and what this might mean for relations between groups of people, and people and place.

Sustainability and early childhood education policy

Sustainability is a key priority area in early childhood education policy, both for the before-school sector and formal years of school. The recently introduced National Quality Framework (NQF) and Standard (NQS) for early childhood education in Australia positions sustainability and related practices under the quality area 'physical environment', with a focus on children 'becoming environmentally responsible and show[ing] respect for the environment' (Australian Children's Education and Care Quality Authority 2013). Furthermore, the newly implemented Australian Curriculum for the formal school years (preparatory to Year 12) identifies sustainability as one of three key cross-curriculum priorities. The sustainability priority is 'futures-oriented and calls on students to act sustainably as individuals and to participate in collective endeavours that are shared across local, regional and global communities'. The priority also 'emphasises the interdependence of environmental, social, cultural and economic systems' (Australian Curriculum and Assessment Reporting Authority 2013). The positioning of sustainability in these two documents provides an interesting comparison in terms of which dimensions of sustainability receive emphasis. Positioning sustainability under the quality area 'physical environment' in the NQF suggests greater prominence on the environmental dimension of sustainability, in isolation from broader areas of concern. The qualifying statement for what children will demonstrate (that is, becoming environmentally responsible and showing respect for the environment) is also positioned solely within an environmental paradigm. I strongly suggest that there is a need for early childhood educators enacting the national policy to *exceed* existing requirements in order to attend to broader, richer and more equitable sustainability practices.

I also suggest that policy directives outlined in the NQF can be interpreted through a reconciliation lens, alongside a focus on environmental elements. To provide examples, I draw on two indicators related to sustainability outlined in *Being, Belonging and Becoming* (Australian Government, Department of Education, Employment and Workplace Relations [DEEWR] 2009), the first nationally endorsed Learning Framework for children aged birth to 5 years, developed as part of the NQF agenda. The Learning Framework introduces five key learning outcomes. In relation to Outcome 2 – 'Children are connected with and contribute to their world' – educators are encouraged to:

- share information and provide children with access to resources about the environment and the impact of human activities on environments (p. 29)
- find ways of enabling children to care for and learn from the land (p. 29).

Here, educators can employ a reconciliation lens to share information about the impact of colonisation on Aboriginal lands and territories, including natural environments and resources. Conversations can be targeted to suit different age ranges, but it is important to recognise that some children will bring knowledge to the classroom about issues that impact relations between non-Indigenous and Indigenous groups, as seen with Albert (aged 5) in the example of practice presented earlier. In terms of the second indicator that recommends that educators enable children 'to care for and learn from the land', there are opportunities to develop values around stewardship while ensuring learning is culturally integrated. For example, educators can incorporate Indigenous technologies (such as digging sticks, baskets and horticultural practices) into learning that occurs in natural spaces, and include Creation Stories as resources that support children's understanding of relationships and responsibilities between people and environments. Indigenous technologies can promote discussion about design, function and process, as well as differences between cultural practices within and across Indigenous groups. Creation Stories contain wisdoms about living with and belonging to the land, and benefit all children, regardless of their cultural background (Connor 2007). An acknowledgement of Traditional Owners could also be incorporated respectfully as part of sustainability initiatives (including bush tucker gardens), playgrounds and local habitats in recognition of Aboriginal and Torres Strait Islander peoples as the First Australians and traditional custodians of the land.

Practical applications of reconciliation are important and provide a basis for more inclusive and reciprocal practices, including consultation with local Indigenous persons and organisations. Working towards shared goals with children, parents and communities around issues that are relevant to the local context is a key component of sustainability initiatives. Educators should also be supported to develop strategies for critical thinking about the influence of their own cultural background on their practices and their motivation for and approaches to interacting with Indigenous communities. Demonstrating preparedness to listen to, and follow the lead of, Indigenous peoples and organisations in ECEfS initiatives is critical to building reciprocity. Ideological work is more difficult, meaning many educators require sustained support and intellectual tools to shift long-held ideas and understandings. Drawing on a range of theoretical perspectives can aid this process; for example, socio-cultural theories promote thinking about historical, social and political influences on an individual's thinking and learning. Critical and post-structuralist theories support understanding about power relations between different groups, including issues around access and equity. These theories are included in *Being, Belonging and Becoming* to encourage educators to 'find new ways of working fairly and justly' and 'investigate why they act in the ways they do' (DEEWR 2009, p. 11). These goals are central to reconciliation and align with key values that underpin sustainability education, including individual responsibility, empathy and concern about the world's peoples.

Conclusion

As ECEfS continues to gain momentum amid calls for greater advocacy and activism, there remains scope and potential for social, political and economic areas of concern to be central to sustainability initiatives alongside the common environmental focus. This chapter considered the place of reconciliation in ECEfS, given that this is one of the most pressing ethical, social, political and economic issues on the Australian landscape. Here, I borrow the words of Selby (2012) to reiterate questions about how ECEfS currently reinforces a dominant Western view of sustainability in terms of motivations to 'go green' at the expense of broader sustainability themes. As Selby (2012) asks, '*Are we missing an understanding of the importance of cultural diversity and democratic processes in our mission to achieve global sustainability?*' (p. 4; my emphasis). I encourage early childhood educators to be reflexive about why they might see and recount issues of water wastage, pollution, inefficient use of energy and other unsustainable practices (see McKeown 2002), but have difficulty developing and articulating a broader understanding of sustainability and related practices – one that recognises appropriate forms of engagement with Indigenous histories, cultures and peoples.

The early childhood field is well positioned to raise awareness and respond to sustainability issues in local and global communities. As explored throughout this text, the Australian field *is* responding well to the environmental dimension of sustainability by drawing on the knowledge and interests of children and providing support to develop positive dispositions towards more environmentally sustainable practices in the early years. This work is crucial given evidence that young children's dispositions towards sustainable practices carry through to adolescence and adulthood, and that children have capacity to influence the attitudes and behaviours of others in their social circles in productive ways (Davis et al. 2008). However, a more critical framework is required to interrogate sustainability practices if the field is to think more deeply about potential long-term consequences of attending primarily to an environmental focus in isolation from social, political and economic areas of concern. If the environmental paradigm prevails as ECEfS continues to gain momentum here and abroad, then questions will need to be asked about the ethical foundations of sustainability employed in ECEfS, and the hidden meanings behind what exactly is being sustained, and for whom.

Review provocations

Silences around aspects of sustainability that are seen to be too 'difficult' or overtly political can be particularly damaging because this sends a message to children that some topics are 'taboo' or too 'uncomfortable' to discuss. Educators should consider their own knowledge base and how they might respond to children's contributions and questions. Reconciliation begins with critical self-awareness. Educators can commence this process by reflecting personally and with others on questions such as:

- How do I frame sustainability work in early childhood education? How is my conceptualisation of sustainability inclusive of a broad range of issues, including those that impact different groups and their circumstances?
- What is my understanding about events in Australian history? How does what I have learned at school, in the media, and in my social circles impact my understanding about Indigenous and non-Indigenous peoples?
- What theoretical resources can I access to move from practical applications of reconciliation to deeper and more critical thinking and forms of action in ECEfS?

References

Ahmed, S. (2004). Declarations of whiteness: The non-performativity of anti-racism. *Borderlands e-journal*, 3(2), paras 1–39.

Ahmed, S. (2012). *On Being Included: Racism and Diversity in Institutional Life*. London: Duke University Press.

Australian Children's Education and Care Quality Authority (2013). Quality Area 3 – physical environment, www.acecqa.gov.au/Physical-environment (accessed 1 May 2014).

Australian Curriculum and Assessment Reporting Authority (2013). Cross-curriculum priorities, www.acara.edu.au/curriculum/cross_curriculum_priorities.html (accessed 13 October 2013).

Australian Government, Department of Education, Employment and Workplace Relations (DEEWR) (2009). *Belonging, Being and Becoming: The Early Years Learning Framework for Australia*. Canberra: Department of Education, Employment and Workplace Relations for the Council of Australian Governments.

Baker, R., Davies, J. & Young, E. (eds) (2001). *Working on Country: Contemporary Indigenous Management of Australia's Lands and Coastal Regions*. Melbourne: Oxford University Press.

Behrendt, L. (2003). *Achieving Social Justice: Indigenous Rights and Australia's Future*. Annandale, NSW: The Federation Press.

Birch, T. (2007). 'The invisible fire': Indigenous sovereignty, history and responsibility. In A. Moreton-Robinson (ed.), *Sovereign Subjects: Indigenous Sovereignty Matters*. Sydney: Allen & Unwin.

Borrows, J. (2004). Practical reconciliation, practical re-colonisation? *Land, Rights, Law: Issues of Native Title*, 2(27), 1–11.

Bowers, C. A. (2001). *Educating for Eco-Justice and Community*. Athens: The University of Georgia Press.

Broome, R. (2010). *Aboriginal Australians: A History since 1788* (4th edn). Sydney: Allen & Unwin.

Burnett, B & McArdle, F. A. (2011). Multiculturalism, education for sustainable development (ESD) and the shifting discursive landscape of social inclusion. *Discourse: Studies in the Cultural Politics of Education*, 32(1), 43–56.

Conley, E. & Bryan, V. C. (2009). Elements needed to support social, ecological, and economic sustainability on a global basis by educational practitioners for Native American Indigenous people. *International Forum of Teaching and Studies*, 5(2): 22–6.

Connor, J. (2007). *Dreaming Stories: A Springboard for Learning*. Watson, ACT: Early Childhood Australia Inc. and SNAICC.

Craven, R. (ed.) (1999). *Teaching Aboriginal Studies*. Sydney: Allen & Unwin.

Davis, J. M. (2008). What might education for sustainability look like in early childhood? A case for participatory, whole-of-settings approaches. In I. Pramling Samuelsson & Y. Kaga (eds), *The Contribution of Early Childhood Education to a Sustainable Society*. Paris: UNESCO.

Davis, J. M., Miller, M. G., Boyd, W. & Gibson, M. (2008). *The Impact and Potential of Water Education in Early Childhood Care and Education Settings*. A report of the ROUS Water Early Childhood Water Aware Centre Program. Brisbane: Queensland University of Technology.

Derman-Sparks, L. (1989). *Anti-Bias Curriculum*. Washington, DC: National Association for Early Childhood Education.

Diller, J. V. (2011). *Cultural Diversity: A Primer for the Human Services* (4th edn). Belmont, CA: Brooks/Cole, Cengage Learning.

Dodson, M. (2010). Challenges and opportunities in Australian Indigenous education. In I. Snyder & J. Nieuwenhuysen (eds), *Closing the Gap in Education? Improving Outcomes in Southern World Societies*. Melbourne: Monash University Publishing.

Elliot, S. (2003). *Patches of Green: Early Childhood Environmental Education in Australia: Scope, Status and Direction*. Sydney: Environment Protection Authority.

Ellyard, P. (1999). *Ideas for the New Millennium*. Melbourne: Melbourne University Press.

Gorski, P. (2008). Good intentions are not enough: A decolonising intercultural education. *Intercultural Education*, 19(6), 515–25.

Graham, M. (2008). Some thoughts about the philosophical underpinnings of Aboriginal world-views. *Australian Humanities Review*, 45, 181–94.

Greenop, K. & Memmott, P. (2007). Urban Aboriginal place values in Australian metropolitan cities: The case study of Brisbane. In C. Miller & M. Roche (eds), *Past Matters: Heritage and Planning History: Case Studies from the Pacific Rim*. Cambridge: Cambridge Scholars Press.

Gundara, J. & Portera, A. (2011). Theoretical reflections on intercultural education. *Intercultural Education*, 19(6), 463–8.

Hickling-Hudson, A. & Ferreira, J. (2004). Changing schools of a changing world? In B. Burnett, D. Meadmore & G. Tait (eds), *New Questions for Contemporary Teachers: Taking a Socio-Cultural Approach to Education*. Frenchs Forest, NSW: Pearson.

Huggins, J. (2003). The figures seem to confirm that practical reconciliation is not enough, www.onlineopinion.com.au/print.asp?article=872 (accessed 15 April 2009).

Human Rights and Equal Opportunity Commission (2003). Why practical reconciliation is failing Indigenous people, www.humanrights.gov.au/news/media-releases/why-practical-reconciliation-failing-indigenous-people (accessed 1 May 2014).

Kalantzis, M. (2005). Conceptualising diversity – defining the scope of multicultural policy, education and research. *Australian Mosaic*, 10(2), 6–9.

McKeown, R. (2002). *Education for Sustainable Development Toolkit*, www.esdtoolkit.org/esd_toolkit_v2.pdf (accessed 12 February 2013).

Magiropoulos, M. & Giugni, M. (2007). Rethinking equity environments and everyday sustainability. *Every Child*, 13(1), 30–1.

Martin, K. (2005). Childhood, lifehood, and relatedness: Aboriginal ways of being, knowing and doing. In J. Phillips & J. Lampert (eds), *Introductory Indigenous Studies in Education: The Importance of Knowing*. Frenchs Forest, NSW: Pearson.

Miller, M. G. (2013a). Action for change? Embedding Aboriginal and Torres Strait Islander perspectives in early childhood education curricula. PhD thesis, Queensland University of Technology, Brisbane.

Miller, M. G. (2013b). Connecting sustainability work with reconciliation. *In the Loop*, Winter 2013, 4–5.

Moreton-Robinson, A. (ed.) (2007). *Sovereign Subjects: Indigenous Sovereignty Matters*. Sydney: Allen & Unwin.

Mundine, K. & Giugni, M. (2006). *Diversity and Difference: Lighting the Spirit of Identity*. Canberra: Early Childhood Australia Inc.

Newman, P. (2001). The politics of hope. ABC Radio National Perspective Program (22 November).

Nordström, H. K. (2008). Environmental education and multicultural education – too close to be separate? *International Research in Geographical and Environmental Education*, 17(2), 131–45.

Nucifora, F. (2007). Indigenous culture and sustainability: Exploring the Great Barrier Reef in the classroom. *Every Child*, 13(1), 18–25.

Phillips, J. (2012). Indigenous knowledge perspectives: Making space in the Australian centre. In J. Phillips and J. Lampert (eds), *Introductory Indigenous Studies in Education: Reflection and the Importance of Knowing* (2nd edn). Frenchs Forest, NSW: Pearson.

Prime Minister Kevin Rudd, MP (2008). Apology to Australia's Indigenous peoples, http://australia.gov.au/about-australia/our-country/our-people/apology-to-australias-indigenous-peoples (accessed 1 May 2014).

Reconciliation Australia (2009). What is reconciliation? www.reconciliation.org.au/about (accessed 1 May 2014).

Schön, D. A. (1983). *The Reflective Practitioner: How Professionals Think in Action*. New York: Basic Books.

Selby, C. (2012). Integrating culture as a cornerstone of success in sustainability education. *Journal of Sustainability Education*, March, 1.

Short, D. (2008). *Reconciliation and Colonial Power: Indigenous Rights in Australia*. Aldershot: Ashgate.

Sisely, D. (2003). Reconciliation: A key component of sustainable development. Paper presented at the Victorian Minerals and Energy Council Annual Sustainable Development Seminar, September.

Skerman, P. (2013). Yarn up: Tok Blo Yumi. My learning journey. *In the Loop*, Autumn, 17–19.

Somerville, M. (2010). A place pedagogy for 'global contemporaneity'. *Journal of Educational Philosophy and Theory*, 42(3), 326–44.

Somerville, M. & Green, M. (2011). A pedagogy of 'organised chaos': Ecological learning in primary schools. *Children, Youth and Environment*, 20(1), 14–34.

UNESCO. (n.d.). Four dimensions of sustainable development, www.unesco.org/education/tlsf/mods/theme_a/popups/mod04t01s03.html (accessed 1 May 2014).

Zink, R. (2007). Outdoor and environmental education, race and ethnicity. Paper presented at the Australian Association for Research in Education (AARE) Conference, 25–29 May, Fremantle.

Chapter 7

The world is getting flatter: ICT and education for sustainability in the early years

Margaret Lloyd

Editor's note

In this revised chapter, **Margaret Lloyd** again makes her arguments for the inclusion of information and communication technologies (ICT) in ECEfS. While some readers think it provocative to include such a chapter, especially given strong arguments about the need to enhance children's engagement with the natural world as a foundation for caring for it, like Margaret I believe that ICT can be harnessed to promote environmental and sustainability learning rather than diminishing it. Nevertheless, we both recognise that there are equity and access issues – computer technologies are still largely artefacts of wealthier economies and societies, though this is changing.

Furthermore, issues of child safety on the internet are of concern: for example, exposure to inappropriate material, cyberbullying and 'grooming' of children. Moreover, the internet is laden with advertisements, potentially contributing to increased materialism and over-consumption that exacerbate unsustainable practices. Nevertheless, many young children now have access to ICT, such as iPads/tablets, at home and/or in school or kindergarten; to ignore its existence is naive and perhaps even irresponsible. To disregard the potential of ICT to enrich ECEfS is an opportunity lost.

Here, Margaret, a specialist ICT educator, reemphasises her perspective on the use and potential of ICT in ECEfS. While the focus remains on opportunities for the young school-aged child there are examples of environmental/sustainability learning using ICT for preschoolers based on Australia's national Early Years Learning Framework. The overall focus of the chapter is on how ICT can reshape early learning for new possibilities.

Introduction

When new technologies are diffused through communities, they bring both expected and unexpected outcomes. We once thought that computers would make industrialised workplaces more efficient, and that the internet would only be used to share data within and between universities and research centres, seamlessly and instantaneously. We did not foresee that computers would be found in homes and schools as small intuitive devices, or that they would 'flatten' the world (after Friedman 2005) by enabling open channels of communication and reducing power relations between experts and learners. Who would have thought that the 'power that [young] children have ... to independently access information and entertainment and to access "adult" knowledge [would challenge] ... traditional images of children as dependent, morally pure and incompetent' (Arthur et al. 2008, p. 13). We now know that, given opportunity and access, young children are capable of 'performing complex web queries in question format' and using 'cognitive abilities such as relevance judgments, multitasking, successive searching and collaborative behaviours at the level of some adult web searchers' (Spink et al. 2010, p. 20). The flattened world is now even flatter.

This chapter introduces digital resources appropriate for ECEfS that range from static dissemination of information through to interactive simulations and active collaboration in 'real time'. It shows how technology, by becoming 'friendlier', displays significant design differences that distance software for children from the productivity tools designed for the adult workplace. ICT has almost accidentally become more attuned to the concepts of play, discovery, guided observation and collaboration that underpin early years pedagogy.

ICT and the 21st-century child

It is tempting to represent 21st-century children as 'digital natives' (after Prensky 2001) with innate capacities to use new technologies. It is similarly tempting to take contemporary data on increasing home ownership and internet access (see, for example, Australian Bureau of Statistics 2008) to mean that all children have equal access to technology. Despite the inherent dangers of such simplistic views, it is important not to completely dismiss the observed phenomenon of many children's facility with, and lack of fear of, the technology they have 'been interacting with and immersed in ... since birth' (Thelning & Lawes 2001, p. 3). Zevenbergen and Logan (2008) explained that many children have:

> been immersed in technology since their emergence into ... [the] world. Their homes have computer technology in all facets of gadgetry – the remote control for the television, the programmable microwave, the remote and mobile telephone, computers, digital games (such as Xbox, as well as those on the computer) (para. 6).

We thus need to accept, using Vygotskyian understandings of children gaining 'spontaneous concepts' through everyday exposure to their environment, that many 'children are competent users of technology, active agents in their own learning and very aware of the world beyond their family' (Arthur et al. 2008, p. 13). This confidence is also said to come – more deliberately – through 'home techno-literacy practices ... unfettered by the pedagogical practices of schooling or their commercial manifestation as designated *education* apps promoting traditional print-based literacy skills' (O'Mara & Laidlaw, cited in Lynch & Redpath 2014, p. 5).

Despite these observations, Zevenbergen and Logan (2008) explained that there are clear pockets of 'have' and 'have nots' and that:

> young children have extensive exposure to computers in their out-of-school contexts and that early childhood settings need to recognise the changes within their clientele; their concomitant dispositions to learning and activity; and the implications these have for the provision of quality learning environments that enhance the learning for many children while seeking to address the potential digital divide for those from digitally poor families (para. 2).

Provocation 7.1

Have you seen young children using ICT? How do children use an unfamiliar phone, digital camera or tablet? Has a child ever shown **you** how to use a particular piece of technology? Have you seen a child use digital devices in ways you had not considered?

Educational systems have unilaterally shown their intention to integrate ICT into learning through the establishment of national and international systemic benchmarks for both teachers and students. This includes the UNESCO (2008) ICT competencies prefaced by the understanding that today's teachers:

> need to be prepared to provide technology supported learning opportunities for their students ... Interactive computer simulations, digital and open educational resources, and sophisticated data-gathering and analysis tools ... enable teachers to provide previously unimaginable opportunities for conceptual understanding (p. 1).

This exhortation extends to early years, previously contested as a technology-free zone in which ICT use was regarded as the antithesis of good practice (Zevenbergen & Logan 2008). For example, an Australian Curriculum Corporation report (McRae 2001) cautioned against using ICT in early years because it might ignore or hinder developmental needs, such as whole-body movement, sensory interaction, language development and the development of personal agency.

Thelning and Lawes (2001) countered by offering that such anti-technological views 'pre-suppose that early childhood educators will disregard well established early childhood learning principles and implement inappropriate didactic, technology-driven and isolating teaching and learning practices in response to the digital age' (p. 7). Reassurance comes in Australia's national *Belonging, Being and Becoming: The Early*

Years Learning Framework (Australian Government, Department of Education, Employment and Workplace Relations [DEEWR] 2009), where known and trusted principles moderate the use of digital technologies, particularly in relation to Outcome 5, 'Children are effective communicators'. The Framework asks educators to:

- provide children with access to a range of technologies
- integrate technologies into children's play experiences and projects
- teach skills and techniques and encourage children to use technologies to explore new information and represent their ideas
- encourage collaborative learning about and through technologies between children, and between children and educators.

Arguably, the anti-technological position is based on an outdated construct of ICT as providing stand-alone, computer-delivered, computer-assisted learning. Things have changed – ICT is not what it used to be. The Glossary of the Early Years Learning Framework offers that ICT:

> includes much more than computers and digital technologies used for information, communication and entertainment. Technologies are the diverse range of products that make up the designed world. These products extend beyond artefacts designed and developed by people and include processes, systems, services and environment (DEEWR 2009, p. 46).

Computers are no longer big, intimidating 'grey boxes' with only a keyboard for input. Newer technologies are marked by lower cost, robustness and more intuitive use. Digital cameras, audio players, mobile phones and microscopes are now made specifically for younger children. Smaller intuitive devices allow input by touch or voice and their accompanying 'apps' (interactive programs that are free or available at low cost) are appealing to children.

Provocation 7.2

This chapter refers to significant design differences that distance software for children from the productivity tools designed for the adult workplace. In relation to this distinction:

1. List and locate information about input devices that are not reliant on typing and may be better suited for use by younger children.
2. Review word processing and other productivity software used in workplace settings. Note how these tools are designed for adults rather than children. Consider how young children could use productivity software creatively and appropriately.
3. Investigate devices such as digital microscopes made specifically for children. What makes these better suited to early years learning environments?
4. Investigate devices such as iPads, iPods and tablets. Consider how interacting through touch and voice, also known as 'gesture-based' technology, impacts on access and use by young children.

New technologies also offer significantly different ways of playing (Zevenbergen 2007). Some electronic toys, for example, lack user input or control but are useful in familiarising young children with 'the concept of operational interactivity in which pushing a button or picture produces a response . . . tape recorders, karaoke machines, electronic keyboards and cash registers also contribute to the child's repertoire of interactions and this process of familiarisation' (Learning and Teaching Scotland 2003, p. 3). Further, Johnson, Adams and Cummins (2012) explained that the gesture-based technology embedded in new mobile devices 'moves the control of computers from a mouse and keyboard to the motions of the body, facial expressions, and voice recognition via new input devices. It makes interactions with computational devices far more intuitive and embodied' (p. 8).

Parallel to changes in hardware, proprietary software and 'apps' have become 'friendlier' and more child-appropriate. These include 'talking books' that use synthesised speech to allow the user to control how text is 'read' and open-ended software that makes intuitive use of 'drag and drop' functionality with menus based on icons as opposed to text. Control by touch – that is, through pointing, swiping or pinching – have made interfaces even more intuitive, and it has been shown that, for young children, 'touch-screen devices ... encourage intuitive participation in open-ended games and apps' (Lynch & Redpath 2014, p. 5).

While software can still be purchased in individual packs or through site licences, teachers are more likely to download learning objects from system websites, or interact with online games in real time. They can locate and download age-appropriate 'apps' for mobile devices at no or low cost. They can also develop their own digital resources through open-ended software, ranging from commonly used tools such as slideshows to customised programs such as animation and movie editors. These resources are described in more detail – as *unconnected interactions* – in the second section of this chapter.

Child-friendly solutions

Using a computer or other ICT device is no longer reliant on typing or textual literacy skills, which frequently precluded their use by younger learners. A prime example of this is the use of VoiceThread with young children.[1] Vasquez and Felderman (2013) have investigated its affordances in supporting 'collaborative and critical discussions of social issues such as racism, sexism and bullying using children's literature as a springboard' (p. 10). VoiceThread makes simple collaboration possible through peer feedback, typically as audio or video. All that is needed is an internet connection,

---

[1] See http://voicethread4education.wikispaces.com/K-2 for examples of VoiceThread in use by young children.

a microphone and a webcam or digital camera. Using their own voices allows children the opportunity to respond spontaneously to a stimulus.

Another similarly appropriate response was noted in this author's field studies in a school in Far North Queensland, Australia. The school's learning management system (LMS) was accessible from outside school through an extranet.[2] One of the teachers discovered that all students in her Year 2 class (aged 6–7 years) had internet access at home. She capitalised on this by having students post weekly journal entries to a secure online discussion forum hosted on the school server. The children experienced a new form of literacy, families were involved and a peer audience was created.

Despite the fears of the anti-technologists, VoiceThread and journal writing have been far from isolating experiences that remove human contact from children's learning. By creatively appropriating digital communication media, these activities have, instead, built bridges between school and home and between children across the globe. It can be argued that such technology has caught up with early years pedagogy, particularly in the affordances for play and interaction that it brings. It seems, also, that newer, friendlier technologies are countering the objections raised by anti-technologists and are opening up new worlds for children and their teachers.

Support and advice for practitioners in the educational uses of ICT are also more readily available (see, for example, Learning and Teaching Scotland 2003; Spink et al. 2010; Zevenbergen & Logan 2008). There have also been genuine attempts, particularly in the United Kingdom, to provide early years teachers with practical advice and models for integrating ICT into their teaching practice (British Educational Communications and Technology Agency 2001). Fine examples are seen in the video recordings of teachers and children at the Southall Early Years Education Centre (see www.schools world.tv/node/162) and the Homerton Children's Centre (http://ictearlyyears.e2bn. org). These show active early learning environments in which interactive whiteboards, connected laptops and cameras are set at child height to encourage independent play. Additionally, devices such as non-operational mobile phones have been used to support children's play. These video vignettes provide clear evidence that 'experiences that challenge children to develop new concepts and processes, especially when scaffolded by an adult or peers, are highly appropriate for young children's development whether they be with manipulatives or symbolic media based on print or digital technologies' (Downes, Arthur & Beecher 2001, p. 143). They also show that technologies other than 'print or digital' can add significantly and authentically to these learning processes.

---

[2] An *extranet* is an extension of an *intranet*, or internal network. It allows external access to the secure network of a school or business through user identification and a password. These networks are distinct from the *internet*, which only provides access to publicly available content.

Thus, when used in combination with time-tested, early years principles and a focus on play, ICT has:

> the potential to provide 'rich and alive' tools/mediums (i.e. attractive, motivating, interactive, positive) for children to engage with learning. The quality technology and programs are multi-sensory, with built-in feedback about success and offer the means to record and reflect on tasks. They support and enhance learning that is child initiated, involves choice, decision-making and problem solving and is fun (Thelning & Lawes 2001, pp. 3–4).

The rationale for the use of ICT in early years education, therefore, appears to revolve around (a) authenticity, in that ICT is the medium of the times, and (b) pedagogy, in that ICT allows new 'rich and alive' learning experiences in the early years classroom.

Despite residual fears that ICT in early years would hinder children's learning and development, new ways of incorporating technologies in learning are being developed and trialled. In keeping with this spirit of experimentation, the examples in the second section of this chapter provide practical advice on how ICT can be used to support EfS in the early years.

Provocation 7.3

Make a digital collection of learning objects and online simulations related to sustainability that are appropriate for young children. Can you identify what makes these digital resources appropriate for these children? What complementary activities might be added to support or extend children's learning?

ICT and EfS

This section positions the use of ICT in the specific context of ECEfS. While the examples provided are relevant to, and appropriate for, young children, they may not have been specifically designed for them, or even for educational purposes. Teachers, therefore, need to make careful, critical decisions about their selections and the kinds of inter-actions they encourage. In your decision making, it is useful to think about ICT use in terms of the types of interactions it affords. Three types of interactions have been identified through my own audit of available resources. These are:

1. *unconnected* – whereby software applications are used on a standalone computer or group of networked computers – that is, not connected to the internet

2. *passive* – whereby users watch or interact with static online resources in simple ways

3. *collaborative* – whereby genuinely collaborative opportunities for learning become available through the internet, and opportunities are available for users to create their own online content.

Provocation 7.4

How is ICT used in EfS within the broader community? Begin by investigating public environmental group websites, such as WWF – World Wide Fund For Nature – or Greenpeace. Ask yourself if these sites are suitable for young children. What might preclude their use?

It should be noted that these categories are not hierarchical, and each serves a specific purpose in teaching and learning. The selected terms are descriptive rather than pejorative; that is, an *unconnected* activity is not disconnected or disengaging, and a *passive* activity is not one lacking in interest, action or reflection. Indeed, many websites and stand-alone applications contain examples of more than one of the possible interactions. What you, as teacher, parent or carer, choose to use – and how you choose to use it – will depend on access, time available, and the aims of the learning experience you have planned. The pedagogy always comes before the technology.

Provocation 7.5

Brainstorm a list of non-digital ECEfS activities. Revise this list in terms of how these activities might be supported through the use of ICT and, if in Australia, how they might meet the intention of the Early Years Learning Framework in regard to the previously cited Outcome 5 ('Children are effective communicators') (DEEWR 2009). For example, you might document the building of a worm farm through VoiceThread replete with digital images collected over time. Use the categories of this chapter – unconnected, passive and collaborative – to structure your list.

The examples of possible interactions in this chapter come with the caveat that the specific resources cited here were available at time of publication. If unavailable, similar sites can be located through an internet search of key terms or via a cached version. You are encouraged to view the sites and other resources as a companion to reading this text.

1. Unconnected

Although this chapter predominantly refers to online resources, let's begin by paying attention to ICT applications that do not require, or only partly require, an internet connection. Unconnected interactions include the following:

- Open-ended software, particularly paint programs, image and audio editors, animation software, spreadsheets with graphing capabilities, and concept-mapping tools. A rich topic for children's animation is 'minibeasts' – insects, spiders, frogs and the like. Several examples can be found on the internet (search terms: 'minibeasts', 'animation', 'early years').

- Teacher-developed resources (such as web pages, animations or slideshows) that:
  - allow reflection on lived events, such as student field trips recorded through audio, still or video images
  - feature local people, places and customs through scanned images
  - highlight local ecology and habitats through a 'virtual' field trip
  - create stories or learning activities using items from the children's known world; for example, taking photos of local foods or modes of transport rather than using 'clip' art, which lacks cultural and environmental relevance.

- Learning objects and simulations, for example, from Scootle (www.scootle.edu.au), that make teacher-recommended resources available.

- Using digital cameras and other devices to record community examples of sustainable practices – such as the construction of a garden – to 'capture the moment' and then share it immediately with families (either online or as printed copy).

- Involvement in school or community projects; for example, documenting the sustainability project at Hallett Cove Preschool (South Australia), involving 'storing and using sunshine and rain' (Bates & Tregenza 2007). Children in this project were involved in a range of learning tasks, including:
  - planning the site; for example, placement of the water tank and plumbing from the roof
  - measuring distances using age-appropriate equipment such as measuring tapes, rulers and blocks
  - recording progress using digital cameras
  - discussing videos and slideshows of the project as it developed
  - helping to plan the launch and issuing invitations.

- Using video or other creative tools to 'explore thinking, planning, communication and media presentation processes with children' (Thelning & Lawes 2001, p. 4). Marsh (2006) studied 3–4-year-old children who had created animations and concluded that they gained technical and visual skills as well as an understanding of narrative and multimodality, awareness of audience, and critical skills in reflecting on what they had produced.

- Using spreadsheeting or graphing software to record 'real' data, such as water use or related sustainability issues.

- Building concept maps to show the relationships between components of a habitat, and to make tacit knowledge explicit. See, for example, Figueiredo et al. (2004) for a description of preschool children using concept maps to describe 'the things we know about a cow'. These authors used a paper-based method that could easily move into digital form using concept-mapping software developed specifically for children, such as Kidspiration.

The advantage of using unconnected activities lies in the additive effect of making multiple uses of digitised images or sounds and in the capacity for reuse and sharing with families. These resources are typically easy to create and have a direct and familiar connection to technologies used at home and in other settings. Importantly, they are not reliant on print literacy or reading. Unconnected activities – as with others described in this chapter – can be scaled to allow young children to deepen their understandings of, and connections to, the world around them.

2. Passive

In this chapter, being *passive* means that you can look at or 'read' online resources, but you cannot 'write' or add to them or personalise them in any way. You may be able to interact in predetermined ways, such as using hyperlinks to choose a pathway through the presented material, or to play simple games. 'Passive' interactions are not isolated and are usually the precursor to further online or offline action.

To understand the difference in impact between print and digital passive resources, consider the effect of holding up an atlas or pointing to a map on a wall, and showing children images of the Earth through Google Earth (www.google.com/earth). The interactivity of Google Earth means that you can literally 'fly' around the planet, looking at aerial and close-up views of known and unknown places. There are now some predeveloped visits to significant landmarks and landscapes that can be used to stimulate discussion and children's understandings of different habitats. There is rapidly growing use of Google Earth and similar geospatial tools to facilitate and enhance student learning (see, for example, Todd 2007).

Another example is NASA's beautifully illustrated 'Welcome to the Planets' website (http://pds.jpl.nasa.gov/planets), which opens with a table of images of the planets in our solar system. From this page, the teacher might show children more detailed images of a selected planet or link to a 'planet profile'. Such interaction allows immediate responsiveness to children's questions. Further, the images of the planets and the skies have a quality not usually possible in print reproductions. This luminosity is particularly evident in the 'Astronomy Picture of the Day' (http://apod.nasa.gov/apod/astropix.html), where, each day, a new image is featured along with a brief explanation written by a professional astronomer. Similarly, there are apps for tablet devices, such as *Pocket Universe: Virtual Sky Astronomy*, *3D Sun* and *Moon Globe HD*.

Digital resources such as these, as well as some online encyclopaedias, often include short explanatory videos or animations that are helpful in explaining concepts such as planetary orbits to young learners. A teacher could, of course, simply turn pages in a book or check the index if a child asks about a particular planet but, generally, a simple click can take the children to where they need to be.

A teacher might also encourage children to explore such sites by themselves – at home with the support of families who could download apps or bookmark sites – and support this by suggesting a learning task appropriate for their age and literacy level. For example, a Year 1 class was observed successfully using a similar website about planets to match the names of planets with particular colours. Giving consideration to the colour and, in turn, the composition, atmosphere and environment of different planets, led naturally to a discussion of what sustains life on Earth and the importance of having clean air and water, and the need to keep temperatures within a range that people, plants and animals can endure.

Websites posted by government departments and organisations such as zoos and museums are fine examples of passive resources. They are reliable, appropriately illustrated and frequently updated. They can generally be counted upon to be comprehensive and authoritative. Despite these general qualities, some sites are not particularly suitable for younger children because of their almost singular reliance on text for both content and navigation. In selecting appropriate internet resources, follow the same rules of thumb as selecting other learning resources. That is, look for comprehension, engagement and suitability of purpose.

Other sites that support EfS are those hosted by environmental and animal welfare groups. There is a continuum of militancy within these groups, however, ranging from mainstream to militant activist. Website selection – with its implicit promotion and advocacy – needs to be based on an understanding of the group's broader agenda and activity. If you are looking to address issues of animal welfare, for example, it may be more appropriate to use mainstream sites, such as those posted by the RSPCA, the World Wide Fund for Nature or the Australian Koala Foundation. Militant animal welfare groups – particularly those opposed to vivisection or animal cruelty – often show quite alarming photographs to graphically reinforce their message. These may be traumatic for young children.

Alternatively, an example of where images have been used to great effect can be seen in the continuously updated photostream posted by the Australian Seabird Rescue Association (www.flickr.com/photos/australian-seabird-rescue). This volunteer group uses Flickr (a free, online image-sharing website) to publish images of the dolphins, turtles, pelicans and other animals they have rescued. Images have immediacy for learners of all ages and can be used as a catalyst for discussion and awareness raising of environmental topics and issues. Selecting and projecting digital images allows closer examination by children than might otherwise be possible, and offers a springboard to further learning and advocacy. Using gesture-based interfaces makes this closer examination an intuitive process.

Local environmentally focused community groups often have websites too and learning may be stimulated by reference to known places and known local individuals. This gives conversations about global issues an immediate and authentic connection. It might also be useful to show children the websites related to special events or initiatives, such as World Environment Day, Earth Hour or the 'Year of' designations. Community and media attention to pressing issues such as water or energy conservation leads easily into discussions and activities in the classroom. Such sites, for example, may be used to illustrate the elements of an ethical framework, such as the 'Little Earth Charter' (www.littleearthcharter.org/LEC_home.html).

'Teachable moments' also arise from negative news. Coverage of natural disasters can be the catalyst for discussions of basic human needs, such as shelter and food. These, in turn, may be expanded to encourage empathy for others. Aid agency sites, such as Oxfam or UNICEF, may be useful as passive resources in these instances, especially for teachers.

Webcams and virtual tours can also be categorised as passive. These can simply be photographs of a place, while others may be animated or offer quite sophisticated navigation. A fine example is the interactive panorama images to be found at 360Cities (www.360cities.net). These allow views of differing world landscapes – from the tops of city towers, to seeing the night sky from Reunion Island in the Indian Ocean. They are so authentic and engaging even the youngest child can become part of genuine conversations about how and where we live, and begin to take note of the diversity of landscapes on Earth.

Authentic examples relating to environmental and sustainability topics that include webcams can be sourced through web searches; for example, those monitored by Californian zoos to observe condors in the wild. Cameras might also be positioned by zoos to unobtrusively allow naturalistic observation of animals such as pandas or tiger cubs. Similarly, some museums host virtual tours of their sites or of particular museum exhibitions.

Passive interactions also include simple games and quizzes. The Children's University of Manchester (www.childrensuniversity.manchester.ac.uk) presents expert information on a range of topics, including Earth and Beyond, Energy and the Environment, and Micro-organisms. Many have simple games and interactions that would appeal to younger children. The Museum of Science, Boston, offers the opportunity to build a virtual fish and to release it into a virtual fish tank (www.virtualfishtank. com). The child-designer of the fish makes a series of decisions that affect the 'life' of the fish as it becomes part of a food chain and interacts with other organisms in the virtual fish tank.

It is important to note that passive sites are not what they used to be. If you have dismissed their use in teaching and learning in the past, they are worth a second look. Passive resources also provide useful learning opportunities in guided instruction and in the consolidation of learning. They can be used to good effect for whole-group interactions, and can be regarded in much the same way as a picture book, poster, video or other artefact used to introduce a new topic. It is often useful to begin a new topic by locating and reviewing resources compiled by other teachers; for example, the Minibeast collection page compiled by the library at St Aloysius College (South Australia) (www.sac.sa.edu.au/Library/Library/Primary/themes/minibeasts.htm).

The resources referred to here are passive simply because of the limited interactions you are allowed with the resources. They can, however, generate learning experiences that are rich and engaging. Using the internet means that there is authenticity and immediacy in accessing resources, particularly relating to current and emerging events. Teachers can use these resources as they would more tangible items to excite or to explain new ideas or difficult issues. They are often the first step in other adventures in learning, and can play a critical role in ECEfS. Being passive does not imply they are used passively!

3. Collaborative

Web 2.0[3] is the term associated with interactive collaborative online activities. The critical difference between the Web 1.0 sites referred to earlier and Web 2.0 is that users 'write to' rather than 'read from' the internet. This has been popularised by the social networking of Facebook, the virtual environments of Second Life and game worlds such as World of Warcraft and EverQuest. Increasingly, the world shares its day through video on such Web 2.0 websites as YouTube, and its images through Instagram and Flickr. Individuals share their views through Twitter, or personal blogs or using email lists. For older children, Web 2.0 learning is facilitated by the blogs and collaborative tools to be found on sites such as Skoolaborate (www.skoolaborate.com) and the Global Kids' Digital Media Initiative (www.globalkids.org) and in online environmental games such as IBM's PowerUp (www.powerupthegame.org). Initially, it may be difficult to see how this type of collaboration can become part of the learning experiences of younger children and, more critically, how learning can be achieved without putting children into potentially risky spaces online. However, this is exactly what is happening as technical and human protocols are put in place to ensure children's safety online.

A teacher who has safely and successfully involved children in online interactions is Maria Knee, a kindergarten teacher from Deerfield, New Hampshire in the United States. She uses Web 2.0 tools to record her class' activities, which are grouped together on the KinderKids site. The site's banner reads: 'Learning Together – Sharing our work with our families and the world.'

---

[3] 'Web 2.0' is an umbrella term coined by Tim O'Reilly in 2004. It describes a new generation of the internet that allows for more user participation, social interaction, and collaboration with the use of blogs, wikis, social networking and sharing of resources (search the terms 'O'Reilly', 'Web 2.0' and 'what-is-web-20.html').

The blog[4] is continuously updated with stories from the classroom, with special attention to field trips taken by the class. The recording of these activities provides a simple way for children to recall their experience and to scaffold ongoing classroom conversations. The moderated blog posts also provide a way to extend the walls of the classroom to home as students share their experiences with their families. Families and others, including the children themselves, can leave comments on the site to further extend the learning opportunities. This is an example of how static resources, such as digital images (addressed earlier in relation to *unconnected* interactions), can be used to generate collaborative interactions. Through activities such as this, Maria Knee shows that the concepts and principles of sustainability provide both the content and context of her teaching practice.

A highlight of Maria Knee's class is their connection to other classrooms around the world. For example, they have had an ongoing relationship with teacher Amanda Marrinan, in Brisbane, Australia, and her students, known as 'The Gems'. Maria explained that:

> Classroom blogging has brought a new excitement into my own teaching. I enjoy using the tools such as *VoiceThread* or slideshows to help make the work we do in the classroom available to families and others around the world. My students . . . enjoy connecting with other students and help 'teach' them about what we learn. Creating, collaborating and communicating are the skills they need for the future and, I believe, the early years are exactly the place where we should begin to develop these skills (Maria Knee, personal correspondence, 28 November 2008).

Provocation 7.6

Visit Maria Knee's KinderKids website. How might parents react to this site? How might children react? Would you maintain a site like this for the children in your care? What might be some of the difficulties or disadvantages in using such ICT tools and strategies?

Children can also be involved in online curriculum projects. These are structured learning activities that use the internet to connect learners with each other or with experts. Individuals informally organise collaborations between schools or through non-profit organisations, such as Global SchoolNet[5] or iEARN.[6] Online projects have clear curriculum goals and frequently involve both online and offline activities.

Collaborative activities are well suited for EfS, particularly in developing understandings of cultures, customs and environments, and also in gaining authentic experience in working with others. They provide a wide range of digital literacies and, when designed with attention to both internet security and early childhood education principles, can contribute positively towards children's learning.

---

[4] Maria Knee's class blogs can be found at http://thekinderkids.edublogs.org.
[5] See www.globalschoolnet.org.
[6] See www.iearn.org.

Conclusion

Al Gore, in writing on global warming, has offered that:

> There is no doubt we can solve this problem. In fact, we have a moral obligation to do so. Small changes to your daily routine can add up to big differences in helping to stop global warming. The time to come together to solve this problem is now (Gore 2006, para. 4).

Attention to sustainability – in all forms, social, environmental, economic, cultural and technological – has become a moral imperative. The responsibility of education to help 'solve the problem' is patently clear and is best achieved through being embedded seamlessly in the 'daily routine' of the classroom. Embedding ICT in authentic ways can be used as an active agent in this process, particularly in encouraging children to 'come together'. This can be achieved within and between educational settings, between home and these settings, as well as between settings in different states, countries and continents.

'Flattening' the world through ICT means that we now 'see' our interdependence. Treating the world as one interconnected community means that we can put that care into focused action. Begin with educating the young, share the world through rich, authentic, hands-on learning experiences and opportunities, but deepen learning through the provision of unconnected, passive and collaborative digital tools that help make the world a better and better-known place. We all need to make the world flatter!

Review provocations

1. One suggestion in this chapter is that the criteria for selecting appropriate internet resources for young children are (1) comprehension, (2) engagement and (3) suitability for purpose. Individually or with others, refine these broad criteria to a specific list to suit the selection of resources relating to ECEfS. Apply your refined list to a selection of the websites mentioned in this chapter.
2. Play with the online resources listed in this chapter. Find where you live on Google Earth, design a virtual fish and release it into the tank at the Museum of Science, Boston, or 'visit' a zoo or museum. Before you can engage children in online activities, you need to immerse yourself in these spaces. Go online! Play!

References

Arthur, L., Beecher, B., Death, E., Dockett, S. & Farmer, S. (2008). *Programming and Planning in Early Childhood Settings* (4th edn), South Melbourne: Thomson.

Australian Bureau of Statistics (2008). *Household Use of Information Technology, Australia, 2007–08*, www.abs.gov.au/Ausstats/abs@.nsf/mf/8146.0 (accessed 5 April 2009).

Australian Government, Department of Education, Employment and Workplace Relations (DEEWR) (2009). *Belonging, Being and Becoming: The Early Years Learning Framework for Australia*. Canberra: Department of Education, Employment and Workplace Relations for the Council of Australian Governments.

Bates, S. & Tregenza, N. (2007). *Education for Sustainability in the Early Years: A Case Study from Hallett Cove Preschool*, www.decs.sa.gov.au/efs/files/pages/HallettCovePreschoolCaseSt.pdf (accessed 31 October 2008).

British Educational Communications and Technology Agency (2001). *Foundation Stage Education and ICT*, http://homepages.shu.ac.uk/~edsjlc/ict/becta/information_sheets/founda.pdf (accessed 4 April 2003).

Downes, T., Arthur, L. & Beecher, B. (2001). Effective learning environments for young children using digital resources: An Australian perspective. *Information Technology in Childhood Education Annual*, (1), 139–53.

Figueiredo, M., Lopes, A. S., Firmino, R. & de Sousa. S. (2004). 'Things we know about the cow': Concept Mapping in a Preschool Setting. Paper presented at Concept Maps: Theory, Methodology, Technology, Pamplona, Spain.

Friedman, T. (2005). *The World is Flat: A Brief History of the Twenty-First Century*. New York: Strauss & Giroux.

Gore, A. (2006). What is global warming?, www.climatecrisis.net/thescience (accessed 1 August 2008).

Johnson, L., Adams, S. & Cummins, M. (2012). *The NMC Horizon Report: 2012 Higher Education Edition*. Austin, TX: New Media Consortium.

Learning and Teaching Scotland (2003). *Come Back in Two Years: A Study of the Use of ICT in Pre-School Settings*. Glasgow: Learning and Teaching Scotland.

Lynch, J. & Redpath, T. (2014). 'Smart' technologies in early years literacy education: A meta-narrative of paradigmatic tensions in iPad use in an Australian preparatory classroom. *Journal of Early Childhood Literacy*, 14(2), 147–74.

McRae, D. (2001). *What to Make, and Why: Principles for the Design and Development of Online Curriculum Content*. Melbourne: Curriculum Corporation.

Marsh, J. (2006). Digital animation in the early years: ICT and media education. In M. Hayes & D. Whitebread (eds), *ICT in the Early Years*, New York: McGraw-Hill International.

Prensky, M. (2001). Digital natives, digital immigrants. *On the Horizon*, 9(5), 1–5.

Spink, A., Danby, S., Mallan, K. & Butler, C. (2010). Exploring young children's web searching and technoliteracy. *Journal of Documentation*, 66(2), 191–206.

Thelning, K. & Lawes, H. (2001). *Information and Communication Technologies (ICT) in the Early Years: The Connections between Early Childhood Principles, Beliefs about Children's Learning, and the Influences of Information and Communication Technologies*, www.earlyyears.sa.edu.au/files/links/ICT_in_the_EYDiscussion_Pa.pdf (accessed 28 October 2008).

Todd, C. (2007). Google Earth as a (not just) geography education tool. *Journal of Geography*, 106(4), 145–51.

UNESCO (2008). *ICT Competency Standards for Teachers*. Paris: UNESCO.

Vasquez, V. M. & Felderman, C. B. (2013). *Technology and Critical Literacy in Early Childhood*. Routledge: New York.

Zevenbergen, R. (2007). Digital natives come to preschool: Implications for early childhood practice. *Contemporary Issues in Early Childhood*, 8(1), 18–28.

Zevenbergen, R. & Logan, H. (2008). Computer use by preschool children: Rethinking practice as digital natives come to preschool. *Australian Journal of Early Childhood*, 33(1), pp. 37–44.

Chapter 8

Healthy and sustainable environments for children and communities

Sue Cooke

Editor's note

Sue Cooke, in this revised chapter, again focuses on the close connections between human health, environmental quality and sustainability issues, especially climate change. Sue outlines how the changing ecology of childhood raises profound challenges for child (and adult) health and wellbeing. She cites research suggesting all is not well. Sue re-emphasises that learning in school community gardens, for example, offers opportunities for linking health/ environmental concerns with positive, integrated educational responses. In updating this chapter, she again outlines the synergies and opportunities offered to educators wishing to create change by international movements such as Health Promoting Schools and Child Friendly Cities. In this edition, she adds Transition Towns to this list. Sue also stresses again the importance of establishing partnerships between health professionals and early childhood educators, advising they continue to strengthen their collaborative work for the common aim of creating 'green and healthy' learning environments for young children, rather than seeing these as two separate goals. In essence, Sue reiterates, living sustainably is not only good for the planet but also for the health and wellbeing of children, families and communities.

Introduction

Research on child health and development has shown that the environments young children experience as they are growing shape their health and wellbeing. Not only their social environments, especially the family, but the physical, built and natural environments play their part, impacting on the developing child arguably from the moment of conception through infancy, childhood and adolescence into adulthood. The importance of relationships between small children and their families, caregivers and educators is now well understood by health and education professionals. Less well recognised as a positive force for children's healthy development and wellbeing is the natural environment, and children's relationships with it.

This chapter explores some positive directions for partnerships between professionals in ECEfS and those in child health and wellbeing. It looks at the synergies between ECEfS and other international, child-centred change movements, such as Health Promoting Schools, Health Promoting Early Childhood Education and Care, Child Friendly Cities and the more recently emerging Transition Towns movement. It argues that the critical factors common to these movements are their focus on individual *and* community empowerment, and action taking for healthy change. Approaches that integrate education for health *and* environment within early childhood education are simply better able to meet the health and wellbeing needs of young children and their families. They also support the cultural shifts required to build healthier, more sustainable communities and societies. We find that what is good for young children's growth and development also supports healthy societies and the planetary ecosystem, our shared life support system. The premise argued here is that early childhood professionals should work together across disciplines – including education, care and health – to simultaneously develop resilient children, societies and environments.

The changing ecology of childhood and its impact on health and wellbeing

While there have been many improvements in children's health over recent decades, rates of childhood obesity, asthma and mental health problems are rising in many developed nations. The Australian Research Alliance for Children and Youth found that Australian children are not faring as well as they could on a range of indicators, in an international context (Australian Research Alliance for Children and Youth [ARACY] 2013). Citing a UNICEF (2007) report on the wellbeing of children and adolescents in developed countries, Eckersley urges us to take a 'big picture' view of the profound social changes occurring in the contemporary world, in order to understand the changes in young people's health and wellbeing (Eckersley 2008, 2011). Family breakdown, dietary changes, increasing individualism, excessive materialism and hyper-consumer lifestyles (Eckersley 2008), increasing time in front of a TV or other screen, and decreasing physical and outdoor play (Shanker 2012a and see Chapter 2 for more on this) all contribute to the changing ecology of childhood. While we cannot clearly predict how these changes will affect children's health and wellbeing, and that of future generations, research suggests that levels of stress experienced by children in developed nations today far exceed those of earlier decades (Shanker 2012a). In light of the links between such changes and children's health, recent decades of rapid economic growth have not delivered the social and environmental dividends they promised (Keating & Hertzman 1999). Some even predict that today's adults could be the last generation to reach higher standards of living and better life expectancy than their parents (Olshansky et al. 2005).

Progress going backwards?

Ironically, at a time when the importance of the natural environment for our health and wellbeing is beginning to gain recognition, pressures on our global and local ecosystems are threatening their capacity to nurture and sustain the children of today and tomorrow. At the macro level, these pressures include climate disruption, diminishing freshwater supplies, heavy reliance on non-renewable energy, population growth, rapid urbanisation and growing numbers of environmental refugees (Davis & Cooke 2007 and Chapter 1).

Climate change has relatively recently been recognised as a major threat to global health in the 21st century. Expectations are for widespread, severe effects on global population health over coming decades, with children being especially vulnerable (Costello et al. 2009; Farrant Armstrong & Albrecht 2012; Hansen et al. 2013). An analysis of climate change threats to children's health in Australia (Sly et al. 2008) identified the following potential impacts:

- changing patterns of infectious and vector-borne diseases, such as dengue fever
- heat stress and health effects of extreme weather events, such as fires, floods and cyclones
- impacts of drought on mental health and suicide rates
- impacts of changing plant growth on allergen levels and asthma
- impacts on water and food security
- impacts on children's mental and emotional health due to concerns about climate change and from any increase in traumatic exposures to fires, floods and storms.

Children's cumulative exposure to climate change-related stresses over their lifetimes is likely to amplify their adverse environmental health impacts, compared to previous generations and today's adults.

To sum up, notwithstanding predictions of widespread health impacts from climate change, many children, particularly in the developed world, *are* doing well. However, the rising rates of childhood obesity, mental health problems and allergies in developed nations are an uncomfortable indication that, even if current lifestyles and circumstances were ecologically and economically sustainable (and clearly they are not), they do not seem to be good for children's wellbeing (Davis & Cooke 2007; Shanker 2012b). Income inequality is also growing (ARACY 2013), with greater social polarisation placing further limitations on the life chances of the poor and their children. Of particular concern is the impact upon children's social and emotional wellbeing, their mental health and resilience.

Children's mental health – social and emotional wellbeing

Already the largest contributor to the burden of disease in Australia's young people, evidence shows that mental health problems in childhood are increasing – occurring at younger ages and at higher rates than ever before – and that more children continue to carry these problems into older childhood, adolescence and adulthood. Indicators of concern include that almost a quarter of children at school entry are assessed as being developmentally vulnerable on one or more domains of the Australian Early Development Index (Australian Institute of Health and Welfare [AIHW] 2012), and a fifth to a third of young people experience significant psychological stress and distress at any one time (Eckersley 2008). Australian and Canadian research has found high (around 40 per cent) and increasing levels of students displaying unproductive, inattentive, impulsive and unmotivated or aggressive behaviour at school (Shanker 2012b).

As well as having personal concerns, such as how they look, being bullied and not fitting in, children are concerned about the state of the world. A 2007 survey of Australian children aged 10–14 years, by the Australian Childhood Foundation (Tucci, Mitchell & Goddard 2007), found that 44 per cent worried about the impacts of climate change. Other significant worries included lack of water in the future, war and terrorism. Disturbingly, a quarter of children were so troubled about the state of the world that they believed it would come to an end before they got older (p. 5).

Children are particularly vulnerable to the distress and anxiety associated with a growing awareness of the risks of climate change (Fritze et al. 2008). In addition, their parents' mental distress and anxiety in response to direct climate change impacts, such as extreme weather events, or the dawning realisation of widespread climate change threats to the global environment, may impact on parenting. The risk of child abuse and neglect, for example, rises following extreme weather events, such as cyclones, bushfires and floods (Self-Brown et al. 2013). Children are therefore at risk of harm due to environmental stress both directly from their own experiences and perceptions, and indirectly through the effects on their parents and broader networks of support.

In Australia, as in many other countries, we are already feeling the effects of extreme weather events arising from climate change. More prolonged droughts, longer heatwaves, and more severe bushfires, cyclones and floods are having a significant influence on the physical and mental health of children (McDermott & Cobham 2012). As our local environments change in unwelcome ways, children and adults may also experience a new kind of place-based distress referred to as solastalgia (Farrant, Armstrong & Albrecht 2012). Solastalgia is a kind of homesickness that is felt without leaving home. Rather, it is the environment we love that has changed around us.

Provocation 8.1

What examples can you identify from your own experiences that illustrate some of the stresses of life's complexities for children and families? Can you identify events or situations that may have resulted in solastalgia?

Addressing the risks: Think globally, act locally, participate personally

Taking a big picture view, for society to rise to the challenges of climate change and other consequences of unsustainable living, we need to cultivate the qualities of critical thinking and optimism, and the competence necessary to take positive action; that is, to change, and to 'make a difference' (Davis & Cooke 2007). Instead, as noted, social and emotional wellbeing in young people seems increasingly threatened. This has led to calls for urgent action to improve early childhood systems in Australia and elsewhere, and to nurture mental health resilience (Eckersley 2008, p. 3; Robinson, Silburn & Arney 2011; Shanker 2012b).

Research (for example, Seligman et al. 2009) indicates that when people, including children, can do something to solve a problem – that is, when they can take actions that lead to success, or to developing mastery over skills – they are better able to move from despair and helplessness to action and optimism. Working together with parents to nurture children's physical, social, emotional and cognitive capacities, early childhood professionals in all fields can play a foundational role in creating caring, healthy environments that build competence, wellbeing and resilience. These are vital for developing healthy, thriving children. Engagement in such 'communities of practice' can help catalyse cultural change through a sociology of creative transformation (Poland, Dooris & Haluza-Delay 2011). Some examples of such approaches are outlined in the next section.

Growing healthy children – what it takes

The importance of the early years for lifelong health and success

Extensive multidisciplinary research shows that good early childhood health and development can have lifelong positive effects, promoting academic success, self-esteem, social skills, employment and health, and reducing the propensity to be teen parents, take drugs or be involved in crime. Babies' and young children's brains are continuously being shaped by what they see, hear, feel and taste, and by their every interaction with the world around them. There are in fact time-critical periods when babies need to be exposed to specific stimuli and experiences for optimal development of their sight and hearing and, perhaps more critically, their ability to delight in learning, and to form loving relationships (Shonkoff & Phillips 2000). It turns out that developing emotional self-regulation, which is essential for 'emotional intelligence', is at least as important for life success and mental health as cognitive development (Keating & Hertzman 1999; Shanker 2012b).

Bronfenbrenner's 'ecological systems' model of child development sees the child as a living system, embedded within and influenced by broader systems. Building on this concept, Figure 8.1 illustrates different layers of social environment having an impact on children. These include the central intrapersonal level (genetics, personal characteristics), extending to the circle of the family and neighbourhood, and then beyond – namely, broader social, economic, political and cultural environments. This model

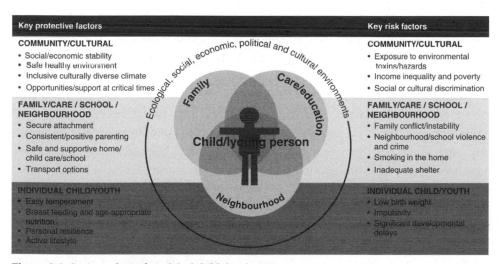

Figure 8.1 *Socio-ecological model of child development*
Source: Queensland Health (2002, p. 20)

makes clear the importance of care and educational environments in children's development and lives. Further, in this case the model explicitly recognises humans' place within the planetary ecosystem, the life support system upon which all individuals, societies and their institutions depend.

The model indicates, too, some of the risk and protective factors that may operate at each systemic level and have an impact on child development, health and wellbeing. Such child health development models can guide early childhood practices aimed at reducing risks and strengthening protective factors. For example, we know that living in a secure, interactive, warm and loving emotional environment, and a safe, stimulating physical environment in early childhood is more likely to produce secure, confident and interested babies and toddlers. They have a good chance of being well prepared for interactions with others, and to learn and thrive when they go from their secure home 'base' into the broader world of an early childhood setting and school. On the other hand, children born to disadvantaged, depressed, stressed or poorly coping parents, particularly those living in chaotic or violent circumstances, are less likely to receive the time-critical stimuli and emotional interactions required for healthy development. They are less likely to develop the strong social, emotional, cognitive and sensory skills they require to help them make sense of the world and to interact confidently within it. These children are more likely to experience health problems and developmental delays, and to be less socially, emotionally and cognitively ready when they enter early childhood educational settings, including school. They are more likely to need extra care and support in early childhood and school environments. Developmental stresses are also experienced by children growing up in physically toxic environments, to which they are often much more sensitive than adults. An example is the incidence of cognitive and behavioural problems in children who are exposed to high levels of lead in the environment, due to living near lead-mining centres.

The logic of reducing risk factors and enhancing protective factors to promote optimal healthy development does not mean that children should be 'bubble-wrapped' (a concept discussed in Chapters 2 and 4) or kept from experiencing challenges. Indeed, healthy child development relies on taking risks, facing challenges and overcoming adversities, within a supportive environment. Positive, stimulating interactions between adults and children, and problem-solving, play-based learning with other children are ideal for early brain development and for building healthy, competent, happy lives. The over-stimulation that can arise from our busy lifestyles and environments, however, is stressful and may contribute to increasing levels of attention and behaviour problems (Shanker 2012b).

What do these findings mean for early childhood education professionals?

Taking into account the research findings about 'growing healthy children', this section highlights three areas that early childhood educators should consider as part of curriculum planning and approaches. These are working partnerships between parents, educators and health professionals; reframing thoughts about health; and appreciating the principles of health promotion. The first two areas are discussed immediately below; health promotion is covered in the next section.

Working partnerships

Family members are a child's first and most important influence, and are also the ones with the best knowledge of their own children. However, many contemporary families do not have extended families nearby to share the challenges and joys of bringing up children and most of us have little training for the role of parenthood. All of us need some support at times. The best outcomes for children happen when early childhood education and care services staff and families work together towards children's health and wellbeing. Negative experiences in one environment may be mediated by positive experiences in another. Just as good early childhood programs that involve parents or other caregivers benefit from those parents' insider knowledge about their children, skilled and knowledgeable early childhood practitioners can also contribute to parents' skills. They can also influence how they relate to and care for their children through respectful, strengths-based partnerships with parents and carers.

Quality early childhood programs that facilitate personalised learning and development experiences for each child are positively linked to good outcomes for children and families. Parents are our most important partners, but early childhood educational practice can also benefit from understanding how children's health develops and from partnerships with early childhood health professionals. Good working relationships with other child and family wellbeing services are also important. Opportunities for multidisciplinary practice in holistic early childhood education and care services, joint professional development programs and reflective practice may be especially valuable in developing interdisciplinary relationships. They can provide opportunities for sharing and developing key skills, such as the capacity to be calm, available and supportive with children, and their families.

Provocation 8.2

What activities can you envisage that might involve partnerships between an early childhood setting and child health and wellbeing professionals?

How might your early childhood education practice support parents' engagement and partnership in the life of your early childhood setting and with the broader community?

Reframing health

The World Health Organization (WHO 2014) defines health as a state of wellbeing that has multiple dimensions, including physical, mental and social, and is more than just the absence of illness and disease. An holistic view of health – one that goes beyond the biological – has led to new understandings of what is necessary to promote the health of individuals, communities and populations. Clearly, what we need goes beyond medical treatments and health services (or, rather, 'illness' services), into everyday life and environments. The Ottawa Charter for Health Promotion (WHO 1986) recognised the importance of *environments* for health, going so far as to identify peace, shelter, education, food and income, a *stable ecosystem*, sustainable resources, social justice and equity as *essential conditions* and resources for health. The Charter states that:

> Health is created by caring for oneself and others, by being able to take decisions and have control over one's life circumstances, and by ensuring that the society one lives in creates conditions that allow the attainment of health by all its members.

The Charter also calls for a commitment to 'address the overall ecological issue of our ways of living' (WHO 1986, p. 4), and sees conservation of nature as essential in any health promotion strategy. In summary, it recognises the importance for individual health of:

- autonomy and independence
- caring relationships with others
- decision making and empowerment
- social justice
- healthy, supportive environments.

Health research increasingly recognises this eco-holistic view. Many studies have demonstrated that contact with nature is good for health, indeed essential for a healthy human habitat, and that steps should be taken to ensure people can have access to the experience (Townsend & Weerasuriya 2010; Kuo 2010; see also Chapter 2). Public health leaders and other health professionals are becoming more outspoken in their involvement and action for healthier environments and a stable climate system (Cooke et al. 2011). Sadly, the recent report card on the wellbeing of young Australians ranks Australia poorly in terms of climate change – we are in the bottom third of OECD countries for carbon dioxide emissions (ARACY 2013), leaving us much room for improvement to safeguard our children's wellbeing.

Provocation 8.3

What does holistic health mean to you? Write your own statement, or draw your own diagram, to illustrate this concept.

Promoting health in schools and early childhood settings: Better health, better learning

In this section I provide an overview of concepts in contemporary health-promotion approaches to child development, as they apply to schools and early childhood settings. The most significant ones are health-promoting schools (HPS) and health-promoting early childhood (HPEC) settings.

Health-promoting schools and early childhood settings

Recognising that health is created and lived by people in the places in which they learn, work, play and love, the WHO established programs focusing on major life settings; for example, schools (including early childhood care and education settings) and work-places, as well as communities, cities and even islands.

Echoing Ottawa Charter principles, key principles for HPS and HPEC are:

- upholding social justice and equity concepts
- encouraging student participation and empowerment
- creating safe and supportive school environments
- linking health and education issues and systems (St Leger 2005).

Fundamentally democratic and participatory, an HPS is ideally a microcosm for how a healthy and sustainable world might function (Davis & Cooke 2007). These schools are deliberately inclusive, valuing diversity in terms of student socio-economic and cultural backgrounds, as well as physical and cognitive characteristics and abilities. The HPS approach has been successfully adopted in a diverse range of developed and developing countries, including Australia, Canada, the United States, China, Singapore, Hong Kong, the European Union, countries in Africa, and Papua New Guinea and other Western Pacific nations and islands (Vince Whitman & Aldinger 2009; Cooke et al., 2011).

Steps in the HPS and HPEC processes embed action learning cycles that achieve the following:

1. Involve *everyone* in creating a *shared vision* of an ideal 'healthy school' or early childhood setting. (Note: This step is critical for ensuring the project looks beyond everyday constraints and identifies the real values and goals that are important to students and the school community.)

2. Identify and prioritise issues for action. (Look across the broad dimensions of health – physical, mental, social, emotional, spiritual, ecological.)

3. Involve students, staff, parents and the community in developing action plans to achieve the desired goals. (Start small – you don't have to do everything at once.)

4. Involve everyone in putting the plans into action.

5. Continuously evaluate progress. (What is working and what isn't?)

6. Celebrate achievements!

7. Plan for the future. (Continue on to the next action learning cycle, the next priority issue.)

HPS practices have been effectively adopted in early childhood educational environments, including childcare, kindergarten and preschool. The comprehensive, whole-of-setting approach of HPS and HPEC (see Figure 8.2) promotes wellbeing and learning through three key components:

- adopting active, participative classroom practices (*curriculum*)

- improving the physical and social environments of the setting (*environment/ethos*)

- forging partnerships with parents, the local community and relevant community agencies (*community partnerships*).

Programs that integrate action in curriculum, the environment, and community partnerships produce better health and education outcomes than those that are mainly information-based and implemented only in the classroom. For example, learning about fresh, healthy food (through the curriculum) is strengthened when food provided in the school tuckshop (canteen) is nutritious, fresh and tasty (that is involving the school's environment and the community through the canteen). The health and learning power of being active and outside in the natural world is demonstrated also when children are involved in growing, harvesting, preparing and sharing the eating of the

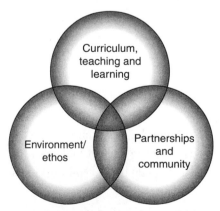

Figure 8.2 *The holistic HPS and HPEC approaches, showing their three interrelated components*

food, as they are in HPS-modelled kitchen-garden activities, such as the Stephanie Alexander School Kitchen Garden program (Yeatman et al. 2013).

For the past 30 years, the HPS concept has enabled health issues to be addressed in more effective, inclusive and empowering ways than traditional, classroom-only approaches. There is good evidence, too, that the process is useful in addressing a range of health issues, especially healthy food intake, physical activity and fitness, and mental health promotion, and that it can be successfully adapted to meet the needs of school communities facing different challenges, all over the world (Vince Whitman & Aldinger 2009). Further evidence of effectiveness is emerging from HPS-based programs focused primarily on developing social and emotional health. For example, MindMatters (www.mindmatters.edu.au) is an Australian national mental health initiative that provides resources and professional development aimed at promoting and protecting the mental health, social and emotional wellbeing of secondary school communities. KidsMatter and KidsMatter Early Childhood are equivalent programs designed for primary schools, and early learning and care environments, respectively.

Evaluation of a trial of the HPEC model in childcare centres in disadvantaged metropolitan suburbs of Queensland, Australia, between 2002 and 2005 demonstrated that many health and wellbeing issues were successfully addressed, including food and nutritional health, sun safety, oral health, staff wellbeing, physical activity, hygiene, head lice, behaviour management, parenting skills, workplace health and safety, communication with families and making links with local agencies (Queensland Health 2006, 2008). The health promotion processes introduced also helped with quality assurance and childcare accreditation requirements.

This early trial demonstrated the need for further early childhood mental health resources and led to the development of a Social and Emotional Early Development Strategy (SEEDS). SEEDS provided teachers and caregivers with a way to reflect on their own knowledge (head), values (heart) and skills (hands), and how they support the social and emotional wellbeing of the children and the adults in their lives (de Plater 2008, p. 28). Benefits experienced by staff, children and families involved in the SEEDS program included improved communication and more open and cooperative relationships between children, staff and parents. For staff in particular, the partnerships with health professionals (such as health promotion staff and child health nurses), and the professional learning associated with the project provided unexpected benefits, such as increased work satisfaction and growing collegiality with other staff in their own and other centres, and with other early childhood disciplines. Staff also expressed increased interest, enjoyment and confidence in working with children and parents. These benefits continue to be found in subsequent, nationally available programs, such as KidsMatter Early Childhood.

The KidsMatter Early Childhood mental health initiative

Following an extensive trial and positive evaluation in 2012, the KidsMatter Early Childhood mental health program is now available nationally (see www.kidsmatter.edu.au/early-childhood). Developed in collaboration with beyondblue, the Australian Psychological Society and Early Childhood Australia, and with funding from the Australian Government, the initiative focuses on four distinct areas (referred to as components). These are:

- creating a positive school community
- teaching children skills for good social and emotional development
- working together with families
- recognising and getting help for children with mental health difficulties.

Note: User-friendly information and resources for staff and parents, including literature reviews, are freely available from www.kidsmatter.edu.au/early-childhood.

Broader benefits of health-promoting approaches

Holistic health-promoting programs, it seems, achieve holistic outcomes. Evaluations of England's National Healthy School Standard program found that 'healthy schools' are effective schools, improving educational outcomes as well as health. Participating schools improved at a faster rate than those not included in the program, and improvements were found in learning environments, student concentration and performance, staff health and wellbeing, and student learning achievement (National Foundation for Educational Research & Thomas Coram Research Unit 2004).

The health issues addressed by using these processes (HPS and HPEC), and the complexity of the responses and actions taken by children and educators, vary with the growing capabilities of students. In Australian primary schools, for example, one of the many issues that have been addressed is dangerous school transport. Most children arrive by car, causing traffic hazards and air pollution and creating barriers to active transport options, such as walking and cycling. The links between health and environmental concerns are obvious. Effectively solving such problems encompasses taking action across all three domains of curriculum and pedagogy, ethos/environment and community. For example, students might survey student and parent school travel practices and research the effects of, and alternatives to, current patterns, through a number of key learning areas such as mathematics, health and studies of society and environment. The social environment and ethos of the school should be supportive of students' active participation in investigations, and should respect their researcher and decision-making roles. Teacher and parent roles might include facilitating student engagement with local community transport authorities – for example, council or state government – and supporting student recommendations for improvements.

Similarly, in early childhood settings, there are many options for action to address local health and environmental issues. For example, children may be assisted in setting up a worm farm to compost their lunch scraps, provide fertiliser for the garden and help them grow their own healthy crops of cherry tomatoes or spinach (see Chapter 4 for a further example of a whole-of-setting approach in action).

Why health-promoting schools work

By overtly including everybody concerned – particularly all children – the democratic HPS/HPEC process allows the various interest groups within the setting to overcome their differences, identify common interests and come together to achieve shared goals. This builds cooperative social skills in adults and children alike. The process mediates between competing interests and builds ownership, commitment and community, as well as achieving better health and educational outcomes for those involved.

Developing personal autonomy, or agency, and a sense of belonging to a community is important. Australian research (see Stewart et al. 2004) found that an HPS environment that engendered 'connectedness' between adults and children and between children and their peers, and that supported autonomy, is a major contributor towards psychological resilience in children. With its focus on active, real-life student participation, the process recognises that even very young children can be competent thinkers about issues that have an impact on their lives and wellbeing. It systematically helps them to develop 'action competence' (Jensen 2002), through critical thinking, planning and taking real-life actions to improve the relevant health issue or situation. In this way, children are learning to question the way things are at present, consciously imagining a more desirable situation, and personally being involved in creating a healthier, more enjoyable classroom, playground, school, community and world. This experience of actually 'making a difference' builds not only hope, but individual and collective empowerment, self efficacy and mental wellbeing. What a lesson for life!

In the next section I further explore reasons for integrating the outdoor, natural environment in all professional early childhood practices.

Natural environments and children's health and wellbeing

Many studies conducted in recent years have demonstrated that engagement with interesting and diverse natural environments in early childhood and school settings is good for young children's physical, social, emotional, mental and spiritual health and development (Maller 2007; Bell & Dyment 2008). Some of the key findings from the literature are summarised in the following subsections. Research has found that contact with nature positively impacts blood pressure, cholesterol, outlook on life and reactions to stress (Maller et al. 2005), directly affecting the pathways to some of the main causes of the global burden of disease, namely cardiovascular and mental health conditions. Therefore, positive interactions with nature are likely to be more and more important in coming years, particularly for children.

The physical characteristics and quality of the environment make a difference to its effects. For example, a study of more than 4000 children in 21 Brisbane (Australian) primary schools found that 'the most active playgrounds with the happiest children were those containing the greatest variety of play areas' (Evans 1998, p. 15, cited in Bell & Dyment 2008, p. 83). Studies in Scandinavia have identified that the size, types and diversity of vegetation, the proximity of trees and shrubs to play structures, the complexity of the environment of preschool landscapes and the opportunities for play afforded by them influence physical activity, motor development and play activities (Fjortoft 2004 and Boldemann et al. 2006, cited in Bell & Dyment 2008). The types of play in which children are able to engage influence social, emotional and mental health outcomes, as well as physical health.

Promoting physical activity, healthy weight and nutrition

Many of our contemporary environments have become 'obesogenic', promoting sedentary lifestyles and over-consumption of food, often highly processed and high in fats and sugars. The rising incidence of childhood obesity, with its physical and social health impacts, makes it important for schools and early childhood settings to support healthy eating and physical activity.

'Greening' school grounds and early childhood environments to provide more 'walkable' and 'playable' environments (Bell & Dyment 2008), grounds with diverse landscape features, and those that create opportunities for boys and girls of all ages, interests and abilities have been found to best support physical activity. Particularly valuable in encouraging moderate and light levels of physical activity are environments that support a range of enjoyable, non-competitive forms of play (Bell & Dyment 2008). Many schools are now finding that, on top of physical activity benefits, participation in edible or kitchen gardening provides opportunities to promote better student nutrition, and has social and emotional benefits (Yeatman et al. 2013). It can also be an engaging first step towards whole-school sustainability.

Social, emotional, mental and spiritual health

While promoting physical activity is vital, playgrounds and environments that provide only *conventional* opportunities for active physical play and sports have been shown to promote social hierarchies, favouring the physically competent but excluding those less physically able or inclined (Bell & Dyment 2008). Children who prefer to play in smaller groups, who have physical constraints or additional needs or are interested in more imaginative or creative play are not well catered for in such grounds.

Figure 8.3 *School community garden at Ashgrove State School, Brisbane*

Limited or boring play environments can lead to frustration and increase aggression. Rather than taking a regulatory approach, creating more interesting, greener grounds can satisfy the needs of a larger variety of students and provide alternative ways to deal with aggression. Studies of 'greened' schools in the United States (California) and Canada found that despite there being fewer opportunities for organised play, there was more free, active, creative, constructive, social and exploratory play compared with the original, less green playgrounds. There was less aggressive play; students were more civil and communicated more effectively. There were fewer discipline problems, and the social climate became more inclusive in terms of gender, class, race and ability (Bell & Dyment 2008; Charles & Senauer Loge 2012).

School community gardens

Gardening activities seem particularly beneficial in promoting positive relations among students, staff and parents. These relationships can be a key element in establishing a healthy school culture or ethos. An HPS – or HPEC – environment would involve children in all stages of these activities, from planning and design to implementation and maintenance. Active involvement is increasingly being recognised as having dramatic benefits for children, who develop important social and life skills, such as teamwork, cooperation and persistence through working together towards a common goal. Such skills are urgently needed for addressing the social and ecological challenges that confront humanity on a global scale.

Greening, gardening and food-growing initiatives also provide excellent opportunities to invite parents and community to become actively involved in the school and to contribute towards the wellbeing of children and the healthy life of the community. The social benefits then extend beyond the immediate childhood setting and influence the social and emotional health of the broader community.

As Sue Elliott indicates in Chapter 2, a growing body of literature attests to the therapeutic role of nature for mental health and stress relief. Stress and stressful events can impair children's disposition for learning, cause anxiety and compromise self-esteem. The stress-reducing effects of exposure to the natural environment, particularly 'hands-on' contact, enhances children's ability to learn and to work with others, increases self-confidence and caring for living things, and creates a more positive attitude towards school and better relationships with peers and adults (Maller et al. 2005; Dillon 2011; Charles & Senauer Loge 2012). These are all important aspects of the educational setting's ethos or social environment – a key component of the HPS approach.

Being able to make decisions and have some control over one's life circumstances is especially important for mental health. Self-determination is associated with psychological wellbeing. This is particularly important for children living with disadvantage or disability. The literature demonstrates that children's participation offers significant benefits for children and communities, especially those experiencing social disadvantage (Hoffmann-Ekstein et al. 2008). Inclusive, participative, health-promoting and greening activities can reduce social exclusion. Maller (2007) found that gardening and greening activities that resulted in tangible changes provided opportunities for all participants to feel good about their accomplishments, and led to a sense of pride, responsibility and self-confidence. These outcomes are especially important for those children who experience few academic or social successes. Interestingly, for children with behavioural problems and non-academic learning styles there were often improvements in overall school performance (Maller et al. 2005; Dillon 2011).

Health benefits may also be related to a spiritual connection with the world, a sense of meaning and purpose to existence. (In Chapter 6, Melinda Miller discusses spirituality in the context of Indigenous Australians' connectedness to country.) Spiritual connectedness includes having a worldview or belief system that provides an ethical path to personal fulfilment, connectedness with self, others and a larger reality. Bell and Dyment (2008) found that as environmental awareness and stewardship increase through involvement in school or community greening activities, students' sense of hope and commitment to the school and to the living world around them also grows. Students' full involvement in the greening process enhanced their skills related to democracy, participation and citizenship, which could be carried into adulthood (Dyment 2004 and Hart 1997, cited in Bell & Dyment 2008, p. 85).

Thus, the research highlights the pivotal role that schools and early childhood education settings can play in providing children with access to nature, and in developing their sense of place in, and connection to, the natural, spiritual and social spheres. Especially critical is their role in nurturing young children's growing autonomy and competence to make a difference for the better. Health professionals, too, must consciously integrate connectedness to nature into public health strategies, including those focused on early childhood. Such approaches not only promote healthy children, but also may nurture family and community resilience and help activate the cultural changes necessary for healthy, sustainable futures.

Provocation 8.4

What effects, positive or negative, have your experiences of the natural environment had on your physical, mental and spiritual health, your sense of self, your connectedness to others and to the world around you?

How might you be able to utilise the natural environment to enhance the learning of young children who have additional social, emotional, physical or economic needs?

Integrating health promotion and EfS

By now you will have noted that educating for health and EfS both involve acknowledging our dependence on the natural world for our material and health needs (for example, air, water, food and shelter). Further, both promote critical thinking, use holistic, whole-of-setting approaches, and seek the active participation of children, parents and community. Both are student-centred and action-oriented to address health and environmental issues of importance to the children in their local settings. Many initiatives designed with health goals in mind also meet EfS goals – for example, the creation of 'green' outdoor spaces and enhanced contact with nature (seen primarily as environmental issues) – that also provide for physical activity and promote mental and social health (seen primarily as health issues) (Davis & Cooke 2007). HPS and EfS are natural partners and mutually reinforcing concepts.

As the research increasingly shows, 'green' *is* healthy, and EfS's explicit focus on the environment increases the salience of health promotion and health education in schools and early childhood settings. Institutions and groups following HPS and HPEC principles value and develop their school grounds for health and learning. When thoughtfully designed, 'green' school grounds were found to be integral to holistic approaches in promoting health in schools (Bell & Dyment 2008, p. 79). EfS and the HPS concept provide processes that go directly to the heart of many of today's student anxieties about the world and their future in it. Given the impact of the early years on lifelong development and health, an integrated foundation of health promotion *and* EfS in early childhood is especially valuable.

'It takes a village to raise a child' – towards integrated child development systems

In today's busy lives, families increasingly seek 'joined-up' solutions to their young children's needs. 'One-stop' access to early childhood education, care and health services is highly desired, and the evidence is growing that integrated responses best meet young children's needs (Miller & Spooner 2004; AIHW 2011). Policy experts recommend we more closely integrate childcare, early learning principles and practice, child protection and child and family health systems to strengthen our early childhood development system (Eckersley 2008; Muir et al. 2010; Queensland Government 2013).

As argued in this chapter, the evidence is clear that effective multidisciplinary approaches are child and family centred, health promoting, participatory and empowering of children and families. The research referred to in this chapter also provides good reasons to design children's health and educational settings to explicitly include experiences with the natural environment, and to support and encourage EfS for healthy child development. I contend that professionals in these fields should find more ways to work and learn together, since it takes a broad range of skills and partnerships across disciplines to meet the complex needs of young children and their families, and to promote all-round human and ecological health.

Child-friendly cities and transition towns

As indicated in Chapter 1, the United Nations predicts that by the year 2025, 60 per cent of children in the developing world will live in cities, and half of these will be poor. The end of cheap energy for transport will increase pressure for the relocalisation of community life, service provision and governance. Cities and their local institutions, including schools and early childhood services, may need to take on greater responsibilities for children, families and communities, including working with them to find solutions to major issues, such as poverty and food security. Health-promoting setting (HPS and HPEC) and EfS processes can contribute to these transitions.

Taking the concept of the village raising children somewhat further, the United Nations Child Friendly Cities Initiative (CFCI) is another holistic, settings-based approach to improving the lives of children and young people. Launched in 1996, the CFCI is based on the premise that the wellbeing of children is the ultimate indicator of a healthy habitat and a democratic society. A child-friendly city is a local system of good governance, committed to fulfilling children's rights and to hearing children's voices. The needs, priorities and rights of children should be an integral part of public policies, programs and decisions. In the nine-step process of becoming a Child Friendly City (CFC), a city becomes 'fit for all' (UNICEF n.d.; and see www.childfriendlycities.org). As Malone (2009) says:

> Ideally, towns and cities should be the site where children socialise, observe and learn how society functions. They should also be places where children can find refuge, discover nature and find tolerant and caring adults who will encourage them to explore and wonder about their world (para. 1).

CFC programs around the world are promoting children's active inquiry into their local environments and are developing their democratic citizenship skills through active participation in decision making and changes that help planners design 'the city they want'. They are helping to shape their local environments to make cities and localities child-friendly. The characteristics of CFC make cities happier, healthier, more liveable places for people of all ages, not just children. They are also cities much better prepared for a carbon-constrained future, preparing children for healthy, just and sustainable lifestyles. Such approaches are effective in a range of settings across urban, rural and remote environments and communities and must not be limited to cities.

A newer evolution of the city/town/community-focused approach is the emerging Transition Town (TT) movement (see, for example, www.transitionnetwork.org). Founded in 2008 by permaculture teacher Rob Hopkins, the TT movement is a practical, positive, even visionary response by ordinary people in local communities to today's challenges of climate change, peak oil and over-consumption. While not *explicitly* child-centred, in fact children are at the heart of the movement. TT initiatives attract people of all ages who are concerned about the world that current generations are creating for future generations. People embarking on TT initiatives empower themselves, each other and their children to build resilient local communities that live lives that are economically, ecologically, culturally and socially sustainable, and richly meaningful. This joyful, exciting and relatively young movement shares many characteristics with the other approaches described in this chapter. Growing fast, the TT movement has established itself in hundreds of localities worldwide, which are 'taking … steps towards making a nourishing and abundant future a reality' (Hopkins 2009, p. 5). The underlying principles of the TT initiative, like those of CFC, HPS, HPEC and EfS, can be applied at many different scales, from home to early learning centre, to community, city and beyond.

CFC and TT processes, like those of HPS, HPEC and EfS, are all providing essential and empowering lessons for life, including how to – individually and collectively – imagine, plan for and take action towards healthier, more sustainable ways of living, now and into the future.

Conclusion

Education and care from early childhood to young adulthood and beyond can and should be positive contributors to sustainability and holistic health, rather than social forces that perpetuate unhealthy and unsustainable ways of living (Davis & Cooke 2007). The evidence is clear that integrated, holistic approaches to children's multi-dimensional health and wellbeing are best – not only for individual children but also for families and communities. Early childhood professionals working in partnership with children, parents and communities can create environments in which children develop and flourish.

Child-centred change movements – such as ECEfS, HPS, HPEC, CFC and TT – are already actively involving children and their families in creating environments that are greener, healthier, fairer and happier. Approaches such as these have the potential to engage children, families and communities in changing society's direction. I assert that what is most important about all these movements is that they empower children and adults alike to examine and to change their current situations in meaningful, ethical ways. Such processes nurture hope and build resilience in individuals and communities. In this chapter I show that together, children, parents, carers, health professionals and teachers in schools and early childhood settings can help lead the way to green, just and healthy futures.

Review provocations

1. How might your early childhood practices support parents' engagement and partnership in the life of the early childhood setting and the broader community?
2. What learning activities can you envisage that might involve partnerships between early childhood services and child health and wellbeing professionals?
3. Consider the effects of your experiences of the natural environment on your physical, mental and spiritual health, your sense of self, your connectedness to people and the world around you. How might these experiences impact on your role as a professional working with a diverse range of young children?

References

Australian Government, Department of Health (n.d.). KidsMatter, www.kidsmatter.edu.au/primary; MindMatters, www.mindmatters.edu.au; KidsMatter Early Childhood, www.kidsmatter.edu.au/early-childhood (all accessed 1 May 2014).

Australian Institute of Health and Welfare (AIHW) (2011). *National Outcome Measures for Early Childhood Development*. cat. no. PHE 134. Canberra: AIHW.

Australian Institute of Health and Welfare (AIHW) (2012). *A Picture of Australia's Children 2012*. cat. no. PHE 167. Canberra: AIHW.

Australian Research Alliance for Children and Youth (ARACY) (2013). *Report Card: The Wellbeing of Young Australians*, www.aracy.org.au/documents/item/126 (accessed 27 February 2014).

Bell, A. C. & Dyment, J. E. (2008). Grounds for health: The intersection of green school grounds and health-promoting schools. *Environmental Education Research*, 14(1), 77–90.

Charles, C. & Senauer Loge, A. (2012). *Health Benefits to Children from Contact with the Outdoors and Nature*. Annotated bibliography prepared for Children and Nature Network, www.childrenandnature.org/downloads/CNNHealthBenefits2012.pdf (accessed 10 March 2014).

Climate and Health Alliance (2013). *Forum on Climate and Health: The Research, Policy and Advocacy* Agenda, http://caha.org.au/wp-content/uploads/2010/01/Report-CAHA-Forum-on-Research-Policy-Advocacy-061113_Final.pdf (accessed 27 February 2014).

Cooke, S. M., Davis, J. M., Blashki, G. A. & Best, A. F. (2011). Healthy children and a healthy planet: A role for education. In E. Bell, B. M. Seidel & J. Merrick (eds), *Climate Change and Rural Child Health*. New York: Nova Science Publishers.

Costello, A., Abbas, M., Allen, A., Bell, S., Bellamy, R. et al. (2009). Managing the health effects of climate change. *Lancet*, 373(9767), 1693–733.

Davis, J. M. & Cooke, S. M. (2007). Educating for a healthy, sustainable world: An argument for integrating Health Promoting Schools and Sustainable Schools. *Health Promotion International*, 22(4), 346–53.

de Plater, L. (2008). Sowing the SEEDS of healthy social and emotional wellbeing. *Auseinetter*, 31(2), 28–30.

Dillon, J. (2011) *Understanding the Diverse Benefits of Learning in Natural Environments*. London: Kings College, www.naturalengland.org.uk/Images/KCL-LINE-benefits_tcm6-31078.pdf (accessed 3 March 2014).

Eckersley, R. (2008). *Never Better – or Getting Worse? The Health and Wellbeing of Young Australians*. Canberra: Australia 21 Limited.

Eckersley, R. (2011). A new narrative of young people's health and wellbeing. *Journal of Youth Studies*, 14(5), 627–38.

Farrant, B., Armstrong, F. & Albrecht, G. (2012). Future under threat: Climate change and child-ren's health. *The Conversation* (9 October), www.theconversation.com/future-under-threat-climate-change-and-childrens-health 9750 (accessed 5 February 2014).

Fritze, J. G., Blashki, G. A., Burke, S. & Wiseman, J. (2008). Hope, despair and transformation: Climate change and the promotion of mental health and wellbeing. *International Journal of Mental Health Systems*, 2(13).

Griggs, D., Stafford-Smith, M., Gaffney, O., Rockstrom, J., Ohman Priya Shyamsundar, M. C. et al. (2013). Policy: Sustainable development goals for people and planet. *Nature*, 495, 305–7.

Hansen, J., Kharecha, P., Sato, M., Masson-Delmotte, V., Ackerman, F. et al. (2013). Assessing 'dangerous climate change': Required reduction of carbon emissions to protect young people, future generations and nature, www.columbia.edu/~jeh1/mailings/2013/20131202_PopularSciencePlosOneE.pdf (accessed 28 February 2014).

Hoffmann-Ekstein, J., Michaux, A., Bessell, S., Mason, J., Watson, E. & Fox, M. (2008). *Children's Agency in Communities: A Review of Literature and the Policy and Practice Context*. ARACY/ARC NHMRC Research Network Seed Funded Collaboration. Sydney: The Benevolent Society.

Hopkins, R. (2009). *The Transition Handbook: Creating Local Sustainable Communities Beyond Oil Dependency*. Lane Cove, NSW: Finch Publishing.

Jensen, B. B. (2002). Knowledge, action and pro-environmental behaviour. *Environmental Education Research*, 8(3), 325–34.

Keating, D. P. & Hertzman, C. (eds) (1999). *Developmental Health and the Wealth of Nations*. New York: The Guilford Press.

Kuo, F. E. (2010). *Parks and Other Green Environments: Essential Components of a Healthy Human Habitat*. National Recreations and Parks Association Research Series 2010. Ashburn, VA.

McDermott, B. & Cobham, C. (2012). *A Road Less Travelled: A Guide to Children, Emotions and Disasters*. Brisbane: TFD Publishing.

Maller, C. J. (2007). Hands-on contact with nature and children's mental, emotional, and social health. PhD thesis summary report, School of Health and Social Development, Deakin University, Melbourne.

Maller, C., Townsend, M., Pryor, A., Brown, P. & St Leger, L. (2005). Healthy nature healthy people: 'Contact with nature' as an upstream health promotion intervention for populations. *Health Promotion International*, 21(1), 45–54.

Malone, K. (2009). Designs for a child-friendly city. *Curriculum Leadership*, 7(2).

Miller, M. & Spooner, C. (2004). *A Head Start for Australia: An Early Years Framework*. Surry Hills & Brisbane: New South Wales Commission for Children and Young People and Commission for Children and Young People Queensland.

Muir, K., Katz, I., Edwards, B., Gray, M., Wise, S. & Hayes, A. (2010). *The National Evaluation of the Communities for Children Initiative*, www.aifs.gov.au/institute/pubs/fm2010/fm84/fm84d.pdf (accessed 1 January 2014).

National Foundation for Educational Research & Thomas Coram Research Unit (2004). *Evaluation of the Impact of the National Healthy Schools Standard*. London: Department of Health and Department of Education and Skills.

Olshansky, S. J., Passaro, D. J., Hershow, R. C., Layden, J., Carnes, B. A. et al. (2005). A potential decline in life expectancy in the United States in the 21st century. *New England Journal of Medicine*, 352, 1138–45.

Poland, B., Dooris, M. & Haluza-Delay, R. (2011). Securing 'supportive environments' for health in the face of ecosystem collapse: Meeting the triple threat with a sociology of creative trans-formation. *Health Promotion International*, 26(S2), ii202–15.

Queensland Government (2013). *Evaluation of the Early Years Centre Initiative: Summary Report*. Brisbane: Queensland Government.

Queensland Health (2002). *A Strategic Policy Framework for Children's and Young People's Health 2002–2007*. Brisbane: Goprint.

Queensland Health (2006). *Promoting Health in Early Childhood Environments Project 2002–2005: Evaluation Report.* Brisbane: Queensland Health.

Queensland Health (2008). *Healthy Bodies Healthy Minds* (2nd edn). Brisbane: Goprint.

Robinson G., Silburn S. R. & Arney, F. (2011). *A Population Approach to Early Childhood Services: Implementation for Outcomes.* Topical paper commissioned for the public consultations on the Northern Territory Early Childhood Plan. Darwin: Northern Territory Government.

Self-Brown, S., Anderson, P., Edwards, S. & McGill, T. (2013). Child maltreatment and disaster prevention: A qualitative study of community agency perspectives. *The Western Journal of Emergency Medicine.* 14(4), 401–7.

Seligman, M. E. P., Ernst, R. M., Gillham, J., Revich, K. & Linkins, M. (2009). Positive education: Positive psychology and classroom interventions. *Oxford Review of Education.* 35(3), 293–11.

Shanker, S. (2012a). How can a five-year-old be stressed? *Huffpost Living Canada* (12 July), www.huffingtonpost.ca/stuart-shanker/stress-in-children-research_b_2252749.html (accessed 4 March 2014).

Shanker, S. (2012b). *Report of the 2012 Thinker in Residence: Self-Regulation.* Commissioner for Children and Young People Western Australia.

Shonkoff, J. & Phillips, D. A. (eds) (2000). *From Neurons to Neighbourhoods: The Science of Early Childhood Development.* Washington, DC: National Academy Press.

Sly, P., Hanna, E., Giles-Corti, B., Immig, J. & McMichael, T. (2008). *Environmental Threats to the Health of Children in Australia: The Need for a National Research Agenda.* Canberra: Australian Research Alliance for Children and Youth.

Stewart, D., Sun, J., Patterson, C., Lemerle, K. & Hardie, M. (2004). Promoting and building resilience in primary school communities: Evidence from a comprehensive 'health promoting school' approach. *International Journal of Mental Health Promotion,* 6(3), 26–33.

St Leger, L. (2005). Protocols and guidelines for health promoting schools. *Promotion and Education,* XII, 145–50.

Townsend, M., and Weerasuriya, R. (2010). *Beyond Blue to Green: The Benefits of Contact with Nature for Mental Health and Well-Being.* Melbourne: Beyond Blue Limited.

Tucci, J., Mitchell, J. & Goddard, C. (2007). *Children's Fears, Hopes and Heroes: Modern Childhood in Australia.* Melbourne: Australian Childhood Foundation, and National Research Centre for the Prevention of Child Abuse, Monash University.

UNICEF (n.d.). *Child Friendly Cities,* www.childfriendlycities.org (accessed 2 January 2009).

Vince Whitman, C. & Aldinger, C. E. (eds) (2009). *Case Studies in Global School Health Promotion: From Research to Practice.* New York: Springer.

World Health Organization (WHO) (1986). *Ottawa Charter for Health Promotion.* Geneva: WHO.

World Health Organization (WHO) (2014). Mental health: A state of well-being, www.who.int/features/factfiles/mental_health/en (accessed 1 May 2014).

Yeatman, H., Quinsey, K., Dawber, J., Nielsen, W., Condon-Paoloni, D. et al. (2013). *Stephanie Alexander Kitchen Garden National Program Evaluation: Final Report.* Centre for Health Service Development, Australian Health Services Research Institute, University of Wollongong.

Chapter 9

Food first: Beginning steps towards children's sustainable education

Nadine McCrea

Editor's note

In this new chapter for the second edition, **Nadine McCrea**, a specialist in early childhood food education, advances a strong case for why food should be considered a fundamental aspect of learning in ECEfS. Nadine links ideas about children's health and wellbeing to the broader topic of living sustainably. She discusses the importance of early childhood educators working collaboratively with children and their families to support food learning and food experiences that build engagement with the natural world and understandings of the socio-cultural foundations of food. Nadine emphasises that critical, transformative approaches to early learning about food offer ways for young children to be empowered future decision makers about matters of importance to their lives.

Introduction

Our 'Eureka' moment arrives with this question: can we, will we, start eating as if our world depends on it? ... Many of society's most profound challenges could benefit from a better understanding of our food ways, from how we select it, grow it, distribute it, eat it, and ruminate on it to, ultimately, how we assign meaning to it (Piper 2007, p. viii).

Food as context

Sometimes when I see a raw vegetable, smell the aroma of a particular dish or taste a certain flavour, I am transported back to childhood with my Gram and her kitchen in an old gold-mining house. I can imagine her deep yellow egg noodle dough rolled out to dry on the kitchen table or her annual summer vegie garden. Later professional memories that I also recall fondly link with food-related events, this time with young children. For example, my mid-1970s work in the children's centre at the University of California at Davis was where I designed 'prep-a-food-a-day'. Every day, 2- to 5-year-olds were 'pitching in' to create morning snacks with a university student. Similarly, my early 1980s community kindergarten work in regional Victoria included prep-a-food-a-day with 4-year-olds designing every morning or afternoon tea with the help of a mum.

Provocation 9.1

Foodways may be described as 'everything about eating, including what we consume, how we acquire it, who prepares it and who's at the table ... [it is] a form of communication rich with meaning. Our attitudes, practices and rituals around food are a window onto our most basic beliefs about the world and ourselves' (Harris, Lyon & McLaughlin 2005, pp. xiii–ix). See also Katz, Goodwin and Gussow (1976).

Stop for a minute to recall something about your foodways: what pleasant childhood food memories about people and place come to mind? Then, do some ruminating about how serious and sensitive you are about family food, the food served at your centre, and even food for the world.

This chapter

When I played with words to create the title for this chapter, I wanted to highlight the vital, yet complex, multifaceted nature of food in our lives and the interactions beyond people influencing the Earth. Thus, I juggled phrases and decided on *'food first'* with a child-oriented learning qualifier. The chapter encompasses ideas about young children living and learning authentically with food. With an 'everyday' approach that intertwines wellbeing and food learning, I suggest six steps ('6Ps') that form recursive cycles-of-food (see Figure 9.1 later in this chapter). When actively engaging with cycles-of-food, children can easily and effectively explore realms of sustainability via the '4Es' – 'Education, Ecology, Economics and Equity' (Edwards 2006). The 4Es link with the dimensions of sustainable development identified by Julie Davis in Chapter 1. In the present chapter, ideas about foods and food learning are undeniably connected with the environmental realm, as foods begin in the natural world primarily as domesticated nature. However, food will also be viewed, advocated for and acted upon in terms of its human connectedness, its anthropocentric lens, with the 4Es continually co-mingling. During food *in, about, for and more* food learning, all sustainability realms can be meaningfully embedded (refer to the discussion of environment education approaches in Chapter 1).

Of course, educators and families are essential and significant partners with young children in relation to foods and food learning, and they are key role models for children (McCrea 1984; Moore 1995). Accordingly, it is important to understand why and how educators commit to food education and particularly to food learning that has a transformative and sustainable ethos. Thus, this chapter's food exploration focuses on people and their relationships with each other and with food, alongside intertwining the 4Es for sustainable living. Food learning is approached purposefully, with a critical lens on looking forward with an eco-worldview, on thinking about whole systems and on challenging ourselves to engage in eco-politics (Huckle 2012). Adults are challenged to have young children alongside 'pitching in' as much as possible. We begin with the concept of *food first*.

Provocation 9.2

1. Consider the Introduction above and reflect on your own food encounters over the last couple of years. Which people and what events or factors (media, marketing) have been most influential in shaping your current beliefs about young children's food learning? How much do you reflect an eco-worldview (Webster 2007 in Huckle 2012)?

2. Consider how family, local, cultural and national foodways have changed in the last half-century and explore this with colleagues. For example, read Eric Scholosser's **Fast Food Nation** (2002), Beverley Kingston's **Basket, Bag and Trolley** (1994) or Michael Pollan's **In Defence of Food** (2008).

3. If you have an interest in historical food origins, locate 'The Food Timeline' (available at www.foodtimeline.org) and consider how you might share this with young children.

Food first

Food plays an ordinary yet extraordinary role in our lives; it is part of everyone's daily experiences. *Food first* reflects human closeness to food's basic life-giving role. Here, we explore this familiar everyday object and subject via *food is* . . . and *food as* ... learning in order to set the scene for children's *in, about, for and more* food learning.

Food is ...

When we look at food and deeply wonder about what it *is*, many ideas and issues arise. Human food is not simple or straightforward. Food is our sustenance and what we eat. But, it has complexity too, as at different ages we need or prefer different foods prepared in unique ways. Various ethnic groups and cultures prize particular food items, which they combine and prepare in distinctive ways (Walker 2002). In such a high-tech, industrialised world, foods today vary tremendously, ranging from fresh, raw, simple and wholesome to very hollow-nutrient, highly processed objects. Michael Pollan (2009, p. 7) warned, 'Don't eat anything your great-grandmother wouldn't recognize as food'. Families eat widely varying meals, from fast, fat/sugar-dense foods with little home cooking to kitchen-prepared, family-traditional and cultural dishes, and to high-end restaurant servings. There are many food-related television shows covering every aspect of the edible; such technologically mediated experiences often deeply influence adult and child foodways.

Even with multiple food temptations, people establish fairly stable food habits. Families, early childhood settings and local communities participate in rituals that often include foods (Fernandez-Armesto 2001). Both daily habits and occasional rituals or celebrations can result in children and adults eating either too little (forms of fasting) or too much (over-feasting); both patterns are defined as malnutrition. Malnutrition is a contemporary societal dilemma for families, educational settings, non-government organisations and governments. Globally, varying access to food means there are families with ongoing hunger, those with sufficient food and general wellbeing, and many families that are part of the obesity epidemic affecting both young and old. (Refer to 'World Hunger' on this United Nations website: www.un. org/Pubs/CyberSchoolBus; see also UNICEF & Bernard van Leer Foundation 2006.) Malnutrition, as a two-sided worldwide challenge, is a reality that early childhood educators should face directly. This dilemma represents a key reason for early childhood professionals fully committing to *food first*. (Refer to this website of the Food and Agriculture Organization of the United Nations and its partners: www.feedingminds. org/fmfh.)

Similarly, food is often referred to as a basic need located at the base of Maslow's Hierarchy of Needs (1970, cited in Sims 2011). However, contemporary perspectives about children focus more on upholding rights rather than simply meeting needs. As an example, Sims' (2011, pp. 23–5) concern about deficit views of children, stemming as they do from needs as a starting point, resulted in her reframing Maslow's model into a hierarchy of rights. Similarly, Kent (2001, 1993) commented: 'Goals do not imply rights, but rights do imply goals. Human rights declarations and covenants express global goals ... [such as] no malnutrition' (Kent 2001, p. 15).

At the global level, the United Nations provides international standards or benchmarks for children's rights to both nutrition and education. In this chapter, these two rights are brought together. However, the words *food* and *food learning* have been used, rather than *nutrition* and *nutrition education*. This emphasises whole foods, their combinations as edible dishes, and food as a familiar object and subject. This position contrasts with an all-too-common focus on the unseen bits of food, such as vitamins and minerals or carbohydrates and proteins. Focusing on whole food is sensible and authentic for young children. I maintain that a broad awareness of foods and healthy bodies (McCrea 2006) also works well for educators and parents. As an extension of rights, what seems to be important about our food and eating habits is feeling in control with choices. Having some personal control ought to be underpinned by food mindfulness, which ties with paying attention to our eating manners and meals.

Many plants and animals from around the world are potential human food items; they come from various geographies and climates. Such variety leads to another key aspect of our foodways – acknowledging the sensory aspects of food (Stevenson 2012). We look at, smell, taste, touch and even hear foods, with sensory links being one source of many of our food memories. In fact, the human sense of taste is thought to be more individual rather than being the same for all (Bartoshuk 1993), with flavour awareness and taste preferences being formed very early (Birch 1999). If we slow down when we eat, we really see various colours, feel multiple textures and taste unique flavours. Being mindful can result in deeper awareness, shared enjoyment and even help us actually eat less.

Food can be related to various countries' early childhood education standards. For example, food has direct links with the National Quality Standard (NQS; see Australian Children's Education and Care Quality Authority n.d.) governing early childhood settings, particularly quality areas 'QA2 Children's health and safety' and 'QA5 Relationships with children'. To move these expectations into actions that intersect with sustainable practices, we turn to another Australian example, the New South Wales Early Childhood Environmental Education Network's ECO SMART tool (Gaul, Nippard & Watson 2012). This tool helps educators identify sustainable perspectives across the NQS through Quality Improvement Plans (QIPs). The ECO SMART tool encompasses the usual categories of sustainability, including:

- maximising connections with nature
- promoting holistic wellbeing
- minimising water usage, waste generation and energy use
- encouraging sustainable transport.

The tool links such everyday practices with socio-cultural perspectives that overlay sustainability values for staff and management decisions and development of community partnerships. Quality areas are extended with 'examples of action' that reformulate whole-site responsibilities and practices into 'Biocentric Belonging, Being and Becoming'.

Provocation 9.3

1. How do you define food needs as opposed to food rights? What is ethical eating (see, for example, Singer and Mason's 2006 book **The Ethics of What We Eat**)? How would Early Childhood Australia's Code of Ethics (Early Childhood Australia 2006) or another code (such as New Zealand's, or that of the National Assocation for the Education of Young Children in the United States) extend your thoughts? What other food principles should your workplace, or professional experience site, if you are a student-teacher, embrace?

2. Having read the **food is** ... section of this chapter, now reflect and share: How much do we address food health and safety in unison with meaningful relationships and rights?

Next, we turn to *food as* learning, which reflects the 4Es (Education, Ecology, Economics and Equity; see Edwards 2006), particularly in relation to social issues, media/marketing orientations and political positions.

Food as ...

There are many ways to investigate *food as* ... This phrase relates to food being viewed and described as something 'other than'. Thus, *food as* may have metaphorical meaning (Hartlage 2011). Let's begin with this key term: 'foodways'. In socio-cultural and anthropological research and literature, a 'foodway' broadly is a 'societal patterning of food consumption' (Katz, Goodwin & Gussow 1976, pp. 8–19). Therefore, *food as* reflects much 'more than a source of nutrition' (McCrea 1996, p. 92). Creating dishes and eating meals as social artefacts reflect micro to macro features of people's everyday lives. For example, influences shaping our foodways encompass:

- family backgrounds
- ethnic and cultural rituals
- local and broader community norms
- societal and media role models.

These collective influences may be called children's personal foodscapes (Hansen et al. 2009). If we think of *food as* in terms of how food may be embraced and valued, then we can sensitively identify with food and do so with the 4Es' sustainable intentions.

Food as . . .

- a deep relationship related to self-image
- life abilities involving love and trust
- politics and history
- learning choices, not just dietetics or serving a biological function
- plant or animal origins, not just organisations' goals or normative statements
- everyday aesthetic servings, not just vitamin and mineral checking
- a transforming lifestyle feature rather than intermittent 'diets'

Provocation 9.4

1. In his book **Holy Cows and Hog Heaven** (2004), Joel Salatin recounts telling Michael Pollan that 'we have a policy here of never shipping food more than fifty miles from the farm'. In the Foreword to Salatin's book, Pollan writes: 'I realised then and there that Joel Salatin was a man dead serious about his principles, and that there was no principle as dear to him as local food' (pp. xii–xiii). Does your service or ones that you have visited consider food purchases in terms of the distances they have travelled? If not, how might you raise this issue with work or student colleagues and create relevant 'food mile' actions with children?

2. Think about food wrappings used in shops today. What approach would you take to audit the amount of food packaging brought into an early childhood setting? What active roles can children take on to help reduce a centre's 'in-and-out' packaging?

Children's food learning with educators and families

Food holds a unique place in early childhood curricula. It is a central aspect of emotionally laden family and community living, as well as an object/subject for exciting, authentic learning. The *food is* and *food as* concepts inform educators' and children's joint engagement with the everyday edible along with *in, about, for* and *more* learning. Children can engage in one or more type of learning:

- *in* food learning, by using seasonal vegie planners and potting up seedlings (*in* is about 'being there' – this is Dighe's *love* approach; see Dighe 1993 cited in Davis 1996)

- *about* food learning, by designing plant growth charts, making representational drawings of food preparations or asking questions about the origins of food items (*about* concerns understanding – Dighe's *know* approach)

- *for* food learning, by purchasing more 'natural' items, such as seaweed nutrients for gardening or sharing 4E-linked food-partaking stories with local elder residents (*for* is about democratic action and working collectively – Dighe's *do* approach with a more critical perspective)

- 'doing' *more* (for example, *through* and *with* food) by engaging with food learning from plot to plate, which can be viewed as an embodied lifestyle of learning and understanding with a thoughtful, ethical 'head'; valuing with a caring heart; and acting with cooperative helping hands that extend beyond self and place.

These potentials can be further enhanced when couched within one or more of the 6P steps of a sustainable cycles-of-food framework (see Figure 9.1). We now turn to an exploration of educators' food learning engagement, children's food learning collaboration and families' food learning foundations.

Educators' food learning engagement

Here, early childhood educators are challenged and encouraged to 'spread their wings' and ponder the saying 'variety is the spice of life'! As important learning partners, they guide young children during investigations, explorations, problem solving, communications and meaningful creations. Educators' personal backgrounds and professional principles, with some founded in national and international standards and laws, underpin who they are, as well as why and how they care. Their professional dispositions, beliefs and behaviours guide the educational principles that they embrace and they frame the pedagogical practices they plan, prepare and implement with children. When food learning is the focus, educators' own life experiences and personal food histories will be influential. This means that 'who we are', in terms of understanding and valuing the everyday edible, shapes how educators then professionally view children's food learning opportunities. Committing to and engaging with food learning as part of an everyday and authentic curricula means that educators depend on a deep understanding of this unique form of learning. Therefore, they need to care about food and for food. It is equally important for educators to acknowledge parents, family life and family involvement when encouraging children's diverse food encounters.

Provocation 9.5

1. What do you believe about children's food learning? As examples, do you value sensory awareness, socialness of meals, staff-child collaboration, the idea of the kitchen as the heart of the home, taking turns with culinary tools, and so on? How might you link sustainable food learning with contemporary early child education standards or accreditation documents? (For an example, refer to McCrea 2012.) Chat with colleagues and record these ideas as a food learning action plan.

2. View the film/DVD **Food, Inc** (A Robert Kenner Film, Fortissimofilms, 2009; go to www.takepart.com/foodinc). What feelings and beliefs did this film 'stir' in you? Why? Also, explore the 20-minute animation **The Story of Stuff** (Director: Louis Fox, YouTube clip, 2007; go to http://storyofstuff.org/movies/story-of-stuff/). Focus your viewing on food-related examples that affect young children and link these with wise consumer issues across the 6P steps discussed further below.

3. Reflect on how you might use David Holmgren's 12 permaculture principles as guidelines for a philosophical statement about children's food offerings and food learning (refer to the box that follows).

David Holmgren's 12 permaculture principles

observe and interact	catch and store energy
obtain a yield	apply self-regulation and accept feedback
use and value renewable resources and services	produce no waste
design from patterns to details	integrate rather than segregate
use small and slow solutions	use and value diversity
use edges and value the marginal	creatively use and respond to change

(Source: Holmgren 2002, p. viii)

Children's food learning collaboration

Children can have active engagement with foods, from everyday edible routines to elaborate waste-to-want processes. Here, food learning is explored through a sustainable cycles-of-food framework (see Figure 9.1). This *in, about, for and more* involvement is linked with both children's right to participate or 'pitch in' (Littledyke & McCrea 2009) at early childhood settings or at home and their taking responsibility for aspects of their lives and for the Earth. Years ago I created a food-cycle approach that was gradually reshaped as I shared ideas with professionals (McCrea 1981, 1979). This became a sustainable cycles-of-food framework with 6Ps for children and educators to engage with:

- producing food
- purchasing food
- processing food
- preparing food
- partaking of food
- processing food wastes (McCrea 2007; see also McCrea 1999 and 1994, and Figure 9.1).

My food-related ideas have always reflected natural, organic, biodynamic and/or permaculture principles and practices, with socio-economic and political angles as key considerations. These ideas are framed here with explicit EfS concepts, including children's actions. Let's first turn briefly to a couple of food learning approaches that offer some *in* and *about*, and potential *for*, engagements.

A routines approach

This learning process means that edible encounters happen as daily routines. If morning tea and lunch are children's primary food learning encounters, then it is important that meal-times are calm and shared. This process represents children's eating for wellbeing, with potential for great variety. Separate meals and solitary eating times, often 'standard' for early childhood health, food and nutrition 'education', are viewed as insufficient. The value of a routines approach can be transformed by thoughtful mealtime conversations, with verbal collaborations about 'here and now' sensory food attributes and a focus on everyday events. In support of this practice, Odegaard (2007) explored what is worth talking about during Norwegian teachers' co-narratives with under threes during their meals.

The prep-a-food-a-day approach

This cooperative early learning process involves children in weekly food-related topics (McCrea 1981), with options such as:

1. *One food prepared variously* – for example, a week of celery or soups.

2. *Foods representing a culture* – for example, a week of Asian or Spanish dishes.

3. *Small muscle preparation skills* – for example, a week of dipping, scrubbing, breaking, stirring, pouring, spreading, wrapping, rolling, peeling with fingers, grinding or peeling with peeler.

4. *Food feature concepts* – for example, a week focused on descriptive language. This could include *sensory concepts* – shape, size, colour, taste; *quantities* – few/more and *qualities* – hard/soft, cold/hot; *spatial* positions, directions or distances – in/out, between/beside; *temporal* relationships with time-intervals – now/later/end; and time ordering – first/next/then/before.

Stories from the field

At our service we believe in the process of food from the garden to the table. This includes learning and discovery about how to grow and care for our produce, followed by preparing foods and caring and sharing these experiences. We aim to teach our children about food being sustenance for healthy bodies. Also, we have the view that they can explore food as a sensory experience; one where they can take time to care for produce in an unhurried way.

We see many opportunities as our children become personally involved in the holistic view of growing their own foods. When children have been involved in the process of preparing the earth, planting, tending to plants and watching them grow, adding worm juice that they have been helping worms create from food scraps, and picking and preparing the foods, they develop connections to food. These are connections that link them to their world, their natural environment, a sense of ability and relevant control of a place.

We all know children with particular tastes; the child reluctant to try new foods. The following story tells of a child's discovery of new foods, as he learnt the process of growing, caring for and tasting foods. 'He doesn't eat anything green', said the mother of one of our boys with special rights; and, it was true! He ate yoghurt, Vegemite sandwiches and fruit bars. His mother bravely packed new foods and a piece of fruit each day, which our little mate refused to try even when educators displayed perseverance and creativity in offering this fruit. We started our garden beds that year and all children were involved in preparations. They helped with digging, planting of seeds and seedlings and then the ongoing care of these plants. We watched our little mate eagerly use the watering can each day as he cared for plants. Then one day he was with his peers; some ate parsley and some did not. We watched him take a small sprig and chew it; almost immediately he spat it out and giggled. He repeated this process as he brought over a small piece to an educator, watched her try it and had another little taste himself – again chewing and then spitting it out. Over the course of the next few weeks, he continually tasted small sprigs of parsley. One afternoon as he was leaving the centre with his mother we noticed him picking a bunch of parsley to take home. His mother commented: 'He now eats one thing green'! During the rest of the year we saw our little mate engage in cooking experiences and begin to try new foods; he became a confident parsley eater.

(Source: Jan Carr, Director of Kindamindi Preschool, Inverell, New South Wales)

Jan's story is so typical of food-cycle learning experiences that I undertook with children years ago in California and Victoria. Each year, one or two very picky eaters provided a pedagogical challenge for us. However, our everyday food learning events involving active preparations, peer modelling and everyday tasting always, over time, led to less pickiness! If children grow their own, prepare for others, place new foods with familiar ones, sit communally at the lunch table and view others eating the unfamiliar food, yes, they will most likely become food tasters too (McCrea 2007, 1981; Pecaski McLennan 2010)!

A sustainable cycles-of-food framework

This framework is explored below in terms of values and then practicalities.

Rationale and values

As a core concept for this chapter, the framework shown in Figure 9.1 supports educators' intentional teaching with authentic emergent learning by children aged about 2 or 3 up to 8 years. The framework's 6P steps integrate findings from research related to children's access to nature; curricula actively involving children and supporting wellbeing and health learning; and scientific explorations that touch on attitudes, processes and concepts (Frances 1995).

Working with the 6P steps results in food learning that intertwines whole-language ideas with a range of intelligences and with socio-constructive ways of learning, including eight Aboriginal ways of learning (see http://8ways.wikispaces.com). To effectively engage with sustainable cycles-of-food, it is helpful to consider natural world systems, including water cycles, carbon cycles and waste-generating cycles. There are food chains and food webs to explore as well as nutrient cycling, with these reflecting the life changes of birthing, living and dying. These sustainable cycles-of-food are about everyday life, with mindful eco-caring and a sense of nature-based place being linked with critically thoughtful acts of socio-economic and socio-environmental advocacy (McCrea in Hughes 2007, p. 32).

By engaging in sustainable cycles-of-food, young children can collaboratively take on a multitude of food-related, often seemingly adult-oriented roles, with explicit attention to sustainability angles. Thus, children can 'pitch-in' (Rogoff 2003 in Littledyke & McCrea 2009, p. 44) both indoors and outdoors, with their 'eco-hands'. I suggest that these 'eco-hands' be reconceptualised, similar to Hayward's (2012, pp. 147–51) reimagining of a social handprint used to establish seeds of ecological

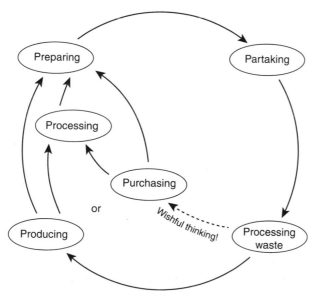

Figure 9.1 *A sustainable cycles-of-food framework for children's learning in, about, for and more via '6P' steps*

The author thanks graphic designer Ivan Thornton from the University of New England for creating this figure.

citizenship for older children. The 6P steps provide recursive and sensory diversity with great potential for meaningful and mindful food engagement (Bays 2009), while also developing a responsible work ethic. The framework is about children exploring foods on a local scale with a sense of place. However, I am not proposing a narrow or parochial position that ignores global food concerns. Educators and children can also 'do' and be global. They may appropriately consider aspects of world food security, such as investigating both socio-political and eco-environmental challenges of balancing cultural, national and global food rights, needs and wants. Such investigation might involve educators and young children in seeking out a local farmer to co-explore geographical, supermarket and customer influences on farming practices, crop selections or distribution channels.

Some writers critically question being local as potentially risky, with the critique ranging from 'defensive localism' to 'diversity receptive localization' (Hinrichs 2003, pp. 36–7, cited in Harris 2010, pp. 361–2). I suggest that the *localvore* concept is relevant for fundamental exploration of such ideas with young children. A *localvore* is a person dedicated to eating foods that are grown and produced locally rather than elsewhere. Identifying with this concept forms a basis for implementing the 6P steps.

Practical learning

For edible learning experiences, plant foods are the suggested focus. If vegetables predominate, all 6P steps can be easily, flexibly and routinely incorporated into everyday curricula. Along with mainly vegies and some fruits, many herbs and spices with some grains or cereals may be added to this food learning mix. Eggs and some dairy products extend the potential repertoire of recipes and tasty dishes. Please note: this is not to suggest that meats or animal by-products be excluded, just that fewer are used so that children's full involvement is maximised. Consideration of vegetarianism and alternative food-eating systems is complex, controversial and beyond the scope of this chapter.

Alongside learning about various food plants and ingredients, three extensions are proposed for the 6P steps:

- engaging with literature (Appleton, McCrea & Patterson 1999; Woodrow & McCrea 2011)

- using lots of everyday questions and storytelling

- facilitating children's meaningful drawing (Brooks 2009).

Questions have many purposes, including 'investigating discovery; eliciting predictions; probing for understanding; promoting reasoning; serving as a catalyst; encouraging creative thinking; and reflecting on feelings' (Harlan & Rivkin 2002 in Littledyke & McCrea 2009, pp. 46, 48–9). There are also many children's books that explore cycles-of-food. These resources and approaches represent ways of creating a place for children's strong food voices. The sharing of books is a key pedagogical tool that helps to introduce, expand and consolidate children's intentional food-related learning.

A kitchen garden to kitchen table plant-food planner (Fanton & Immig 2007) can help guide educators and children through cycles-of-food. A handy planner can detail the following: plans; plots; pace; plants; planting styles; propagating and pampering; picking and pre-preparing; preparing with picto-recipes; presenting table; partaking; re-processing plant pieces as wastes/wants; plant clipboards and portfolios; past-future pondering; and succession planning (McCrea 2008).

From broad planning, we now turn to exploring the practicalities of the 6P steps one by one. Each step is explored via a general description, children's roles, and ways of being multi-sustainable. Educators and children can begin with any of the 6P steps and cycle around or simply engage with individual steps. However, for a recursive, over-time, project approach, educators will usually begin at producing or purchasing.

Producing food

This step engages children with a range of food-producing activities, including:

- creating glass containers that may sprout mung beans, mustard-and-cress seeds, and 10-day microgreens (vegetables harvested at 'first true leaf stage')
- growing herbs in containers
- planting vegetables with edible companion flowers in a garden plot
- keeping watch over a box of rising mushrooms stored in a dark place.

'Cut and come again' gardening with lettuces, silverbeet and the like results in living 'reusable' plants. This P step is about encouraging green thumbs for planting summer and/or winter vegies so that children can produce a variety of edible plant parts for tasting – root, leaf, stem, bark, flower, fruit and seed. Soil is vital (National Wildlife Federation 2012) and how we care for and use it is important. Related tools and containers are significant artefacts for outdoor kitchen gardening.

Within this P step, children can be the edible no-dig gardener, carer of plants, garden tool user, seed saver, bush tucker guardian, organic seedling planter, seasonal crop rotator, weather watcher, mulch spreader, soil steward, climate/temperature change documenter, or harvester. Being sustainable with food producing is about children participating in the nurture of wild-looking and domesticated nature; using drip watering; creating local seasonal food security; acknowledging and incorporating local and Indigenous cultures (Perey & Pike 2011); returning to practical skills that were common in the past; gardening without commercial pesticides/herbicides or artificial fertilisers; and growing extra garden produce for community outreach, neighbourhood engagement and local advocacy.

Purchasing food

This step engages a few children at a time with an educator in buying vegetables from a neighbourhood greengrocer, buying one lamb chop each from the neighbourhood butcher, or being a hunter-gatherer of ethnic/cultural food ingredients from a local delicatessen.

Within this P step, children can be the shopping-list creator, natural fabric shopping-bag maker, wise and competent consumer, shelf selector, label reader, packaging evaluator, finance negotiator/purchaser, or marketing message critic. Being sustainable with food purchasing is about being more aware and sensible; indeed challenging our pervasive consuming lifestyle habits (McCrea 2005; Offer 2012). Such thoughtfulness includes selecting cooking utensils and serving dishes based on their manufactured composition (for example, stainless steel vs aluminium; glass and plastic vs pottery); their potential health risks (for example, plastics and Bisphenol A, or BPA, compounds); and where they are made (local, regional, imported). In particular, it may encompass educator actions for engaging children and families in conversations about mindful food-related shopping; purchasing the most natural, least processed and minimally packaged foods; helping children evaluate television advertisements; and campaigning with families *for* greater wellbeing-friendly food labelling and advertising.

Processing food

This step engages children directly with 'putting by' (that is, conserving or preserving) food through activities such as:

- sun-drying apricot halves
- making mustard pickles from cucumbers
- steaming miniature cloth-wrapped Christmas puddings and Chinese New Year buns
- smoking fish
- drying mushrooms
- curing green and black olives.

Many food processing experiences result in transformed edibles that will keep for some time. They can be shared through gift giving. This P step can be incorporated into the curricula regularly or when making edible items for special events, such as local festivals and neighbourhood cultural celebrations. Within this step, children can be the food processor, edible-gift creator, ritual participant or food-gift giver. Being sustainable with food processing is about children replacing some packaged and travelled foods with community-based, personally hand-prepared tastes that may be eaten sooner or later; and deciding to create foods for personal health and local economic reasons, with cycle-of-food stories shared publicly in a local newspaper or at a community market or fete.

Preparing food

This step engages children in working with a rainbow of raw and some cooked ingredients. They may participate in:

- breaking and cutting vegies for a soup or dip
- spreading mashed banana and grated carrot on multigrain toast
- creating a round vegetable tower with mashed avocado as 'cement' between the layers of vegies.

There is a focus here on working with a varied and balanced array of plant foods each week. It is important to give sensitive attention to incorporating cultural styles, celebration dishes and a range of seasonings. Culinary equipment and utensils, along with using processes of applied science (chemical and physical changes), are central to these socio-physical experiences. Change processes include, if working with raw food, changing a whole food into bits by tearing or cutting; or, if cooking with heat, steaming, baking and sautéing so that children can see food changing from hard to soft. Such processes may be extended when prep-a-food-a-day topics are incorporated. Food preparations can occur in a quiet corner of the playroom or on a verandah. For actively involving children, 'no heat' is suggested for this vegetable- and fruit-focused food making. Picto-recipes (see Figure 9.2) are effective and meaningful taste-making props that children, even as young as age 2, can easily follow, moving left to right along a table with ingredients displayed for combining (Appleton, McCrea & Patterson 1999, pp. 71–106; Woodrow & McCrea 2011). Within this P step, children can be the vegetable scrubber, ingredient combiner, or chef or cook. Being sustainable with food preparing is about children using many seasonal, local and organic foods; considering their serving sizes; reducing food wastes; and helping monitor kitchen energy uses.

Partaking of food

The social potential of food tastings and shared meals is extensive; this goes way beyond the *routines approach* noted earlier. Children can select small nibbles during morning

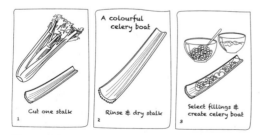

Figure 9.2 *An example of a picto-recipe with a card for each ingredient/preparation step – a colourful celery boat*

The author thanks graphic designer Ivan Thornton from the University of New England for creating this figure.

tea, a smorgasbord self-serve lunch or an intimate mid-afternoon snack. The settings for these tastings could be a home corner table for three, under a tree on a blanket or at a standard playroom table for six. Children can assist with setting tables and creating an aesthetic atmosphere for edible experiences, with attention to pottery containers, glass dishes and woven baskets, instead of the all-too-common plastic dining sets. Children may participate in a clay pottery experience by designing a personal bowl or plate with a local potter, who fires their wares for later use during meals. Within this P step, children can be the table-setter, sensory detective, taster, food appreciator, gourmet or clearer-upper.

Being sustainable with food partaking is about children taking small serves and eating all, rather than wasting; helping separate leftover food scraps; and using 'magic' microfibre cleaning clothes with biodegradable dish-washing soap. This P step is also about educators reducing the number of plastic utensils in the kitchen; scrubbing sinks and surfaces with natural products (such as ground limestone, Eucalyptus oil or vinegar and salt), rather than petrochemical options; and reducing hot water service temperatures to use less gas or electricity, and even installing solar hot water systems.

Processing food wastes

This step engages children in changing 'wastes' from food preparing and partaking experiences into 'wants' or useful by-products that are returned to the producing P step or sent off for community recycling. Children may be engaged in 'trash to treasure' by:

- feeding stale bread to bantam chickens
- layering vegetable and fruit scraps with some black and white newspaper in a worm farm for conversion to worm poo and worm wee garden nutrients
- placing green prunings in a compost bin for future garden compost soil.

Beyond plant materials, this P step is about using fewer 'disposable' containers and, after using them, recycling them. Within this P step, children can be the recycle sorter, garden mapper, ultimate recycler, sweeper not washer, and worm farmer. Being sustainable with food waste processing is about children observing and documenting decaying plant matter becoming reusable compost, mulch or worm by-products; incorporating these by-products into ongoing gardening projects; and encouraging families and community members to recycle and reuse more.

In concluding the 6P steps, educators can create many links from the cycles-of-food framework to professional and government guidelines, various organisational principles, as well as sustainability education resources. The cycles-of-food framework supports children along with adults as interpreters of biophilia to actively move from the important but rather simplistic mantra of reduce, reuse and recycle towards a deeper level of socio-political activity encompassing refuse, reconstruct and redirect (Gough 1997, cited in Feng & Newton 2013, p. 349). This political angle may be shared with families.

Provocation 9.6

Consider the following ethical dilemma using the 4Es. A seed-to-seed cycle involves gardening but raises questions; for example, what will we plant seedlings in? This situation arose at The Point Preschool, in the southern suburbs of Sydney, when egg cartons were to be used (Lee 2012, p. 13). The dilemma raised more questions for staff: What about our sustainable philosophy and practices? How much of a stand will be taken? What kind of cartons will we ask for? In the end, staff wrote: **'Dear families, we will be having a planting activity at our Sustainability Expo and are asking for donations of egg cartons. In keeping with our philosophy of caring for and nurturing all life on our planet, we ask that you only donate cartons that have held free-range chicken eggs.'** This note raises ethical considerations for you: What is your professional feeling about this dilemma? Would you take the same socio-environmental or socio-economic stand? How might you raise such a dilemma with children?

Families' food learning foundations

Educators and families cooperate in many ways to strengthen home action links; some of these can be related to children's food learning. One creative way to encourage local, yet global, advocacy is to identify national and international celebration/advocacy events that link with food and use these for reflective caring for the world and about sustainable practices. There are many such events: Nude Food Day, Food Revolution Day, World Food Day, Clean Up Australia Day, National Tree Day, National Recycling Week, National Dental Health Week, Earth Watch Day, Give Now Week and National Nutrition Week. Local engagement *with* and *for* global issues reflects Amin's 'call for a shift from "... politics *of* place to politics *in* place"' (Amin 2002, cited in Harris 2010, p. 363). Families can display this 'politics *in* place' during celebrations and community gardening, when actions are couched within concepts of public pedagogy and social movement learning (Walter 2012).

Provocation 9.7

Using NQS quality area 'Collaborative partnerships with families and communities' or a similar standard as background, work with families and colleagues to create an eco-calendar (see www.un.org/en/events/observances). Jointly decide which celebrations you will commit to and consider children's involvement and citizenship desires.

Conclusion

Young children may well develop personal food lifestyle repertoires through a sustainable cycles-of-food framework by actively engaging with reciprocal *in, about, for and more* learning. This learning helps lay foundations for values of 'care and conserve' with less 'compete and consume' (Sterling 2003, p. 2). There is a sense of spontaneity – yet considered design – with these kinds of opportunities. They represent a form of kindness and kinship for building equitable and egalitarian principles for people and the Earth. If these ideas are gathered together as a few holistic principles, then early childhood pedagogical leaders have the tools to purposefully engage in and critically reflect on ways to interlink *food first*, the 4Es and cycles-of-food. With professional and international guidelines about leading and managing services holistically, such leaders can reflect further to build on strengths, act responsibly, and continually adjust principles related to slow, mindful foodways with young children.

References

Food

Bartoshuk, L. (1993). The biological basis of food perception and acceptance. *Food Quality and Preference*, 4(1–2), 21–32.

Bays, J. (2009). *Mindful Eating: A Guide to Rediscovering a Healthy and Joyful Relationship with Food*. Boston: Shambhala Publications, Inc.

Dighe, J. (1993). Children and the Earth, *Young Children*, 48(3), 58–63.

Fernandez-Armesto, F. (2001) *Food: A History*. London: Macmillan.

Harris, E. (2010). Eat local? Constructions of place in alternative food politics. *Geography Compass*, 4(4), 355–69.

Harris, P., Lyon, D. and McLaughlin, S. (2005). *The Meaning of Food*. Guilford, CT: The Globe Pequot Press.

Hartlage, C. (2011). We are what we eat. In D. Wright, C. Camden-Pratt & S. Hill (eds) *Social Ecology: Applying Ecological Understandings to Our Lives and Our Planet*. Gloucestershire, UK: Hawthorn Press.

Katz, D., Goodwin, M. & Gussow, J. (1976). *FOOD: Where Nutrition Politics and Culture Meet. An Activities Guide for Teachers*. Washington, DC: Centre for Science in the Public Interest.

Kent, G. (1993). Children's right to adequate nutrition. *International Journal of Children's Rights*, 1(2), 133–54.

Kent, G. (2001). Goals and targets in the realm of nutrition rights. *SCN News – Nutrition Goals and Targets* [United Nations System's Forum on Nutrition; ACC Sub-Committee on Nutrition]. 22, 15–7.

Odegaard, E. (2007). What's up on the teachers' agenda? A study of didactic projects and cultural values in mealtime conversations with very young children. *International Journal of Early Childhood*, 39(2), 45–64.

Offer, A. (2012). Consumption and well-being. In F. Trentmann (ed.), *The History of Consumption*. Oxford: Oxford University Press.

Piper, O. (2007). Foreword. In F. Allhoff and D. Monroe (eds), *Food and Philosophy: Eat, Think and Be Merry*. Malden, MA: Blackwell Publishing.

Pollan, M. (2009). *Food Rules: An Eater's Manual*. Camberwell, Vic.: Penguin Group (Australia).

Stevenson, R. (2012). The role of attention in flavour perception. *Flavour*, 1(2).

Walker, H. (ed.) (2002). *The Meal: Proceedings of the Oxford Symposium on Food and Cookery 2001*. Devon, UK: Prospect Books.

Food learning

Appleton, J., McCrea, N. & Patterson, C. (1999). *There's More to Food than Eating: Food Foundations for Children from Birth to Eight Years*. Castle Hill, NSW: Pademelon Press.

Birch, L. (1999). Development of food preferences. *Annual Review of Nutrition*, 19, 41–62.

Fanton, J. & Immig, J. (2007). *Seed to Seed: Food Gardens in Schools*. Bryon Bay, NSW: The Seed Savers Network.

Frances, M. (1995). Children's garden: Memory and meaning in gardens. *Children's Environments*, 12(2), 1–16.

Hansen, G., Hillen, S., Huotilainen, A., Jensen, T., Johansson, B. & Makela, J. (2009). Nordic children's foodscapes. *Food, Culture and Society*, 12(1), 25–51.

McCrea, N. (1979). *Australian Experiences with Plants and Animals*. Early Childhood Resource Booklet, No. 1, Watson, ACT: AECA.

McCrea, N. (1981). A down-under approach to parent and child food fun. *Childhood Education*, 57(4), 216–22.

McCrea, N. (1984). *Nutrition and Food Education, Community responsibilities during early childhood*. North Carlton, Vic.: Melbourne Lady Gowrie Child Centre.

McCrea, N. (1994). Early Childhood Foodcycle Learning: Revealing food beliefs, happenings and management in three child care centres. PhD thesis, University of Queensland, Brisbane.

McCrea, N. (1996). A sociocultural perspective of foods and food habits – learning beyond nutrition. In NNESP, *Food and Nutrition in Action: Teacher Handbook*. Carlton, Vic.: Curriculum Corp.

McCrea, N. (1999). Approach 3 – Food cycles. In J. Appleton, N. McCrea & C. Patterson. *There's More to Food than Eating: Food Foundations for Children Birth to Eight Years*. Castle Hill, NSW: Pademelon Press.

McCrea, N. (2005). Challenging consuming lifestyles – children being able and active with appetite in Australia. *The Australian Health Consumer*, 2, 9–10.

McCrea, N. (2006). *Everyday Learning about Healthy Bodies*. Watson, ACT: Early Childhood Australia.

McCrea, N. (2007). Food as shared living-and-learning. In B. Neugebauer (ed.), *Child Development II: A Beginnings Workshop Book*. Redmond, WA: Exchange Press, Inc.

McCrea, N. (2008). What are your green educational values? Consider: Children as veggie gardeners. *Every Child*, 14(4), 6–7.

Moore, R. (1995). Children's gardening: First steps towards a sustainable future. *Children's Environments*, 12(2), 66–83.

Pecaski McLennan, D. (2010). 'Ready, Set Grow': Nurturing young children through gardening. *Early Childhood Education Journal*, 37(5), 329–33.

Walter, P. (2012). Theorising community gardens as pedagogical sites in the food movement. *Environmental Education Research*. 1–19.

Woodrow, S. & McCrea, N. (2011). *Eating My Colourful Vegies and Fruit: An Avocado Sampler of Sensory Food Learning Experiences for Children Aged 3 to 5 Years – Educators' Resource Book*. Sydney: Horticulture Australia Ltd & Australian Avocados.

Sustainability and other concepts

Australian Children's Education and Care Quality Authority (n.d.). National Quality Standard, www.acecqa.gov.au/national-quality-framework/the-national-quality-standard (accessed 1 May 2014).

Brooks, M. (2009). Drawing, visualisation and young children's exploration of 'Big Ideas'. *International Journal of Science Education*, 31(3), 319–41.

Davis, J. (1996). Early childhood environmental education. *Educating Young Children: Learning and Teaching in the Early Childhood Years*, 2(4), 38–9.

Early Childhood Australia (2006). *Early Childhood Australia Code of Ethics* (rev. edn), Watson, ACT: Early Childhood Australia.

Edwards, A. (2006). *The Sustainable Revolution: Portrait of a Paradigm Shift*. Gabriola Island, BC: New Society Publishers.

Gaul, J., Nippard, H. & Watson, D. (2012). *ECO SMART for Early Childhood: A Sustainable Filter for Quality Improvement Plans*. Sydney: NSW-ECEEN & NSW Office of Environment and Heritage.

Gough, A. (1997) in Feng, L. & Newton, D. (2012). Some implications for moral education of the Confucian principle of harmony: Learning from sustainability education practice in China. *Journal of Moral Education*, 41(3), 341–51.

Hayward, B. (2012). *Children, Citizenship and Environment: Nurturing a Democratic Imagination in a Changing World*. Milton Park, UK: Routledge.

Holmgren, D. (2002). *Permaculture, Principles and Pathways Beyond Sustainability*. Hepburn, Vic.: Holmgren Design Services.

Huckle, J. (2012). Even more sense and sustainability. *Environmental Education Research*, 18(6), 845–58.

Hughes, M. (2007). *Climbing the Little Green Steps: How to Promote Sustainability within Early Childhood Services in Your Local Area*. Gosford & Wyong, NSW: Gosford City Council & Wyong Shire Council.

Lee, C. (2012). *'Stories from the Heart': Connecting Children and Families with Our Earth*. Deakin West, ACT: Early Childhood Australia.

Littledyke, R. & McCrea, N. (2009). Starting sustainability early: young children exploring people and places. In M. Littledyke, N. Taylor & C. Eames (eds), *Education for Sustainability in the Primary Curriculum: A Guide for Teachers*. Melbourne: Palgrave Macmillan.

McCrea, N. (2012). Sustainable provisions and provocations. In Lee, C., *'Stories from the Heart': Connecting Children and Families with Our Earth*. Deakin West, ACT: Early Childhood Australia.

National Wildlife Federation (2012). *The Dirt on Dirt: How Getting Dirty Outdoors Benefits Kids*. Reston, VA: NWF.

Perey, R. & Pike, R. (2011). *Outline for the Teaching Module Country and Sustainability: Applied Holistic Thinking from an Aboriginal Perspective*. Sydney: ARIES at Macquarie University, http://aries.mq.edu.au/projects/deewr_indigenous_concepts/ARIES_Country&Sustainability_Teaching_Plan.pdf (accessed 1 May 2014).

Sims, M. (2011). *Social Inclusion and the Early Years Learning Framework: A Way of Working*. Castle Hill, NSW: Pademelon Press.

Sterling, S. (2003). Sustainable education – putting relationships back into education, http://ecommunities.tafensw.edu.au/pluginfile.php/12139/mod_page/content/145/Stephen%20Stirling%20article.pdf (accessed 1 May 2014).

UNICEF & Bernard van Leer Foundation (2006). *A Guide to General Comment 7: 'Implementing Child Rights in Early Childhood'*. The Hague, Bernard van Leer Foundation, www.bernardvanleer.org/a_guide_to_general_comment_7_implementing_child_rights_in_early_childhood (accessed 1 May 2014).

Chapter 10

Early learning for sustainability through the arts

Lyndal O'Gorman

Editor's note

In this new chapter for the second edition, **Lyndal O'Gorman** explains how the arts and sustainability can be successfully integrated into early childhood curricula to enrich learning in both areas. She explains that arts experiences are well recognised – for both children and adults – as opportunities that engage learners, build self-concept, and tell stories about social and physical worlds. Lyndal introduces the works of social realist artists such as Picasso, and contemporary artists such as Banksy, Chris Jordan and Andy Goldsworthy, as examples of the arts engaging with universal moral issues such as poverty, war and environmental damage, as well as emphasising the beauty and fragility of the natural world. Lyndal then discusses a drawing project with 5-year-old Ava to exemplify key points about a pedagogical approach that sees this young child draw her natural world on a regular basis and engage in a project about birds. The experiences that Lyndal describes illustrate how bringing the arts and sustainability together for Ava simultaneously develops her artistry and intimately deepens her knowledge of the natural world. Lyndal challenges us to consider how the arts can provide 'ways of seeing' sustainability from new and different perspectives and how the arts might provide adults and children with important ways of making their understandings about sustainability visible to others.

Introduction

This chapter is about how early learning for sustainability can be enhanced through adults' and children's engagement with the arts. The chapter begins with an examination of how, over the centuries, the arts have provided human beings with alternative languages for understanding and expressing big ideas. You will be challenged to think about your personal attitudes to sustainability and to the arts, and you will be encouraged to think in new ways about both by examining how they can come together synergistically. This chapter also includes a detailed example illustrating how young children can use the arts to make their learning about sustainability visible.

Sustainability and the arts – the big picture

The arts, which include visual arts, dance, drama, music and media arts, have provided humanity with diverse means of expression for millennia. The Aboriginal rock carvings of the Burrup Peninsula in Western Australia are some of the oldest know artworks in the world. Possibly more than 30 000 years old, they depict the social world of Indigenous peoples and the animals that connected them to the natural environment many years ago. These artworks continue to speak to us through the passing of centuries, providing a glimpse of important features of Aboriginal lifeworlds. Indigenous cultures, languages and traditions continue to evolve in the present, with contemporary Indigenous Australian artists communicating important aspects of rich and diverse cultures through the arts.

Each strand of the arts is its own language, providing fresh and sometimes challenging ways for people to send and receive universal messages about the world. The arts, for example, have played – and continue to play – a significant role in raising human consciousness about social justice and controversial social issues that include all the themes of sustainability – human, economic, social and environmental (McArdle, Knight & Stratigos 2013; Leavy 2009). Picasso, for example, painted *Guernica* in the 1930s to reveal the horrors of the Spanish Civil War, bringing the impact of war to the world's attention when the painting was taken on a brief world tour. *Guernica* has now become an anti-war symbol and one of Picasso's most famous works, even in recent times packing a 'potent political punch' (Darts 2004, p. 318).

In contemporary times, the work of enigmatic street artist Banksy is another salient example. Banksy uses stencil art to make powerful, satirical statements about Western culture, social justice and politics. He started his work on the streets of London, but now his art can be found in major cities across the world. Some of his most famous works are placed on the West Bank barrier, drawing international attention to the ongoing conflict in Israel and Palestine. Other works by this artist address majority world poverty, consumerism, war and popular culture.

Provocation 10.1

Spend a few moments searching online for the many easily accessible examples of Banksy's stencilled street art. As you browse the images, consider how Banksy has used art to challenge his audience about culture, social justice, politics and other themes. Which of his images amuse you? Which of them confront you? Identify one image that you find particularly powerful. What is it about this picture that 'paints a thousand words' for you?

More recently, children's artwork has entered the domain of politics. In February 2013, Australian Senator Sarah Hanson-Young released to the media and tabled in parliament a collection of images drawn by children in immigration detention on Manus Island, Papua New Guinea. The powerful visual imagery of children and families behind bars as they sought asylum in Australia created significant media attention. In 2014, drawings by children in detention were again used to raise awareness of Australia's policy of detaining children in offshore processing centres. One collection of images was used to create a television advertisement (see http://outof sight.org.au/).

Provocation 10.2

What do you think it is about the artworks of the asylum seeker and refugee children that conveys their messages so powerfully? Do you think there are any ethical implications of using children's artwork in this way?

You can read more about these incidents by accessing Bianca Hall's (2013) and Sophie Peer's (2014) online articles (see references list).

People have been interested in the views of children with regard to sustainability and the environment for some time. In 1992, Lannis Temple documented the writings and drawings of children from every continent except Antarctica in his collection *Where Would We Sleep? Children and the Environment*. For this book, children aged 5–14 years, from a diverse range of cultural, socio-economic and geographical backgrounds, were asked to write and draw a message to the world. Their drawings depicted children's special places, their concerns about the destruction of the natural environment and about pollution, and their hopes for a more environmentally sensitive and sustainable future. More than 20 years later, we might ask ourselves how far we've come.

When children use the arts to communicate their thoughts, they sometimes do so in unexpected ways. McArdle and Spina (2007) worked with refugee children in urban Brisbane, Queensland, to explore the ways in which the arts might provide children with opportunities to engage with learning, build self-concept and tell the stories of their experiences as recent arrivals in Australia. Rather than depicting stories of war and trauma, the children became engrossed in the arts materials and processes, creating self-portraits full of colour, life and the depiction of their current social circumstances – friendships, teachers, and hopes for the future. The arts provide children with languages to tell their own stories rather than stories that adults might predict that they will tell.

In addition to these examples of the ways in which the arts help us to connect with social issues, artists across the world are increasingly using the arts to explore themes specifically relating to the environment and sustainability (Curtis, Reid & Ballard 2012; Steiner 2007; Young 2012). The arts hold the potential to encourage transformational approaches to sustainability, as they can enable people to see the world differently and challenge us to enact change at a personal and community level. The old adage 'a picture paints a thousand words' acknowledges the ways in which the arts cross boundaries of culture, language, age, geography and time to speak of the human, and natural, condition.

Chris Jordan, for example, is an artist from the United States who uses his large-scale works to address issues of social, economic and environmental sustainability. One of his images, *Stone of the Sun* (2011), depicts 92 500 agricultural plant seeds, equal to one hundredth of 1 per cent of the number of people in the world today who suffer from malnutrition. To illustrate the entire statistic with 925 million seeds would require 10 000 prints of this image, covering more than eight football fields. Chris Jordan's piece *Plastic Cups* (2008) is another example of how visual imagery can drive home the message of (un)sustainability. *Plastic Cups* portrays 1 million plastic cups, the number used on airline flights in the United States every six hours.

Jordan's more recent work confronts the viewer with the horror of marine debris and unsustainable use of plastics. *Midway: Message from the Gyre* (2009 to present) is a collection of photographs of dead albatross chicks on Midway Atoll, more than 3000 kilometres from the nearest continent. Parent birds feed their young on pieces of plastic from huge floating garbage patches polluting the ocean, mistaking the plastic for fish. In Chris Jordan's photographs, humans' impacts on nature are brought to our attention, vividly alerting us to a tragedy usually played out in places far removed from our consciousness.

Provocation 10.3

The work of artists such as Chris Jordan helps us to understand the scale of environmental and sustainability problems, such as world poverty and marine debris. Hearing or reading the statistic that 925 million people in the world suffer from malnutrition is incomprehensible to most of us, but seeing this statistic illustrated visually can help us go some way towards understanding the extent of the problem. Hearing that seabirds are feeding plastic debris to their young is one thing, but seeing the terrible images of dead baby albatross with stomachs full of plastic forces us to confront an uncomfortable reality. But do you think it would be appropriate to show these confronting images to young children? Why or why not?

Visit Chris Jordan's website (www.chrisjordan.com) to explore his collection of images that investigate themes relating to sustainability. Listen to his TED talk (www.ted.com/talks/chris_jordan_pictures_some_shocking_stats.html) to learn more about why he uses his art to highlight the problems facing the world as a result of mass consumption and overuse of resources.

The arts also help us to celebrate the beauty of the natural world. Scottish artist Andy Goldsworthy is internationally recognised for his ephemeral artworks celebrating both the splendour and destructive capacity of the natural environment. Goldsworthy uses found materials – such as sticks, stones, flowers, icicles and shells – to make *in situ* installations that are then photographed and left to return to the earth, stream or ocean. These works draw our attention to both the beauty and the harsh realities of the natural world around us, and remind us that we, too, will one day return to the earth.

The examples described in this section promote strong connections between the arts and sustainability. All strands of the arts – visual arts, music, dance, drama and media arts – have this potential to powerfully explore social, political and environmental sustainability, connecting us with these ideas deeply, and beyond words. Traditionally, issues associated with sustainability have been tackled within the domains of science and geography. The arts can help us to access complex concerns and messages about the environment and sustainability by connecting we humans at an emotional level as well as intellectually, something that approaches grounded in the sciences generally don't do very effectively.

Start with yourself – what are your attitudes to the arts and sustainability?

If we are to consider the place of the arts and EfS in early childhood education programs, and how they can work together in transformational ways, it is important to consider our own attitudes to both fields. In my work with pre-service early childhood teachers, one of my goals is for teachers entering the profession to take with them a commitment to high-quality arts learning experiences for young children and to transformational approaches to ECEfS. This, sometimes, means that pre-service teachers are required to confront their own preconceived ideas and patterns of behaviour in relation to the arts, and to address their understandings of what is meant by personal sustainability. I have found that the first step – of examining personal attitudes – can be the most critical, with powerful implications for students' future roles as early childhood professionals.

It is well documented that generalist teachers often enter the profession with feelings of anxiety and apprehension about art teaching (Russell-Bowie 2012). If teachers have low confidence in their own artistry, they are likely, also, to have low confidence in their capacity to teach art to young children (Duncum 1999). The arts are often marginalised in crowded school and early childhood curricula, while traditional subjects, such as literacy and numeracy, are privileged (McArdle & Boldt 2013). The combination of low teacher confidence and pressure to focus on 'the basics' means that children may be spending less and less time on the arts during their schooling and preschooling, the arts being relegated to out-of-school hours, in classes that are available only to those who can afford them (McArdle 2008). This means that children are being offered fewer and fewer opportunities to interpret the world through an arts lens and to use the languages of the arts to express their perspectives about the world.

Pre-service teacher education has an important role to play in preparing early childhood teachers to be effective and confident teachers of the arts. Miller, Nicholas and Lambeth (2008) underscore the importance of personal and emotional engagement with the arts as a way of increasing confidence and helping beginning teachers to see the value of arts-based approaches in early childhood education. I teach arts units in both undergraduate (four-year) and graduate entry (two-year) pre-service teacher education programs in Queensland, Australia. In a number of our arts units, I require students to draw every day for 20 days as part of their assessment, and to use their developing skills to create a significant artwork over time. Students often tell me that this applied and regular engagement with the artistic process helps them to enhance their artistic skills, see the world in new ways, see themselves differently, and to transform their attitudes to the arts and arts pedagogy. While these pre-service teachers can choose to draw any subject in their daily drawings, I encourage them to make links with environmental sustainability. When students complete their daily drawing task, they frequently describe how this process has also assisted them to see the natural world differently. Learning to *draw* is as much about learning to *see*. It is very common for students to tell me that they will 'never look at a leaf or a flower the same way again' because drawing the leaf or flower caused them to attend closely to lines, patterns, colours and shapes and, therefore, to see these natural objects in new ways.

I also promote daily drawing as a strategy for teachers to use with young children. It is common for pre-service teachers to return from their field-based experiences in schools and early childhood centres describing the successful implementation of a daily drawing program in their particular early childhood context. Success and confidence in the arts at a personal level has the potential to lead to increased confidence in arts teaching.

Provocation 10.4

How confident do you feel about the arts? Think specifically for a moment about how confident you feel with drawing. If you had to give yourself a score out of 10 for 'drawing confidence', what would you score?

Challenge yourself to draw every day for at least 20 days, for as little as 5–10 minutes each time. Consider drawing subject matter from the natural environment – leaves, flowers, animals, clouds. Consider also including themes of social justice in your drawings. How might you communicate your thoughts in images rather than words? As you draw these things, think about how the time you are spending drawing them might be enabling you to think about social justice and the environment in new ways.

Personal attitudes and values towards sustainability have a similarly powerful influence on teachers' approaches to EfS in early childhood contexts (Ferreira & Davis 2010). If teachers understand that sustainability is an immediate global imperative and that local and personal actions can make a difference, they are likely to ensure that EfS is a core component of their early childhood programs.

When I explore with my pre-service teachers the works of artists such as Banksy, Chris Jordan and Andy Goldsworthy, they are introduced to social, economic and environmental sustainability themes through visual languages. For many pre-service teachers, this is the first time they have experienced the potential of the arts to express powerful ideas in ways that go beyond the written and spoken word. Another way to introduce people, whether they are pre-service teachers, in-service teachers, parents or the broader community, to the importance of personal sustainability is through the use of Ecological Footprint Calculators (EFCs). EFCs can be applied to assist individuals and institutions, such as schools and universities, to connect their sustainability practices with associated impacts, identify the sources of their greatest impacts, adopt more sustainable habits, and implement effective mitigation and education measures (Barrett et al. 2004; Chesterman 2008; Cordero, Todd & Abellera 2008; Flint 2001).

At the individual level, ecological footprints are usually translated into the number of 'Earths' required to maintain an individual's lifestyle. For instance, the ecological footprint of people living in Australia averages four, meaning that four Earths would be required to sustain Australian consumption at the present level (Environmental Protection Agency Victoria 2005). As there is only one Earth, this is clearly unsustainable as people living in other parts of the world, and future generations, should also be able to access an equitable share of the world's resources. Something has to change.

In my work with pre-service early childhood teachers, I encourage students to complete an online EFC. This typically prompts powerful reactions and reflections about what causes large 'footprints'. O'Gorman and Davis' (2013) paper outlines these responses in detail. Suffice to say, engagement with EFCs can prompt people to take immediate action to live more sustainably, to advocate for social change and to commit to incorporating sustainability into their early childhood programs upon graduation. A word of caution, though; it is easy to become disheartened when we calculate our ecological footprints. Students used words such as 'disappointed', 'surprised', 'shocked', 'embarrassed' and 'guilty' when they discovered how many Earths it would take if everyone on the planet lived like they did (O'Gorman & Davis 2013). The results of using EFCs are known to trigger feelings of hopelessness and apathy (Kaplan 2000). Responses such as these are not helpful for inspiring early childhood teachers to include sustainability at the heart of their teaching. Hence, I have to ensure that I also focus on remedies, such as inspiring examples, and new approaches to early education that engender positive, transformative and hopeful responses to sustainability issues. The arts can help with this.

Provocation 10.5

How sustainable is your present lifestyle? Is your personal sustainability important to you? Do you think you can make a difference? Enter 'Ecological Footprint Calculator' into your search engine and spend a few minutes engaging with one of the many online tools that are available. Document your reactions to the result you are given. Go back over the tool to work out which areas of your lifestyle are contributing to your footprint. Are there any aspects that you think you can change immediately? Are there some things that you think you could plan to change in the short term? What longer-term actions are necessary?

The arts and sustainability working together in practice

The field of early childhood education has traditionally demonstrated deep interest and strong advocacy for the arts. Art-making, ingenuity, creativity and imagination typically flourish during the early childhood years (Wright 2012). The arts deserve their place in early childhood contexts as fields of knowledge in their own right. They also have the potential to strengthen, and to be strengthened by, other fields of knowledge. Integration of the arts across the curriculum increases the possibilities of cross-curricular learning (Gibson & Ewing 2011) that transcends boundaries and transforms thinking, particularly in relation to social justice (McArdle, Knight & Stratigos 2013) and sustainability. It is possible and indeed important for teachers to find meaningful ways for the arts and EfS to work together.

The arts and sustainability have more in common than might be obvious at first glance. High-quality arts programs provide children with avenues for actively creating their futures through critical thinking, problem solving and openness to change (Wright 2012). High-quality arts programs involve so much more than the all too common provision of colouring and cutting templates that require children to follow adult-provided instructions. Rather, arts programs should engage children in opportunities for collaboration, risk taking, and challenging stereotypical assumptions, thus enabling children to see the world from a range of perspectives (Ewing 2012). Developments in the field of early childhood arts education over the last two decades recognise the importance of children making meaning through art (Wright, 2012). In addition, the relational nature of art-making is emphasised, in which children co-construct their knowledge while working with supportive adults and peers to make their learning visible (Giudici, Rinaldi & Krechevsky 2001). When we start to think about arts programs with these characteristics, the synergies with EfS become obvious.

High-quality ECEfS should provide opportunities for young children to appreciate the sensory and aesthetic beauty of the natural world, to imagine possible futures, to think outside the square and to make their learning about sustainability visible in a variety of ways, and to speak about sustainability using a range of languages. As the arts, too, hold the power to transform (Ewing 2012; Gibson & Ewing 2011), their inclusion can enrich the transformative potential of EfS.

If children are to experience opportunities in which they can make their learning about sustainability visible through the arts, they need time and support to do so. Teachers must resist the temptation to design segmented programs that allocate parcels of time to discrete subject areas. Rather, a project approach (Katz & Chard 2000) in which children engage in integrated, collaborative learning across boundaries, and over time, is likely to promote the powerful and transformational learning for which I am advocating in this chapter. (See Sharon Stuhmcke's Chapter 11 and Okjong Ji's Chapter 14 for further examples of the use of the Project Approach in ECEfS.)

The following section provides a detailed description of how one child, Ava, engaged in a self-directed, yet supported, informal learning project that provided many opportunities for her knowledge of the natural world to be consolidated, extended and made visible through the arts.

Ava's bird project: Making learning about the natural world visible through the arts

Ava's name, appropriately, derives from 'bird' in Latin. Ava (5 years) has always loved birds. She loves to read about them and to draw them. Living in suburban Brisbane, Ava is fortunate, as a huge variety of birds, insects and reptiles frequent her backyard.

I suggested to Ava and her mum, Megan, that she might like to keep a visual journal to document the creatures that she finds in the natural environment. Ava loves this diary and regularly refers back to it, adding new animals to the pages as she encounters them. On her recent school holidays, Ava took her nature journal outside most days after breakfast and sat quietly on the steps in the garden. Megan told me that she would often hear a dramatic little gasp when Ava finally found an ant or, even better, a cicada. A whirlwind drawing would take place as she captured her found creature on the page. She would then often spend some time drawing grasses or plants and making attempts at labelling them as she had seen in many of the picture books with an environment/ sustainability focus that Ava's family has in the house.

Ava is a great fan of Australian author and illustrator Narelle Oliver. This author uses beautiful linocut illustrations to represent natural Australian landscapes and to highlight for children the creatures that live there. Ava particularly likes finding and naming the animals and insects hidden in Narelle's books, such as *The Hunt*. Narelle often labels her illustrations as occurs in a botanical book. Other favourite books include *Leaf Litter* by Rachel Tonkin, *Tree* by Danny Parker and Matt Ottley, and Tania McCartney's *Eco Warriors to the Rescue! Leaf Litter* in particular has inspired Ava to create many collages of found materials and drawn or painted flora and fauna.

Ava loves to use the visual arts to express her knowledge of the natural environment. She spent hours on the illustration shown in Figure 10.2, returning to it over a number of days to create her collage of favourite birds. Inspired by a couple of her favourite books, *Don't Let a Spoonbill in the Kitchen* by Narelle Oliver and *Feathers for Phoebe* by Rod Clement, Ava and Megan studied the illustrations in these and other picture books to work out the parts of the birds and what shapes they were. Even though Ava had been making sketches of birds for a long time, when she really studied the artwork in these picture books she took additional, detailed note of the shapes of the birds and refined her drawings in response. Figure 10.1 shows one of Ava's drawings of a spoonbill, inspired by one of her favourite books, *Don't Let a Spoonbill in the Kitchen*.

After weeks of drawing birds daily, Ava became confident in drawing a range of birds and then began inventing her own new species on a daily basis. When she was satisfied that her bird pictures looked like actual birds, her drawings really came to life. Ava's mum, Megan, then talked with Ava about the colours of trees, the bush and nature, and they discussed which colours Ava would use. Ava's natural inclination is to use bright colours and lots of them. When she went to feed the family chickens,

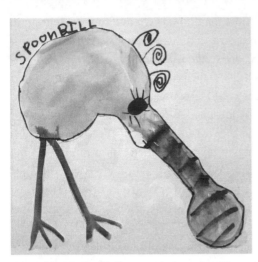

Figure 10.1 *Spoonbill*

Figure 10.2 *Bird collage*

Megan asked Ava to look at the colours around her and then, when they went back inside, Megan suggested to Ava that she pull those colours out of the pencils, crayons and paints she owned and use them in her illustrations to create pictures that reflect the natural colours of the birds, animals and plants that she'd found. This co-construction of knowledge about the arts and the natural environment suggests Wright's (2012) Guided Learning Approach, in which adults work with children to scaffold their learning, extending their thinking through dialogue and interaction.

Creating the collage depicted in Figure 10.2 became a slow process of exploring colours, adding detail with black pen, drawing a tree with crayons, cutting out each bird, and finally assembling all of the pieces as a collage. The conversations that took place during the creation of the artwork helped to make Ava's knowledge of the natural environment visible, and provided opportunities for that knowledge to be extended in new ways. At one point Megan asked Ava what birds she was drawing. Ava said, *'Can't you TELL?! They're spoonbills! They have a beak like a wooden spoon and pelicans have a beak like a bag'*. This is how Narelle Oliver describes the beaks in *Don't Let a Spoonbill in the Kitchen*. Ava then asked if she could look up spoonbills on the internet. She watched some YouTube clips and used the knowledge she had gained to refine her spoonbill, adding stripes to its bill.

The collage technique is something Ava has favoured since she attended an art workshop that focused on leaf rubbings. Megan says that Ava is often frustrated by her drawings and, though she is constantly told that her artworks are her own creations, and that they do not need to look any particular way, that art is a process and sometimes it takes lots of practice, she never wants to discard her many rough sketches. Consequently, drawings that are not quite as she wants are cut out and used to make collages. For example, she reuses cut off legs that didn't 'work' for her, or cuts out sections where the colour is not quite right in her eyes, and glues all these pieces together into arrangements with which she is happier.

Applications for early childhood settings

The example of Ava's bird project highlights the rich learning that can occur when high-quality visual arts and EfS come together. This example demonstrates that integration of the arts and sustainability can be powerful, enhancing and deepening the learning offered by both fields – and yet without the requirement for expensive materials and high levels of expertise.

In this description of Ava's project we see that she took time every day to engage in two important activities: observation and drawing. Every morning she would go outside into her garden to spend time alone, pondering and observing the natural environment and eagerly awaiting the arrival of the creatures that inevitably emerged. Ava also had time to engage in daily drawing – an activity that I've outlined above. Regular engagement with the artistic process – for adults as well as children – enhances our ability to see the world in new ways and to appreciate what is often overlooked. Drawing is as much about our eyes and our minds as it is about our hands.

Throughout this project, Ava was given the gift of time. And time truly is a gift for children in a busy world. So often we find the need to rush from one intense activity to the next without spending time just sitting, thinking, observing and experimenting. The time that Ava was given allowed her to return to her project over days and weeks, to experiment with her drawings, to conduct research into the natural world so that she could learn more about the birds and creatures that were the objects of her fascination. Ava had time to imagine new types of birds and to experiment with these ideas, making them visible to herself and others through the arts. Imagination is the cornerstone of creativity and foundational to both the arts and sustainability. Without opportunities to exercise imagination, we deny children (and adults) the means by which they can play with possibilities, solve problems and construct alternative futures.

While Ava frequently worked alone on her project, it is important to note that there were also many instances in which she engaged the support of an adult to co-construct her arts and sustainability learning. When Megan posed questions about the colours, shapes and textures that Ava was using in her bird drawings, and when she took Ava outside to look at the bush colours and the chickens, she was co-constructing some important learning about the arts and sustainability. This is very much a *hands-on* approach to arts and sustainability education. In the past, teachers have frequently fallen into the trap of believing a *hands-off* approach is best for early childhood arts pedagogy, leaving children alone to explore and experiment. When Ava worked along-side Megan to discuss her drawings, she was co-constructing her knowledge of shapes, colours, textures and animal anatomy, making the most of opportunities for Ava to extend her knowledge of the arts and the natural world.

Ava's project also highlights to us the benefits of children's exposure to the work of established artists. One of the most accessible ways for children to appreciate art is through the illustrations in picture books. Picture books focusing on environmental sustainability provide children with readily available examples of how artists make their knowledge and appreciation of the natural world visible for others, opening up endless possibilities for children to learn about the beauty of the natural world and the arts processes that might illustrate that beauty. Arts learning doesn't occur in a vacuum. Artists over the centuries have been inspired by other artists and have used this inspiration to inform their own work. The new Australian Curriculum underscores the importance of not just *making* art, but *responding* to it. By responding to author and lino print artist Narelle Oliver's works, Ava is learning about the spoonbills and pelicans at the same time as she is learning about line, colour, shape, pattern and texture – the elements of the visual arts.

Ava's project shows us that there are many ways in which children's knowledge of the arts and sustainability can be extended – real observations of flora and fauna (see Sue Elliott's Chapter 2, which focuses on children and nature), illustrated picture books, and electronic resources such as the internet (read Margaret Lloyd's Chapter 7 for more on this). Ava's example shows us that the arts can be the conduit for making children's observations and interpretations of the world around them visible to others. When we examine Ava's collage and we know about the conversations she had with Megan as she created it, we learn something of her understandings of the shapes, colours, patterns and behaviours of her favourite birds. Ava's bird project speaks to us of her love of the natural world, and is testament to the time she has been given to explore it, alongside a supportive adult. Chawla (2006) suggests that it is precisely these types of experiences that form the foundation of children's advocacy for the natural world:

When children have access to the natural world, and family members encourage them to explore it and give it close attention, they have a strong basis for interest in the environment. To turn this interest into activism, they later need to build on this foundation through education, membership in organizations, or the careers that they pursue; but from their childhood experiences in nature through their own free play and in the company of significant adults, they carry the memory that the natural world is a place of such full and positive meaning that it justifies their most persistent efforts to protect it (p. 76).

Conclusion

This chapter has explored the ways in which the arts hold rich potential to tell stories of the world around us. Unlike other areas of learning and communication, the arts help us to express and interpret meaning in ways that transcend verbal and written texts, breaking down barriers of language, time and culture. In this chapter, you have been introduced to the works of a number of artists who use their work to engage audiences with moral issues, such as poverty, war and the natural environment. You have also been encouraged to consider how the arts and EfS might come together in ways that enhance your thinking about both fields. We have explored in depth the example of Ava's bird project to illustrate how the arts and EfS can work together to enrich the learning potential of both. The arts provide alternate ways of seeing sustainability and communicating understandings about sustainability, for both adults and children.

Finally, learning to draw is about learning to see. The arts provide children, and adults, with opportunities to learn to love and appreciate the natural world by seeing it in new ways. In order to draw something, one must give it close attention. Close attention leads to appreciation, appreciation leads to love, and love leads to a determination to protect. When the arts and sustainability work together, they hold the potential to transform the ways in which we see, and represent, the world around us.

Review provocations

1. Reflect on your attitudes to the arts and sustainability. What personal and professional learning needs have you identified? How can you build or maintain your own confidence as a teacher of the arts?
2. Visit an art gallery and identify themes of sustainability in the works that are on display.
3. Can you see new possibilities for exploring sustainability through the arts?
4. How will you bring the arts and sustainability together in your work with young children?
5. Has this chapter prompted your thinking about your approach to arts and sustainability education?

References

Barrett, J., Birch, R., Cherrett, N. & Simmons, C. (2004). *An Analysis of the Policy and Education Applications of the Ecological Footprint*. Stockholm: Stockholm Environment Institute.

Chawla, L. (2006). Learning to love the natural world enough to protect it. *Barn*, 2, 57–78.

Chesterman, M. (2008). *Eco Footprint*. Brisbane: Queensland University of Technology.

Clement, R. (2010). *Feathers for Phoebe*. Pymble, NSW: Angus & Robertson.

Cordero, E., Todd, A. & Abellera, D. (2008). Climate change education and the ecological footprint. *Bulletin of the American Meteorological Society*, June, 865–72.

Curtis, D. Reid, N. & Ballard, G. (2012). Communicating ecology through art: What scientists think. *Ecology and Society*, 17(2), 3.

Darts, D. (2004). Visual culture jam: Art, pedagogy and creative resistance. *Studies in Art Education*, 45(4), 313–27.

Duncum, Paul (1999). What elementary generalist teachers need to know to teach art well. *Art Education*, 52(6), 33–8.

Environmental Protection Agency Victoria (2005). *The Ecological Footprint of Victoria: Assessing Victoria's Demand on Nature*. Melbourne: EPA Victoria.

Ewing. R. (2012). Competing issues in Australian primary curriculum. Learning from international experiences. *Education 3–13: International Journal of Primary, Elementary and Early Years Education*, 40(1), 97–111.

Ferreira, J. & Davis, J. (2010). Creating deep and broad change through research and systems approaches in early childhood education for sustainability. In J. Davis (ed.), *Young Children and the Environment: Early Education for Sustainability* (1st edn). Melbourne: Cambridge University Press.

Flint, K. (2001). Institutional footprint analysis: A case study of the University of Newcastle Australia. *International Journal of Sustainability in Higher Education*, 2(1), 48–62.

Gibson, R. and Ewing, R. (2011). *Transforming the Curriculum through the Arts*. Melbourne: Palgrave Macmillan.

Giudici, C., Rinaldi, C. & Krechevsky, M. (eds) (2001). *Making Learning Visible: Children as Individual and Group Learners*. Reggio Emilia, Italy: Reggio Children.

Hall, B. (2013). Manus Island children draw on desolation of detention. *Sydney Morning Herald* (5 February), www.smh.com.au/federal-politics/political-news/manus-island-children-draw-on-desolation-of-detention-20130204-2dukg.html

Kaplan, S. (2000). Human nature and environmentally responsible behaviour. *Journal of Social Issues,* 56(3), 491–508.

Katz, L. & Chard, S. (2000). *Engaging Children's Minds: The Project Approach* (2nd edn). Stamford, CT: Ablex.

Leavy, P. (2009). *Method Meets Art: Arts-Based Research Practice*. New York: The Guilford Press.

McArdle, F. A. (2008). The arts and staying cool. *Contemporary Issues in Early Childhood*, 9(4), 365–74.

McArdle, F. & Boldt, G. (eds) (2013). *Young Children, Pedagogy, and the Arts*. New York: Routledge.

McArdle, F., Knight, L. & Stratigos, T. (2013). Imagining social justice. *Contemporary Issues in Early Childhood*, 14(4), 357–69.

McArdle, F. & Spina, N. (2007). Children of refugee families as artists: Bridging the past, present and future. *Australian Journal of Early Childhood*, 32(4), 50–3.

McCartney, T. (2013). *Eco Warriors to the Rescue!* Canberra: National Library of Australia.

Miller, M., Nicholas, E. & Lambeth, M. (2008). Pre-service teachers' critical reflections of arts and education discourse: Reconstructions of experiences in early childhood and higher education. *Contemporary Issues in Early Childhood*, 9(4), 354–64.

O'Gorman, L. & Davis, J. (2013). Ecological footprinting: Its potential as a tool for change in preservice teacher education. *Environmental Education Research* 19(6), 779–91.

Oliver, N. (1995). *The Hunt*. Melbourne: Lothian.

Oliver, N. (2013). *Don't Let a Spoonbill in the Kitchen*. Parkside, SA: Omnibus Books.

Parker, D. & Ottley, M. (2012). *Tree: A Little Story about Big Things*. Richmond, Vic.: Little Hare Books.

Peer, S. (2014). Pictures of misery: What children draw in detention on Christmas Island. *The Guardian* (26 March), www.theguardian.com/commentisfree/2014/mar/26/pictures-of-mis ery-what-children-draw-in-detention-on-christmas-island (accessed 1 May 2014).

Russell-Bowie, D. E. (2012). Developing preservice primary teachers' confidence and competence in arts education using principles of authentic learning. *Australian Journal of Teacher Education*, 37(1), http://dx.doi.org/10.14221/ajte.2012v37n1.2.

Steiner, A. (2007). *Art in Action: Nature, Creativity and Our Collective Future*. San Rafael, CA: Natural World Museum, Earth Aware Editions.

Temple, L. (1992). *Where Would We Sleep? Children and the Environment*. Sydney: Random House.

Tonkin, R. (2006). *Leaf Litter*. Pymble, NSW: Harper Collins.

Wright, S. (2012). Ways of knowing in the arts. In S. Wright (ed.), *Children, Meaning Making and the Arts* (2nd edn). Frenchs Forest, NSW: Pearson.

Young Imm Kang Song (2012). Crossroads of public art, nature and environmental education. *Environmental Education Research*, 18(6), 797–813.

The children's environment project: Developing a transformative project approach with children in a kindergarten

Sharon Stuhmcke

Editor's note

This is another new chapter for the second edition. **Sharon Stuhmcke** bases her contribution on her recent doctoral studies in which she investigated the use of the Project Approach, a longstanding pedagogical strategy, with roots in the reformer John Dewey's work, to engage kindergarten children (aged 4–5 years) in environmental and sustainability learning. Sharon sought to apply the pedagogical strengths of EfS, which focuses on transformative learning and teaching, to co-constructivist early childhood education, which she had been practising for many years in her classroom. In so doing, she supported children's investigations of environmental and sustainability questions that resulted in some significant changes in thinking and practice within the kindergarten. Not only did the children show that they were able to learn some quite sophisticated concepts, they also demonstrated their capabilities as change agents for sustainability.

Introduction

In this chapter, I share part of my journey – derived from my own teaching experience in conjunction with doctoral studies – as I adapted my long-held early childhood teaching approaches to calls from within the early childhood profession to respond to children as competent and capable. As a consequence of these stimuli for change, I now believe that EfS should begin at birth. Here, I outline my experiences as I engaged in an action research project with a class of kindergarten children (aged 4–5 years) who developed a project about 'the rainforest'. This project lasted for seven weeks, and resulted in a great deal of learning *in*, *about* and *for* the environment, and many changes to the kindergarten's pedagogical and management approaches. I draw on my research to discuss and explain what was learned.

Initial impetus for this project came from my desire to broaden my existing teaching practices to more completely embed EfS into the kindergarten's program. Although I had incorporated environmental learning into past programs and projects, I recognised that this could best be described as teaching and learning that occurred *in* the environment or *about* the environment. It had become evident to me that contemporary EfS, with its focus on critical examination of issues and a desire to create sustainable change, was much more concerned with learning *for* the environment, whereby change is created and action is taken towards positively sustaining the natural environment (Davis 2010).

Provocation 11.1

How do the personal values you hold influence and impact on your teaching and learning practices?

What are your personal values? Are these articulated in your teaching philosophy?

How are these reflected in your daily practice?

Background

The Project Approach was already in use at the kindergarten, and was a fundamental aspect of my teaching for several years. I understood that the Project Approach was founded in Deweyian democratic approaches to teaching and learning and utilised Vygotsky's co-constructivism and that it has merit in early childhood classrooms because it is child-centred and builds teaching and learning around topics and issues that are of interest to, and have meaning for, children. I concur with Harris Helm and Katz (2011), who describe the Project Approach as a means of achieving a child-responsive, meaningful and engaging curriculum for young children.

Chard (2011) defines a project as 'an in-depth investigation of a real world topic worthy of children's attention and effort' (para. 1). A project generally begins from an observed child or children's interest and, throughout the course of the project, the teacher scaffolds children's explorations of this interest in a variety of ways as suggested by the child participants. This approach forms a teaching and learning cycle that is a continuous and ongoing process. During a project, artefacts and documentation, such as children's drawings and photographs of activities, are kept as records of learning and discovery. Harris Helm and Katz (2011) define the Project Approach as providing structure to teaching and learning rather than a 'prescription'. Although emergent in nature, a project would typically follow this format:

Phase 1: Introductory phase

- An 'interest web' is recorded (words and/or pictures).

- Children's questions are listed – for example, 'What do we want to know?'

- A list of 'What do we already know?' is recorded.

Phase 2: Synthesising phase

- An in-depth exploration of an interest area is conducted through a variety of open-ended methods.

Phase 3: Culminating phase

- What has been discovered during the course of the project is communicated. This might involve putting documentation on display (Katz & Chard 2000; Chard 2011; Sloane 2004).

In relation to the project that is the focus of this chapter, in the next section I provide details of each of the three main phases.

Provocation 11.2

Have you used the Project Approach? If so, was it successful? What were the benefits/difficulties?

Can you see value in such an approach within an early childhood setting?

Phases of the environment project

Introductory phase

A number of pre-cursors were relevant to the project; these are outlined in Table 11.1.

Of significance in relation to the pre-cursors is that the Project Approach was already the major pedagogical strategy used within the kindergarten. Children were

Table 11.1 *Summary of project pre-cursors*

PHASE	KEY EVENTS	KEY PARTICIPANT CO-CONSTRUCTED ACTIVITIES	KEY PARTICIPANT TRANSFORMATIVE ACTIVITIES
	Project Approach was established as central to the kindergarten's curriculum.	**Children, teacher** and **teacher aide** are involved in child-centred and play-based pedagogy. Curriculum is planned from observations of children interests. Environmental education 'in' and 'about' is occurring.	**Children, teacher** and **teacher aide** are involved in democratic decision-making about the curriculum.

also familiar with the use of democratic practices as an embedded part of daily kindergarten life; these included choosing their own interests to investigate, and directing their own learning by suggesting avenues to follow, such as Googling information, researching in books or asking experts. Children were also familiar with engaging in projects over lengthy periods of time ranging from a couple of weeks through to a whole term (up to 10 or 11 weeks).

Other pre-cursors to this project that may have contributed to the children's environmental interest in the rainforest include:

- the kindergarten's physical location on the edge of a nature reserve
- the large playground that features natural grasses and plants in its landscaping
- a planting policy that aligns with the management of the neighbouring reserve
- the kindergarten's existing environmental policy and the way it influences the educational program
- everyday environmental practices, such as composting; environmentally friendly cleaning practices; use of water-saving sensor taps and a water tank to address water conservation; and litter-less lunch practices, with families encouraged to provide food in containers to be washed and reused, rather than providing food in plastic film or disposable packaging.

Table 11.2 outlines the introductory phase proper. The five key learning events that occurred in the introductory phase included:

- One child's rainforest collage sparked interest in environmental issues.
- We developed a list of children's learning interests about rainforests.
- We went on a 'nature hunt' in the playground.
- We collected parents' and children's ideas for a new playground.
- The children constructed a waterfall and rainforest model.

Table 11.2 *Phase 1: Introductory phase of the environment project*

PHASE	KEY EVENTS	KEY PARTICIPANT CO-CONSTRUCTED ACTIVITIES	KEY PARTICIPANT TRANSFORMATIVE ACTIVITIES
Week 1	Children's list of learning interests was drawn up. Playground plans were made. Rainforest collage was created. Nature hunt was held.	**Children** made representations and drawings about what they would like to see in the playground. **Teacher** and **teacher aide** made observations of children's activities and reflected on these. **Teacher** read *The Nature Hunt*. **Collaborative activities:** – Current interests were listed and one key interest identified. – Nature hunt held in the playground.	**Children** suggested and implemented rules about treatment of flora and fauna.
Week 2	Construction of environment model begins.	**Children** asked questions about waterfalls and indicated they wanted to make a waterfall. **Children** co-constructed knowledge about the water cycle. **Teacher** and **teacher aide** provided materials to facilitate model construction and educational resources with an environmental focus. **Teacher** read Jeannie Baker books to children – these contain pro-environmental messages. **Teacher, teacher aide** and **children** 'Googled' pictures of waterfalls and discussed plans to construct a waterfall.	**Children** enacted pro-environmental attitudes. **Children** proposed solution to environmental sustainability issue – 'people homes and animal homes should be together'.

After a busy morning at kindergarten, the children came together (as was normal practice) to share about their various play and learning experiences. One child's discussion about the rainforest collage that she had made sparked quite a bit of interest with other children in the class. This raised conversations about camping, pollution, rubbish in the rainforest, and some rainforest animals. After this sharing time, the children then expressed ideas about their future learning interests. I recorded their suggestions as:

- jungles
- forests
- waterfalls
- rainforests
- dinosaurs
- water
- dinghies
- beaches (class discussion, 23/8/2010).

The class discussed each option for further exploration and developed several plans, including plans to construct a waterfall and rainforest model, 'cos then we can see what a waterfall and a rainforest is like ... because we don't have any at kindy' (class discussion, 23/8/2010).

It is important to note that, while this chapter focuses on this particular project related to the environment, a lot of other learning was also occurring within the wider kindergarten program. In other words, the rainforest project (and use of the Project Approach) did not constitute the entire curriculum; rather it complemented and enriched the kindergarten program. Within the scope of this chapter, however, other learning (outside the project) is not included here.

The nature hunt

Also of significance in this introductory phase of the project was the book *We're Going on a Nature Hunt* (2007) by Steve Metzger, which was intentionally selected as a follow-up to the children's emerging interests. Sharing this text prompted the children to want to conduct their own nature hunt and to emulate the behaviours of the book's characters, such as not touching the flora and fauna and instead appreciating the plants and insects in their natural habitats. Accordingly, the children chose to take magnifying glasses and the class camera to allow them to 'capture' what they observed without causing disruption. Their pictures were later printed and laminated and used in a variety of learning experiences, including matching, camouflaging, comparing and contrasting.

Redesigning the playground

Occurring simultaneously with the start of this project was the kindergarten committee's regular meeting during which there was discussion about allocation of funding. It was decided to investigate plans to fund some upgrades to the playground and to repaint the external building. I discussed these plans with the children too, and suggested that they might like to contribute their ideas about what they'd like to see in the playground. As a result, some children made drawings or collages depicting what they would like; others brought pictures from home. Parents were also informed and a community noticeboard was set up so that everybody could have input into what they would like to see considered in a revamped playground. As part of my doctoral study, I then analysed the various contributions in some depth.

The children's representations showed grass, water, plants, trees, birds, nests and stepping stones. Where children represented constructed features, these occurred alongside natural phenomena; for example, bridges were built over water, tree houses were built within the trees, and pot plants were provided for strawberries grown along the patio. Bridges were the most common human-made feature. One picture showed a slide going into water. All pictures contained multiple natural elements, including water, stones, trees and plants.

Based on an analysis of the children's artwork in conjunction with conversations with children, my interpretation was that the children were showing a partiality for natural phenomena. As Wright (2010) states, 'children's drawings provide a natural-istic way to witness children's creative meaning-making, because the source of the content emerges from the child's own thoughts, feelings and imagination' (p. 26). The teacher aide, in some ways a co-researcher with me, agreed with my view that the children had a preference for natural elements in their ideas for the revamped play-ground. She commented:

> The children made a lot of references to mushrooms, quiet spaces in the yard, rockeries and coves that we could make around the rocks we already have. They talked about long, green, wavy grass for hiding and they asked for sticks so they could make bridges in their pictures (conversation with teacher aide, 18/8/2010).

Analysis of the children's artwork also revealed the absence of play gym style structures (often vibrantly coloured, fixed metal structures with swings, slides and platforms). I interpreted this to be a reflection of the children's preference *not* to have such structures in their playground. One child wanted a sign in his playground that said 'No crying allowed'. This prompted me to pay particular attention to the facial expressions repre-sented in the children's artworks. All other children's pictures contained representa-tions of people with smiling faces. I considered that the smiling faces, combined with children's representations of predominantly natural features, indicated their positive feelings towards being in a natural environment.

Parents' contributions also featured predominantly natural phenomena. These included fairy gardens; a tee-pee with bean vines; a sensory garden; meandering pathways; water features; food plants; plants to touch, smell and feel; a native bee-hive; possum boxes; bird-feeders; stumps for sitting on; and wind-chimes. Magazine clippings were also added to the ideas board by some parents. Many of these featured playspaces designed around and within trees. This suggested that parents, too, pre-ferred to see natural elements featured in the kindergarten's playground, as well as materials, structures and plantings that would encourage wildlife onto the site.

The waterfall model

The final significant 'event' of the introductory phase was that the children began constructing their rainforest and waterfall model. This commenced with the children mostly focused on the cascading nature of a waterfall. To assist with this process, we engaged in learning experiences, such as searching on Google and looking at various images of waterfalls. The children were able to view a variety of waterfalls, some flowing quite heavily and others just trickling. Children then began asking questions about water, water quality and the water cycle. In response to these questions, resources including books, posters and calendar pictures of different environments were made available. Some children shared their existing knowledge about what they knew of the water cycle and water pollution. This learning was then represented further in children's art and play in the sandpit. At this point, I intentionally read *Lester and Clyde* (Reece 1995), a picture book that tells a story but also educates about polluted water.

Synthesising phase

As Table 11.3 shows, there were a number of key events in the synthesising phase; these included the following:

- New topics, such as recycling and nature conservation, emerged.
- Construction of the rainforest and waterfall model continued.
- Children proposed solutions for environmental issues.
- A rainforest puppet show visited the kindergarten.

During this phase of the project, the children devised their own 'rules' and practices around recycling and conservation. These were additional to centre-wide practices already in place, such as the use of sensor taps and the rainwater tank aimed at reducing town water consumption. During this period, I shared more picture books with the children from the series written by Jen Green (2006), including *Why Should I Recycle?*, *Why Should I Protect Nature?*, *Why Should I Save Energy?* and *Why Should I Save Water?* I also read *Michael Recycle* by Ellie Bethel (2008). As the titles imply, these texts have pro-environmental themes and characters that model responsible environmental behaviours. The kindergarten children were becoming experts at identifying environmental issues (such as water wastage, and water and air pollution) and were able to relate the stories to practices at the kindergarten. Additionally, they were able to suggest additional sustainable practices to improve the kindergarten's sustainability.

Learning about recycling and water pollution

In particular, the children had been expressing concern during this phase of the project about polluted water and the impact this could have on native animals. They began to

Table 11.3 *Phase 2: Synthesising phase of the environment project*

PHASE	KEY EVENTS	KEY PARTICIPANT CO-CONSTRUCTED ACTIVITIES	KEY PARTICIPANT TRANSFORMATIVE ACTIVITIES
Week 3	Children taught about recycling and nature conservation. Work on environment model continues.	**Children** identified environmental issues and positive practices. **Teacher** and **teacher aide** shared texts about recycling and conservation. **Teacher, teacher aide** and **children** observed their water usage and rubbish disposal practices.	**Children** devised and implemented further practices about water usage, pollution and recycling. **Children** created and distributed drawings about recycling to remind shopkeepers to recycle. **Children** influenced parental shopping practices regarding purchase of recyclable goods, packaging and using green shopping bags.
Week 4	Solutions proposed for environmental issues. Work on environment model continues.	**Children** demonstrated understanding of the impact that unclean water can have on animals. **Children** engaged in the 'Earth Game' on the interactive whiteboard and were observed saying that animals could live there when the pollution was removed.	**Children** designed 'water cleaning' devices and incorporated these into play in the sandpit. **Children** role-played pro-environmental behaviours.
Week 5	Rainforest puppet show held. Work on environment model continues.	**Children** transferred learning from rainforest puppet show into their play and work around their environment model. **Children** represented their learning and understanding (from the puppet show) in their drawings. **Teacher** and **teacher aide** scaffolded children's demonstrated interests by providing related books and materials **Teacher, teacher aide** and **children** explored rainforest animals (in particular those from the puppet show). They also discussed /explored issues, such as camouflage, human threats to wildlife and habitat losses.	**Children** continued to identify and discuss environmental issues, such as human impacts on animals and environments (habitat destruction and pollution). **Children** designed a 'rubbish crane' to remove pollution from trees and air. **Children** expressed their choice for pro-environmental behaviours through drawings.

enact their ideas about how this problem could be solved through their sandpit play, devising ways to clean sand from the pipes they were using. As they played, they made comparisons to the pipes that had polluted water draining out into the pond as seen in the picture book *Lester and Clyde* (Reece 1995) that I had read to them earlier. One child commented: 'we can see the baby animals ... we have to clean the water ... if there's rubbish in the water the baby animals will die' (30/8/2010). What these children were doing was role-playing pro-environmental behaviours by 'pretending' to clean the waterways. They showed understandings about what was natural to a waterway, and what did not belong. Their dialogue demonstrated their understandings of the consequences of polluted water on animal life. Such role-play, on this theme of cleaning water, was repeated frequently over a number of weeks after this first occasion.

Another example of children being active citizens was when they played a game on the kindergarten's interactive whiteboard. This was called *Earth Day* (Starfall Education 2002–12), available on an educational website for young children (www. starfall.com). The game shows a polluted natural environment, including a pond, trees and grassed areas. Children 'click and drag' the polluting items and place them in the correct recycling bins: paper, plastic or glass. While the children were playing this game, they noticed that, as they cleared more pollution away, animals began to reappear in the pond, stream and trees. They hypothesised and problem solved:

> They (animals) can come out now because the rubbish is gone ... animals can live here now because the rubbish has been cleaned up ...
>> ... it's (the game) about picking up the rubbish so the animals won't die ...
>> ... they're special (the bins) because you can make new stuff out of them (31/8/2010).

These comments indicated that the children were able to make connections between pollution and the presence or absence of animals in the pond. The children also deduced that the animals were more able to live in an unpolluted environment and that if animals ingested polluted water it could have detrimental effects.

At this point of the project children also began to identify solutions to environmental issues, particularly when they revisited picture books that had been shared with the group. I observed several children browsing through various books related to their current environmental interest. I overheard and recorded comments made by several children as they revisited *Michael Recycle* (Bethel 2008), for example. Comments included:

> ... see ... you roll up paper so it doesn't get wasted ... once upon a time people threw rubbish on the ground ... and then along comes a super guy to teach us not to throw rubbish everywhere ... When we learn it he goes somewhere else and says 'no more throwing rubbish on the world' ...
>> ... she's sad because they are wasting water ... they should save the water 'cos we'll run out and the animals will be thirsty (31/8/2010).

While looking at the text *Why Should I Recycle?* (Green 2006) one child took on the role of the book's main character using her voice to imitate the character and, using facial gestures for emphasis, she said:

> Stop! Stop! We don't put rubbish around the house . . . put it here [points to recycling bin] . . . wash it up and use it again . . . it will be a little bit new . . . we can drink from it . . . we can play with it . . . it can go to the 'newer shop' and they will make it new again (31/8/2010).

Analysis of this data revealed that these children were able to propose and implement solutions to environmental issues, such as recycling and water conservation, and that the children could apply these to their own lives. For example, they suggested further recycling measures be implemented at meal times at the kindergarten. The kindergarten already observed a 'litter-less lunch' policy; however, the children decided to recycle the commonly used, individually portioned yoghurt containers often sent from home by introducing a specific yoghurt container recycling bin. They also suggested that these containers be washed and reused for painting and craft activities. They encouraged each other to adhere to these recycling 'rules' until the end of their kindy year. To further illustrate their interest in practical recycling strategies within the kindergarten, the teacher aide shared the following observation:

> The children are very aware about their wrapping [cling wrap] and the tops of their yoghurt containers, they tell one another 'quick, quick . . . get it before an animal picks it up . . .'. They (the children) seem to be transferring their learning into their practices without any intervention by us (conversation with teacher aide, 6/9/2010).

Arising from their initial interest in the waterfall, recycling and water conservation continued to be key interests for the children in this second phase of their environment project. Water conservation measures additional to those already in place in the kindergarten were proposed and implemented by the children. For example, during group time, several children suggested that 'you need to have a plan in your head about what the water will be used for . . . you can't just fill up the bucket and tip it out . . . you need a good reason' (31/8/2010). The following is an excerpt from my weekly curriculum plan (1/9/2010):

> Today the children came up with the idea to fill one small trough with water and then used small containers to carry water to the sandpit. This was discussed straight after our morning song (9.15 am) as a follow up from yesterday's discussion and book about saving water. The children also decided they needed 'good' reasons to use water such as 'for the animals' and 'to fill up rivers' rather than 'just tipping it out'.

During this discussion, the children suggested that only small containers should be used for water play and that only the tap connected to the rainwater tank should be available for use. They also identified that completely filling up a drinking cup was wasteful when only a small drink was wanted, 'cos you should only fill it up with what you need . . . and . . . if you have leftover water in your cup you should pour it on the plants or the grass . . . not just down the drain . . .' (1/9/2010). The teacher aide also commented on children's continuing interest in water conservation. For example, she reported that children were 'chastising' each other if they saw water being wasted (conversation with the teacher aide, 1/9/2010).

Learning about the rainforest

Based on the children's interest in environmental issues, we organised for a rainforest puppet show to visit the kindergarten. We chose a show by Evergreen Theatre, which specialises in puppetry with environmental themes for young children (Stewart 1990). The show identifies features of the Australian rainforest (including its special flora and fauna), focuses on human impacts on rainforest habitats and presents ways in which children can act to preserve rainforests. The children capably answered many of the puppeteer's questions related to wildlife protection, habitat destruction and pollution. Their responses illustrated that these children had developed quite deep understandings about issues affecting native rainforest wildlife.

During this phase, too, the children continued to engage with the rainforest and waterfall model. However, their involvement had evolved; they were now incorporating new and environment-related ideas into their play. Harris Helm and Katz (2011) describe young children as being involved in increasingly advanced play throughout the course of a project, and that children often become protective of living things when involved in projects about nature. For example, their new play included creating and camouflaging animals' homes: 'It's a burrow where the echidna can live . . . he can hide from people so they can't kill his home or eat him . . . I put trees around the burrow to camouflage it . . . I want him to be safe from people' (15/9/2010). Children's creations included burrows, tunnels and trees using rocks and craft materials. Their awareness that introduced species (such as toads) posed a threat to wildlife was illustrated when I heard a child saying 'no . . . no . . . they [toads] can kill the rainforest animals' (15/9/2010). This occurred when another child approached holding a toy toad.

Children also started to make references to animal characteristics, commenting that wombats and echidnas live on the ground and in burrows because 'they have short legs and strong bodies so they are good at digging . . . but gliders can glide so they live in trees' (15/9/2010). I deduced from these observations and comments that the children had learnt about concepts such as the need for animal camouflage from their participation in the puppet show and that an animal's unique characteristics will impact on where a particular animal might live; for example, in a tree or in a burrow. Children then applied this learning, more broadly, to other environments and habitats (other than their created model). For example, the children started to ask questions about the features of desert animals and related these to the desert environment. I deduced from

Figure 11.1 *Wombat burrow*

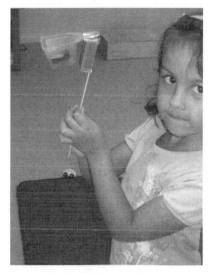

Figure 11.2 *Child with rubbish crane*

this that the children were transferring their learning from one context to other contexts, and were engaging in quite high-level thinking.

After engaging with the puppet show, the children began to represent their new ideas. For example, one child made a 'rubbish crane' designed to remove pollution from trees and the air, indicating her understanding that pollution cannot always be 'seen'. This child also used this rubbish crane in subsequent play in and around the waterfall model. She used her rubbish crane to 'scoop' (unseen) pollution and remove it from around the environment model. Children also frequently made references to specific animals that they had learned about through the puppet show, commenting on their particular needs and the potential threats posed by humans. Harris Helm and Katz (2011) report that young children often process and extend their learning through play. This was certainly the case in this project.

As the second phase progressed, I continued to collect children's drawings and I recorded their comments the day after the puppet show. Their conversations contained many references to environmental and sustainability issues, as the following list shows.

- We need to dispose of rubbish properly: 'you don't leave rubbish on the floor or the animals might die'.
- People should not build in the rainforest: 'people shouldn't build there because animals have houses there'.
- Rubbish can harm wildlife: 'the paddymelon [small wallaby] had a cut on its foot because the campers had left broken glass ... you shouldn't leave glass in the rainforest'.
- Trees should not be cut down: 'we don't cut down trees because of the food for animals and the nests ... no birds will come if there are no trees'.
- Pets should be restrained as they are a threat to wildlife; native wildlife should not be caged: 'I put my pet bird in a cage but we don't put catbirds [a native Australian rainforest bird] and scrub turkeys in cages ... they live in trees and they scratch in the dirt ... we don't scare them and we can't let cats near birds ... we can't let pets in the rainforest because they will kill the animals ... and we take rubbish home' (15/9/2010).

Speaking generally, the children demonstrated a strong sense that wildlife had the right to live peacefully without threat from humans.

In summary, my reflections during this synthesising phase identified that the children developed many understandings about environmental issues and topics, including that:

- there are human impacts on flora and fauna
- there is seen and unseen pollution
- food chains and ecological systems are fragile
- there are appropriate practices for dealing with rubbish
- native wildlife should not be caged
- domestic animals need to be restrained
- pollution and polluted environments are harmful to wildlife and humans.

Culminating phase

As Table 11.4 shows, key events of the culminating phase were:

- documenting the children's environment project
- continuing construction of the rainforest and waterfall model
- producing a class book.

Table 11.4 *Phase 3: Culminating phase of the environment project*

PHASE	KEY EVENTS	KEY PARTICIPANT CO-CONSTRUCTED ACTIVITIES	KEY PARTICIPANT TRANSFORMATIVE ACTIVITIES
Week 6	Documentation of children's environment project begun. Work on environment model continues.	**Children** reflected and recalled their learning and involvement. **Teacher** and **teacher aide** recorded what children said and chose (e.g. pictures from PowerPoint presentations). **Teacher, teacher aide** and **children** decided on the narrative and photos for documentation.	**Children** continued to practise and implement strategies that they learnt about in relation to recycling, water conservation and pollution. **Children** continued to demonstrate pro-environmental preferences during play.
Week 7	Class book created. Work on environment model continues.	**Children** suggested words and drew pictures for their book. **Teacher** acted as the 'editor' by combining similar ideas and recording children's words. **Teacher, teacher aide** and **children** 'published' the book.	**Children** saw themselves as teachers when they indicated their desire to 'make a book to teach others' about ways to care for the environment.

As noted earlier, documenting learning is an important feature of the Project Approach. Accordingly, the seven-week learning journey was recorded by the class in some depth. This was essentially a narrative account of the key events presented as large display posters. We also revisited PowerPoint slideshows (everyday photographs taken by the teachers and aide and used in a daily slideshow viewed by staff, children and parents each afternoon); reviewed art and craft artefacts; selected items from children's individual portfolios that contained evidence of their learning and participation during the project; and summarised of discussions held at group times. This collated poster documentation was hung from lines across the kindergarten classroom. Harris Helm and Katz (2011) describe this process as beneficial for children as it helps them develop a sense of their learning process. As was customary at the kindergarten, children and teachers selected photos and text to represent the project chronologically and to summarise what had been learnt.

Further to creating this class documentation that told the 'story' of the children's environment project, the children also wanted to produce a book 'so we can teach other people' (class discussion, 5/10/2010). Harris Helm and Katz (2011) state that 'another way that children can educate others is to create books about their nature topic' (p. 65). This desire to make a book indicated the children's prior learning about, and recognition of, books as important means for learning. Suggestions about the text for the book

We look after the animals.

We make places for animals to live.
You can put possum boxes in the trees.

We don't scare animals and we are quiet.

Figure 11.3 *Page from children's book*

came from the children, while I was the editor and grouped similar ideas and helped with sentence construction. Book illustrations were created from children's drawings and photographs suggested by the children. The class book was then reproduced and copies were distributed to families as the children wanted to *teach other people* about ways to act for the environment.

Creating the class book allowed the children to feel that their efforts and knowledge about the environment and sustainability were valued by others, including their teachers, teacher aide and parents. Chawla and Flanders Cushing (2007) describe a sense of 'collective competence' resulting from such shared experiences when children come together around a common goal, in this case to share their knowledge and to educate adults about environmental matters. In this project the children worked collaboratively and cooperatively, achieving consensus through negotiation and discussion. This is an example of democracy at work in the classroom as children were engaged in democratic processes and decision making based on knowledge they co-constructed (Chawla & Flanders Cushing 2007).

At the conclusion of the children's environment project, both the project documentation (which summarised the project for the children) and the class book (designed to educate others) remained in the classroom, available for later use by the children. The children continued to access and refer to these resources until the end of their kindergarten year – that is, for several months after the project was completed.

All the while, the environment model continued to be a popular play area within the kindergarten classroom, similar to the book corner and puzzle area, which are standard room areas within many kindergartens. The children regularly used animal

Figure 11.4 *Environment model*

replicas, trees they had made themselves and rocks they had collected from the playground as part of their play.

The picture in Figure 11.4 shows the environment model that the children made with strings of beads and craft materials threaded onto lengths of wool and twine to represent the rainforest canopy. This feature was added in the latter stages of the project, after the children revisited a book they had used earlier in their learning and realised that *their* environment model did not have a rainforest canopy.

After the project

Even when the children's environment project was officially over, the learning that occurred continued to influence the educational program of the kindergarten and the ongoing practices and actions of both staff and children. This happened in three ways. First, the children made continuing, frequent references to learning and actions developed during the course of the project. Second, the project influenced the learning of the other class that shared the kindergarten, who had access to the environment model and the resources that were being used for the project. For example, children in this other group became concerned that local possums needed more homes so they organised for a possum box to be built and installed at the kindergarten. Third, the project was the highlight of the children's end-of-year concert, a public production that summarised their learning throughout the whole kindergarten year.

Table 11.5 *Post-project phase summary*

PHASE	KEY EVENTS	KEY PARTICIPANT CO-CONSTRUCTED ACTIVITIES	KEY PARTICIPANT TRANSFORMATIVE ACTIVITIES
	End-of-year 'celebration of learning'	**Children** suggested that trees, flowers, animals, a possum box, etc. be incorporated into the backdrop they were making for their end-of-year production. **Children** frequently referred to their involvement and learning from the environment project. **Teacher** and **teacher aide** continued to observe children's behaviours, practices and references to their learning and involvement in the environment project. **Teacher, teacher aide** and **children** constructed backdrops and chose songs for the end-of-year production.	**Children** continued to implement strategies about recycling, pollution control and water conservation (and encourage others around them to implement these strategies also). **Children** displayed pro-environment behaviours, attitudes and practices. For example, **children** instigated installation of a possum box in the playground. When the 'celebration of learning' was held, **children** chose songs and backdrop. These were explained with statements such as the 'possum box' (part of the backdrop) was made because **children** had suggested that people and animals should live together.

My reflections on the project: Developing the Transformative Project Approach

Compared with previous projects at the kindergarten, this project clearly illustrated that the children were not only active participants in decision making about their learning, but were also active participants in enacting change within their kindergarten and home contexts. I believe, however, that this outcome did not occur simply as a result of the choice of the project topic; rather, it was the result of a new kind of educational program. As noted earlier, children's ideas were already central to the curriculum before the project began, and a culture of discussion and shared decision making was well established. The difference, this time, was the influence of EfS principles and pedagogies on curriculum delivery. This new way of thinking about the two fields of early childhood education and EfS is represented by Figure 11.5.

The impact of this synthesised thinking was that I more consciously decided to scaffold and facilitate learning in ways that encouraged children to not only co-construct knowledge, but to consider ways they could act upon this new knowledge.

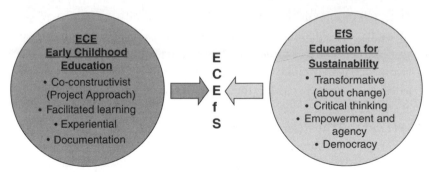

Figure 11.5 *ECEfS – key features*

The new kinds of open-ended questions I used assisted this process. For example, rather than just asking the children questions that would stimulate knowledge co-construction, I asked questions that supported and encouraged the children to consider possible actions they could take based on this knowledge. For example, I asked questions such as 'What can we do to help?' and 'Will what we do help change this situation?'

Provocation 11.3

In what practical ways can you broaden your current teaching and learning practices to incorporate EfS?

How can you include transformative practice into existing practices?

How can you support and encourage children to enact change?

These changes enabled the children to take charge, problem solve, and make and effect environmental decisions much more than they had been able to in the past. This shift, from co-construction of knowledge to enacting change, seemed a natural progression and enhancement of the kindergarten's use of the Project Approach. Although I feel that the children already had a favourable predisposition towards the natural environment, they really drove the learning throughout this new project. As a result of changes to my pedagogy, the children were able to better negotiate, debate and discuss the various issues and topics as they arose. They were more able to devise solutions to problems and to enact these. I became a better learning facilitator – one who scaffolded learning by making more use of open-ended questioning, encouraging critical thinking and supporting children's ideas to create change.

Further, by researching my own practice as a kindergarten teacher, I was able to theorise about my own teaching. Essentially, this meant discontinuing practices

(Kemmis 2009) that I felt did not adequately address sustainability – a paradigm shift (Kemmis 2009) away from my longheld co-constructivist practices using the Project Approach towards the integration of transformative practices had become necessary. This synthesis of approaches resulted in revised curriculum planning and renewed teaching approaches. In other words, the focus on co-constructing knowledge was broadened to include teaching and learning strategies that assisted young children to *enact change*. I call this the **Transformative Project Approach**.

The project also raised questions for me in terms of how aspects of sustainability, such as the social and political dimensions, might be addressed using this Transformative Project Approach. As noted, the use of democratic practices (the social dimension) had been part of my teaching repertoire for many years. In this action research project, however, democratic practices were implemented more fully and for longer. The children freely articulated their thoughts with one another and with the teachers all the way through the project. Moreover, the children's democratic behaviours influenced their peers within the kindergarten to behave in more democratic and environmentally friendly ways. Additionally, the project focused more overtly on empowerment, agency and children enacting change (the political dimension). During the project, emphasis was placed on ways for children to create change based on their own suggestions and ideas. An example of this was when the children chose to publish the class book. Their first step was the co-construction of knowledge about caring for the environment. Their second transformative step was to enact a change.

Latter stages of the project saw the children become more empowered, as they exercised agency and enacted change in relation to a range of sustainability issues. This was evidenced when children influenced their families and the local community to take up environmentally sustainable practices. An example was when posters were made for a local bakery to remind the bakers to recycle their empty packaging.

Participation in the project also caused me to consider the educative influence on children of myself as a teacher. Jenkins (2009) advocates a teacher-facilitator approach for effective EfS. This occurs when the teacher establishes the learning environment so that it responds to children's needs and interests by paying attention to materials and interactions, ensuring these are appropriate (MacNaughton & Williams 2009). This approach aligns with EfS as it provides children with opportunities to examine possibilities for change. MacNaughton and Williams (2009) describe teacher-facilitators as encouraging independent learning and self-discovery. The argument made in this project is that a teacher-facilitator style, rather than a 'teacher as leader' one, is necessary for a Transformative Project Approach. Teachers should facilitate both co-constructivist and transformative learning through questioning, discussing, critiquing and scaffolding. Strategic questioning (Peavey 1995), for example, can encourage children to co-construct knowledge but also to consider ways to act upon this knowledge.

Conclusion

Three key ideas about young children's capabilities in relation to environmental and sustainability issues emerged from my use of the Transformative Project Approach. These are:

1. Young children *can* think critically about environmental sustainability issues.
2. Young children *are* able to create change in their local contexts.
3. Young children *are* able to be educators of adults.

With regard to the first point, throughout the project I became very aware that the children were able to think critically about issues. This was evident from the earliest stages of the project, when children discussed environmentally sensitive ways to treat flora and fauna during their nature hunt and expressed disapproval of habitat destruction when shown Jeannie Baker's picture books. The Transformative Project Approach also supported children towards a more complete understanding of complex issues. They came to the understanding, for example, that water is a finite resource, and illustrated this understanding when they implemented water conservation measures into their daily routines and water play. They demonstrated their ideas and proposed solutions to issues through their words, play, artwork and actions.

With regard to the second point, young children can create change in their local contexts. For example, as a response to their interest in native animals and their suggestion that animal houses and people houses should be together, a possum box was placed in a tree in the playground. Change was also created by children within the kindergarten when they introduced new water conservation and recycling practices.

With regard to the third point, young children are able to take on the role of educators as demonstrated by the production of the class book. The reason children gave for making the book was 'to teach our parents about what we can do' (teacher reflection, week 6). The children felt they had important knowledge to share with others and demonstrated empowerment when they took on a role usually assumed by adults. They were able to see themselves as having the resources and independence to direct their own activities (MacNaughton & Williams 2009). Furthermore, some families reported that, at their children's instigation, they changed their shopping habits to more sustainable practices, such as using environmentally friendly shopping bags and purchasing items with little packaging, or packaging that displayed recycling symbols. These are examples of intergenerational learning (Gambino, Davis & Rowntree 2009) that is shared and experienced between different generations, such as parents and children.

To conclude, this project began with the interest of one kindergarten teacher who wanted to make a difference. This was undertaken through examining my own teaching in response to concerns for the environment and sustainability, combined

with recognition that my existing practices were insufficient in terms of being transformative. The resulting project – and one child's idea that sparked learning about the
rainforest – became the catalyst for many changes within and beyond the kindergarten gates.

References

Ballantyne, R., Connell, S. & Fien, J. (2006). Children as catalysts of environmental change: A
framework for researching intergenerational influence through environmental education.
Environmental Education Research, 12(3–4), 413–27.

Bethel, E. (2008). *Michael Recycle*. Mascot, Sydney: Koala Books.

Chard, S. (2011). Project Approach. www.projectapproach.org/project_approach.php (accessed
25 April 2012).

Chawla, L. & Flanders Cushing, D. (2007). Education for strategic environmental behaviour.
Environmental Education Research, 13(4), 437–52.

Davis, J. (2010). *Young Children and the Environment: Early Education for Sustainability*
(1st edn). Melbourne: Cambridge University Press.

Gambino, A., Davis, J. & Rowntree, N. (2009). Young children learning for the environment:
Researching a forest adventure. *Australian Journal of Environmental Education*, 25, 83–94.

Green, J. (2006). *Why Should I Protect Nature?* New York: Scholastic.

Green, J. (2006). *Why Should I Recycle?* New York: Scholastic.

Green, J. (2006). *Why Should I Save Energy?* New York: Scholastic.

Green, J. (2006). *Why Should I Save Water?* New York: Scholastic.

Harris Helm, J. & Katz, L. (2011). *Young Investigators: The Project Approach in the Early Years*.
New York: Teachers College Press.

Jenkins, K. (2009). Linking theory to practice: Education for sustainability and learning and
teaching. In M. Littledyke, N. Taylor and C. Eames, *Education for Sustainability in the
Primary Curriculum: A Guide for Teachers*. South Yarra: Palgrave Macmillan.

Katz, L. G. & Chard, S. C. (2000). *Engaging Children's Minds: The Project Approach* (2nd edn).
Stamford, CT: Ablex.

Kemmis, S. (2009). Action research as a practice-based practice. *Educational Action Research*,
17(3), 463–74.

MacNaughton, G. & Williams, G. (2009). *Techniques for Teaching Young Children: Choices in
Theory and Practice* (3rd edn). Frenchs Forest, NSW: Pearson Prentice Hall.

Metzger, S. (2007). *We're Going on a Nature Hunt*. New York: Scholastic.

Peavey, F. (1995). Strategic questioning: An approach to creating personal and social change, www.context.org/iclib/ic40/peavey (accessed 11 May 2014).

Reece, J. H. (1995). *Lester and Clyde: Running Scared*. Sydney: Scholastic.

Sloane, M. W. (2004). Tailoring your teaching with the Project Approach. *Kappa Delta Pi Record*, 40(4), 175–9.

Starfall Education (2002–12). *Earth Day* (interactive web game), www.starfall.com/n/holiday/earthday/play.htm?f (accessed 28 July 2012).

Stewart, J. (1990). *The Rainforest Experience* (puppet show), www.evergreenchildrenstheatre.com.au (accessed 10 October 2012).

Wright, S. (2010). *Understanding Creativity in Early Childhood: Meaning-Making and Children's Drawings*. Los Angeles: SAGE.

Part 2

Caring for oneself, others and the environment: Education for sustainability in Swedish preschools

Eva Ärlemalm-Hagsér
and Ingrid Engdahl

Editor's note

In this new chapter, the authors from Sweden provide a context for ECEfS by first describing key features of the Swedish early education system. They highlight that there is an underlying framework that supports sustainability education and the active participation of children in decision making around sustainability issues, even though sustainability, as such, is not overt within Sweden's key national early childhood curriculum documents. They then discuss recent Swedish research related to ECEfS, identifying that, while advances are being made, there is a way to go in upskilling practitioners in ECEfS understandings and practices. They finish their chapter by outlining an example of ECEfS in practice that integrates all dimensions of sustainability – environment, economics and the social – and illustrates how young children can be actors and change agents within their communities.

Introduction

In this chapter we introduce readers to early childhood education in Sweden, and how Swedish preschools work for sustainability. Democratic values, a cornerstone of EfS,[1] are looked upon as a foundation for learning and interactions. The Swedish preschool curriculum stipulates respect for human rights and fundamental democratic values (National Agency for Education 2011a). Each and every person working in a Swedish preschool needs to promote respect for the intrinsic value of every individual, respect for others and respect for our shared environment. The overall purpose is to give children opportunities to understand how democracy works, specifically to take part in democratic decision making and accept responsibility for their actions both within the preschool environment and outdoors in nature, and to actively participate in society (National Agency for Education 2011a).

Provocation 12.1

What thoughts and meanings arise when you think about the following fundamental values, as stated in the Swedish preschool curriculum:

- inviolability of human life
- individual freedom and integrity
- equal value of all people
- gender equality
- solidarity with the weak and vulnerable
- respect for our shared environment?

Preschools in Sweden

This section provides background to the organisational structure and development of preschools in Sweden, from a societal perspective. The first Swedish preschools began in the early 1800s. The modern preschool, however, was launched in the middle of the 20th century, when day care, kindergarten and family policy came together as areas of intense political interest. The first Preschool Act was passed in 1975 and introduced the overall concept of the 'preschool' that encompassed all previous forms of early childhood education and care. After 1996, the Swedish preschool moved from being part

---

[1] In Sweden, the concept of education for sustainable development (ESD) was first introduced into public policy and politics, and also in research contexts (Öhman 2011). In this chapter, we use the concepts education for sustainability (EfS) and early childhood education for sustainability (ECEfS).

of the social services sector and came to be seen as the first step in Swedish education. All preschool children, from babies to school age, are looked upon as preschoolers. There are no separate institutions for the under threes; the sections in the Education Act and the National Curriculum for the Preschool are common for all children, whether they are 1, 3 or 5 years of age (Engdahl 2011).

During the last 35 years, the preschool has become a major pillar of Swedish society – all children, regardless of family income and whether or not parents are in the workforce, on parental leave or are new immigrants, are welcome to participate. Parents are supported by a generous parental leave insurance system (480 days) financed through the Swedish welfare system. Most children start preschool in their second year (National Agency for Education 2011a).

Access to preschool

The Education Act of 2010 establishes the right for all children from 1 year of age to be offered preschool education. Preschools are opened all day and parents choose how many hours daily their children will spend in the preschool. Children have the right to free general preschool education from the autumn of the year they turn three – 525 hours per year in total, aligned with school semesters. The demand for preschool education is expected to be met for each family without undue delay, usually within four months, and as close to the child's home as possible (Education Act 2010).

Preschools are open all year round, with daily opening times varying to fit parents' working hours, study schedules or other commitments. All education services are provided by municipalities that allocate resources to all preschools in their local community, regardless of who 'owns' the preschool. Preschools can be run by municipalities, companies, parent cooperatives or non-profit organisations. Resources are based on the number of children, with variations for individual, economic, social and cultural backgrounds, and child and staff turnover levels. Municipalities receive state contributions based on demographic data, and also allocate their own municipal resources. A low flat fee for full-day preschool attendance was introduced in 2002 and remains relatively low in 2014.

Preschool groups are organised locally, and can consist of mixed ages (1–5 years), toddlers (1–3 years), older preschoolers (3–5 years) or age-specific groups (1, 2, 3, 4 and 5 years). Early childhood professionals work in teams of 2–4 teachers and preschool attendants per group. In 2011, the average group size was 16.9 children, with a child–staff ratio of 5.4 children per adult. Fifty-four per cent of staff have a university degree in education, while around 40 per cent have professional training post-secondary school (National Agency for Education 2011b). In 2011, attendance levels for children were 47 per cent of 1-year olds, 87 per cent of 2-year olds, 92 per cent of 3-year olds, 94 per cent of 4-year olds and 94 per cent of 5-year olds (National Agency for Education 2011b).

Provocation 12.2

What are the key reasons for offering early childhood education in your country?

Compare your understandings of your own context with the Swedish history and experience of preschool education.

Characteristics of the Swedish preschool system

The main steering documents for preschools in Sweden are the 2010 Education Act and the National Curriculum for the Preschool (National Agency for Education 2011a). The Swedish preschool is founded on a comprehensive and holistic view of children, whereby children are described as individuals with competencies, and as active beings with experience, interests, knowledge and skills. These attributes are emphasised as the starting points for everyday activities. The Swedish preschool strives for a pedagogical approach that sees care, nurturing and learning together forming a coherent whole, often referred to as 'educare'.

View of the child

With reference to the United Nations Convention on the Rights of the Child (United Nations 1989), children are increasingly looked upon as citizens with their own rights to influence the content and teaching in Swedish preschools. The national curriculum describes children as active and competent, with the right to influence their everyday life and surroundings, to play with friends, and to be challenged and supported by their teachers. Teachers are also expected to address gender equity in the everyday curriculum: girls and boys should have the same opportunities to develop and explore their abilities and interests without limitations imposed by stereotyped gender roles (National Agency for Education 2011a).

Education and evaluation perspectives

The national curriculum (National Agency for Education 2011a) articulates the main task, fundamental values and overall goals of preschool education, which are then implemented locally by a collaboration of teachers, principals, children and parents. Teachers are expected to use approaches whereby a variety of children's voices are listened to, and children's interests are taken into account. According to the curriculum and general guidelines, learning should be promoted through interactions with other children, reflecting the view that children are important and active partners in their own development and learning (Engdahl 2011). Learning should be planned so that children have fun, are involved in meaning making and have the right to influence matters that relate directly to them. Preschool education is to be 'enjoyable, secure and rich in learning for all children' (National Agency for Education 2011a, p. 4).

Given this child-oriented approach, all forms of evaluation should also adopt a child perspective. In Swedish preschools, assessment is more about obtaining knowledge of the quality of the preschool – that is, its organisation, learning content, and the pedagogical actions used to improve possibilities for children to 'learn, develop, feel secure, and have fun in the preschool' (National Agency for Education 2011a, p. 14); it is less about focusing on the children themselves. Using a range of forms of pedagogical documentation, teachers make learning, development, and the conditions for learning and development visible. Documentation is oriented towards communication and interaction with and between children, their participation and influence, and capturing children's experiences, as illustrated later in this chapter.

EfS in Sweden

EfS has its history in environmental education in Sweden. Activities in early childhood include learning in and about the natural environment, often through outdoor play, gardening and natural science practices profoundly rooted in the Fröbelian tradition (Fröbel [1826] 1995). Since the 1970s, learning about environmental issues has been included in the Swedish early childhood education steering documents. Here, we discuss sustainability in the Swedish preschool looking at past and present perspectives (through the national preschool curriculum and how it is enacted). We then outline challenges for EfS in the Swedish preschool.

The EfS curriculum in early childhood education

The current National Curriculum for the Preschool (National Agency for Education 2011a) does not specifically use the terms sustainability/sustainable development or EfS even though the value of making the world a better place has informed Swedish early childhood education from the outset (Dahlbeck & Tallberg Broman 2011). Nevertheless, our conclusion is that the important social, economic, environmental and political dimensions of sustainability are clearly present in the document. How preschools fulfil these tasks in everyday practice is another question, discussed later.

Specific tasks concerning environment and nature in the preschool curriculum are awareness of environmental and nature conservation issues; adoption of an ecological approach, a positive belief in the future and a caring attitude to nature and the environment; and an understanding of nature's recycling processes. The curriculum identifies that the preschool should help children understand that daily living and work practices can be organised in ways that can contribute to a better environment, now and in the future (National Agency for Education 2011a, p.11).

From projects to research in EfS in Sweden

Although Sweden is often seen as a pioneer country in sustainability, there are only a few research studies within this field related to Swedish preschool education. Nevertheless, many practical EfS projects have been implemented in preschools since the early 1970s (Ärlemalm-Hagsér & Sandberg 2013; Sandell & Öhman 2012), and especially since the mid-1980s.

For example, in the 1980s, preschools could apply for grants from the National Board of Health and Welfare for local development projects focused on enhancing environmental awareness (Gustavsson 1993). Other early collaborators were the Environmental Protection Agency and the Keep Sweden Tidy Foundation that instigated a national litter pick-up day, which is still active. Nowadays, around 1500 preschools are certified with the Green Flag, part of the international Eco-schools movement, and may be accredited with an environmental education award from Keep Sweden Tidy. The 'Diploma of Excellence in Sustainable Development' is another award that is granted by the National Agency for Education. The diploma focuses on social and economic awareness alongside environmental issues. In spring 2012, 206 preschools were certified with this diploma (Ärlemalm-Hagsér 2013).

Provocation 12.3

Discuss whether there are any obvious influences of Fröbel or other early childhood education pioneers in your preschool context.

Have you been involved in an ECEfS project? If so, tell a colleague about it.

As noted, there is general, practical interest in sustainability in Swedish preschools; however, the number of research studies has only recently begun to expand, with a vibrant discussion emerging focused on the relevance and purpose of EfS. For example, Hägglund and Pramling Samuelsson (2009) argue that children have competencies and skills, as well as rights, to participate in working for a sustainable world. Johansson (2009) introduces the idea of children as global citizens that involves both individualism and a sense of community, with caring for oneself, others and the world all fundamental concepts. Dahlbeck and Tallberg Broman (2011) stress that from the start of the Swedish preschool movement, the preschool child was given the task of bringing new knowledge and ideas to families to improve their quality of life, leading, ultimately, to an improved society. Dahlbeck (2012) emphasises, however, that there are hidden ethical values about individuality, attitudes and behaviours embedded in EfS and that 'sustainability values' are seldom problematised or challenged in the preschool setting. He comments that some forms of EfS seem to proclaim, rather too strongly, quite rigid ideas of 'what the human social world should be like' (p.35). This and other discussions arising from current research raise important questions about early childhood EfS. One such question, for example, is: *Is there a gap between the envisioned curriculum, as promulgated in the national curriculum, and the enacted curriculum as played out in Swedish preschools in relation to EfS?* Here, we offer responses to this particular question by reporting on two recent studies.

Study 1: Ärlemalm-Hagsér & Sandberg (2011) focused on 32 preschool attendants'[2] understandings of the concept of sustainable development and related pedagogical practices in their preschools. They found that these attendants defined sustainable development in three possible ways: (1) an holistic, multifaceted concept; (2) an environmental concern only; or (3) an aspect of democracy. These differing ways of approaching sustainable development then created different attitudes and day-to-day practices within the educational programs of preschools. The study also showed that while almost all participants commented that preschools are characterised by environments where questions of values, morals, human rights, democracy, participation and relationships with nature are raised, nevertheless, as Dahlbeck found, there appeared to be limited critical reflection on these concepts. On a positive note, however, these preschool attendants indicated that they were working to improve EfS within their settings.

Study 2: Ärlemalm-Hagsér (2013) conducted a meta-analysis of studies about EfS in the Swedish preschool. As already noted, EfS is seen as an important task of Swedish preschool education, and preschool children participate regularly in activities dealing with sustainability issues. The findings of the meta-analysis, however, point to a complex web, with today's education activities containing ideas stemming from the early days of preschool education. For example, traditional nature education is often integrated with contemporary understandings of children and childhood, with the preschool seen as a place where sometimes opposing political and practical agendas are expressed. Such complexities highlight the need for more to be done to build early childhood practitioners' understandings of ECEfS and how it might be practised.

The egg project – a case study

We now discuss an example of how EfS *could* be enacted thoughtfully in a preschool in Sweden. This exemplary EfS case study (Engdahl & Ärlemalm-Hagsér 2008) was carried out in a suburban Stockholm preschool where 5-year-old children and their teachers worked on a project aimed at holistically integrating the social, economic, environmental and political dimensions of sustainability. The project started with a discussion about dinosaur eggs and ended with an analysis of the economic and ethical cost of eggs produced from alternative ways of egg farming, such as those produced

---

[2] Preschool attendants have a 2–3-year vocational qualification, and work in teams with preschool teachers.

by battery hens and those by free range hens. The learning process empowered the children involved, who then demanded changes in their local setting.

The starting point was a visit to the Museum of Natural History following a three-month dinosaur theme. One of the children looked at the huge dinosaur egg and asked: 'Is there something alive in this egg?' The new project was born!

Back in the classroom, the teachers and children discussed questions such as: *What is alive? Do all eggs carry life? What is not alive?* The children's varied answers pushed the project along and led to many ideas about and strategies for learning more about life, eggs and hens. With the help of different forms of pedagogical documentation, including illustrations, drawings and texts, to answer the question *How come some eggs carry chickens and some don't?*, learning in the project was made visible. The children's questions and the production of rich documentation fully engaged children, teachers and families.

The children used many ways to access new knowledge about the topics that were part of the egg project, including: 'We can ask Anna's grandmother.' 'We can read a book about eggs.' 'We can go to a farm and ask.' As in all research, questions came up continuously, which then gave inspiration for a study visit to a nearby farm. The children brought their questions about life, eggs and hens to the farm; they included: 'Where does life come from?', 'Can a cock mate with any hen?', 'Why are the eggs different?' and 'Do eggs come from the poo-poo hole?'

After the farm study visit, the children began making their own hens, in replica sizes, from chicken wire stuffed with shredded paper. This activity re-energised the project, capturing every child's interest. The children identified personally with their hens, which then led to new investigations about hens and chicken farming around questions such as: 'Can they go outside?', 'Can they fly?', 'How much do they eat?', 'Do they like bathing?' and 'How do they find worms?' The children began to discuss the existential and ethical aspects of being a hen, focusing on the living conditions of hens and human responsibilities for nature.

Next, the children searched for information about the living conditions of commercial egg-laying hens. When they found out how small many of the cages were, they became very upset. They took notes of the sizes of the cages and made two-dimensional replicas of hens. The next step was to build two-dimensional replicas of the cages. With the help of applied mathematics, and measuring and counting with tapes and carpenter's rules, they constructed 'realistic' cages for their hens. The children's studies revealed that life for hens is not always nice, as many hens live in very small coops and do not always have a perch, and many stay indoors all their lives.

Three types of cages were built by the children: one for battery hens that live all their lives in small cages without perches; one for cage-free barn hens with more space and a perch; and one for free-range hens that can walk around freely indoors and outdoors.

Figure 12.1 *Hens in a cage in a battery farm*

Figure 12.2 *Cage-free barn hens, with a perch and more indoor space*

The cages were then put on show in the preschool. For each cage, there was a sign showing how many eggs from each type of egg-farming system could be bought for two krona: battery farm hens – six eggs; cage-free barn hens – five eggs; free-range hens – four eggs. The children were exploring economics!

The final part of the project took off when the children asked the preschool cook about the eggs she served for lunch. They were appalled by her answer: the eggs came from battery hens in cages, a decision forced by municipal regulations requiring the preschool to buy the cheapest eggs. This prompted the children to start a political campaign involving the municipal office, the Directors of Education and Finance, and local egg producers. They were successful! After a meeting with the mayor and her staff, the rules were changed and preschools in this particular municipality were allowed to buy eggs from ecologically certified farms. Needless to say, the teachers, children's families and their relatives also switched to eggs from hens with the better living conditions!

Figure 12.3 *Free-range ecological hens, with access to indoors and outdoors*

Provocation 12.4

Could a project such as this occur in your preschool? Why? Why not?

How can preschool children reach out to their neighbourhood and invite joint actions for sustainability?

What are the social, environmental and economic aspects of sustainability that this project addresses?

Challenging adults and the municipal system

The egg project covered all pillars of sustainable development – ecological, social and economic (UNDESD n.d.), as well as the political dimensions of empowerment and agency. Learning was kept going due to the children's ideas, questions and action initiatives. As engaged co-learners, the teachers supported children's learning through relevant forms of pedagogical documentation and challenged the children by enlarging the scope of the learning with further questioning. The overall impact was that learning occurred in a democratic and empowering way that supported children's participation and the power to change things, seen as fundamental aspects of EfS. We believe that the children and teachers were demonstrating competencies and ethical understandings that help create a culture of sustainability (Davis 2010) in their preschool.

Conclusion

Here, we have provided an overview of the Swedish preschool system and of EfS in Swedish preschools. We have illustrated this with reference to current research and a case study of EfS practice. Looking back on the chapter's themes, however, an important question emerges: *Why don't more teachers engage in empowering forms of EfS in preschools in Sweden, especially as the steering documents support such practices?*

While we don't have clear answers to this question, we are convinced that embedding EfS into the pedagogical practices of preschools needs to become more widespread. Children's thoughts and initiatives are not taken seriously enough, and they often have limited power to influence their preschool's daily programs or the actions of their local communities. It is a fundamental democratic task for preschool teachers to create opportunities for shared critical thinking and child participation in society. Children should be supported as active citizens, and given opportunities to challenge existing practices that are unsustainable.

To conclude, it is well understood that habits, attitudes, values and self-esteem form in the early years. Thus, it is of vital importance to address children's agency, values, attitudes and behaviours in preschool education. EfS is about empowerment, aimed at addressing sustainability issues and developing fundamental values such as caring for oneself, others and the environment. As such, it offers ways to show solidarity, equality, respect for life, and recognition of the dependence of humanity on a healthy biosphere.[3] We challenge preschool educators to keep this broad goal in mind and to look for opportunities to design holistic, child-centred learning projects aimed at advancing sustainability and active citizenship. This is not a simple task as we recognise the complexities of working with a diversity of values, attitudes and behaviours related to both education and to sustainable development. Perhaps a starting point for early childhood educators is to consider – and to regularly return to – the following question: *How does EfS in my preschool lay the groundwork for lasting changes to everyday life that contribute to sustainable futures?*

---

[3] See also *The Gothenburg Recommendations on Education for Sustainable Development* (University of Gothenburg & Chalmers University of Technology 2008).

References

Ärlemalm-Hagsér, E. (2013). *'An Interest in the Best for the World'? Education for Sustainability in the Swedish Preschool* (Doctoral thesis, Gothenburg Studies in Educational Sciences 335). Gothenburg: Acta Universitatis Gothoburgensis.

Ärlemalm-Hagsér, E. & Sandberg, A. (2011). Sustainable development in early childhood education: In-service students' comprehension of SD. *Environmental Education Research Journal*, 17(2), 187–200.

Ärlemalm-Hagsér E. & Sandberg A. (2013). Outdoor play in a Swedish preschool context. In S. Knight (ed.), *International Perspectives on Forest School: Natural Spaces to Play and Learn*. London: Sage.

Dahlbeck, J. (2012). *On Childhood and the Good Will: Thoughts on Ethics and Early Childhood Education* (Doctoral thesis, Malmö Studies in Educational Sciences 65). Lund: Lund University.

Dahlbeck, J. & Tallberg Broman, I. (2011). Ett bättre samhälle genom pedagogik: Högre värden och barnet som budbärare [A better society through education: Values and the child as a messenger]. In P. Williams & S. Sheridan (eds), *Barns lärande i ett livslĺngt perspektiv*. Stockholm: Liber.

Davis, J. (2010). What is early childhood education for sustainability? In J. Davis (ed.), *Young Children and the Environment Early Education for Sustainability* (1st edn). Melbourne: Cambridge University Press.

Education Act (2010:800). Swedish Government, www.skolverket.se/regelverk/skollagen-och-andralagar, (accessed 4 October 2013).

Engdahl, I. (2011). *Toddlers as Social Actors in the Swedish Preschool* (Doctoral thesis). Stockholm: Stockholm University, Department of Child and Youth Studies.

Engdahl, I. & Ärlemalm-Hagsér, E. (2008). Swedish preschool children show interest and are involved in the future of the world. In I. Pramling Samuelsson & Y. Kaga, *The Contribution of Early Childhood Education to a Sustainable Society*. Paris: UNESCO.

Fröbel, F. (1826 [1995]). *Människans fostran* [Die Menschenerziehung]. Lund: Studentlitteratur.

Gustavsson, B. (1993). *Börja bland barn: En miljöfostrande pedagogik [Begin with Children: An Environmental Pedagogy]*. Socialstyrelsen: Allmänna förlaget.

Hägglund, S. & Pramling Samuelsson, I. (2009). Early childhood education and learning for sustainable development and citizenship. *International Journal of Early Childhood*, 41(2), 49–63.

Johansson, E. (2009). The preschool child of today: The world citizen tomorrow? *International Journal of Early Childhood*, 41(2), 79–95.

National Agency for Education (2011a). *Curriculum for the Preschool: Lpfö 98*. Stockholm: The Swedish National Agency for Education, www.skolverket.se/publikationer?id=2704 (accessed 4 October 2013).

National Agency for Education (2011b). *Facts and Figures 2011: Preschool Activities, School-Age Childcare, Schools and Adult Education in Sweden* (Summary of Report 363). Stockholm: The Swedish National Agency for Education, www.skolverket.se/publikationer?id=2768 (accessed 4 October 2013).

Öhman, J. (2011). Theme: New Swedish environmental and sustainability education research. *Education and Democracy*, 20(1), 3–12.

Sandell, K. & Öhman, J. (2012). An educational tool for outdoor education and environmental concern. *Journal of Adventure Education and Outdoor Learning*, 13(1), 36–55.

UNDESD (n.d). About ESD, www.desd.org/aboutesd.htm (accessed 1 May 2014).

United Nations (1989). *The UN Convention on the Rights of the Child*. New York: United Nations.

University of Gothenburg & Chalmers University of Technology (2008). *The Gothenburg Recommendations on Education for Sustainable Development*, www.esd-world-conference-2009.org/fileadmin/download/Gothenburg_RecommendationsAndBackground.pdf (accessed 5 February 2009).

Chapter 13

Beyond traditional nature-based activities to education for sustainability: A case study from Japan

Michiko Inoue

Editor's note

In this updated chapter, **Michiko Inoue** first outlines key features of the early childhood education system in Japan. She then discusses the place of nature-based education and environmental education in Japanese early childhood education and makes a connection to EfS. In this discussion, Michiko incorporates case studies that show specific aspects of ECEfS. These include a case study about renovating a playground and another involving children and teachers learning about the origins of daily food. The latter case illustrates the use of 'practice study' as a form of professional development that can be utilised to support pedagogical change aimed at implementing ECEfS. Michiko finishes her chapter by discussing initiatives in Japan that support ECEfS and some of the challenges to be overcome for wider uptake of EfS within Japanese early education.

Introduction

Early childhood education in Japan

Japan has a dual early childhood education system with two types of authorised services: kindergartens and nursery centres (National Institute for Educational Policy Research 2009). Each type has two kinds of governing bodies: public (city councils and the national government) and private (such as religious organisations and private education foundations). In Japan, primary schools for children aged 6–11 years, and lower secondary schools for children aged 12–14 years, are compulsory. Preschool education is not compulsory. Children's enrolment rates in early childhood education in Japan for the under threes is low (24.5 per cent in 2008). The rate for 3-year-olds, however, is 79.8 per cent and for 5-year-olds is 97.8 per cent.

The Japanese government developed national standards for early childhood education as far back as the 19th century. Currently, there are two sets of guidelines: the Course of Study for Kindergarten and the Guideline for Care and Education in Nursery Centres. Although these two guidelines are managed under different governing ministries, the educational objectives for children aged 3–5 years have been aligned since the early 1990s. In 2006, the government founded a new service type called 'centres for early childhood education and care' to enhance further cooperation between kindergartens and nursery centres.

In terms of qualifications, the certificate for a kindergarten educator is the 'Teacher's License' awarded by the Ministry of Education, Culture, Sports, Science and Technology, of which there are three levels. The certificate for a nursery centre worker is the 'Qualification as a Nursery Teacher' from the Ministry of Health, Labour and Welfare. Most early childhood educators have both national certificates. The training curricula for both certificates are strictly regulated by the national government. A recent report of the Organisation for Economic Co-operation and Development (OECD) described Japan as having highly qualified staff in early childhood education, with its nursery workers singled out (Taguma, Litjens & Makowiecki 2012).

Environmental education in Japan

'Environmental education' was imported from Western countries to Japan in the early 1970s, although education about pollution and nature conservation has been taught in schools and communities since the 1960s (see, for example, Kawashima, Ichikawa & Imamura 2002). The Japanese government introduced environmental education into its environmental policy in the 1980s and into the national curriculum for schools in 1989.

The government also enacted the Law for Enhancing Motivation on Environmental Conservation and Promoting of Environmental Education in 2003 (revised in 2011). Consequently, both the environment and education government sectors in Japan mostly use the term 'environmental education' in their official discourses across law, education, environmental management and other related areas. Neither the concept 'sustainable development' nor 'education for sustainability' (EfS) has been adopted in any laws, environmental policies or educational guidelines in Japan. Following this tradition, in this chapter, I use 'environmental education' as the main terminology. However, I recognise that environmental education is an important part of the broader concept of EfS.

Stories from the field

When visiting early childhood centres in autumn in Japan, we see many forms of arts and crafts made by children using natural materials, such as acorns, coloured leaves, nuts and sticks. The children usually gather these materials themselves. Many centres also plan to give children experiences in harvesting sweet potatoes, which symbolises autumn. After the harvest, children commonly engage in art activities with a 'sweet potato' theme, and sometimes cook and eat sweet potatoes at their centres.

These activities are nature-based activities. Children also play in outdoor natural spaces, plant flowers, take care of animals, collect natural materials and use them in creative activities. Do you regard these kinds of activities as contributing to EfS? Explain your response. Are nature-based activities enough of a contribution towards building a sustainable society? Explain.

Figure 13.1 *Playing with plants*

Nature education in early childhood in Japan

As noted, Japan has a long tradition of national early childhood curricula. The first national law and regulations for early childhood education – the Kindergarten Order and the Enforcement Regulations for the Kindergarten Order – were established in 1926. Following these official initiatives, nature-based activities became standard practice in Japanese kindergartens. At that time, many kindergartens built gardens and acquired animals for children to care for. After World War 2, the government amended its education laws and guidelines for early childhood and, since then, in every version of the guidelines, there are two specific objectives that relate to nature-based activities; these aim to facilitate scientific ways of thinking and foster humanitarianism in children (Inoue 2000). These descriptions have not fundamentally changed. Therefore, nature-based activities, such as outside play, caring for animals, and gardening, have been regarded as integral for children's development in the long history of early childhood education in Japan, as has the development of care and concern for others in society.

Kindergartens are legally required to have playgrounds in Japan. Although this same regulation does not apply for nursery centres, most have their own playgrounds. Half of all services have garden beds, spaces for wild grasses, fruit trees, and areas where children can freely pick and use flowers and leaves while playing. Traditionally, Japanese children have used wild plants in their play – for example, to make reed pipes and clover flower crowns, and to extract natural dyes from petals. Children also use outdoor playgrounds for making mud balls and catching or observing small creatures, such as woodlice, grasshoppers and cicadae. In a 2003 survey conducted by this author, it was found that children played in centre playgrounds every day, on average, for 105 minutes. Animals were cared for in 90 per cent of services and each centre cared for an average of 4.4 animals, such as crayfish (58%), rabbits (53%), goldfish (46%), and butterfly larvae (43%) and other insects (41%) (Inoue & Muto 2009). Most services also organised short excursions (to parks, shrines and open spaces in the community), on average, once or twice a month (Inoue & Muto 2010).

Every official early childhood education guideline describes nature-based activities as significant for child development and health; educators accept the importance of such activities and do include them in their educational practices. However, this raises an important question: *Does repeating such traditional practices contribute to environmental education?* I question the assumption that it does, because it appears obvious that the continued use of traditional, nature-based activities over generations in Japan has failed to prevent the ongoing depletion of natural resources in Japan caused by rapid, often injudicious, economic development, even though generations of children have learned about the natural world in early childhood under the guidance of national curricula. Additionally, the natural environments of the early 20th century in Japan, when these guidelines were first introduced, were remarkably different from those of the present. Then, most people were engaged in pre-industrial occupations, such as fishing and agriculture. There were more undeveloped natural areas, and streets were not paved with asphalt, even in urban areas. Children lived in greater proximity to a wide variety of plants and animals within their daily lives. They played with natural materials because most children did not have manufactured toys, and they engaged frequently in nature-based activities because no other choices existed. However, such experiences, while undoubtedly contributing to children's development and health, were not at all aimed at fostering an ecological worldview. I believe, therefore, that it is now time to rethink and redesign nature-based activities, not only for child development and health benefits, but for establishing an ecological worldview that many consider essential for building a sustainable society.

An ecological worldview

Ecology is a relatively new academic field, born of the late 19th century. The concept 'ecosystem' emerged in the 1930s. In Japan, national curricula for primary schools and secondary schools refer to concepts such as ecosystem, food web and biodiversity as ideas to be taught at school. Thus, Japanese people have a basic knowledge of ecology. However, after presenting an ecology lecture to my university students where I emphasised that humans were part of the planet's ecology, many commented that they had never regarded themselves as a part of any ecosystem. While these students had knowledge about ecology, this knowledge did not make direct connection with themselves or their everyday lives (Inoue 2005). Basically, environmental issues are ecosystems issues. An ecological worldview develops an understanding of how the natural world works and how humans interact with the planet's natural ecosystems. Living organisms, including human beings, cannot survive outside natural ecosystems. It is important, therefore, to foster an ecological worldview that connects humans to a shared natural environment. This should be the main aim of contemporary environmental education. *What do you think of these ideas?*

Provocation 13.1

How do you define an ecological system?

What part do you think human beings play within the Earth's ecological systems? What past experiences have contributed to your definition of an ecological system?

How might you foster an ecological worldview with young children through your early education practices?

Redesigning nature-based activities for sustainability

How can nature-based activities be redesigned for environmental education in Japan, in order to foster an ecological worldview that contributes to sustainability? As mentioned above, for a long time, the value of nature-based activities for child development has been recognised under national educational guidelines. Some educators, however, have also begun to realise that the role and impact of nature-based activities needs to change. For example, children in contemporary Japanese society play outside much less often than children in the past, and it is beginning to be recognised that our society is confronting an unsustainable future. Such critique presents a good opportunity to rethink existing Japanese early childhood practices. Here, I propose two ideas to promote change: (1) redesigning children's playgrounds to fully support outdoor learning in nature, and (2) refocusing on connecting children with nature on a daily basis.

Redesigning children's playgrounds

Playgrounds in early childhood services in Japan are appropriate places to experience nature. As mentioned, Japanese children play in the playgrounds of early childhood services for around 1.5 hours per day, and it is usual for playgrounds to have some trees, flowers and vegetable gardens (Inoue & Muto 2006). However, the quality and quantity of natural spaces varies greatly between services. To foster an ecological worldview, the quality of outdoor natural spaces is very important. For more on this topic, read Sue Elliott's Chapter 2. For example, spaces such as butterfly gardens that invite butterflies, caterpillars, bees and predator insects are significant for experiencing biodiversity and ecological cycles. Note: Indigenous plant species are preferred in playgrounds as it is possible to damage the local ecosystem if invasive species are introduced.

Case study 1: Kwansei-Gakuin Seiwa Kindergarten

Kwansei-Gakuin Seiwa Kindergarten is located in a residential district in Nishinomiya City (Hyogo prefecture) in the middle of Japan, with nearly 200 children attending, aged 3–5 years. This kindergarten, a leading kindergarten that offers high-quality education using child-centred approaches, has a beautifully renovated, forest-like playground. Twenty years ago, its playground area was a parking space for cars. The present Director started to improve the soils by planting clover. After this improvement, the Director intentionally planted a variety of species, including evergreen trees, deciduous trees, vines, edible fruit trees, oaks producing acorns, herbs and wild grasses, with which Japanese children have traditionally played. Having a wide range of plants offers a variety of leaves, fruits and nuts of different textures,

Figure 13.2 *Forest-like playground*

shapes, smells and colours. Now, there are many kinds of flowers, herbs and wild grasses growing at this kindergarten, and the children can freely use this wide range of botanical materials in their play. Scents of various plants fill the whole playground and stimulate children's olfactory senses. Fallen leaves give nutrients for decomposers and help fertilise the soils, and now there is a great variety of birds and insects in this kindergarten. This forest-like playground comprises a small ecosystem that is also part of the wider community ecosystem.

Moreover, this playground has a variety of play spaces, including a small hill, a pond and a sand pit. Play equipment, such as cubby houses, a trampoline and a Tarzan rope, has been made from original designs mainly using natural materials. Some equipment was even constructed by the teachers themselves. These play spaces and their apparatuses provide many ongoing opportunities for children to use all parts of their bodies and senses, and contribute to their overall health, wellbeing and environmental learning. This kindergarten provides inspiration to other early childhood services, showing them what is possible.

Connecting children with nature in their daily lives

To connect children with nature in their daily lives and to help them realise the close ecological relationships between human beings and other living organisms, food is a most appropriate teaching and learning resource. Through food, children can learn how society works and how we are all involved in the economy as consumers. Food is an excellent resource for learning the complexities of the social, environmental and economic factors that make up sustainability in our everyday lives. For more on this topic, read Chapter 9 by Nadine McCrea.

In Japan, the Child Welfare Act requires that a nursery centre offers lunch to children, and that each centre has its own kitchen and professional kitchen staff (for the over

Figure 13.3 *Outdoor play equipment*

threes, a registered food provider can be used who does not have to be onsite). Thus, nursery centres are most suitable for learning about and through food. The Japanese government also enacted the Basic Act on Food Education in 2005 to enhance the 'acquisition of knowledge about food as well as the ability to make appropriate food choices' (Preamble of this Act). Under this law, food education is included in the national curriculum for all education services from kindergartens to secondary schools, as well as in the Guidelines for Care and Education in Nursery Centres in 2008 (Cabinet Office, Government of Japan 2011).

All food is produced in supermarkets?

There are many humorous (and concerning!) stories of children's knowledge about food. When teachers ask children 'Where does rice come from?', children often answer: 'Supermarket!' or 'Rice shop!' Such answers are also common when children are asked about the origins of vegetables, eggs, meat and other basic foods. One teacher told me that she had been surprised to find a drawing of a fish fillet when a child was asked to draw a fish. Such responses and misrepresentations are also common with older students. Even college students sometimes draw figures of chickens with four legs (Masuda 2012)!

Humans are major consumers within the Earth's ecosystems. The fact is that our food comes from living organisms – plants, animals, fungi and bacteria – and we humans cannot live without sacrificing other animals and plants. Many humans, however, appear to live without this basic understanding, especially in urbanised, contemporary societies. If we forget that our own lives depend on other organisms, we do not fully understand the value of the natural world to humans, and do not have an ecological worldview.

Case study 2: Tomioka-nishi Nursery Centre

Tomioka-nishi Nursery Centre is located in a residential district in Sakai City (close to Osaka City), with 120 children attending from 57 days after birth up to 5 years of age. This centre has conducted a 'practice study' (Jissen Kenkyu) since 2010 using the theme of environmental education; I have been the supervisor of this study. The educators renovated the centre's playground in order for children and educators to better experience nature and to improve the overall educational environment. They documented what they were doing and discussed their experiences once a month in order to improve their practices.

Practice study (Jissen Kenkyu)

In Japan, teachers in primary schools and secondary schools undertake 'lesson study' (Jugyo Kenkyu) to improve their educational practices as part of ongoing professional development (Arani, Fukaya & Lassegard 2010; Lewis 2000). For kindergartens and nursery centres, educators engage in a similar process called 'practice study' (Jissen Kenkyu). Such study is conducted as a whole-centre approach. Educators decide on a study theme and then practise, reflect and evaluate their educational practices in relation to this theme. Documentation is a fundamental part of the study, with teachers engaging in reflection by observing each other's practices, then discussing these after the practice has been observed. 'Practice study' is common especially in public kindergartens. The governing city council selects particular kindergartens each year that then conduct 'practice study' for one or two years. Such study is usually supervised by city council officers who are former experienced educators, and by researchers at universities. At the end of the study, the kindergarten conducts a final study meeting that is open to all kindergarten teachers in the area, and usually includes a model practice, a presentation of the whole study process, and a talk by professionals and researchers. In the process of 'practice study', educators develop their professional skills and deepen their understandings of the study theme.

As part of the new practices developed through their practice study at Tomioka-nishi Nursery Centre, children in the class for 5-year-olds visited a local pig farm. This was one of a series of events for the class because the educators wanted the children to understand where the meat used in their everyday meals came from. Initially, the children reacted negatively to the smell of the farm. However, they changed their attitude when they realised how thoughtful the farmer was about his pigs, and how much work he did for their welfare. This experience then became exciting for the children; they actively questioned the pig farmer about what he did as a farmer.

Figure 13.4 *Pig farm visit*

Figure 13.5 *Butcher's shop visit*

Several days after the visit, the children visited the butcher shop from where the centre usually bought its meat for the children's lunch. The owner told the children about how the meat was named according to the animal's body parts. The children asked eagerly: 'Which part of the body does this meat come from?' 'How do you use the meat-cutting machine?' and 'Does meat go rotten straight after being cut?'

As the cooking staff at the children's centre were using pork for lunch that day, the teachers planned to build on the children's earlier learning and, therefore, before lunch, explained what was being served: 'We eat pork because the farmer looks after his pigs; pigs are then killed; the butcher processes the meat; our cooking staff cook the meat for our lunch.' The children then remarked: 'Pigs are killed to give meat to us.' 'We have to thank pigs because they give us our meat.' 'When we say "Thank you for our food" before eating, this means we are giving thanks to the pigs.' From such experiences, the children came to know where their food comes from and how their daily lives depend on other people in the community. Through learning about pigs, these children also learned how food used in their daily lives is environmentally, socially and economically connected.

Conclusion

What are the ways to promote EfS in early childhood education in Japan? Recently, there have been some hopeful changes. For example, the environmental education sector has begun to include early childhood as a target group, and the number of nature education centres and non-profit groups that offer nature-based activities to young children is growing. For example, the Forest Kindergarten Network, a nationwide non-profit association for sharing knowledge and experience of outdoor activities for young children, noted a significant increase in membership in 2013.

Furthermore, kindergartens and nursery centres are now expected to refurbish their playgrounds and to offer children more opportunities for nature-based activities as a result of recent revisions to the national guidelines that have re-emphasised their significance. While this is a good start, the main concern among early childhood educators is still with improving *individual* child development, rather than thinking about the greater *social* purpose of sustainability. This is a huge, unresolved issue for early childhood education in Japan, and much more work needs to be done in this area. It is vital that early childhood educators become engaged in EfS because they are key for reflecting on, rethinking and changing early learning environments, educational theories and educational practices as they relate to EfS. Through such changes, then, early childhood education in Japan can make a stronger contribution to a healthier, more sustainable world, not only for Japanese children but for all children.

References

Arani, M. R. S., Fukaya, K. & Lassegard, J. P. F. (2010). 'Lesson study' as professional culture in Japanese schools: An historical perspective on elementary classroom practices, *Japan Review*, 22, 171–200.

Cabinet Office, Government of Japan (2011). *Basic Program for Shokuiku Promotion*, www8. cao.go.jp/syokuiku/about/pdf/plan_ol_eng.pdf (accessed 14 October 2013).

Inoue, M. (2000). An historical study on the significance of 'nature' in early childhood education in Japan – from a viewpoint of environmental education [in Japanese], *Environmental Education*, 9(2), 2–11.

Inoue, M. (2005). Practices of environmental education in liberal arts courses at university level [in Japanese], *Journal of Kinki Welfare University*, 6(1), 1–10.

Inoue, M. & Muto, T. (2006). A survey of the natural environment of playgrounds in kindergartens and nursery schools [in Japanese], *The Japanese Journal for the Education of Young Children*, 15, 1–11.

Inoue, M. & Muto, T. (2009). A survey on nature activities in kindergartens and nursery schools (2) [in Japanese], *The Bulletin of Education and Social Welfare*, 35, 1–7.

Inoue, M. & Muto, T. (2010). A survey on nature activities in kindergartens and nursery schools (3) [in Japanese], *Bulletin of Osaka Ohtani University*, 44, 117–32.

Kawashima, M., Ichikawa S. & Imamura, M. (eds) (2002). *Introduction to Environmental Education* [in Japanese]. Kyoto: Minelva Shobo.

Lewis, C. (2000). *Lesson Study: The Core of Japanese Professional Development*, American Educational Research Association Meetings, www.csudh.edu/math/syoshinobu/107web/aera2000.pdf (accessed 14 October 2013).

Masuda, H. (2012). *Why University Students Draw a Picture of Chickens with Four Legs?* [in Japanese]. Maebashi: Jomo-Shinbun-sha.

National Institute for Educational Policy Research (2009). *Preschool Education and Care in Japan*, www.nier.go.jp/English/EducationInJapan/Education_in_Japan/Education_in_Japan_files/201109ECEC.pdf (accessed 23 March 2013).

Taguma, M., Litjens, I. & Makowiecki, K. (2012). *Quality Matters in Early Childhood Education and Care: Japan*, OECD Publications, www.oecd-ilibrary.org/education/quality-matters-in-early-childhood-education-and-care-japan-2012_9789264176621-en (accessed 23 March 2013).

Chapter 14

Education for sustainable development in early childhood in Korea

Okjong Ji

Editor's note

In this new chapter, **Okjong Ji** provides us with an overview of the early childhood system in the Republic of Korea (South Korea, or 'Korea' for short). This is followed by an account of how the Korean government has stimulated national educational changes that promote and support education for sustainable development across all education sectors in Korea, including early childhood education. These initiatives have led to increasing engagement with sustainable development concepts and pedagogies, and new resources and strategies for early childhood teachers to put into practice. In this chapter, Okjong presents a case study of a kindergarten that successfully used the Project Approach to engage young children in an authentic, locally relevant sustainability project where they identified issues in their local park and then worked with the City Hall to tidy up and improve the park's safety and aesthetics. An engaging feature of this project was the children's use of 'Quick Response' (QR) codes to communicate about and engage the local community in their project.

Introduction

General background to early childhood education in Korea

In Korea, there are two kinds of formal education institutions for children in the birth to 5-year-old range. One is a 'childcare centre' for those in the birth to age 5 group; the other is a 'kindergarten' for 3- to 5-year-olds. Previously, childcare centres focused more on caring for children, while the kindergarten focused primarily on education. Now, however, care is considered as important in kindergarten as education because most kindergartens now operate whole-day programs and children spend much longer periods in the institution than previously. Also, in childcare centres many parents are demanding high-quality education as well as actual childcare. Therefore, the differences between these two types of early education institutions have gradually diminished in Korea, supported by efforts for integration at the national level. Still, in 2013 there remain several differences between these two types of institutions, as shown in Table 14.1.

Education for sustainable development (ESD) efforts in Korea

Current efforts of the Korean government for ESD

After the Rio Summit of 1992, and according to the United Nations' recommendation, the Korean government created the Presidential Commission on Sustainable Development in September 2000 to implement sustainable development (SD) at a national level. Then, in August 2007, a related law, the Framework Act on Sustainable Development, was also

Table 14.1 *Differences between childcare centres and kindergartens in Korea*

	CHILDCARE CENTRES	KINDERGARTENS
Responsible to	Ministry of Health and Welfare	Ministry of Education
Teacher qualifications	Three kinds: Level 1, 2, 3, managed through Ministry of Health and Welfare	Two kinds: Level 1, 2, managed through Ministry of Education
Related law	Infant and Child Care Act	Early Childhood Education Act
Target age of children	Birth to 5-year-olds	3- to 5-year-olds
Curriculum framework	Care curriculum for 0- to 2-year-olds Common curriculum: 'Nuri' for 3- to 5-year-olds	Common curriculum: 'Nuri'

established. This act specified that, for 'the realisation of SD, education programs need to be developed' (Article 21, Education and Public Relations). Later, in the revised national school curriculum of 2007 for elementary and middle schools, it was mentioned that 'ESD needs to be stressed across the content of the curriculum'. More recently, specific materials for teachers of elementary and middle school have been developed, including 'Reference Materials about ESD for Elementary Teachers' (Korean Government, Ministry of Environment 2009). However, it is important to note that prior to this, there was no interest or concern for ESD at the kindergarten level, even though there was a change of perspective within the revised national kindergarten curriculum of 2007, from a human-focused orientation to one that promoted respect for both humans and nature.

National promotion of ESD in kindergarten became official with the enactment of the Environmental Education Promotion Law in February 2008. According to Article 2 of the Law, 'environmental education is aimed towards SD'. The law also clearly specifies that environmental education for SD should begin from kindergarten level, as set out in Article 9.

Meanwhile, on 15 August 2008, at the national address for the 60th anniversary of the Republic of Korea, Lee Myung-Bak, the former President, announced a 'low-carbon, green growth' strategy as a new vision to guide the nation's long-term development. Following this announcement, the Presidential Committee on Green Growth was established in February 2009. The Committee announced a Five-Year Plan for Green Growth (Korean Government, Presidential Committee on Green Growth 2009) on 6 July 2009 to serve as a medium-term plan for the implementation of the National Strategy for Green Growth over the period 2009–13. According to this plan, Korea has a vision 'to become one of the top 7 green growth countries in the world by 2020 and in the top 5 by 2050' (Korean Government, Presidential Committee on Green Growth 2009, p. 31).

As part of this process, green growth education, as a practical way of implementing ESD, has stood out strongly in the education field. As a concrete example, the Green Growth Committee, the Ministry of Education, the Ministry of Environment, and the Ministry of Public Administration and Security have worked together to publish the Activation Plan of Green Growth Education (Korean Government, Presidential Committee on Green Growth et al. 2009). The main components of this plan include three strategies and eight policy tasks. The first strategy is 'reinforcement of green growth education for elementary and secondary school'. As a result of this strategy, in the curriculum revisions of 2009, the subject of 'environment' was changed to 'environment and green growth' for the middle school. In the same context, in 2011 'green growth education' was added to the 'Nuri' curriculum that was developed as a common curriculum for 5-year-olds in both kindergartens and childcare centres. Then, in 2012, green growth education was also included as one of the characteristics of the new Nuri curriculum for 3- to 5-year-olds.

'Green growth education': A practical way of implementing ESD in kindergarten in Korea

In December 2012 the Ministry of Education published *The Green Growth Education Program for Supporting Kindergarten Curriculum Operations*. To be used by every kindergarten in Korea, the goal of this program is 'to form a foundation of global green citizens who can contribute to sustainable life and green growth in the future' (Korean Government, Ministry of Education 2012, p. 18). The objectives of the program are in three domains: knowledge and understanding; feelings and affection; and attitudes and participation. Following on from these objectives, the content of the program consists of four key aspects: basic understanding of the Earth's environment; awareness of environmental problems; appropriate lifestyle for sustainability; and increasing green citizenship and participation for a sustainable life.

Since the promulgation of the Nuri curriculum and the development of the green growth education program for 3- to 5-year-olds in 2012, the Ministry of Education has offered a professional development program based on this curriculum and program for teachers and directors working in kindergartens. As a consequence of all these new initiatives, specialist groups such as the Korean Society for Early Childhood Education (KSECE) are now trying to introduce ESD to the early childhood field by way of seminars, conferences and short-term training programs.

The Maebong Park Project as an example of early childhood ESD in Korea

Here, I discuss the Maebong Park Project conducted by Surim Kindergarten in Cheongju city as an example of ESD in Korea's kindergartens. Surim Kindergarten is a member of the 'Chungbuk Early Childhood Educators' Community for Nature Appreciation', which consists of eight early childhood institutions supervised by Okjong Ji, the author of this chapter. These eight institutions conducted the Maebong Park Project once a year during 2011–13, focusing on the relationships between children and the community. As a result of the project's success, in 2012 the Korean National Commission for UNESCO authenticated the 'park project connected with their community' as an excellent model of ESD. Then, in 2013, the Chungbuk Early Childhood Educators' Community for Nature Appreciation received a citation from the Mayor of Cheongju city for creating a better community environment. The Maebong Park Project discussed here is just one successful example among the eight projects conducted by these institutions in 2013.

The Maebong Park Project used the Project Approach as its key curriculum strategy (Katz & Chard 2010). In accordance with the main features of the Project Approach, the project began with topic selection and initial teacher planning, followed by three phases that were undertaken by both the teacher and the children of Surim Kindergarten. These phases were Phase I (getting the project started), Phase II (project in progress) and Phase III (consolidating the project).

Preparation for the Maebong Park Project

Prior to commencing the project, the teacher made a topic web and checked possible curriculum areas related to Maebong Park in order to find suitable learning activities, and to set educational objectives. Specifically, the objectives focused on developing children's understandings that the park is an important community place for its citizens, including the kindergarten children, and that taking care of the park contributes to sustainable living. Then the teacher compiled a resource list including potential local experts for the project, and prepared a picture book about the park, with pictures of interesting play objects and other park features. During this phase, the teacher also visited Maebong Park with the Director of the kindergarten and the teacher aide to scrutinise possible activities for young children in the park.

Phase 1: Getting the Maebong Park Project started

Twenty-eight 5-year-old children, one teacher and one teacher aide from the Surim Kindergarten together carried out the project, from 25 March 2013 to 3 May 2013, supported by the Director. The park is located 10 minutes away, by walking, from the kindergarten.

In the beginning stage of the project, the teacher realised that several children did not know anything about the park, and that some children who did know the location of the park thought it was simply 'the place for playing'. Also, the children did not have any special interest in or concern for the park. So, for an interesting introduction to the park, the teacher took photographs of several places in the park, such as a big stone, some play apparatus and a strangely bent tree.

On the first field trip to the park, the teacher gave each pair of children a photograph. They were then asked to cooperatively search for the subject of the photo as 'the mission' of the day. The children were delighted to have this mission where they could act as detectives. When the children found the subject in the photo, they shouted out loudly 'Here! We found it'. The teacher then confirmed the discovery by taking the children's photos alongside their found object.

Continuing in this way of discovery, exploring here and there in the park, the teacher and children found some dangerous-looking equipment for doing sit-ups, some broken electric apparatus and an abandoned tyre in the pond. Also during this time, the children became intrigued with the 'QR' codes attached to several items in the park by Cheongju City Hall. 'QR' is short for 'Quick Response'; a QR code is a two-dimensional code of block pattern that encodes a URL address to connect to a

(a)

(b)

Figure 14.1 *a. Dangerous sit-up apparatus b. QR message saying 'If anybody finds a problem, please report using this QR code'*

website. The teacher helped the children to learn about QR codes, and how a QR code is made. Because of the investigation into the QR codes, when the children visited the park again, they were able to check the codes quickly on the teacher's smart phone and obtain the necessary information, such as the name of the maintenance office for the physical equipment, and the phone number to ring to ask about repairing the apparatus.

Phase 2: Progress in the Maebong Park Project

Asking City Hall to repair objects in the park using a QR code

After finding information using the QR codes, the children then sent a request letter to the maintenance office of Cheongju City Hall asking City Hall to deal with the problems they had found. Moreover, they made their own QR code for this letter, and printed out the QR code, with the teacher's help, so that their parents could also access the letter at home via the QR code. The parents showed huge interest in the letters. As a point of reference, Korea is a country with advanced digital technology; most parents have smartphones and even young children are familiar with these devices. Several days later, the children received an official letter from the maintenance office saying that their request was accepted and that the problems in the park would be fixed in a few days. The children also read the officer's appreciation of the children's efforts to improve the park environment.

Provocation 14.1

Have you ever used or made a 'Quick Response' (QR) code? If you are a teacher of 4- to 5-year-olds, how might you use a QR code for education for sustainable development? If you have never used a QR code yourself, find out how to do this!

Resolving the problems the children asked City Hall to solve

One week later, when they visited the park again, the children ascertained that most of the problems they had identified had been resolved. For example, the broken equipment had been taken away (including the dangerous-looking sit-up apparatus), the broken electric apparatus had been changed, and the abandoned tyre in the pond had been removed. Seeing the results, the children, with great fervour, tried to find more things that needed repair in the park. As a result, the children and their teacher were able to change the park into a more safe and comfortable place for the wider community. The pond was totally changed as a result of the continuous efforts of the children.

Extended activities centred on the QR code

At the same time, because of the high interest the children had in the QR code, they began to make QR codes for all their ongoing activities in the project. For example, a QR code was made for a poster that asked the community's citizens to 'Keep the park clean'. After making this QR code, each of the children made an armband with the code attached. Then, whenever they visited the park to pick up rubbish, they wore the armband proudly, as the photo in Figure 14.3 shows. Furthermore, the children wanted to wear the code even when coming to kindergarten and going back home each day. Thanks to the children, the parents and the citizens became more interested in QR codes and the quality of the park's environment.

Figure 14.2 *Abandoned tyre in the pond*

Figure 14.3 *Children proudly wearing their armbands*

Part of the children's ongoing activity in the park was picking up the rubbish every Wednesday. The children realised that most of the rubbish was being thrown away by students from a nearby elementary school because the rubbish was mostly game cards and elementary students' exam papers. The kindergarten children and their teacher discussed how they could deliver their message of 'No litter in the park' to these elementary school students. They decided to make a flyer for the students asking them to respect the park environment. However, a problem was raised in that the school students might throw the flyers away as soon as they received them. Therefore, the children modified their way of delivering their message by using another QR code connected to the flyer and a flash mail that showed their message as an audiovisual letter.

After making these items, the Director of the kindergarten visited the elementary principal to deliver the flyers and the flash mail. The Director explained about the park project, focusing on the changes to the park created by the efforts of the kindergarten children. The elementary principal was very admiring of the kindergarten children's mindful concern for the park and the various tasks they undertook during the project.

A week later, the elementary principal led a meeting between the kindergarten children and the first-grade students of the elementary school in order to develop a cooperative activity for the park. As a result, the children of both institutions met at the park on 31 May 2013, and participated in several activities together, including singing a song entitled 'Keep Maebong Park clean together', which was composed by the kindergarten children. They also wiped the scribbles from the bulletin board and campaigned together in front of citizens who were in the park, asking them to take care of the park. These combined children's activities were reported in the local newspaper so that many people in the community found out about the children's efforts to make the park safe and clean.

Provocation 14.2

If you were to carry out a project similar to this 'park project', with whom could you cooperate in your local community to support and encourage children to participate in community problem solving?

Phase 3: Consolidating the project

Finally, as events of the project were culminating, the kindergarten children made a play about their project that included characters such as the bent tree and the broken bench and the other physical apparatus. These were all-important elements of the project, and were items about which the children now had intimate knowledge. The key message of the play was 'Let's love and keep clean the Maebong Park forever'. The play was recorded, and a QR code was also made for the play so that the children could watch it at home with their parents at any time.

As the last step of the project, the teacher and children gathered all the QR codes they had made and bound them together as a small book. This book was sent to each child's parents and also to the officer at Cheongju City Hall, the elementary school principal, and other people who had helped with the project.

After finishing the Maebong Park Project, the children's understandings of the park changed from simply being 'the place for playing' to 'the important place that they should take care of continuously with deep concern'. It must be noted that, during the same period, the other seven institutions of the Chungbuk Early Childhood Educators' Community for Nature Appreciation also involved in the Maebong Park Project brought similar results for their young children. Collectively, this means that the young children of all eight early childhood institutions were engaged in implementing ESD values, such as showing real concern for a local community issue, active participation in solving a problem in their community, evoking the wider community's interest in a community issue, and contributing to making the park a better place for the community.

Figure 14.4 *QR code for the play*

Provocation 14.3

Make a topic web about a special place in your community that would be suitable for carrying out a community sustainability project with young children. Then, make a list of possible learning activities that could arise from your topic web.

Issues/challenges for ESD in early childhood in Korea

Since the beginning of 2010, interest in ESD in early childhood has been rapidly increasing in Korea. Because of this high interest, many seminars on ECEfS and associated topics – such as the 'forest kindergarten', 'eco early childhood education', 'green growth education for young children', 'environmental education for sustainable development' and 'ESD for young children' – have been held by the government and professional associations. Nevertheless, many teachers and directors clearly do not know much about ESD, and the differences between ESD and environmental education. In Korea, ESD in early childhood is a very new concept for kindergarten directors and teachers; many have never heard these terms used before. Therefore, one of the biggest issues for the application of ESD in early childhood in Korea is to clearly explain many of these overlapping and ambiguous concepts in order to create common understanding of how ESD relates to early childhood education.

The next important challenge is how teacher professional learning can be focused in practical ways so that teachers can apply ESD in their classrooms in ways that connect children with their parents and the wider community around local sustainability issues and topics. Early childhood teachers and directors do not know the most effective methods to use even though they may want to apply ESD. I suggest that the Project Approach offers an appropriate way to practise ESD in early childhood in Korea; it offers a pedagogical approach that supports 'learner initiative' and 'learning all together'. Children's real participation in community issues can come to light through the project approach as demonstrated in the Maebong Park Project case study.

A further issue is to find an effective way to connect early childhood ESD with Korea's newly emerging environmental education centres that are being built following the implementation of the Environmental Education Act of 2008. To achieve this, early childhood professionals should actively cooperate with professionals from fields such as environmental education, environmental science and ecology in order to provide rich environmental and sustainability learning for young children.

As well, early childhood education professionals need to find effective ways to communicate with government officers who make policy and strategies on ESD so they can advocate for a 'whole-systems approach' for ESD in Korea, where all of early childhood education contributes to sustainability. Current policies favour formal school education and tend to neglect the potential of early childhood education to contribute to Korea's ESD goals.

Other issues that need to be dealt with, and can be seen as being a part of the previous key points, include parent education about the place of ESD in early childhood education, and how to more effectively demonstrate sustainable practices in the operation of kindergartens, such as using renewable energy, conserving water and reducing food waste.

Conclusion

In Korea, there have already been many early childhood education initiatives, such as programs to increase children's creativity, energy-saving programs, environmental education programs, economic education programs and Korean traditional culture programs. These are all aimed at making early childhood education more desirable to both children and parents. Such programs mean that young children have already been learning the broad values that underpin ESD in one way or another. However, until recently, we have been in a position to view what we have been doing through the lens of a comprehensive ESD approach.

Fortunately, the Korean government, academics, teachers and centre directors are now ready to learn about ESD and to apply it to the early childhood education field. To do this effectively, we must also learn from and communicate with colleagues in other countries across the globe. Hopefully, in the future, all children in all nations on Earth will strive to live sustainable lives together.

References

Katz, L. G. and Chard, S. C. (2000). *Engaging Children's Minds: The Project Approach* (2nd edn). Stamford, CT: Ablex Publishing Corporation.

Korean Government, Ministry of Education (2012). *The Green Growth Education Program for Supporting Kindergarten Curriculum Operations*. Seoul: Ministry of Education.

Korean Government, Ministry of Environment (2009). *Development of Reference Material about ESD for Elementary Teachers*. Seoul: Ministry of Environment.

Korean Government, Presidential Committee on Green Growth (2009). *The Five-Year Plan for Green Growth (2009–2013)*. Seoul: Presidential Committee on Green Growth.

Korean Government, Presidential Committee on Green Growth (and Ministry of Education, Ministry of Environment and Ministry of Public Administration and Security) (2009). *The Activation Plan of Green Growth*. Seoul: Presidential Committee on Green Growth.

Early childhood education for sustainability in the United Kingdom

Louise Gilbert, Janet Rose and Paulette Luff

Editor's note

In this new chapter for the second edition, the three authors from the United Kingdom share their perspectives on ECEfS, using the four strands of UNESCO's Education for Sustainable Development initiative (2012) to shape their discussion. In short, they examine responses in the United Kingdom to EfS through the lenses of access to quality basic education; professional education provision; changes to existing educational programs to address sustainability; and public understanding and awareness of sustainability. They expand on these themes with reference to two 'Stories from the field' vignettes that highlight aspects of the four UNESCO strands. The authors argue that, even though there appears to have been a diminution of central policy support for sustainability and EfS across the country, and an economic recession, sustainability initiatives should not be left to flounder. The authors make the point that, by building on the strength of current initiatives and making the most of adversity to stimulate creativity, new opportunities can be generated to further legitimise and integrate ECEfS into lifelong educational experiences that promote sustainable living.

Introduction[1]

> We are the music makers and we are the dreamers of dreams . . . yet we are [also] the movers and shakers
> of the world for ever, it seems (O'Shaughnessy 1874).

Our world, as we know it, is a human construct; we are both social products *and* social producers. If we accept that human behaviours affect and are affected by our engagements with physical, social and economic environments, then early years practitioners are potential 'movers and shakers of the world' (O'Shaughnessy 1874), and well placed to promote and facilitate sustainable development. This chapter explores this possibility, using the four strands of UNESCO's Education for Sustainable Development initiative (UNESCO 2012, p. 11) to discuss ECEfS in England. The four UNESCO strands are improving access and retention in quality basic education; training provision; reorienting existing educational programs to address sustainability; and increasing public understanding and awareness of sustainability.

Siraj-Blatchford, Smith and Pramling Samuelsson (2010, p. 5) note that if early education practice and policy do not recognise the necessity to 'balance human and economic wellbeing with cultural traditions and respect for the environment', they are likely, at best, to be ineffectual and, at worst, to fail. This review of ECEfS in the United Kingdom, therefore, adopts a consilience approach to the discussion, one that combines 'knowledge from the natural sciences with that of the social sciences and humanities . . . [to] provide a clear view of the world' (Wilson 1998, pp. 13–14). The chapter includes three case studies presenting different ways that sustainability might be embedded into ECEfS, and concludes by noting that early childhood education (ECE) requires an evolutionary approach to change. Such change should create opportunities for early years practitioners to explore and experience the values and relevance of ECEfS, to work in partnership with families and communities, and to celebrate personal and professional transformation.

Provocation 15.1

We have used lines from the inspirational ode 'We are the music makers and we are the dreamers of dreams'. The poem describes writers as 'movers and shakers'. Do you think that early childhood teachers can also be 'movers and shakers' who can change the world through their work? What differences do you aim to make through your work with children and families?

---

[1] Please note that this chapter focuses on developments in England that reflect similar developments in the rest of the United Kingdom. While the term 'early childhood education' is used, an educare framework is assumed.

Early childhood education (ECE) in the United Kingdom

Improving access and retention in quality basic education

The economic benefits of education are tacit and universally accepted (Fien, Maclean & Park 2009); however, societal progress is also shaped by the availability of human, social and environmental resources, or 'capital'. Higher levels of capital bestow:

> social, emotional, and academic foundations that will serve [children] throughout life [and provide a] better prepared workforce … while society will benefit [from] children who are better prepared to participate in democratic processes (Committee for Economic Development 2006, p. 1).

With a need and desire to reduce national childhood inequities, break cyclical inter-generational deprivation and promote human rights and equal opportunities, the previous United Kingdom government (1997–2010) scrutinised children's health, education and care services as one of its governmental tasks. This led to radical alterations in the structure and delivery of early years education, with responsibility for children's services devolved from central government. An integrated approach to service delivery was adopted to ensure that services reflected and satisfied local needs and that statutory and voluntary organisations shared service provision budgets. To generate local social, human and economic capital, early childhood services were centred on community-based Children's Centres. These were modelled on the work of the Sure Start initiative (National Evaluation of Sure Start 2010), which initially focused on early years provision to those in disadvantaged areas, but was later extended to support universal provision.

A change of government in 2010 refocused priority on those children and families identified as 'most in need'. Despite this apparent 'turnaround', government rhetoric continues to support improving provision for *all* children in the United Kingdom, promotion of equal opportunities for all, and localised and integrated service delivery across the nation. The current government's goal is to create a nation 'inspired by the values of freedom, fairness and responsibility' and the desire to build 'a stronger society, a smaller state … [with] power and responsibility in the hands of every citizen' (Great Britain, Cabinet Office 2010b, p. 8).

At a broad level, these aspirations echo values and principles underpinning education for sustainable development (ESD), with education believed to be foundational to the national development plan. For example, the UNESCO vision for ESD promotes issues related to freedom and fairness, such as human rights and cultural diversity (UNESCO 2012). Thus, prior to compulsory schooling at 5 years of age, 3- and 4-year-olds are eligible for free ECE, with some provision available for disadvantaged 2-year-olds (Great

Britain, Department for Education [DfE] 2013). This encompasses a range of contexts, including private and state-funded nursery schools, day care nurseries, play groups, children's centres and child minders. Recognition of ECE provision is also reflected in the government's pledge to continue with the ambition of developing a graduate-led ECE workforce.

ECE and ESD training

Historically, there has been limited oversight of ECE, with minimal professional qualifications required for those seeking to work in early years education. In keeping with global recognition of the importance of the early years, ECE is now accepted as a specific and significant domain of study in higher education in the United Kingdom and beyond (Baldock, Fitzgerald & Kay 2009). With a desire for ECE to be led and enacted by committed, knowledgeable, enthusiastic, reflective and lifelong-learning practitioners, the Early Years Professional Status (EYPS) initiative was launched in 2006 (Great Britain, Department for Education and Skills [DfES] 2006a). 'Early Years Professionals', now known as 'Early Years Teachers' (Great Britain, DfE 2013), are early years specialist graduates who lead ECE in community settings.

In terms of curriculum, the Early Years Foundation Stage (EYFS) (Great Britain, Department for Children, Schools and Families [DCSF] 2007; DfE 2012) provides national statutory guidance for fostering children's learning and development from birth to age 5, and the work of their teachers. One principle of the EYFS is to promote enabling environments, considered to play a 'key role in supporting and extending children's development and investigation' (Great Britain, DCSF 2007; DfE 2012). The word 'environment' appears regularly throughout the EYFS (Great Britain, DfE 2012); however, the term reflects multiple meanings rather than being operationalised exclusively to represent ESD philosophy (Luff et al. 2013). Although the term 'sustainability' is not referenced in this document, the underlying commitment to supportive relationships, nurturing experiences and enabling environments to ignite 'children's curiosity and enthusiasm for learning, [and] build their capacity to learn, form relationships and thrive' (Great Britain, DfE 2012, p. 4) evidences key principles of ESD.

Another element of overlap between the intentions of the United Kingdom curriculum and ESD relates to a focus on respectful communication, trusting relationships and democratic participation, which are all considered essential to 'empower young children to strengthen their role as citizens in their communities today and for tomorrow' (Mackey & Vaealiki 2011, p. 85). Nutbrown and Clough (2009) identify that, for children, a:

> sense of inclusivity and belonging in their early years settings stems from practitioners ensuring that young children feel good about themselves, feel positive about the differences they see in other children and are secure in their own sense of place in their early years community (p. 203).

Drayson et al. (2013) note that growing numbers of higher education students recognise that environmental and social skills are important and relevant; however, there is less consensus as to what specifically these skills are. Moreover, Bell (2011, p. 264) cautions: 'self-reflection upon sustainability may be possible for all people; but, to be truly effective, it needs to be consciously and deliberately applied and not left to chance.' If the role of ECEfS is to make 'values and characteristics visible and "lived" in daily settings' (Pramling Samuelsson & Kaga 2008, p. 60), early education practitioners require skills to facilitate learning opportunities that challenge and reflect on tangible, personal experiences, inviting children 'to be, to do, to learn and live together' (Hughes 2009, p. 140).

Too much information, and possible disinformation, however, can lead to information overload that can inhibit engagement in positive actions for sustainability and promote feelings of disempowerment (Buchanan 2012). Practitioners working with young children must be mindful of imposed sustainability mantras that lead to feelings of being 'browbeaten or terrified into towing [sic] the environmental line' (Williams 2010, p. 81) or a belief that to question and criticise will 'mark one as ethically suspect' (Williams 2010, p. 78). ECE training programs, therefore, should model an interactive approach to learning (Rose et al. 2011), recognising that 'real life is rich and messy with complexity, diversity and the unexpected' (Nimmo 2008, p.10). The 'Stories from the field' case study below is an example of complex and diverse ways of doing ESD in early childhood contexts.

Stories from the field

A small-scale qualitative research project was developed that focused on the use of reclaimed materials as play resources within four early years settings in different locations in eastern England. Researchers were interested in how and why reclaimed resources are used in early childhood settings; how these materials are presented to children; and the affordances of these materials as play resources.

Findings from the study showed that the amount and type of reclaimed resources differed considerably between settings, with a wide range of materials being used from fabric scraps to tractor tyres. Children of all ages were observed to use these reclaimed materials in a wide variety of ways, including construction and role play both indoors and outside. The early years practitioners were aware of the importance of exploratory play and outdoor provision for the birth to 5-year age group and recognised the potential of reclaimed resources for fostering creativity.

In general, the early years practitioners commented that England's EYFS curriculum gives no guidance on what is meant by the term 'environment' or how sustainability links to young children's learning and development; however, some interviewees identified that leaving this open to interpretation allows for flexibility rather than prescriptions about how to integrate ESD into ECE. Importantly, managers and staff identified *a need for initial training and continuing professional development* in relation to early childhood education for sustainability.

(Source: Luff et al. 2013)

Reorienting existing educational programs to address sustainability

In England, commitment to the values and aspirations of ESD and promoting sustainable environmental practices began in the 1980s. This led to the identification of sustainability and global citizenship as cross-curricular themes within the statutory National Curriculum for children aged 5–11 years. The Sustainable Development Action Plan (Great Britain, DfES 2006b) encouraged all schools to join the United Kingdom's 'Sustainable Schools Programme'. This program evidenced a positive impact on raising academic standards, enhancing wellbeing and promoting community cohesion (Great Britain, DCSF 2010).

The change in government in 2010 saw reorganisation and redistribution of responsibility for sustainability, with the Department for the Environment, Food and Rural Affairs (DEFRA) taking overall leadership of ESD. Every government department was then tasked with ensuring that its policies and activities were 'stimulating economic growth and tackling the deficit, maximizing wellbeing and protecting our environment, without negatively impacting on the ability of future generations to do the same' (Great Britain, DEFRA 2013).To empower local people and communities to see themselves as active in, and responsible for, community development, the 'Big Society Initiative', with both national and local focus and funding, was launched (Great Britain, Cabinet Office 2010a).

Consequently, the Sustainable Schools Programme is now supported through Sustainability and Environmental Education (SEEd). As a registered charity, it acts as a hub for educational settings, providing primary, secondary schools and further education colleges with online resources, training, news updates, practitioner forums and campaign information. However, for ECE there is no specific forum to support engagement. Duhn (2012, p. 27) notes that 'making ECE more than a sheltered enclave that is dominated by romantic notions of childhood and nature requires imagination and courage [of] heart, body and mind'. This lack of attention to ECEfS is possibly premised on an historical hegemonic discourse that, first, views the youngest members of society as needing protection; second, considers issues related to sustainable futures as too complex for young children's developmental capabilities; and, finally, implies that involvement of young children in ESD learning is of little relevance or worth (OECD 2006; Siraj-Blatchford 2009).

Yet, there is a palpable shift afoot that challenges the dominance of the discourse of childhood development founded on adult protection and restriction and recognises child capability through engagement and empowerment. Evidence abounds that young children are able to be successful, active participants in practices that promote sustainable, ecological and social wellbeing and have abilities from an early age to develop foundational notions of global citizenship and social justice (Chan, Choy & Lee

2009). Nutbrown and Clough (2009) advocate that inclusion, citizenship and belonging can and must underpin ECE policy, and recent revisions to the EYFS (Great Britain, DfE 2012) have strengthened the focus on these elements.

Moreover, as in other parts of the world, ECE in the United Kingdom is already well aligned with ESD even if this is unrecognised. ECE follows traditions of valuing co-constructive pedagogical approaches to children, practitioners and families. Integrated learning, based on personal experience and the local environment, normalises the notion of children as active, participating citizens (Pramling Samuelsson & Kaga 2008). As Davis et al. (2009) state, ECE is recognised as the natural starting point for ESD, providing 'great potential to nurture values, attitudes, skills and behaviours that support sustainable development' (Pramling Samuelsson & Kaga 2008, p. 12). The 'Stories from the field' case study below reveals how, through child-led, multisensory experiences, children and the local community can become engaged in promoting more sustainable lifestyles through growing and eating their own food.

Stories from the field

Redcliffe Children's Centre is an inner-city location in the southwest of England. Here, children, parents and staff are engaged in learning about continuous cycles of growth. An allotment site provides an ideal environment for improving wellbeing and engaging with concepts of sustainability. Children visit the allotment to plant a variety of crops that are fast growing, easy to maintain and pick. Children, parents and staff maintain the space with Julie, our farm worker.

The children are involved in the process of growing produce, such as beans, strawberries, potatoes, salad leaves and herbs, and have free access to equipment and tools. Sessions are child-led and multisensory; children taste, smell, play, create and learn for themselves about health and homegrown food. Children are encouraged to save seeds to use at the beginning of the cycle. The seeds are planted at the nursery and the children care for them daily and watch them grow.

These activities complement our food project, which has children working in partnership with our artist and chef, Jo. Produce is picked and the children explore crops, at the allotment and back in the nursery kitchen. They create their own recipes, picking fresh herbs to supplement their dishes from the kitchen garden. Homegrown produce is included in the children's lunchtime menu. Children also take produce home to cook and share with their family.

These projects have helped create new partnerships within the local community and have helped us all to recognise and value the importance of sustaining a home-grown cycle of food, to share and enjoy together.

(Source: Jeanette Hill, Deputy Head, Redcliffe Children's Centre)

Provocation 15.2

The allotment garden and linked food scheme provide examples of ways in which adults and children learn about living sustainably. Are you familiar with any similar projects? What activities could you plan and implement that would make a difference to children's wellbeing? How would you decide on a project? What sources of advice and support would you need to put it into action?

Increasing public understanding and awareness of sustainability

In order to break intergenerational cycles of dysfunction and underachievement, parents and key professionals must have clear understandings of how to build children's social and emotional capability (National Institute for Health and Clinical Excellence 2012). Researchers have highlighted early childhood as a time during which:

> genetic potential interacts in infinitely complex ways with early experience to construct the neural pathways and connections that quickly become both the foundations and the scaffolding for all later development (UNICEF 2013, p. 34).

Recognition that nurturing relationships are critical to the development of empathy, motivation, memory and resilience skills in children (Siegel 2012) informs the government's commitment to safeguarding and preserving ECE provision for children from birth to 5 years of age. The current government pledges to foster community wellbeing and support public service provision to 'promote fairness and social mobility and to break cycles of poverty and deprivation' (Bamfield 2011, p. 2). A key goal of ECEfS for early years practitioners is for these professionals to become change agents, who facilitate the development of children, families and organisations (Rose & Rogers 2012), rather than maintaining the status quo that is recognised as contributing to unjust and unsustainable practices. Although traditional environmental concepts of resource sustainability – *reduce, reuse, repair and recycle* (Pramling Samuelsson & Kaga 2008) – are tacit to the ECE curriculum, employers are increasingly seeking employees who show awareness of, and responsibility for, social sustainability as well as for environmental concerns (Park, Majumdar & Dhameja 2009). Recognition that 'we interpret our experiences in our own way and that how we see the world is a result of our perceptions and our experiences' (Cranton & Taylor 2012, p. 5) necessitates broadening the early childhood curriculum beyond the exploration of environmental issues to also include the wider sustainability agenda of *respect, reflect and responsibility* (Pramling Samuelsson & Kaga 2008). Thus, we see this widening of the four 'Rs' as more representational of an holistic curricular approach that addresses not just environmental concerns but also promotes human and social capital. This is a view also expressed by Melinda Miller in Chapter 6.

The peer mentoring program described in the following case study is one primary school's efforts to empower children with the skills to promote greater understanding and empathy of behaviour and create more supportive learning environments.

Emotion Coaching Peer Mentoring Project

Emotion Coaching is a strategy that helps children to self-regulate their emotions and behaviour, and creates opportunities for sustainable wellbeing and resilience. It enables early childhood practitioners to promote an ethos of positive learning behaviour and to empower children to take ownership of their behaviour. Emotion Coaching recognises the powerful, symbiotic relationship between learning, experience and the environment, and fosters improved communication and relationships, contributing to skills that promote resilience and sustainable citizenship.

As part of a research project undertaken by Bath Spa University focused on building community resilience, 60 children aged 9–10 years were trained as peer mentors in Emotion Coaching. This involvement extended the work of school staff to empower children to support their peers and younger children. Research data showed that, after training, the children felt more empowered to overcome difficulties, resolve issues by engaging in problem solving, and were better able to support their peers in self-regulation. They also stated that becoming Emotion Coaching peer mentors helped them to have a greater understanding of how others were feeling. As one participant put it: 'It shows that you care for your friends and all that kind of stuff.' Another child explained how 'it helps you to comfort other people when they're upset and know what they're feeling' while another declared: 'I do it every day because almost always everybody in my class gets upset.'

Evidence from the project suggests that Emotion Coaching can play a part in building human and social capital and, thus, help to create a more caring and just society.

(Source: Team led by Dr Janet Rose, School of Education, Bath Spa University, 2013)

Where to from here for ECEfS?

Aspirations to foster ECEfS are being challenged by the recent economic consequences of the national and worldwide recessions that have led to sweeping cuts to health, education and care services in the United Kingdom. Consequently, since 2010 in England, there has been less policy emphasis on sustainable development and less evidence of ESD informing pedagogy (UNESCO 2013). With the marginalisation and decentralisation of responsibility for ESD, many established networks have fragmented, lost impetus or been disbanded. Thus, aspirations for ESD are now negotiated through services that are experiencing severe funding curtailment or withdrawal. Allied with a lack of consensus on what constitutes excellence in ESD, early childhood practitioners are reporting that they feel confused and isolated about how to take practice forward (Nolan, Raban & Waniganayake 2005); accordingly, there are 'increased uncertainties amongst educational institutions and practitioners about how much emphasis to place on sustainability within teaching and learning' (UNESCO 2013, p. 17). This is a worrying trend for, as Buchanan (2012, p. 118) cautions, 'if the cost of action is high, the cost of inaction or procrastination would appear to be absolutely beyond our means'.

Conclusion

Although the United Kingdom government claims that sustainability remains at the heart of British education, currently there seems to be a lack of impetus, cohesion and focus for ECEfS, with developments remaining largely reliant on localised, small-scale projects with limited resources. If the goal of ESD is to empower children, families and communities in their roles, rights and responsibilities to each other and future generations, then major systemic changes to societal perceptions about sustainability and the role of ECEfS are required. This necessitates that requisite skills and knowledge to promote ESD must be integral to both early childhood practitioner education and curriculum.

Devoting more time and opportunities to explore, discuss, reflect and experience the values and relevance of ESD as 'not [just] techniques but rather attitudes of the spirit' (Ettling 2012, p. 545) is fundamental to the construction of personal and collective identities. Powerful symbiotic, recursive relationships between learning, experience and environment need to be harnessed, for 'in the work of sustainable development . . . all change must be implemented by *people* . . . in order to eventually evolve the system as a whole' (Bradbury 2007, p. 279, original emphasis). Embodied learning that emanates from living with and through experience is a catalyst for personal and professional transformations, encouraging ongoing experimentation and engagement, and resulting in increased practitioner confidence and competencies within early years education (Gilbert et al. 2013).

Economic recession is a universal challenge, but it can also provide opportunities for change, creative restructuring and growth (Vaitilingam 2009). The closing lines of O'Shaughnessy's (1874) poem echoes this sentiment, suggesting that 'each age is a dream that is dying, or one that is coming to birth'. As seeds of ESD are sown in families and communities, and nurtured through ECE, there is an opportunity, right now, to create a national ESD policy that identifies ECEfS as integral to lifelong learning. This would legitimise and integrate early informal and formal learning experiences into the lifelong educational experience, and support an evolutionary, deep-seated, cultural shift towards ESD, rather than a revolutionary approach that might not be sustained (Davis 2009). Historically, ECE is community-based practice that embraces working in partnership with families and communities, and adopts holistic approaches to development and learning. Therefore, it is well placed to nurture opportunities, skills and knowledge that empower children to celebrate their roles, rights and responsibilities as 'music makers', 'dreamers of dreams' and 'movers and shakers of the world' (O'Shaughnessy 1874).

Review provocations

This chapter is framed around the four strands of UNESCO's Education for Sustainable Development (ESD) initiative: improving access and retention in quality basic education; training provision; reorienting existing educational programs to address sustainability; and increasing public understanding and awareness of sustainability. Having read this chapter, can you use these four dimensions to compare ECEfS in England with the context in another country with which you are familiar? What do the two places have in common? What different challenges do they face? What could teachers in each place learn from one another in order to contribute to global change for sustainability?

References

Baldock, P., Fitzgerald, D. & Kay, J. (2009). *Understanding Early Years Policy* (2nd edn). London: Sage Publications.

Bamfield, L. (2011). Beginning the Big Society in the early years. *The Political Quarterly*, 82: 158–77.

Bell, S. (2011). From sustainable community to Big Society: 10 years learning with the Imagine approach. *International Research in Geographical and Environmental Education*, 20(3), 247–67.

Bradbury, H. (2007). Social learning for sustainable development: Embracing technical and cultural change as originally inspired by The Natural Step. In A. E. J. Wals (ed.), *Social Learning Towards a Sustainable World*. Wageningen: Wageningen Academic Publishers.

Buchanan, J. (2012). Sustainability education and teacher education: Finding a natural habitat. *Australian Journal of Environmental Education*, 28(2), 108–24.

Chan, B., Choy, G. & Lee, A. (2009). Harmony as a basis for education for sustainable development: A case example of Yew Chung International Schools. *International Journal of Early Childhood'*, 41, 35–48.

Committee for Economic Development (2006). *The Economic Promise of Investing in High-Quality Preschool: Using Early Years Education to Improve Economic Growth and the Fiscal*

Sustainability of States and the Nation. Washington, DC: Committee for Economic Development.

Cranton, P. & Taylor, E. (2012). Transformative learning theory: Seeking a more unified theory. In E. Taylor & P. Cranton (eds), *The Handbook of Transformative Learning, Theory, Research and Practice*. San Francisco: Jossey Bass.

Davis, J. (2009). Revealing the research 'hole' of early childhood education for sustainability: A preliminary survey of the literature, *Environmental Education Research*, 15(2), 227–41.

Davis, J., Engdahl, E., Otieno, L., Pramling Samuelsson, I., Siraj-Blatchford, J. & Vallabh, P. (2009). Early childhood education for sustainability: Recommendations for development, *International Journal of Early Childhood*, 41, 113–17.

Drayson, R., Bone, E., Agombar, J. & Kemp, S. (2013). *Student Attitudes Towards and Skills for Sustainable Development*. York, UK: The Higher Education Academy.

Duhn, I. (2012). Making 'place' for ecological sustainability in early childhood education. *Environmental Education Research*, 18(1), 19–29.

Ettling, D. (2012). Educators as change agents. In E. Taylor & P. Cranton (eds), *The Handbook of Transformative Learning: Theory, Research and Practice*. San Francisco: Jossey-Bass.

Fien, J., Maclean, R. & Park, M. G. (eds) (2009). *Work, Learning and Sustainable Development, Opportunities and Challenges*. Berlin: Springer.

Gilbert, L., Rose, J., Palmer, S. & Fuller, M. (2013). Active engagement, emotional impact and changes in practice arising from a residential trip. *International Journal of Early Years Education*, http://dx.doi.org/10.1080/0966760.2013.771320 (accessed 25 July 2013).

Great Britain, Cabinet Office (2010a). Building the Big Society, www.gov.uk/government/uploads/system/uploads/attachment_data/file/78979/building-big-society_0.pdf (accessed 1 November 2013).

Great Britain, Cabinet Office (2010b). *The Coalition: Our Programme for Government*. London: Cabinet Office, www.gov.uk/government/publications/the-coalition-documentation (accessed 10 October 2013).

Great Britain, Department for Children, Schools and Families (DCSF) (2007). *Statutory Framework for the Early Years Foundation Stage*. Nottingham: DCSF Publications.

Great Britain, Department for Children, Schools and Families (DCSF) (2010). *Evidence of Impact of Sustainable Schools*. Nottingham: DCSF Publications.

Great Britain, Department for Education (DfE) (2012). *Statutory Framework for the Early Years Foundation Stage*. Nottingham: DCSF Publications.

Great Britain, Department for Education (DfE) (2013). *Graduate Leaders in Early Years: Early Years Teachers*. Nottingham: DCSF Publications.

Great Britain, Department for Education and Skills (DfES) (2006a). *Children's Workforce Strategy: Building a World-Class Workforce for Children, Young People and Families. The Government's Response to the Consultation.* Nottingham: DfES Publications.

Great Britain, Department for Education and Skills (DfES) (2006b). *Learning for the Future: The DfES Sustainable Development Action Plan 2005/6,* Nottingham: DfES Publications.

Great Britain, Department for Environment, Food and Rural Affairs (DEFRA) (2013). Vision for sustainable development, http://sd.defra.gov.uk/gov/vision (accessed 5 August 2013).

Hughes, P. (2009). Education for all and TVET: The creative synergy. In J. Fien, R. Maclean & M. Park (eds), *Work, Learning and Sustainable Development: Opportunities and Challenges.* Berlin: Springer.

Luff, P., Austin, P., Emre, S., Mandra, J., Matamba, R. & Ryder, G. (2013). The four 'Rs' – Reclaim, Reduce, Reuse, Recycle: Resources for early childhood education, http://4recrg. blogspot.co.uk (accessed 16 December 2013).

Mackey, G. & Vaealiki, S. (2011). Thinking of children: Demographic approaches with young children in research. *Australasian Journal of Early Childhood,* 36(2): 82–6.

National Evaluation of Sure Start (2010). *The Impact of Sure Start Local Programmes on Five Year Olds and Their Families.* London: Department for Education, www.ness.bbk.ac.uk (accessed 13 June 2013).

National Institute for Health and Clinical Excellence (2012). Social and emotional wellbeing in early years (PH40), http://guidance.nice.org.uk/PH40 (accessed 1 May 2014).

Nimmo, J. (2008). Young children's access to real life: An examination of the growing boundaries between children in child care and adults in the community. *Contemporary Issues in Early Childhood,* 9(1), 3–13.

Nolan, A., Raban, B. & Waniganayake, M. (2005). Evaluating a strategic approach to professional development through guided reflection, *Reflective Practice,* 6(2), 221–9.

Nutbrown, C. & Clough, P. (2009). Citizenship and inclusion in the early years: Understanding and responding to children's perspectives on belonging. *International Journal of Early Years Education,* 17, 191–206.

OECD (2006). *Starting Strong II: Early Childhood Education and Care.* Paris: OECD Publishing.

O'Shaughnessy, A. (1874). Ode, www.bartleby.com/101/828.html (accessed 5 September 2013).

Park, M., Majumdar, S. & Dhameja, S. (2009). Sustainable development through a skilled, knowledge-based workforce. In J. Fien, R. Maclean & M. Park (eds), *Work, Learning and Sustainable Development: Opportunities and Challenges.* Berlin: Springer.

Pramling Samuelsson, I. & Kaga, Y. (eds) (2008). *The Contribution of Early Childhood Education to a Sustainable Society.* Paris: UNESCO.

Rose, J. and Rogers, S. (2012). *The Role of the Adult in Early Years Settings.* Milton Keynes: Open University.

Rose, J., Fuller, M., Gilbert, L. & Palmer, S. (2011). Transformative empowerment: Stimulating transformations in early years practice. *Learning and Teaching in Higher Education* (LATHE), 5, 56–72

Siegel, D. (2012). *The Developing Mind: How Relationships and the Brain Interact to Shape Who We Are.* New York: Guilford Press.

Siraj-Blatchford, J. (2009). Education for sustainable development in early childhood. *International Journal of Early Childhood*, 41(2), 9–22.

Siraj-Blatchford, J., Smith, K. & Pramling Samuelsson, I. (2010). *Education for Sustainable Development in the Early Years.* Florence: World Organization for Early Childhood Education (OMEP).

UNESCO (2012). *Shaping the Education of Tomorrow: 2012 Report on the UN Decade of Education for Sustainable Development (Abridged).* Paris: UNESCO.

UNESCO (2013). *Policy Brief 9: Education for Sustainable Development (ESD) in the UK – Current Status, Best Practice and Opportunities.* London: UK National Commission for UNESCO.

UNICEF Office of Research (2013). *Child Well-being in Rich Countries: A Comparative Overview. Innocenti Report Card 11.* Florence, Italy: UNICEF Office of Research.

Vaitilingam, R. (2009). *Recession Britain: Findings from Economic and Social Research.* London: Economic and Social Research Council (ESRC).

Williams, A. (2010). Corroding the curriculum: Sustainability v education. *Academic Questions*, 23, 70–83.

Wilson, E. (1998). *Consilience: The Unity of Knowledge.* New York: Vintage Books.

Chapter 16

Using research and a systems approach to mainstream change in early childhood education for sustainability

Jo-Anne Ferreira and Julie M. Davis

Editor's note

In this revised chapter, **Jo-Anne Ferreira** and **Julie M. Davis** reiterate two matters they consider essential for the future development of ECEfS. The first 'essential' is the necessity to create deep foundations based in research. Although there have been some steps forward in recent times, research in ECEfS remains meagre at a time of rising practitioner interest. A robust research base is crucial for enhancing quality curriculum and pedagogy in ECEfS and for promoting learning and innovation in thinking and practice.

The second 'essential' for mainstreaming EfS in early childhood education is a systems approach to changing the field. All levels within the early childhood education system – individual educators and their classrooms, whole centres and schools, early childhood professional associations and networks, accreditation and employing authorities and teacher educators – must work together to create and reinforce the cultural and educational changes required for sustainability. This chapter provides explanations of systems theory and processes for engendering system-wide change, illustrated with reference to recent studies on mainstreaming EfS in teacher education. These emphasise the apparent contradiction that the answer to large-scale reform lies with small-scale changes that build capacity and make connections across the whole of a system.

Introduction

Many educational policymakers, particularly in early childhood education (ECE), which has come late to the environmental and sustainability agenda, are unaware of the scale of change required if education is to contribute towards the achievement of sustainable societies. This chapter draws together themes and perspectives from previous chapters, emphasising the necessity for further change within ECE – deep changes to how we think, learn, teach and act. What is clear from all the previous chapters is that replicating 'business as usual' in ECE will not help to achieve sustainable societies. Instead, we must rethink daily educative practices, leadership approaches, ethical foundations and ideas relating to reconciliation between Indigenous and non-Indigenous Australians; we need to revalue nature for both environmental and human health; we have to replace worn-out, unengaging pedagogies with those that stimulate; and we must more fully recognise the powerful role that young children can play as agents of change for sustainability. Many early childhood educators *are* seeking to address the challenges of sustainability through changing their curriculum and pedagogical practices; this book provides readers with ideas and insights into how such change might happen through EfS within their own classrooms, centres and schools.

While small-scale changes in individual classrooms and centres are vitally important, they are not enough on their own. As has been observed, the 'patches of green' identified within ECE are required to become more than the 'exemplary individuals, organisations and centres that share a passion and commitment' for EfS (New South Wales Environmental Protection Agency 2003, p. 1). A new evolutionary point is necessary that constitutes broad coverage across, and deep infiltration into, ECE. This requires system-wide changes, driven by a strong research and evidence base, within and across the field.

This chapter focuses, therefore, on how the ECE sector can leverage its current position – arguably still at the fringes of endeavours to embed sustainability into everyday educational practices – to make a more significant contribution towards the cultural and educational shifts that are necessary for sustainability to be realised. Two key ways are proposed. The first is the development of research and evidence to help the field grow on solid foundations. The second is the use of systems theory for creating system-wide changes within ECE. Systems approaches to creating change are well known in management and organisational change circles, but are newly emerging in education.

Creating change within ECE: The role of research

Ramping up research and research capabilities is essential in creating deep and effective engagement with and within ECEfS. As this book shows, the ECE field *is* beginning to engage with EfS. Furthermore, research that was almost invisible a decade ago is being transformed, admittedly off a very low base. Since Davis (2009) reported on how little research there was in ECEfS, there has been a whole special edition on this topic in the *International Journal of Early Childhood*, while 2014 saw the publication of the world-first research text on ECEfS, *Research in Early Childhood Education for Sustainability: International Perspectives and Provocations* (Davis & Elliott, in press). Additionally, an increasing number of theses, research papers and chapters addressing this topic have been published across the globe.

As identified in the first edition, research in ECEfS is important for three reasons. First, as the field engages with EfS, practitioners look for exemplars of good practice. Without studies and reports of success in the conception and implementation of ECEfS programs and strategies, practitioners are denied the benefits of learning from others. If success stories remain hidden, this slows the process of turning 'patches of green' into a 'patchwork quilt' (Elliott 2006, p. 1). Second, without research, there is little program and practice review and critique. Common implementation mistakes, for example, are more likely to be replicated, thus limiting the field's evolution. Third, without a rich and growing source of studies, there is less likely to be discussion and critique around the wide range of topics and issues that are indicative, as Reid and Scott (2006) note, of a 'healthy field of inquiry, brimming with ideas and perspectives on its past, present and future' (p. 1). A robust research culture aids lively exchanges and rich collaborations within the field, across disciplines and around the world, and helps to enhance our thinking and our practice.

Practical research strategies for ECEfS

To continue to advance the place and power of research in ECEfS, we again propose the three strategies iterated in the first edition of this book, and propose a fourth strategy consisting of these elements:

1. Explicitly include ECE within EfS research funding pools that target formal education (too often, terminology such as 'school' or 'schooling', as a catch-all phrase, serves to perpetuate the marginalisation of the ECE sector, even when this is not intended).

2. Target the ECE sector for specific research projects, especially case studies of exemplary practice. These should then be disseminated broadly – in professional journals, academic publications, on the web and in print, and taken directly to practitioners through 'roadshows' and conferences.

3. Continue to build research capacity for both new and experienced researchers in the field of ECEfS. Dedicated research scholarships focused on ECEfS are vital.

4. Continue the new practice of including ECE strands in the programs of national and international environmental education/EfS conferences (such as the World Environmental Education Congress) and EfS strands in the programs of national and international early childhood education conferences (such as the World Organisation for Early Childhood Education). These measures provide outlets for researchers to discuss their work with a wide range of practitioners and researchers and normalise ECEfS.

The continuing growth of a research base for ECEfS will also enable the field to make the most of rising interest in interdisciplinary research, especially for addressing complex issues, such as climate change and sustainability. As Sue Cooke (in Chapter 8) shows, there is potential for new partnerships between ECEfS practitioners and health researchers, and with those in fields such as urban design and planning. Environmental psychologists also offer perspectives on education and sustainability issues, as shown by the Australian Psychological Society's (APS) recommendations for assisting young children to cope with the current and future challenges presented by climate change. Further, Melinda Miller (Chapter 6), in exploring a post-colonialist perspective on ECEfS, sees potential for collaborations with researchers and practitioners from non-Western settings. This is a theme also advocated for by Michiko Inoue (Chapter 13). Systems theory offers another potentially fertile perspective for ECEfS researchers and practitioners. The necessity of and potential for 'whole-of-system' change within ECE is outlined below.

Creating system-wide, sustainable change within ECE

There are two key approaches to achieving change across systems. The first is what can be termed the 'scaling-up' approach, where a particular initiative is developed and then implemented, as is, across a system. While such an approach can lead to rapid and widespread change, the problem is that it lacks flexibility and is, therefore, not context-specific. As a result, such initiatives tend to have a short lifespan. The second key approach is a related, but markedly different, approach. Rather than implementing a new initiative in the same way throughout a system, a mainstreaming approach 'infuses key elements of the model into all aspects of the education system, including the processes and parameters that shape the system. This means the planning, implementation, financing, staffing, management, supervision, monitoring and evaluation of education' (UNICEF 2009, ch. 9, p. 2) are all aspects that are involved in the process of change. Thus, a mainstreaming approach does not seek to implement one new initiative across a system, but rather seeks to find ways for new ideas or change to '[become] an integral part of the education system' (UNICEF 2009, p. 2).

As a mainstreaming change approach is underpinned by systems theory, we turn our attention to the insights that systems theory offers to ECEfS about how to ensure that EfS becomes an integral part of the ECE system. To illustrate systems theory in practice, we refer to two studies that sought to embed EfS into pre-service teacher education in Queensland, Australia (Stevenson et al. 2014; Ferreira et al. 2009). These studies demonstrate that local changes within individual settings can be achieved along with, and at the same time as, system-wide change that involves, for example, government departments and teacher accreditation authorities. This is the power of a system-wide approach to change. These projects – while not specifically targeted at early childhood pre-service teacher education – have already impacted on hundreds of early childhood teacher graduates with regard to EfS and will continue to do so into the future. These projects are discussed in more detail in the 'Stories from the field' case study on page 311.

Models of educational change: Engineering versus cultural change

Resistance to change is a characteristic of educational systems (Fullan 2013; DuFour & Fullan 2013; Cuban 2013; Hargreaves & Shirley 2012; Tyack & Cuban 1995), with many teachers appearing afraid to explore issues outside their comfort areas (de la Harpe & Thomas 2009). EfS falls into this category for many early childhood teachers, with few having had exposure to the content and pedagogical processes of EfS in either their pre-service teaching qualification or through professional education in the field (Ferreira, Ryan & Tilbury 2007). A number of theories have been put forward about why education systems appear to be resistant to change. Fullan (2013), for example, argues that this is because traditional rationalist models of change are used, while Hargreaves and Shirley (2012) argue that the problem is that we prioritise and support planning and orderly change over other forms of change.

The idea that system-wide change can be brought about through linear processes is underpinned by a technocratic view of change that came into vogue in the 1970s and 1980s. This perspective is increasingly challenged by educators (Fullan 2013; DuFour & Fullan 2013; Cuban 2013; Hargreaves & Shirley 2012), including by those within environmental education/EfS (Elliot 1991; Johnson & Mappin 2005; Sterling 2006, 2008). Elliott (1991), for example, argues that the orthodox view of change is underpinned by an 'engineering model'; she equates it with an engineer designing a system to fulfil a particular function and then supervising its implementation. Such a model enables engineers to control the process by communicating their requirements to the workforce and providing criteria for monitoring and supervising progress. This approach assumes a certain rationality of behaviour in following a 'good', orderly planning process. However, as these theorists all argue, the traditional, rationalist view of change does not take into account the complexities and social realities of human actions and interactions.

In addition, viewing change as rational and orderly also treats each educational setting as a unique organisation – more or less as an island – with only loose connections with other organisations. Here, change is understood as remaining within an organisation, and is not diffused more widely. Such understanding fails to recognise that individual settings are actually part of a larger, more complex organisational system. Therefore, we argue that in order to achieve sustainability, the whole system, as well as individual sites, must change. The real aim is for large-scale, system-wide educational transformation. Large-scale reform, however, cannot be construed as monolithic social restructuring, because such reform does not alter the set patterns that have historically constructed the idea of education (Farrell 2000; Fullan 2013; Fullan & Scott 2009; Tyack & Cuban 1995). Indeed, as experience has shown, rather than changing a situation, such reforms tend to become assimilated into previous patterns, and these then become even harder to change.

Ideas about system-wide transformation, therefore, need to forgo notions of large-scale mandated reforms. Instead, ideas of complexity and diversity must be considered. This means looking for, and appreciating, the potential in small-scale change. The apparent contradiction here is that the answer to large-scale reform lies with small-scale reform. The new wave of organisational change specialists (Dawson & Andriopoulos 2014; Kotter 2012) argue that thousands of local, small-scale changes will lead to innovation and capacity building – these will be developed from the bottom up, emerging from events within local settings that cannot be readily planned for or forecast in advance. When efforts are made to 'join up' these small-scale changes, they become a major change in the overall educational effort that then reaches across the whole system. As Farrell (2000) states, 'under this conception, the task of the planner is not to invent and/or implement the innovation or reform across the whole . . . territory, but, rather, to develop and unleash a capacity to innovate throughout the system' (p. 95). The focus, then, is on enhancing capacity for change.

One of the real difficulties of creating change in the ECE 'system' is that it is highly complex and fragmented – there are multiple modes of service delivery and multiple levels of governance. In addition, the ECE system has numerous stakeholders, varying interconnections between parts of the system, interest groups with differing agendas, and institutionalised rules and hierarchies. In such complex and uncertain organisational environments, the conceptualisation and practice of sustainability requires a change process that takes account of this fragmentation and complexity; this is what a system-based approach to change offers.

Cultural change through systems thinking and practice

System-based approaches to change emerged as a discipline as a result of the failure of reductionist approaches to cope with the complexity and uncertainty inherent in biological and social domains, and have developed sophisticated ways of dealing with uncertainty and creating possible models for future action. Thinking systemically provides a way of looking at the world, not as a range of disparate problems, but as an interconnected set of factors situated within an environment. As already noted, efforts to bring about change tend, traditionally, to focus on only a part of a system, such as an individual early childhood centre or individual teachers. These small-scale changes, while positive on their own, need, however, to be connected into a large-scale movement if an innovation such as EfS is to take hold.

We argue that change in the ECE sector is more likely to occur – and to be widespread – if we understand the various parts that together form a larger system, and find ways to facilitate change in all of them concurrently. For example, early childhood teacher registration bodies, government education and welfare departments, and childcare accreditation authorities all impact on an early childhood setting, and each has a role to play in bringing about change in the ECE system. What a system-based approach to change encourages is engaging with all of these stakeholders in order to ensure that everyone in the system is 'marching to the beat of the same drum'.

What is a system?

In seeking to effect change using a systems approach, it is important to understand what constitutes a system, and how systems function. A system is made up of discrete elements that are interrelated. Systems are bounded – that is, there are features that are within a system and features that are outside a system in what is referred to as the contextual environment, meaning the environment in which the system is located. Systems can be hierarchical – that is, contain sub-systems within the system – as illustrated in Figure 16.1. It is important to note that a system is not an actual thing but a constructed entity. Indeed, a system boundary is defined by those within the system itself. Boundaries are important to consider as they set the types of exchanges that occur between the system and its sub-systems and its contextual environment. The participants' very act of defining and negotiating the system and sub-systems, and the boundaries and interactions, deepens mutual understandings of the forces at play and develops possibilities for action that have a more holistic focus.

Figure 16.1 shows that sub-systems are nested inside the larger system, which in turn is situated in a broad contextual environment. Each system has a permeable boundary through which information and resources can pass. For example, the sub-systems of the ECE system include early childhood centres, schools, childcare and teacher education institutions, accreditation bodies and professional associations. Each of these sub-systems is itself a system that contains additional sub-systems.

While complex, a system-based approach to change allows those seeking to bring about a change within each system and sub-system to define the system from their own

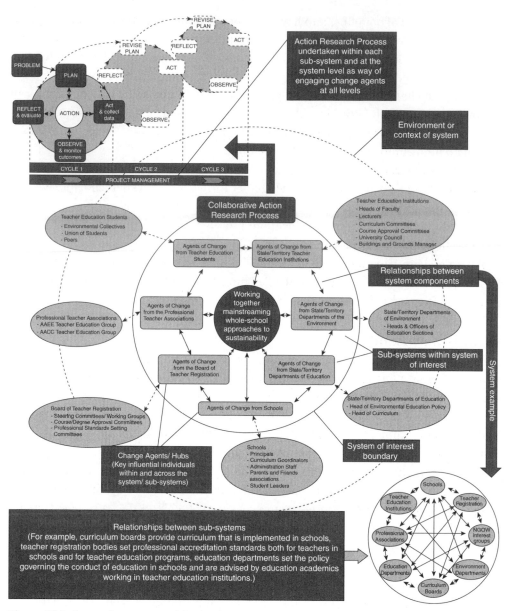

Figure 16.1 *A generic system model*
Source: Ferreira & Ryan (2012, p. 40)

perspective. It is through the processes of interpretation, co-construction and development of shared understanding of the system's elements, interactions and drivers that system-wide change is brought about. Making a boundary judgement improves one's understanding of the system in which one is operating. It also helps to clarify one's own role and the role of others in the processes of change. Additionally, demarcating a system boundary helps to identify and clarify feasible opportunities – and people – for enacting change. Identifying a system of interest and its sub-systems thus forms the first important step in efforts to think and work systemically.

Interactions among system elements

As stated, a system-based approach to change seeks to explore and better understand the whole system rather than acting solely on a part of the system in isolation of its larger context. Stakeholders from throughout the system explore the ways in which the parts of a system are interdependent, the nature of the connections between the parts, external influences, and the roles of themselves and others in the system. As a result of this inclusive process, members of the system develop their understandings of the larger system through appreciating the patterns of activity and their many influences that exist within a system. A systems focus, though, goes beyond incorporating information from multiple perspectives and disciplines. Rather, it involves a deliberate method of synthesising distinct findings into a coherent whole (Gharajedaghi 2011).

Taking an holistic view is important because the behaviour of a whole system emerges from the interactions among its parts. Trying to 'solve' a problem by reducing it to its parts and acting on them separately can produce unpredictable outcomes and even make a situation worse. The roles that individuals play within a system also influence the behaviour of a whole system. Thus, thinking systemically also focuses attention on relationships and roles (Meadows 2009). The focus of a system-based approach to change, therefore, is on the several layers of the system, the nature of their connections, and the relationships among the elements at each level of the system that the participants are trying to change or better understand. On this basis, a more holistic perspective emerges, encompassing the patterns in the system and the broader contextual environment.

Hierarchical levels

In systems theory, systems have properties of hierarchy and subsidiarity. It is generally useful to consider three hierarchical levels of a system: the environment, the system and the sub-system. The labels of 'system' and 'sub-system' can change depending on what level you are considering at a particular point in time. There is a system of interest that is embedded within a contextual environment, and also contains within it sub-systems, as illustrated in Figure 16.1.

The properties of hierarchy and subsidiarity illustrate how a sub-system cannot directly control a larger system of which it is a part. In turn, the larger system has varying degrees of partial influence or incomplete control over a sub-system. For example, if a single early childhood centre or service is seen as a sub-system, then it is influenced by, but has no direct influence over, childcare accreditation bodies. Nevertheless, while a sub-system has no direct influence, changes within the sub-system can affect the larger system of which it is a part by increasing diversity and options that can be drawn upon by those within the system and other sub-systems. Collectively, these small-scale changes *can* impact on the larger system, causing it to change. This illustrates the paradox of large-scale change emerging out of small-scale change, and exemplifies the 'butterfly effect' (Hilborn 2004), the concept of chaos/complexity theory that promises magnification of small changes and achievements beyond their initial impacts.

Hubs

Another important concept within systems thinking is the notion of 'hubs' (Meadows 2008, 2009). In a complex system, hubs are the nodes that link with a disproportionate number of other nodes – often hundreds of times more than other nodes. Hubs act as connectors and are a fundamental part of networks, 'present in very diverse complex systems, ranging from the economy to the cell' (Barabasi 2003, p. 56). Identifying and working with the hubs in a system is vitally important for leveraging influence within a system. The idea of a hub is allied to the concept of a leverage point in systems dynamics: a place in a complex system where a small change in one area can bring a disproportionate change to a whole system (Hjorth & Bagheri 2006; Meadows 2009). Key to bringing about change across a system – such as the ECE system – is locating those individuals who are crucial leverage points. It is important to note that they are not always individuals who are in 'positions of power'. Such individuals often only become clear during a systems mapping exercise that seeks to identify roles, requirements and interactions between members of a system of interest. Systems mapping thus makes visible hubs of activity and those individuals who are acting as hubs.

Hubs are crucial in scaling up changes within a system or sub-system, because they build capacity and momentum for change. They do this by bringing more and more individuals and centres into the innovation and change processes. This is vital if a change is going to have longevity and become embedded within a system. As Fullan (2011) suggests, an important aspect of capacity building is the transferability of capabilities, rather than products, across a system. Therefore, creating change is not simply about appropriating someone else's successful program or policy and transplanting it to your own setting.

For example, Campus Kindergarten's Sustainable Planet Project (discussed in detail in Chapter 3) is a unique approach to ECEfS that has grown from the particular circumstances, resources and people associated with this centre; it could not simply be replicated elsewhere – though it does provide ideas and inspiration for others to implement in their own unique contexts. As an exemplar, the centre itself and individuals within the centre are hubs who help show the way, motivate and build capacity for EfS across the early childhood system through showcasing, networking and other important outreach activities. They do not promote a 'model' of ECEfS, though, for other to follow. Rather, they encourage others to create 'hybrids' suited to their own particular contexts (Tyack & Cuban 1995). With this in mind, therefore, policies and processes aimed at creating change within a system are best stated as general aims and principles – instead of ready-made plans – to be modified in light of local experiences and embodied into practices that vary setting by setting, and even classroom by classroom.

In summary, creating widespread educational change – such as that needed for the implementation of EfS across the early childhood sector – requires both capacity building at the local early childhood setting or service level, as well as changes to the multi-level systems to which these services and settings belong. Only then can small changes resonate in significant ways throughout the system and throughout society. Those committed to new ideas in education need to think and act at both levels: to be reformers inside their educational settings and activists in the infrastructures surrounding them (Fullan 2013, 2011).

To illustrate how these ideas about a systems approach to change can work in practice to achieve, in this example, the not-so-modest goal of embedding EfS into teacher education, a case study of a system-wide change process is presented (for more detailed reports, see Ferreira et al. 2009 and Stevenson et al. 2014).

Stories from the field

Embedding EfS in pre-service teacher education

Implicit in creating the cultural changes necessary for EfS to be widely taken up in early childhood is the need to change teaching and teachers. There are two challenges here: changing teachers already in the ECE 'system' and preparing pre-service teachers, the next generation of educators about to join the profession. Campus Kindergarten's initiative (Chapter 3) illustrates the processes of change among teachers already 'in the field'. The case study discussed below relates to the latter group, pre-service teachers.

Project background

This action research project was conducted in two phases in Queensland, Australia (Ferreira et al. 2009; Stevenson et al. 2014). These phases involved participants (lecturers and student teachers) from the education faculties/schools of all universities in Queensland that offer teacher education programs (including several with early childhood teacher education courses). Each of these universities forms a sub-system of the larger education system in Queensland. The project also involved participants from other parts of the broader education system, specifically representatives from government education and environment departments, environmental education centres, a state-level policy think tank, an environmental education consultant, representatives of professional and non-government organisations concerned with sustainability and EfS, and, in the first phase, a change management consultant.

The process

The project combined action research with a systems approach in order to create change at both the small-scale level (that is, within the education faculties to include EfS in subjects and courses) and at the large-scale level (that is, seeking policy changes, such as the inclusion of EfS as a teacher education requirement).

Project leaders began the process by identifying their educational system and sub-systems. This helped to name possible partners – organisations and individuals (hubs) – to be brought into the project to leverage change. In the first stage project, a change consultant (another 'hub') was hired to help facilitate the process of change by drawing upon and introducing the participants to organisational change management theory and approaches, in particular Kotter and Rathgeber's (2007) '8-Step Process of Successful Change'. In the second-stage project, there was a focus on becoming agents of change and learning to lead.

In both phases, university participants worked individually in their own institutions to raise the profile of EfS, while sharing, liaising and supporting each other's efforts through regular meetings and electronic communications. These interactions strengthened the connections between sub-systems. The participants were focused on the following: changing their own internal sub-system (their faculty) by changing curriculum and pedagogy; addressing colleagues in meetings and forums; seeking support from deans and others of influence; sitting on faculty and university teaching and learning committees; publicising their activities; and reflecting on the processes in which they were engaged. Concurrently they met with and lobbied personnel within the broader teacher education system, including the Minister for Education and staff of the teacher registration authority (who approve teacher education courses). In these ways, engagement, learning and change occurred within sub-systems, between sub-systems and within the broader system.

Sample activities

In the first phase, a key way in which the project leaders sought to leverage support for EfS to become a fundamental component of teacher education was to engage with student teachers to encourage them to become advocates for change. Paradoxically, this is a sub-system often ignored in more traditional approaches to change. To build their capacity, a forum was organised by student teachers from all universities. Using Facebook as their primary medium of communication (this was a medium that students were already using and helped overcome the fact that students were located throughout Queensland, some living 2000 kilometres from the main student body), these students developed a 'Student Teacher Charter for Education for Sustainability'. The student teachers then invited the Minister for Education and the Director of the Office of Climate Change, and other high-level stakeholders with influence within the wider teacher education system, to a forum where they presented their Charter to the Minister of Education. This Charter outlined their concerns about sustainability and climate change and detailed their aspirations for EfS to be embedded within all their teacher education courses.

In the second phase of the project, in addition to curriculum and pedagogical changes within faculties, engagement within and across the system occurred by working through sub-system structures, such as high-level learning and teaching committees within universities, and with disciplines not traditionally engaged with EfS, including drama and the arts.

Key changes achieved through these projects

Within universities

- EfS was written into subjects and courses in all the universities involved in the projects.
- In one university, EfS was embedded as a cross-disciplinary theme in all teacher education courses (including early childhood courses).
- New academic partnerships and upskilling around EfS occurred within all faculties involved.
- A body of committed, connected and engaged student teachers were mobilised with the potential to influence practising teachers when on field experience, and later as teachers in early childhood settings and schools.

Within the wider system

- New partnerships/networks between all Queensland universities were formed to continue to lobby for further systems change, develop joint research projects around EfS in teacher education, present at conferences and write research papers.
- New connections were established with key individuals (hubs) in government agencies who have the potential to influence future policy directions related to EfS, such as revising Teacher Standards so that they include EfS, and having EfS as a curriculum requirement in all educational settings.

Conclusion

In this chapter we have argued that for ECEfS to continue to grow, a flourishing research culture and research base is required to underpin good practice. We have also argued that strengthening the field can come from increased engagement in cross-disciplinary research, methods and approaches. In particular, we argue that engaging with systems theory literature and processes has much to offer in helping the ECEfS field to really 'take off' and contribute to the societal changes required, especially with the growing sense of urgency around local and global sustainability issues. Taking a research-based and systems approach to change will ensure that EfS becomes part of the everyday culture of every early childhood education setting – marginal no more.

Review provocations

1. Undertake a literature review of an area of ECEfS that interests you – this text has provided many potential starting points! What have you learnt from this review that will help inform your practice as an early childhood educator? What issues or topics are not discussed in the literature? What questions remain unanswered? How might you design and implement your own research study to help answer these questions? How could you creatively and innovatively publish and share your findings so that they add to the body of knowledge in ECEfS?

2. Map out the system, sub-systems and environment of an ECE setting or service with which you are familiar. What and who are the key organisations and hubs in the system? What are their relationships with each other? In what ways could you work with these organisations and individuals to begin to leverage change for sustainability, more broadly, across and within this system?

References

Barabasi, A. (2003). *Linked: How Everything is Connected to Everything Else and What It Means for Business, Science, and Everyday Life*. New York: Plume.

Cuban, L. (2013). *Inside the Black Box of Classroom Practice: Change without Reform in American Education*. Cambridge, MA: Harvard Education Press.

Davis, J. (2009). Revealing the research 'hole' of early childhood education for sustainability: A preliminary survey of the literature. *Environmental Education Research*, 15(2), 227–41.

Davis, J. & Elliott, S. (eds) (n.p.). *Research in Early Childhood Education for Sustainability: International Perspectives and Provocations*. London & New York: Routledge.

Dawson, P. & Andriopoulos, C. (2014). *Managing Change, Creativity and Innovation*. London: SAGE.

de la Harpe, B. & Thomas, I. (2009). Curriculum change in universities: Why education for sustainable development is so tough. *Journal of Education for Sustainable Development*, 3(1), 75–85.

DuFour, R. & Fullan, M. (2013). *Cultures Built to Last: Systemic PLCs at Work*. Bloomington, IN: Solution Tree Press.

Elliott, J. (1991). Environmental education in Europe: Innovation, marginalisation or assimilation. In *Environment, Schools and Active Learning*. Paris: OECD/ Centre for Educational Research and Innovation.

Elliott, S. (2006). Beyond patches of green: A turning point in early childhood environmental education. Paper presented at the Turning Points in Environmental Education Conference, New Zealand.

Farrell, J. (2000). Why is educational reform so difficult? Similar descriptions, different prescriptions, failed explanations. *Curriculum Inquiry*, 30(1), 83–103.

Ferreira, J. & Ryan, L. (2012). Working the system: A model for system-wide change in pre-service teacher education. *Australian Journal of Teacher Education*, 37(12), 29–45.

Ferreira, J., Ryan, L., Davis, J., Cavanagh, M. & Thomas, J. (eds) (2009). *Mainstreaming Sustainability into Pre-service Teacher Education in Australia*. Canberra: Prepared by the Australian Research Institute in Education for Sustainability (ARIES) for Australian Government, Department of the Environment, Water, Heritage and the Arts.

Ferreira, J., Ryan, L. & Tilbury, D. (2007). Mainstreaming education for sustainable development in initial teacher education in Australia: A review of existing professional development models. *Journal of Education for Teaching*, 33(2), 225–239.

Fullan, M. (2011). *Change Leader: Learning to Do What Matters Most*. San Francisco: Jossey-Bass.

Fullan, M. (2013). *Motion Leadership in Action: More Skinny on Becoming Change Savvy*. Thousand Oaks, CA: SAGE/Corwin Press.

Fullan, M. & Scott, G. (2009). *Turnaround Leadership for Higher Education*. San Francisco: Jossey-Bass.

Gharajedaghi, J. (2011). *Systems Thinking: Managing Chaos and Complexity – A Platform for Designing Business Architecture* (3rd edn). Burlington, MA: Elsevier.

Hargreaves, A. & Shirley, D. (2012). *The Global Fourth Way: The Quest for Educational Excellence*. Thousand Oaks, CA: SAGE/Corwin Press.

Hilborn, R. (2004). Sea gulls, butterflies, and grasshoppers: A brief history of the butterfly effect in non-linear dynamics. *American Journal of Physics*, 72, 425.

Hjorth, P. & Bagheri, A. (2006). Navigating towards sustainable development: A system dynamics approach. *Futures*, 38, 74–92.

Johnson, E. & Mappin, M. (2005). *Environmental Education and Advocacy: Changing Perspectives of Ecology and Education*. Cambridge, UK: Cambridge University Press.

Kotter, J. (2012). Accelerate! *Harvard Business Review*, 90(11), 43–58.

Kotter, J. & Rathgeber, H. (2007). The 8-step process of successful change, www.kotter international.com/our-principles/our-iceberg-is-melting (accessed 10 March 2014).

Meadows, D. (2008). *Thinking in Systems: A Primer*. Vermont: Chelsea Green Publishing.

Meadows, D. (2009). Leverage points: Places to intervene in a system. *Solutions*, 1(1), 41–9.

New South Wales Environmental Protection Agency (2003). Patches of Green, www.environ ment.nsw.gov.au/education/patchesofgreen.htm (accessed 10 March 2014).

Reid, A. & Scott, W. (2006). Researching education and the environment: Retrospect and prospect. *Environmental Education Research*, 12(3–4), 1–17.

Sterling, S. (2006). *Sustainable Education: Revisioning Learning and Change*. Cambridge, UK: Green Books.

Sterling, S. (2008). Sustainable education: Towards a deep learning response to unsustainability. *Policy and Practice: A Development Education Review*, 6, 63–8.

Stevenson, R., Davis, J., Ferreira, J. & Evans, S. (2014). *A State Systems Approach to Embedding the Learning and Teaching of Sustainability in Teacher Education*. Sydney: Office of Teaching and Learning.

Tyack, D. & Cuban, L. (1995). *Tinkering Towards Utopia: A Century of Public School Reform*. Cambridge, MA: Harvard University Press.

UNICEF (2009). *Child Friendly Schools: Manual*. New York: UNICEF.

Index